The Blue Ridge Parkway
by Foot

CONTRIBUTIONS TO SOUTHERN APPALACHIAN STUDIES

1. *Memoirs of Grassy Creek: Growing Up in the Mountains
on the Virginia–North Carolina Line.* Zetta Barker Hamby. 1998

2. *The Pond Mountain Chronicle:
Self-Portrait of a Southern Appalachian Community.*
Leland R. Cooper and Mary Lee Cooper. 1998

3. *Traditional Musicians of the Central Blue Ridge: Old Time, Early Country,
Folk and Bluegrass Label Recording Artists, with Discographies.*
Marty McGee. 2000

4. *W.R. Trivett, Appalachian Pictureman:
Photographs of a Bygone Time.* Ralph E. Lentz, II. 2001

5. *The People of the New River: Oral Histories from
the Ashe, Alleghany and Watauga Counties of North Carolina.*
Leland R. Cooper and Mary Lee Cooper. 2001

6. *John Fox, Jr., Appalachian Author.* Bill York. 2003

7. *The Thistle and the Brier: Historical Links and Cultural Parallels
Between Scotland and Appalachia.* Richard Blaustein. 2003

8. *Tales from Sacred Wind: Coming of Age in Appalachia.
The Cratis Williams Chronicles.* Cratis D. Williams.
Edited by David Cratis Williams and Patricia D. Beaver. 2003

9. *Willard Gayheart, Appalachian Artist.*
Willard Gayheart and Donia S. Eley. 2003

10. *The Forest City Lynching of 1900: Populism, Racism, and White Supremacy
in Rutherford County, North Carolina.* J. Timothy Cole. 2003

11. *The Brevard Rosenwald School: Black Education and
Community Building in a Southern Appalachian Town, 1920–1966.*
Betty Jamerson Reed. 2004

12. *The Bristol Sessions: Writings About the Big Bang of Country Music.*
Edited by Charles K. Wolfe and Ted Olson. 2005

13. *Community and Change in the North Carolina Mountains:
Oral Histories and Profiles of People from Western Watauga County.*
Compiled by Nannie Greene and Catherine Stokes Sheppard. 2006

14. *Ashe County: A History.*
Arthur Lloyd Fletcher (1963). New edition, 2006

15. *The New River Controversy.*
Thomas J. Schoenbaum (1979). New edition, 2007

16. *The Blue Ridge Parkway by Foot: A Park Ranger's Memoir.*
Tim Pegram. 2007

17. *James Still: Critical Essays on the Dean of Appalachian Literature.*
Edited by Ted Olson and Kathy H. Olson. 2007

18. *Owsley County, Kentucky, and the Perpetuation of Poverty.*
John R. Burch, Jr. 2007

19. *Asheville: A History.*
Nan K. Chase. 2007

The Blue Ridge Parkway by Foot

A Park Ranger's Memoir

TIM PEGRAM

CONTRIBUTIONS TO SOUTHERN APPALACHIAN STUDIES, 16

McFarland & Company, Inc., Publishers
Jefferson, North Carolina, and London

LIBRARY OF CONGRESS CATALOGUING-IN-PUBLICATION DATA

Pegram, Tim, 1951–
    The Blue Ridge Parkway by foot : a park ranger's memoir /
    Tim Pegram.
        p.   cm. — (Contributions to Southern Appalachian studies ; 16)
    Includes bibliographical references and index.

    ISBN-13: 978-0-7864-3140-3
    softcover : 50# alkaline paper ∞

    1. Blue Ridge Parkway (N.C. and Va.)— Description and travel.
    2. Blue Ridge Mountains— Description and travel.   3. Pegram,
    Tim, 1951– — Travel — Blue Ridge Parkway (N.C. and Va.)
    4. Backpacking — Blue Ridge Parkway (N.C. and Va.)   5. Pegram,
    Tim, 1951–   6. Park rangers— Blue Ridge Parkway (N.C. and Va.)—
    Biography.   7. Blue Ridge Parkway (N.C. and Va.)— History—
    Anecdotes.   I. Title.
    F217.B6P37 2007
    917.55 — dc22

                                                2007022802

British Library cataloguing data are available

On the cover: Mabry Mill (milepost 176.2). Photographs ©2007 Shutterstock.

Manufactured in the United States of America

McFarland & Company, Inc., Publishers
    Box 611, Jefferson, North Carolina 28640
        www.mcfarlandpub.com

To every girl and boy
with dreams of someday becoming a park ranger,
and to every man and woman
who dreamed but never did.

Acknowledgments

I am most indebted to my courageous wife, Patty, who supported me throughout the process of living and writing this book and endured the recitation of every paragraph as it was written. To my patient and talented daughter, Laura Pegram Benoit, I express my gratitude for living most of this book with us and laboriously conducting the initial editorial review of the manuscript. Neighbor Jennifer B. Apple, accomplished author Susan S. Kelly, and dear friend Betsy G. Miles I thank for critical reviews of parts of the manuscript.

The Blue Ridge Parkway staff was cordially helpful at every turn, and I sincerely thank the following members for their valuable contributions: civil engineering technicians Dott Abernethy and Debbie Northrop for access to historic plans and drawings; park rangers Janet Bachmann and Kathryn Brett for locational assistance; interpretive specialist Peter Givens for a gutsy statement of fact; chief ranger John Garrison for counsel and permissions regarding sensitive issues; cultural resource management specialist Al Hess for providing helpful research materials; park curator Jackie Holt for access to the Parkway archives; and chief of interpretation Patty Lockamy for access to the Parkway library and a critical review of the complete manuscript. Thanks also to Sam Weddle, former Parkway ranger and current chief ranger at Chickamauga and Chattanooga National Military Park, for permission to use an original work, and Gary Candelaria, National Park Service deputy manager of the Harpers Ferry Center, for permission to use numerous oral history transcripts.

Other contributors deserving of special thanks include: Esther Cope, president general of the United Daughters of the Confederacy, for permission to use the name of their organization; Tom DeVaughn of Troutville, Va., for the vertical calculations contributed to a Parkway bicycling brochure; Daniel Grosch of Forest, Va., for providing a copy of that brochure; Jeff Morgan of Carolina

Steel Corporation for a better understanding of I-beam anatomy; Karen Searle, regional manager of Eastern National, for suggested publishers; and all those who agreed to the use of their photographs.

Requesting forgiveness from any whose names are misspelled or have been unintentionally omitted due to an imperfect memory, I sincerely thank the following colleagues without whose association this book would never have been possible:

THE ROANOKE VALLEY GANG

Janet Bachmann
Ken Barfield
Duke Barr
Laree Bradley
Dan Brown
Bud Carter
Pinky Dayton
Wes Earnest
Dave Fisher
Edith Garst
Leon Gibson
Bobby Gillespie
George Goodwin

Randy Griffin
Dick Harholdt
Jeff Hash
Jim Hix
Bill Holda
Mary Hudson
Jim Keller
Joe Kelley
Butch Kelly
Bob Krzywicki
Art Lawrence
Hartman Maunz
Richard Morefield

Mavis Murray
Bill Overstreet
Joyce Pence
Robert Price
Hoyt Rath
Robert Rider
Ferrell Saunders
Dick Stokes
Whitt Sutphin
Jeff Swortzel
Marvin Tucker
Sam Weddle
Bonnie Whitlock

THE BALSAM GAP GANG

Thad Beach
Grady Birchfield
Marcia Bowers
Rick Branagh
Ernest Bryson
Clifford Burnette
Melissa Cahn
Bud Cantrell
Clifford Cogdill
Don Coleman
Joe Curtis
Ken Davis
Merle Eggin
Sue Elderkin
Patsy Everhart

Richard Griffin
Don Hannah
Marsha Harris
Kent Holley
Sam Hoyle
Joe Humphrey
Kristine Johnson
David Ledford
Bobby Little
Brian Loadholtz
Marshall Lovedahl
Keith Martin
J.C. Morgan
Fred Nicholson
Charlie Norman

Nancy Ohlsen
Ted Olson
George Pace
Junior Payne
Nila Peebles
Al Phillips
Dave Phillips
Peggy Rives
Seth Smith
Mike Sneed
Steve Staley
Al Thacker
Heather Todd
Jim Watkins
Bob Whiteman

And finally, I shall remain forever indebted also to every other progenitor and perpetuator of the North Carolina state park system and the Blue Ridge Parkway whose names and numbers exceed the bounds of this book.

T.W.P.

Contents

Preface

I thought I had seen an apparition as it faintly appeared and just as quickly disappeared in the thick fog as I patrolled past it — a man sitting on a stone wall, dressed in full Scottish attire and its own lack thereof, playing a bagpipe. I found a safe place to park and, as reverently as could be expected of a uniformed park ranger, walked invisibly back toward the sound of the most pristine music I had ever heard. The combination of talent, fog, and the amphitheater effect of a steep mountain cove made it so. "I try to come up here at least once a year when it is foggy. It plays its purest at this very spot," the man told me during a break in his solitary performance to an audience of one.

I knew then that the Blue Ridge Parkway, the most visited unit of the National Park Service, had captured more hearts than my own. I felt also a compulsion to preserve such rich encounters and to convey the character and spirit of this unique park in a way that had never before been attempted. How to do that with words became a hand-wringing struggle between the choices of fact or fiction, poetry or prose. Truth and, for the most part, prose eventually emerged as the appropriate format for this project. Blame it on the lyrical personality of this park where I have surrendered to its poetic clutches.

The idea to create such a place was born in the travail of the Great Depression, and a casual conversation between an American president, his secretary of the interior, and a U.S. senator slapped it on the bottom and forced it to breathe. Designed primarily to be enjoyed from the comfort of a motor vehicle with stop-awhile opportunities, only a small percentage of its visitors ever drive its complete 469-mile length from Shenandoah National Park to the Great Smoky Mountains National Park. Fewer still ever bicycle its entire length. Not until 2003, as far as I have been able to determine, did anyone ever backpack its entire length — not through its backcountry on a foot trail, but along its very shoulder, exposed to the same features its more mobile visitors were experiencing.

This adventurous undertaking became the supporting trunk of the book on which I was able to hang the storied limbs and branches of my own experiences as a ranger on the Parkway. Obscure, anecdotal tidbits of its history and accounts of some of the Parkway's earliest rangers, gleaned primarily from the park's library and archives, are shared in the interest of adding the ornamental finery to what I intended to become a tree as lovely and uplifting as the Fraser fir which adorns this park's highest elevations.

Clearly understanding the emotional gamble to which I was subjecting myself, I began writing this book with much trepidation. First book. Scant formal education in writing. Some raw talent. Zero experience in the world of publishing. The disclosure of deeply revealing personal information. And the terrible risk of professional failure.

Upon receipt of my fourth rejection letter from a publishing company, I determinedly resolved to seclude myself with pen and ink to produce — as did the monks of old — the first edition of the book by hand. At least my grandchildren, I hoped, might someday appreciate the effort. I further resolved to produce — in like manner — as many subsequent editions for any buyers willing to pay its justifiably exorbitant price. But, alas! My declining skill of penmanship failed to mar the first page; the fifth letter, from McFarland, spared me the necessity of beginning a stubborn course that would have certainly led to a humped posture and gnarled right hand. I can hardly believe what my labors are now about to yield.

To the millions of people who have already experienced the Blue Ridge Parkway, I hope something warmly familiar will be discovered within these pages. To the millions who have never paid it a visit, I hope you will beat a path to it soon before the tide of adverse forces erodes its splendor any further. No place will ever again be created quite like it. And every Parkway ranger has a tale as unique as my own to share.

1

Once Upon the Parkway

"Without a diary, their travels would 'be no better than a flight of birds through the air,' leaving no trace."
—*John Adams*, by David McCullough

Emily is a bright child, of course. She is my firstborn grandchild, and that is the sort of thing you say about such a creature. Her little five-year-old mind absorbs new discoveries as quickly as she can gulp down one of those frozen grape treats. Still, her innocence allows her to stray in the direction of gullibility. And, at times, I take advantage of this narrow breach in her developmental progress.

On a recent drive to the zoo, I had Emily convinced that the blown truck tires strewn along the highway were alligators. This was a perfect time for this trick; she had wild animals on her mind. The adults in the van could hardly contain themselves as she excitedly pointed out all of the twisted, rubbery beasts she could spy, strapped in her car seat, whizzing past them at 70 mph. Speed gave me the advantage, while her precocious mind pondered why alligators would venture onto such dangerous territory.

One of the inalienable rights associated with becoming a grandparent is the privilege of choosing the title by which your grandchildren will address you. I chose "Granddaddy." In her earliest attempts to say this, Emily corrupted it to "G-Daddy" (pronounced jee-daddy), and I have proudly accepted this version. Besides, this variation was original, and I *had* worked for the government for a few years. Plus, everyone thinks it is cute. But cute she was not as we slowed on the exit ramp to the zoo, whereupon Emily inspected an "alligator" at a more recognizable speed of 20 mph. "G-Daddy. That's not an alligator. It's a truck tire!" she screamed into my ear past a seriously scornful countenance. Short-lived was our fun with no harm done, excepting a temporary hearing loss.

My only regret was that I had not been as alert on all of those Sunday afternoons visiting my Papaw Corn. He had *me* convinced that I could catch a bird by sprinkling salt on its tail! So much time I had wasted that could have been spent eavesdropping on the adult conversations! Now I have come to understand that this is one of the ways grandfathers show their love to their grandchildren while humoring themselves in the process.

Fathers do the same with their own children. Not many years ago, I continue to believe, I similarly tricked Emily's mother. We were a young family living in western North Carolina. I was a park ranger on the Blue Ridge Parkway, and we made occasional trips to central North Carolina to visit relatives. Interstate 40 was our primary route, and about fifty miles shy of our destination, we always encountered Exit 146–Stamey Farm Road. The name of this exit bore a striking resemblance to the name of our favorite barbecue restaurant located near our destination. And these visits usually included a meal there. Finally, on one such trip, my daughter conjectured that Stamey Farm could be the very farm that raised the hogs for this restaurant. Unknowingly, she had set her own trap, and I quickly came in for the kill, praising her insightful deduction.

I told her she was absolutely correct and proceeded to describe the Great Annual Hog Drive and how thousands of hogs would be herded down the median of this busy highway every November. I had an answer to nearly all of her questions. November was the best season to butcher hogs. The long journey reduced their fat content and made the meat tastier. Yes, a few unfortunate animals strayed onto the roadway, as evidenced by occasional smudges along the drive. But I could not explain how they negotiated the overpasses and underpasses without causing massive traffic jams. She just could not accept the preposterously revealing explanation that the Highway Patrol would stoop that low to assist with traffic control at these problem areas. Every trip thereafter, though, we laughed hilariously while counting the smudges on the road between Statesville and Greensboro, making mockery of the poor representatives of other species who had met their own untimely demises.

At one time, a movie production company used a clever technique in presenting its trademark introduction to the film. A white horse would begin trotting in a serpentine course from a darkened background. As it approached the foreground of the screen, it would transform into a magnificent representation from Greek mythology by sprouting wings and taking flight. It looked very real. But my daughter never fell for my assertion that I had seen such an animal on the Parkway. She knew *that* story was a fairy tale, and I knew she was growing up on me.

The title of this chapter might suggest the following to be a work of fiction, a fairy tale of sorts. But fiction it is not. And a fairy tale it is, in the context that I remain in awe that this story happened to me.

2

Door Number Three

"I've never intended to be exceptional. I just want someone
to say I have promise."
— *How Close We Come*, by Susan S. Kelly

Nearly every sport the Wolfpack of North Carolina State University touched
in 1974 turned to gold. Basketball coach Norm Sloan was edging his team toward
a national championship with superstars David Thompson, Monte Towe, and
Tom Burleson. Campus was bundled up for the winter. The sunbathing "beach"
between Owen and Tucker dormitories was unofficially closed. Students of den-
drology could be seen struggling to identify trees naked of their leaves by means
of bud and twig characteristics. The student newspaper warned streakers to
"wear adequate foot coverings to prevent cut and bruised feet." John Denver
was a musical sensation, and Daniel Ellsberg was a political sensation. President
Richard Nixon was becoming more distant with the press. Students were enraged
over the price of parking decals. The Eastern timber wolf, our school mascot,
had been placed on the endangered species list. Robotic engineering majors and
their kind wore black-rimmed glasses. Dreamy design majors and their kind
wore wire-rimmed glasses. Natural resource recreation majors, such as myself,
wore hiking boots, no matter the surface or weather.

Like thousands of different species of insects all wrapped in a single winter's cocoon, we grew and developed, munching away at books, viewing the
world outside with a narrow eye. Each of us would someday emerge in fluttering brilliance to become that which we were destined to be. Since childhood, I
had just assumed that my mere attendance at such an institution would magi-
cally transform me into a park ranger at Hanging Rock State Park upon successful graduation.

I had come to love that park as a little boy, swimming in its cold, spring-fed lake and picnicking under a rustic shelter built by the Civilian Conservation Corps. There were sights, sounds, and smells there that a boy could experience nowhere else. Growing into adolescence and more courage, my brother Bob, my friend Charles, and I ventured first onto its many trails and eventually bushwhacked our way into every corner of its backcountry, discovering and examining, in close detail, its every mountain, waterfall, cave, and stream. Fearlessly and foolishly, we scrambled over rock cliffs without the protection of safety lines. We frightened ourselves to death with the discovery of an old airplane crash. We clambered through rock fields that we learned years later to be prime rattlesnake habitat. We named our favorite camping spot "The Shelves" and rationalized that it was located just a few feet outside of the park boundary. Old hatchet marks on a boundary tree, we gambled, would justify our case to any park ranger who challenged our legal right to camp and build a fire there. We named a prominent rock face "Jason's Wall" and pledged that the first son born amongst us would be named Jason. My brother kept that pledge.

From its lofty peaks to the south, we could see our hometown of Winston-Salem, North Carolina, a place from which we regularly fled but to which we always scurried back when we became tired and hungry. Our view to the east was one of flatter land, for which we had little use. To the north rested Virginia, a land about which we knew little. To the west, just a few miles beyond the Dan River Valley, stood the Blue Ridge Mountains running northeast to southwest in a long line as far as the eye could see. Somewhere out there, we knew, was our future; for the time being, we were quite content to leave it there.

In the movie *The Good Old Boys*, C.C. Tarpley, a ruthless banker and land baron played by Wilford Brimley, chastises Hewey Calloway, a good-hearted cowboy played by Tommy Lee Jones, for his presumed wandering and shiftless life. Hewey humbly and reflectively replies that his work had once taken him into the glacier country of Canada. C.C. then asked him how much of it he owned, to which Hewey replied, "In a way I own it all." We lads owned not a single acre in that park, but we knew it belonged to us.

I was about thirteen years old the day our Scout troop took a trip to Hanging Rock that I would never forget. We had just completed a long hike and were enjoying a wiener roast in the picnic area when a man drove into the parking lot in a green pickup truck sporting an official-looking insignia on its door. He was a park ranger, neatly dressed in green trousers and a grey shirt, wearing a name tag and a badge. Experience had probably taught him that young Scouts could ravage the place he was sworn to protect, regardless of their espoused conservation virtues. He had once been a boy himself, and stopping to chat with us was no more than a thinly veiled excuse to survey the surrounding area for litter and incriminating initials carved on trees. Satisfied that we had bridled our mischief, at least in that spot, he took a few extra minutes to fascinate us with tales of living and working in the park. At that very moment, I decided that I would be HIM someday, despite the urgings of Miss Kinnamon, my seventh grade English teacher, to become a writer.

I walked confidently into Biltmore Hall that winter morning, certain that I would work my internship the following summer at Hanging Rock State Park. I left the building in a nearly catatonic state, carrying the monstrous Standard Form 171 federal job application.

Dr. William E. Smith supervised the summer internship program and was a friend to all of his students. The manner in which he cocked his head slightly to one side and interlocked his fingers while lecturing revealed his gentle nature. I liked him as a professor but despised his class in which I had been forced to enroll. Recreation programming was a required core course, but I had no intentions of ever working in a sport or municipal recreation setting.

We met in his office at the appointed time, and he calmly asked where I preferred to complete my internship. Following my quick reply, he smiled and apologized that all of the slots available at my first choice were filled and asked for my second choice. What? I had never considered a second choice! I frantically explained to Dr. Smith that my enrollment at that institution had been undertaken only so I could spend the rest of my life at Hanging Rock.

His sympathetic chuckle caused his chair to rock backward, and with a fatherly seriousness, he leaned forward, and with convincing demeanor, counseled that my focus was far too narrow and offered what he thought would be a better opportunity. He was fairly certain that he could place me on the Blue Ridge Parkway as an interpretive ranger. He was not aware of any State student that had ever been placed there before. My only consolation was that I would be employed by the National Park Service, an opportunity which far exceeded my boyhood dream.

But the duty station was in that unfamiliar land of Virginia at an oddly named place called the Peaks of Otter. An extremely shy Tim would be stretched far beyond his comfort zone conducting guided walks, working in a visitor center, and presenting campfire programs to large groups of visitors. Contractually, he would be required to work through Labor Day and would miss enrollment for the fall semester of his senior year and the first two weeks of class.

In a token effort to mend my unraveled world, Dr. Smith kindly offered to enroll me in all of my classes and make proper explanation to each of my professors for my delayed attendance. How could I decline? He offered no other choice.

3

Twelve Years, Eight Months, Forty-One Days

"I learned this, at least, by my experiment; that if one advances confidently in the direction of his dreams, and endeavors to live the life which he has imagined, he will meet with a success unexpected in common hours."
—*Walden,* by Henry David Thoreau

The tombstone of my great-great-grandfather, John Fletcher Pegram, fully denotes his birth date as September 5, 1824, and his death date as February 8, 1882. Yet, also neatly chiseled into the stone — which required additional painstaking effort and some probable extra expense — is his age, expressed as fifty-seven years, five months, and three days. I have observed this practice to be fairly common on my family history forays into older cemeteries, and it evidences an apparent emphasis upon the length of a life.

The sum total of my life on the Blue Ridge Parkway can be expressed similarly, beginning with that summer internship in 1974. Twelve years denotes the approximate length of full-time employment as a protection ranger from 1978 to 1990. Eight months denotes the approximate length of seasonal employment as an interpretive ranger during the summers of 1974 and 1975. And forty-one days denotes the exact length of time I took to backpack the entire length of the Parkway during the autumn of 2003, confessedly, as one of its most unconventional park visitors to date.

Quite frankly, I had grown a bit weary of the early morning carpool arrangement with the two civil engineering majors from my neighborhood. They had little interest in my perfect knowledge of the scientific name of the sweetgum tree —*Liquidambar styraciflua.* Outnumbering me, they dominated the conversation with garbled references to stress, load, and equations quite foreign to me. They simply trusted the trees to grow as I trusted the bridges to stand.

Once on campus, I was confined for the day until my wife, Patty, concluded her work at the standard time of 5:00 P.M. at a local interior design firm. This schedule allowed more time on campus than I needed or desired for study purposes, and I was spending far too much time in the student center watching the Senate Watergate hearings on television. The time had come for us to become a two-car family. More importantly than for convenience, I needed a second vehicle to complete this summer internship work on the Blue Ridge Parkway, while Patty continued living and working in Raleigh, North Carolina.

And so I found one, a 1960 Valiant with a second coat of exterior white paint that had been applied, if one looked closely, with a paint brush. For the bargain price of $130, I now owned a "device" that ran perfectly but was no valentine on which to gaze. It later revealed further secrets inconsequential to its ability to convey a body across land. The linkage forks for the standard transmission were held together with a knotted wad of rubber bands. One side of the rear floorboard, covered cleverly with a carpet sample, had rusted completely through. And the fuel gauge was stuck on empty. Surviving a ride in this car merely required one to ride with the windows rolled down to avoid carbon monoxide asphyxiation, occasionally lift the rubber boot at the base of the stick shifter to check the condition of the rubber bands, and stop frequently for fuel.

Patty chose to follow me to the Peaks of Otter that warm, sunny day in May 1974 in our real car. I appreciated her interest in where I would be spending the summer, but as I watched her follow in the rear-view mirror, I developed a nagging feeling that a shortage in confidence that my old Valiant would make it up the mountain better defined her role on the trip.

Our tiny caravan entered the Parkway near Roanoke, Virginia, and headed north. We had a thirty-five mile drive from that point to my home for the summer. Prior to that moment, I had no memory of ever visiting the Parkway. Perhaps we had driven a short section of it on that proverbial childhood trip every North Carolina family took, at least once during that era, to see the Cherokee Indian Reservation, the Great Smoky Mountains National Park, and Rock City — all in one hurried trip. I just had no recollection of it.

My first impression was that the Parkway looked and felt like everything that a park should be, and I was captivated by its beauty and design. As we rounded a curve near a place called Pine Tree Overlook, high on the crest of the Blue Ridge Mountains, a scene of cathedral proportions came into view. Ahead loomed twin mountain peaks standing a good 1,500 feet higher than the road on which we were driving. We had already driven twenty-six miles up to that point through a park that seemed to have no visible boundaries. For the next nine miles, the road spiraled in and out of rich coves of hardwood forest and then abruptly entered a small, open valley. Something about the scene before me suggested that we had merely been traveling over a long, beautiful driveway to something even more spectacular. A dark, beautiful lake sparkled in the foreground, surrounded triangularly by the majestic twin peaks of Sharp Top and Flat Top Mountains and little Harkening Hill. A lodge, restaurant, campground, visitor center, and picnic area all seemed to fit perfectly into the scene. Visitors were enjoying themselves, and park employees appeared to be loving their jobs immensely. We had arrived at the Peaks of Otter.

The district ranger was prompt in meeting us, and before I could get unpacked and settled into the male dormitory — an old house trailer — he offered Patty a job for the summer collecting fees in the campground. An employee he had hired for the summer had just declined the job, and he had been given emergency hiring authority. We both looked at each other, dumbfounded, having already accepted the fact that we would not be seeing much of each other for the next three months. I was further shocked when Patty accepted the offer and explained to me that, if her employer would not give her a three-month leave of absence, she would simply resign. She had fallen in love with the Peaks of Otter at first sight and was determined to spend the summer there with me.

She headed back to Raleigh for her things, and I found us an apartment in the nearby town of Bedford. I was quite relieved to learn that her boss not only granted her request but offered her a salary increase if she would return to work for him in September. He even brought his wife up for a weekend visit that summer just to see for himself what would cause an otherwise stable young woman to make such a brash decision.

By the time Patty returned a few days later, I was well into the business of helping visitors enjoy and better understand the park through guided walks, slide programs, and campfire programs. In the heat of the afternoon, I took visitors on creek walks and explained how surface tension permitted the water strider to walk on water. In the cool of the night, I took visitors on night walks and cleverly "sniffed out" spiders with a flashlight. One of my campfire programs introduced visitors to an array of wild edible foods and a sampling of freshly brewed sassafras tea. This kind of work became perfect medicine for my timid nature, and I thoroughly enjoyed becoming a better-versed naturalist while trying to find an answer to every question a visitor could pose. I was receiving an education that no university could teach and getting paid to boot.

Meanwhile, Patty made friends with every camper who kindly paid the fee for their campsite. Those who attempted to avoid the fee she dutifully hunted down and captured on her government-issued bicycle equipped with a battery-operated siren.

The protection rangers, though, seemed to have the most exciting job. I was fascinated with their radio chatter and tales of stalking ginseng poachers and providing lifesaving first aid to victims of motor vehicle accidents. Their road patrols also brought relief to the careless visitor who had run out of gasoline and justice to the one who attempted to negotiate the curvy road under the influence of alcohol. They were duty-bound, as has often been said, to protect the park from the people, the people from the park, and the people from the people.

A most memorable event occurred that summer. One Patty Hearst, a Federal fugitive at the time, had supposedly been sighted in the area riding as a passenger in a certain make and color of vehicle bearing a certain license plate number. An observant patrol ranger spotted this very vehicle traveling down the Parkway and began following it while requesting back-up units. The driver of the suspect vehicle eventually made a sudden U-turn in the road and was greeted by a train of six ranger patrol units who had not quite completed their plan for a textbook felony stop. Nevertheless, one was clumsily executed, and both occupants were ordered out of their vehicle and onto the pavement at gunpoint. The rangers had no other choice; the suspects were thought to be armed with automatic weapons. The right car was arrested but it contained the wrong people, and apologies were quickly made. Some poor couple on vacation did, however, receive a complimentary dinner and stay at the Peaks of Otter Lodge and Restaurant.

Or so the story went, as it was told to me. Unless one were present, one never knew to what degree these stories were afterwards embellished. Fortunately, for my own career aspirations, this incident occurred as I was innocently busy at the summit of Sharp Top Mountain sharing with visitors the many theories of how the Peaks of Otter might have acquired its name.

A sense of family developed that summer between a group of employees who represented a wide range of cultural and professional differences. Our camaraderie peaked in bloom on July 25, when we decided to celebrate Christmas six months early. A suitable tree was found and decorated. A traditional dinner was served. Gifts were exchanged. Live string music was played. And all were happy in that rustic log cabin that memorable night.

For my swan song performance, I spent many hours carefully choreographing the best of the district color slide collection to some enchanting instrumental music. With a remote in each hand and a silent prayer that a slide would not jam in the tangle of four projectors and two dissolve units, I splashed the artful photography of rangers past onto the screen at precisely timed intervals. The crowd of visitors that evening in the amphitheater gave a standing ovation. I had shared with them the best I and the park had to offer, and they knew it. Like a shooting star, our glorious summer quickly streaked to a rapid, unwanted conclusion. Patty returned to her former job, and I started down the home stretch of my final two semesters.

In a 1958 interview, Stanley W. Abbott, the Parkway's first resident landscape architect, thusly described his 1934 mandate to connect Shenandoah National Park to the Great Smoky Mountains National Park with a 469-mile scenic highway:

> Now we are coming in here amidst this natural beauty. We had better design and
> build thoughtfully, sensitively, creatively. We had better not have dull, insensitive

The author and wife Patty in front of the Peaks of Otter Visitor Center, Virginia, summer 1974.

people doing it. It requires sensitivity to design even such a comparatively minor detail as a sign and a signpost, as you usher men and women into the presence of the natural gods, as at the foot of Old Faithful.... I can't imagine a more creative job than locating that Blue Ridge Parkway, because you worked with a 10-league canvas and a brush of [a] comet's tail. Moss and lichens collected on the shake roof of a Mabry Mill measured against the huge panoramas that look out forever.

Abbott's vision of the Parkway included widenings or bulges of several hundred to thousands of acres sprinkled along an otherwise narrow, linear park, described as "beads on a string; the rare gems in the necklace." His vision is crystallized in the widening known as the Peaks of Otter. Abbott Lake, its focal point, now quietly honors his name and contributions.

An old photograph taken of Patty and me, standing in front of the visitor center, skinny and dressed in our flat hats and National Park Service uniforms, immortalizes that summer. Abbott's chief assistant, Edward Abbuehl, compared the interpretive services offered by the Parkway as the "frosting on the cake ... the final finishing touches." Dr. Smith had blessed me with a rare opportunity to participate in such work, but it took me a number of years to finally forgive him, not for derailing my career plans, but for failing to keep half of his promise regarding the internship. He had, indeed, registered me for six courses, totaling nineteen semester hours, but had failed to explain my delayed reporting date to some of the professors. Some had dropped me from their rosters, and none had a neatly arranged folder of make-up work waiting for me, as I had envisioned. In my frenzy to salvage the semester, I applied myself so intently on playing catch-up that I "accidentally" earned my first and only 4.0 grade point average for a semester. I am, however, forever grateful to Dr. Smith for stretching me beyond my own head.

Only one student out of a total of 198 graduating from the School of Forest Resources in May 1975 was offered full-time employment with a Federal agency. His appointment was with the U.S. Forest Service. Most Federal agencies, including the National Park Service, were hiring from registers of applicants who had taken the PACE exam (Professional & Administrative Careers Examination). I had taken this excruciatingly painful exam twice prior to graduation. Unable to score higher than the low nineties, I refused to be tortured by it a third time. Without the benefit of veteran preference, which added points to the score, the prospect of my name ever floating high enough on a register to be reachable looked rather dismal. Besides, I was going to become a park ranger at Hanging Rock State Park and had an application on file with the N.C. Division of State Parks well before graduation. Meanwhile, seasonal rehire privileges landed me another interpretive ranger position for a second summer on the Parkway, stationed this time at another widening known as Linville Falls in North Carolina.

Our marriage had miraculously survived the cramped quarters of a ten-foot by fifty-foot house trailer for four years. The narrow, one-way hallway had been the cause of many stubborn standoffs, and we had no regrets selling it to another student. The old Valiant, despite its haggard appearance and hazardous secrets, had served us well and sold for a net profit of thirty dollars. With college behind us, we headed up another mountain to an uncertain future with everything we owned in a borrowed pickup truck.

One product of President Franklin D. Roosevelt's New Deal program to provide economic relief to a nation reeling in the throes of the Great Depression was the Resettlement Administration. The first five recreation areas, or widenings, constructed along the Parkway were purchased from impoverished landowners through funds from that program. Conversely, Linville Falls was acquired through the generous philanthropy of John D. Rockefeller Jr. Worlds apart in visual comparison to the Peaks of Otter, it requires a modest hike to view its focal point, a dramatic waterfall plunging into a rugged gorge. Still, the area hooked us just as deeply.

Apparently the Parkway had stumbled onto a good deal when it acquired several surplus mobile homes from a flood disaster area for use as ranger quarters. Our new home at Linville Falls could not be cleansed of the musty smell of mud, and the front door had a hole in it the size of a baseball. But, alas, it was much larger than the one we had just sold, and Jody Marody, our pet Siamese cat, was a skilled mouser.

Left to right: Leigh Ann Medford, Sonya Askew (visiting cousin), Rhonda Medford in the summer of 1975 in the driveway of the ranger quarters located at Milepost 317.5 near Linville Falls, North Carolina.

Our lives became quickly intertwined with neighbors Ronnie and Robbie Medford and their two young daughters, Rhonda and Leigh Ann, who also lived in the same cluster of ranger quarters. Ronnie was a permanent protection ranger and took me under his wing. He sensed my interest in the protection work and invited me to ride night patrols with him. From him, I learned how to shoot a revolver and the clever intricacies of catching a speeder with a radar gun and a poacher spotlighting deer. I was always welcome to join him on any call-out in the middle of the night if I could get dressed in time. We had no telephone so, upon receipt of a call, he would bump the siren on his patrol car as my cue that he would be leaving momentarily. Rhonda and Leigh Ann idolized singer Olivia Newton-John, who must have been just as adorable at their ages. Their flirtatious renditions of "Please Mr. Please" and "Have You Never Been Mellow" were as entertaining as their playful traffic control antics with a "Stop-Slow" paddle they had borrowed from the trunk of their dad's patrol car.

Claude and Vivian McKinney's nearby country store became our connection to the local folks in that part of Avery County. The McKinneys treated us like family and introduced us to everyone in the community who used the purchase of a soda as an excuse for stopping to chat. Game wardens, foresters, park rangers, and their kind used it as an informal rendezvous point to swap tales and tips. The frequent sight of one or more official vehicles in its small parking lot rendered a wholesome, law-abiding atmosphere to an otherwise quaintly dilapidated structure by which a cautious tourist might otherwise pass.

Linville Falls was a base of operation for my work, which included duties farther south on the Parkway at the Museum of North Carolina Minerals and Crabtree Meadows. I expanded my campfire program theme of wild edibles, developed the previous summer, to include cooking demonstrations of trout caught in the Linville River and crayfish plucked from the more shallow waters of Camp Creek. Off-duty days were justifiably frittered away in the hunter-gatherer fantasy that we could live off the land and forever in Avery County when my appointment terminated on Labor Day.

My immediate supervisor, friend, and mentor for the summer was none other than Harley E. Jolley, professor of history at nearby Mars Hill College, author of the scholarly historical work *The Blue Ridge Parkway,* and veteran seasonal interpretive ranger. Dr. Jolley, as we called him, traveled about all summer in an old Volkswagen with the back seat filled with props, including a rocking chair, that he used for his own campfire programs. His vast knowledge of the Parkway and genuine demeanor, yes indeed, charmed the visitor in a way that could never be duplicated.

One busy day, while working the counter at the Museum of North Carolina Minerals, I was approaching my limit on how many times I was willing to give visitors directions to the restroom. Visitation was heavy that day, and my thumb ached from the steady clicking of the little hand-held device I was required to use to count every person who walked through the door. Dr. Jolley arrived to assist, and I expressed to him my concern that perhaps the Parkway had reached its carrying capacity for the day. This was a term I had learned in an advanced recreation theory course in college. In simple terms, it is the measurable limit that a recreation resource can tolerate before irreversible damage occurs to it or the users' enjoyment of it is appreciably diminished (or the employees managing it just cannot take it any longer).

I thought this observation would impress Dr. Jolley, but he simply smiled and replied that he only lost sleep over the millions in the world that had never experienced the Parkway. I was dazzled momentarily by his vision, until a gentleman approached the counter and innocently asked for directions to the restroom. I tensed and twitched. Graciously, Dr. Jolley gave me an "allow me" nod and worked his magic. I am certain this man forgot that he even needed to use the restroom as he excitedly exited the building with a map and directions to a nearby emerald mine.

Lying in the afternoon shadow of the massive range of the Black Mountains, which includes Mount Mitchell, the tallest, North American peak east of the Mississippi River, is another Parkway widening known as Crabtree Meadows. Here I beheld the architecturally precise design of the wild columbine flower for the first time. It was also the place where I triumphed one day as an interpretive ranger.

A cardinal rule of this trade is to never pretend to know the answer to a visitor's question with a hopeful guess. A stealthy few of them are always lurking to embarrass a weakling ranger with a question to which they already know the answer. They travel from park to park every summer looking for victims of their sick game. Another cardinal rule is to know the identification of every slide in your program, even if it is only being used as window dressing for an unrelated theme. A polite lady in the audience, with no malice aforethought, will inevitably ask the name of the wildflower blooming next to a timber rattlesnake in your program about snakes.

One afternoon I was scheduled to give a guided walk at the campground. About a dozen visitors had gathered for the walk at the Crabtree Falls trail head. A gentleman in the group found a bird sitting on a nest near our gathering point and asked if I could identify it. I was fairly certain it was a solitary vireo, not through any expertise of my own, but because I had a slide of that very species in a program to be presented that evening in the campground amphitheater. The gentleman gleefully judged my identification to be incorrect, citing another species. As he hurried to his nearby camper and returned with the best bird identification books money could buy to prove me wrong, I silently prayed that my slide had been labeled correctly. With a puzzled look, he mumbled references to spectacles and wingbars as he nervously flipped through the pages of his books and, exasperated, finally conceded defeat. The group that had gathered for the walk gave me a kind applause, and the humiliated gentleman faded back to his campsite in disbelief.

As our blissful summer raced toward Labor Day, the prospect of becoming simultaneously homeless and unemployed appeared inevitable. Since graduation, I had made weekly calls to Bill Webster, the hiring official for the state park division. Each time I was advised there were no vacancies.

The small staff of about a dozen seasonal interpretive rangers in North Carolina were scattered across 250 miles of Parkway. At the beginning of the season, wise managers gave us a three-day training and orientation tour of the entire North Carolina section. Disastrously foggy weather on the entire trip and a blown engine on our bus could not thwart the intended objectives. Our group bonded and received masterful instruction. Dr. Jolley gave a demonstration campfire program that was an example of perfection. Bob Bruce, the Parkway's chief interpreter, gave a demonstration slide program riddled with imperfections for our delightful critique. Near summer's end, Jim Warner, our state supervisor, brought us all together again for a final staff meeting and farewell picnic. As Jim thanked us all for our work with the usual formalities, I was snatched from my light daydream when he unexpectedly announced to our group that I had been selected to work for two additional months, if I was available. "Yes, I am available!" I shouted with relieved delight.

My duties for the months of September and October were simplified to operation of the Craggy Gardens Visitor Center and presentation of a slide program at Mount Pisgah every Friday night. What a glorious experience I had, witnessing the complete progression of autumn color—from its earliest tinges to leaf drop, from summit to valley floor — on those daily round trips of nearly a hundred miles. One Sunday afternoon, much to the surprise of visitors in search of autumn color, snow made a visit to the colorful heights of Craggy Gardens.

Winter weather was knocking also at the door of our drafty mobile home, and we knew we had to find other quarters. Parkway maintenance could not afford to winterize it, and we could not afford to heat it. A kind lady who owned a summer cabin in the community heard of our plight and offered it to us for forty dollars per month. It sat high on a knoll with a splendid view of Jonas Ridge. If she would have sold it to us, we would be living there today. This unexpected treat buoyed our spirits as winter, unemployment, and an uncertain future settled upon us.

Suddenly, about mid–November, one of those weekly calls to Bill Webster yielded an interview that led to an offer of employment as a full-time state park ranger. The job was not at Hanging Rock State Park, but it was a step closer in that direction. Mr. Webster later amusingly complained that I had become a gadfly with my persistent tactics. Without them, he confessed, my application would have floundered with hundreds of others in his file cabinet; everybody, it seemed, wanted to be a park ranger. Ronnie Medford begged me not to accept this job and urged me instead to hold out for a permanent position with the National Park Service. But hope and uncertainty were empty bowls at my supper table, and I quietly accepted in the practical recesses of my mind that no such offer would ever be tendered. One thing, however, became solidly certain. The day we drove off that mountain headed for the flatlands of Harnett County, N.C., I left my heart on the Blue Ridge Parkway.

Two and one-half years later, I was enjoying lunch one day with Patty and our infant daughter in our fairly sound, comfortable ranger quarters. I had just been promoted and moved to Crowders Mountain State Park, and most of our belongings were still packed in boxes. The benefits of a steady paycheck and affordable health insurance had brought enough peace of mind to begin a family. But some of the inevitable trials of life, which come to everyone in different forms, were resting heavily on our minds.

Our baby was healthy, but her alert pediatrician diagnosed Patty with lupus. Our home had just been burglarized by a local drug addict, and we lost our first newly purchased color television. My purest sense of fairness had been recently violated through political maneuverings that cost me a sure promotion to Hanging Rock State Park. The reality associated with a $9,000 annual salary was beginning to come into focus, too.

The phone rang, interrupting lunch, and a man at the other end of the line introduced himself as Dan Brown, a supervisory protection ranger on the Blue Ridge Parkway. For several minutes he expounded on the advantages of living and working as a ranger on the Parkway in the Roanoke, Virginia, area. My heart was racing. I knew a little bit about that district. It was an area that had unfairly given ranger work on the Parkway, at the national level, the poor reputation of being no better than that of a glorified highway patrolman. I finally interrupted Mr. Brown's sales pitch and asked if he was offering me the job. When I hung up the phone, Patty sighed and quietly inquired as to where and when we would be moving. Two weeks later we were living again on the Blue Ridge Parkway, and I was employed as a full-time protection ranger.

Just before transferring to another Federal agency twelve years later, an odd thought occurred to me one day. I had stopped at a nondescript location on the Parkway to investigate some faint skidmarks on the pavement to settle my conscience that a vehicle had not plunged over the mountain. I was relieved to discover no mishap and pleasantly surprised at the discovery of a beautiful waterfall cascading down the mountain just below the road grade. I had patrolled past that spot hundreds of times and had never seen the waterfall. Someday, I thought, I would have to return to the Parkway to discover more of its hidden secrets by walking its entire length.

4

Deliberately, Reflectively, Randomly

"Although many people had run the river in boats, no one seemed to have forced a passage of the Canyon on foot."
— *The Man Who Walked Through Time*,
by Colin Fletcher

The opportunity to retire from Federal service at the age of fifty came rather unexpectedly and suddenly, a pardon of sorts from a career choice to which my nature was not suited. And to borrow a line from *Forrest Gump*, "That's all I have to say about that."

The morning of June 3, 2002, found me voluntarily and uncharacteristically rising from bed at 5:48 A.M. for a morning walk. The trees had never looked greener. The sunrise had never looked more glorious. I was certain I heard the chorus of bird species not yet discovered. The great blue heron, standing motionless by the pond, apparently detected a snap in my walk which triggered a survival response to forfeit breakfast. I could have walked ten miles at that pace before my own breakfast. A bleary-eyed neighbor heading to work that Monday morning stopped to congratulate me on my first, official day of retirement. I had not experienced such a feeling since the birth of my daughter. Then, instead of walking five miles a day, I was jogging that distance. The day she came home from the hospital I ran a personal best of five miles in exactly thirty minutes. Such are the rewards of patience, suffering, and endurance as these rare days become the unforgotten lines of demarcation between the chapters of our lives.

The term "retirement," though, is such a hideous word, suggesting an abrupt halt in meaningful productivity, with connotations of laziness if undertaken too early and whisperings of diminished capacity if delayed too long. Prior to its institutionalization by the Social Security Administration, its usage was uncommon in the lexicon of the average American worker. I prefer to avoid its utterance altogether. The modest pension I now receive is no more than just reward for an investment choice made many years ago. If it were to suddenly vanish, I trust that my descendancy from ancestral farming stock would yield the same attitude expressed by Herman Melville in an 1851 letter to Nathaniel Hawthorne, when he said:

> People think that if a man has undergone any hardship, he should have a reward; but for my part, if I have done the hardest possible day's work, and then come to sit down in a corner and eat my supper comfortably — why, then I don't think I deserve any reward for my hard day's work — for am I not now at peace? Is not my supper good?

Oh, but what a blessing it is to live in a time and in a land that permits the happy pursuit and choice of meaningful productivity for an entire lifetime, yielding a harvest far greater than the reward of a good supper.

Words can hardly describe the feeling, following decades of educational and professional pursuits accompanied by their attendant stresses, when the day arrives that you can rise from bed and do anything you please. The world now revolves on your axis. No more alarm clocks, 8:00 A.M. classes, or exams. The recurring nightmare that Dr. Smith informs you, two weeks before graduation, that you are one course short of completing the degree program has finally subsided. No more angst associated with getting to work on time. The morning traffic report is now entertaining rather than distressing. No more performance evaluations that leave you with a nagging feeling that your supervisor is really saying, "This employee is going far, and the sooner he starts, the better." No more applications for vacation leave only to hear your supervisor reply, "But who will work in your place?" No more sinking feelings in the stomach on Sunday afternoon, as the weekend fades, because Mondays now equal Fridays. But you are faced with the certain reality that there is less time ahead of you than behind you and are prompted by an urgency to tackle all of those wonderful postretirement goals and dreams. In my case, retirement came as a rebirth and an opportunity to hearken to the unforgotten counsel of a seventh-grade English teacher. In her opinion, I had not yet achieved my greatest potential and had less time to do so.

The first order of business was to celebrate the occasion, which conveniently dovetailed close to our thirty-first wedding anniversary. Peaks of Otter was a mere two hours from our home now, and the season and route were pleasantly reminiscent of our first journey in the old Valiant. This time, however, we rode together, in a much more reliable vehicle and gasped together in awe again as we rounded the same curve at Pine Tree Overlook.

We stopped first at the visitor center and were a bit disappointed to find it closed, particularly at that time of the year. Had budget cuts become that severe? As we were walking away from the door, astonished by once-timid deer now walking boldly through the parking lot, two women dressed in ranger uniforms exited from a side door of the visitor center. We knew them both, Patty Lockamy and Jamie Parker. I had worked years ago with Patty, who now headed the park's interpretive operations. Jamie was the daughter of veteran park ranger Gene Parker, a friend and colleague from whom I had learned much of rangering. Gene, by his own stubborn choice, had spent his entire career stationed at the Peaks of Otter. Jamie was now working as a seasonal interpretive ranger and, much to our relief, had become a beautiful young woman, having outgrown a baby face closely resembling that of her father.

Patty and Jamie explained that the visitor center was closed due to remodeling and installation of new interpretive exhibits, yet graciously invited us in for a sneak preview. We were most intrigued and humored by the exhibit of the Smith sisters, who revolutionized the Parkway mowing policy with their stealthy photography and embarrassing revelations of wildflower debauchery. During their heyday, those members of the park staff most irritated by their cause affectionately referred to them as the "Snoop Sisters." Their work not only enhanced wildflower diversity along the Parkway but spawned a nationwide interest in wildflower beautification of the interstate highway system. Justly had they been honored and their unique story preserved, and I was pleased.

The day of this particular visit had been carefully planned to coincide with the famous seafood buffet, an every-Friday institution offered at the Peaks of Otter Restaurant, one of the many concession services along the Parkway. Our enjoyment of this tantalizing meal was amplified by a window seat, which framed gentle Abbott Lake in the foreground and the fatherly, rocky peak of Sharp Top Mountain in the background. Had the original plans been implemented, as depicted on an archival drawing bearing Stanley Abbott's signature of approval, dated June 8, 1939, our view would have been reversed. From the opposite side of the lake, we would have been viewing the rounded, motherly crest of Flat Top Mountain and a swimming beach and boat dock on the yonder shore. The moment would have been sublime in either case.

This had not been our first return to the Peaks of Otter since the glory days of the summer of 1974. Photographs taken in front of the visitor center now included some with a daughter, son-in-law, grandchildren, and ourselves, minus the uniform and a little older, weightier, and wiser. One particular Valentine's Day of late fell on a cold, rainy, wintry Sunday. Following church and a lunch of homemade vegetable soup, Patty curled up on the sofa with a magical, sleep-inducing blanket. Just prior to her reaching that point of no return, I suggested that we take an afternoon drive on the Blue Ridge Parkway. Her look, with a single, open eye, felt more chilling than the weather. So I noisily climbed up to the attic to retrieve a travel bag, which caused her other eye to open, reflecting a countenance of growing consternation mixed with bewilderment. The precise moment had arrived to announce that reservations had been made for the evening at the Peaks of Otter Lodge. Zoom, we were off! What I had not planned was a winter landscape scene that could have been taken directly from the movie *Doctor Zhivago*. The lake was frozen. The ground was covered with newly fallen snow. Deer were ambling about the grounds. The wind was blowing just enough to make the stiff, naked trees sway and creak. And the crackling fire in the lobby of the lodge was warm.

What should have been a quick breeze for me through the small gift shop, following that delicious seafood dinner, became a heart-rending experience. At a music preview station equipped with headphones, I discovered the compact disc entitled *The Blue Ridge Mountains*, a pure mix of instrumental music and sounds of nature. I turned my back to the other customers to hide the tears that welled up in my eyes as the first selection, "The Morning Sun," touched something deep inside me. I had experienced every sound I was hearing. This park and I had become best friends the day we met. Spirit to spirit, we understood each other. The time was drawing near for us to become reacquainted.

Quickly then, we drove a few miles north up the Parkway, through gigantic natural gardens of rhododendron in full bloom, in time to witness the setting sun from Thunder Ridge Overlook. A short path from the parking area merged onto the Appalachian Trail and led to a splendid western view across the Great Valley and distant Alleghany Mountains. A buck deer standing along the trail appeared to be attracted to the same spectacle. Near this place, I began my first backpack experience on the Appalachian Trail. Patty and I had nearly perished from dehydration and exhaustion in 1974 backpacking about twenty miles in two days from this point south to the trail's intersection with the Parkway at Bear-wallow Gap. On the second day of our trip, we traveled an uphill stretch with no water resupply points on a very hot, humid day. Years later, I would participate in an emergency rescue of a backpacker suffering from sunstroke on this same stretch of trail and come to the stark realization that Patty and I had been in more serious trouble than we realized. Her interest in future Appalachian Trail experiences waned from that day forward and was ultimately extinguished the next summer on a two-day trip in rain and fog. Despite its perils and sacrifices of comfort, my interest in the trail expanded to section hikes of fifty to sixty miles over the next few years and a goal to thru-hike its entire length someday.

Our celebratory day continued as we enjoyed an informative program, presented by Jamie at the amphitheater, about the life cycle of the gypsy moth and the devastation it was causing the Appalachian forest. I had given many similar programs myself in this very amphitheater and thoroughly enjoyed my role on this occasion as a spectator. Lastly, we stopped at Great Valley Overlook to witness the snuffing of the final vestiges of the afterglow and the debut of sparkling lights in the heavens above and in the valley below. The time was far past midnight when we finally returned to our home back in Oak Ridge, North Carolina.

Fourteen months later I found myself scurrying about the house in a frenzy, making hasty plans to backpack the entire length of the Blue Ridge Parkway, beginning on Labor Day, which conveniently fell on the first day of September that year. The day of the month would exactly coincide, at least for the first thirty days, with the number of days hiked, my mathematically challenged mind wryly surmised. The thought had come suddenly a few days earlier, on the sixth day of August to be precise, that my circumstances had become perfectly aligned to begin such an adventure at that time. Colin Fletcher, renowned author and backpacker, spent a year making preparations to become the first person to hike the length of the Grand Canyon. But the scale of his undertaking far exceeded my plans in terms of risks and unknowns. Navigating through dangerous terrain, alone, in a desert climate, his life depended on a carefully planned schedule and resupply points. I would be backpacking down a paved highway sprinkled with visitor centers, campgrounds, picnic areas, lodges, and restaurants along its path. More of the same and in greater variety could I find not far off its path. People encounters would be frequent. This adventure had been evolving in my head for many years, despite the outwardly impetuous appearance of my hurried planning process. Nevertheless, I had given myself only twenty-five days to make all of the final preparations, and there was much to do.

On June 20, 1936, Congressman Jesse P. Wolcott from Michigan took the floor in a debate of House Resolution 12455 and declared, "Mr. Speaker, I think that this is the most ridiculous undertaking that has ever been presented to the Congress of the United States." He was referring to the Blue Ridge Parkway, which was well under construction as a relief project under the temporary management of the Public Works Administration. Wolcott viewed the project as a "colossal steal" and fought unsuccessfully to block this bill, which placed the Parkway under the administration of the National Park Service and Department of the Interior. I hoped that my adventure would not be perceived as a "most ridiculous undertaking" and began jotting down all of its justifications before taking the first footstep.

Rarely does a single reason explain any significant course of action a person might take. Deliberately, reflectively, and randomly would become the proper adverbs to describe my intentions. The time had come to take the whaling expedition of Herman Melville prior to his writing of *Moby Dick*. My first novel would, likewise, marry actual experience with the embellishment of fictional imagination which, in my case, would most assuredly be of lesser talent and scale, more safely anchored on preferred dry ground.

The attic had been searched for old documents, and the memories of a former park ranger had been scoured, but the material needed to be freshened. I would begin backpacking the Parkway at Milepost Zero, its northern terminus in Virginia, taking an estimated fifty days to reach Milepost 469, its southern terminus in North Carolina. Meticulous notes would be recorded in a journal, documenting every milepost, overlook, and elevation reference for logistical purposes. Forgotten memories and new experiences would be packed between these details. The adventure would become the postlude experience to a former career and a prelude experience to a new one.

I would visit this park in a way that its designers had never envisioned. Instead of whizzing along its scenic, winding course on some conveyance, its intended means of enjoyment, I would slowly and deliberately walk every foot of its path, exposed to every sensory experience its landscape had to offer. I had not forgotten the hidden waterfall I had discovered years earlier and knew there were many more hidden treasures to be found. I would perhaps become the only person to know the location of every pipe spring, the secret refreshment stand of every thirsty mower operator on a hot day. Where motor vehicles were prohibited from stopping along the shoulder of the road, as they are through a scenic watershed area, I could meander unbridled.

This would not be a hike of solitude. There were far superior locations for that sort of experience. Of necessity, it had to be a solo venture. A hiking companion would disrupt the reflective thought process and would surely go insane with the frequent stops I would be making for note taking. Random interaction, though, with visitors, employees, wildlife, and the weather was preferred and of paramount importance. I would have no scheduled appointments except a start date.

As a ranger, I had met numerous visitors who swelled with pride in their proclamation to me that they had driven the entire stretch of "their Parkway." A motorcyclist, who apparently viewed the park as a mere race course, had once boasted to me of having completed it from one end to the other in record time. Many had also bicycled its torturous 469-mile route, pedaling their own weight and equipment a vertical distance of over nine miles. I had even heard of a park ranger who had jogged it. But I was not aware of a single person who had backpacked the thing and neither had a Parkway official who replied to my anonymous e-mail inquiry on the park's official Web site. A preposterous thought, I supposed, for an avowed backpacking enthusiast to consider trekking down a highway, albeit scenic by design. Nevertheless, to test the hypothesis that I might be the first, I mailed a brief press release entitled "Former Park Ranger Plans To Become First Person To Backpack The Entire Blue Ridge Parkway" to a few selected newspapers I thought might have an interest in the venture. Before I could even begin the trek, the *Kernersville* (N.C.) *News*, a local paper, declared in a headline, "A 469-mile nature hike — Oak Ridge man preparing to hike the Blue Ridge Parkway." *The Floyd* (Va.) *Press* declared, "Man plans to hike entire Parkway." My longest hike to date had been sixty miles, and I had never quite attained the "trail legs" spoken of by distance backpackers. This would be an excellent test of my body and equipment for a future hike of the entire Appalachian Trail. The press had now trapped me in my own words, and I would complete this thing if I had to crawl to its finish.

5

Means of Engagement

"There are some enterprises in which a careful disorder-
liness is the true method."
     —*Moby Dick*, by Herman Melville

Mothers and wives are welcome only by invitation in the final, frenetic
stages of preparation for a backpacking trip. Their solicitous, hands-on-the-hips
presence, wrinkled foreheads, questions, and reminders are genuine displays of
concern for safety and comfort. But the party to whom such posturing is directed
generally considers such interest a distraction and annoyance, until an essential
item needs to be located. Such tender ones are then demandingly called upon
to find and deliver said items instantly. A safe return home always guarantees a
more relaxed, loving countenance and a favorite dish for supper. But first, the
sentry blocking the doorway, with garden hose in hand, displaying the disposition of a policeman decked in full riot gear, must first be obliged by dropping
all gear and clothing before entering the premises. Boys and men would become
despicable animals without them.

I am reminded of a boyhood romp. My mother, at our request, dropped
us boys off at a point on N.C. Route 8 where we could take a direct compass
bearing on the Hanging Rock, situated a good five miles in the distance. Stubbornly undeviating on our bearing, we walked through woodlands, briar thickets, and creeks. Through freshly plowed fields and past laundry hung out to dry
within the curtilage of private property we traipsed. In many parts of this country, such folly would have resulted in buckshot rash. The good country folk of
Stokes County, however, just gave us curious stares and nodded approvingly as
we climbed over their fences as carefully as we could. They had sense enough to
know that boys needed "wood to chop" and granted us safe passage.

Tired, dirty, and hungry following three days of exploration, we bushwhacked our way out of the park to another road. Charles's mother, by prior arrangement, had been requested to retrieve us at noon "somewhere along N.C. Route 66." Eager for the comforts of home, we strategically placed ourselves near the highway on someone's mowed lawn. Soon she arrived, and in precisely the exact order that Charles had predicted, asked firstly if our trip had been fun, secondly if we had gotten cold, and thirdly if we had brought enough to eat. We laughed so hard that Mrs. Parsons threatened to never assist us with logistical support again.

The only item of gear left over from those days that I still continued to use was a Boy Scout poncho, which should have been mothballed years ago. Under no circumstances did it ever offer any protection from rain from the waist down. Some protection was afforded to the head and vital organs of the torso region if I could get it snapped properly while wearing the backpack. A second person could be helpful with this maneuver but was not always available. Even so, with the slightest wind, I always felt like a girl wearing a dress too short for the occasion. The time had come to upgrade my rain gear to a respectable pack cover, pair of rain pants, and rain jacket at my favorite provision company. Gambling for a fifty-day stretch of fair weather on the Parkway, I knew, would be a losing bet.

Self-imposed Ground Rule #1 prohibited me from spending a single night in a motel. There would be plenty of temptation to do so at the fine Parkway concession facilities, namely the Peaks of Otter Lodge, Rocky Knob Cabins, Bluffs Lodge, and Pisgah Inn. Many more privately owned facilities could also be easily accessed just off the Parkway in towns and villages. Philosophically speaking, the thought reeked of hypocrisy to a veteran backpacker. Practically speaking, it could become quite an expensive habit, and my travels no longer qualified for government per diem. From the onset, I had every intention of spending every single night in a tent or under the stars.

But choosing a campsite would be a challenge. Park regulations permitted camping only in designated campgrounds, and they were spaced much farther apart than I planned to walk in any single day. Even bicyclists touring the Parkway have difficulty timing their evenings to campgrounds spaced anywhere from about twenty to seventy miles apart. With a fair understanding already of the location of much of the park boundary, which could usually be found not too far from the roadway, I would practice leave-no-trace camping on U.S. Forest Service and privately owned lands. Self-imposed Ground Rule #2 would prohibit me from building a fire at these carefully selected campsites. Though a solo hiker's best companion after sunset and legal in many places, I worried that it might attract the unnecessary attention of well-meaning firefighters or a second violation notice and fine from an irritated park ranger unsympathetic to an inaccurate determination of the park boundary.

I had spent the night in a motel only once in my entire backpacking history, in justifiable concern that a true medical emergency might develop during the night. About halfway through a sixty-mile section hike of the Appalachian

Trail in one of the driest Octobers on record in southwest Virginia, maps and plans failed me miserably. Already short on my water supply by noon, I passed up the plentiful waters of the North Fork of the Holsten River. Pure in appearance and swift in flow, its lush algae content and dense snail population warned my better senses that, though boiling might render its water safe from upstream manure runoff, it would not eliminate other unknown toxins seeping from farms and highways. I had not yet purchased a water purification pump and had yet to become ill from carefully selected mountain springs. My trail guide showed two good water sources and two ascents of about eight hundred vertical feet apiece over Big Walker and Gullion Mountains along the next ten miles to Interstate 81, the next highway crossing.

Both springs, however, proved to be bone dry, and the normally modest climbs became killers. Driven by thirst and a fear that I would become delirious and wander off the trail, I doggedly staggered forward from one white blaze to the next. I had never been thirsty to the point that my tongue felt like it was stuck to the roof of my mouth. Teasingly, a thunderstorm developed at dusk, yielding more lightning than rain, just as I came off the last wooded ridge into an expansive pasture. Two miles in the distance glowed the lights of an oasis, at which the trail crossed the interstate highway right in front of a fast food restaurant. The cows must have thought me silly, wearing that airy poncho, walking through their living room, holding my aluminum cooking pot high in the air trying to catch a few raindrops. If I was going to die from a lightning strike, I would do so without my tongue stuck to the roof of my mouth. Halfway to the oasis of choice, I stopped at a farmhouse, where a kind, elderly couple shared all the water I could drink.

At the restaurant, I basically ordered a large size of everything on the menu and, out of respect to the more civilized customers, excused myself to the outdoor dining area under the handy shelter of a gazebo. Meanwhile, the weather deteriorated to a driving rain and chilling wind. Uncertainty of the trail direction in the darkness, a nauseous feeling from either eating too quickly or failing to remove the pickles from a triple cheeseburger, and genuine concern for ill effects from my dehydrated condition caused me to take notice of a cheap motel a short distance down the road. Only one room remained vacant, and I took it. The next morning the kidneys seemed to be working properly, and I completed the trip in good health. Soon thereafter, I purchased a reputable water purification pump and now consider it a mandatory piece of equipment.

For the Parkway trek, and with much nostalgic anguish, I retired my old two-man tent, relegating it to the abuse and amusement of grandchildren. Nearly thirty years old, it was so familiar that I could pitch it without the aid of light on the darkest of nights. Younger backpackers snickered at its bright, two-tone green and yellow color scheme and its maze of guy lines. In its defense, the weather — no matter how dark and gloomy outside — always appeared deceptively better from within its flashy interior. But its eight guy lines required a roomy site, were tedious to stake down and adjust, and I would not miss trip-

The author's old tent on a solo backpacking trip taken about 1988 in the Shining Rock Wilderness Area, Pisgah National Forest, Haywood County, North Carolina.

ping over them at night answering the call of nature. Though stalwart in a strong wind, it had long ago lost its ability to efficiently repel water and was more tent and weight than I needed on a long solo trip.

Its replacement was a modern, lightweight, three-season, one-man model that could be pitched in seconds in a small space. A handy vestibule by the zippered doorway provided a perfect location for pack storage outside of the tent but still within easy reach. Its interior fit me perfectly. Over half of the roof was constructed of mosquito netting which, minus the rainfly, offered a superb view of the heavens. I could not decide if it looked more like an Alaskan dog sled or the soap box derby I had built as a kid. A lightweight, positive-pressure foam pad, topped off with a few exhalations of air, would provide the most efficient comfort and insulation between me and the ground. A heavy, musty, military-surplus, down-filled sleeping bag had long ago been replaced with a lightweight, three-season model with a twenty-degree Fahrenheit rating.

With shelter and bedding thusly described, some interpretation might be helpful. It is offered apologetically to the skilled, sincerely to the unskilled, and satirically to the manufacturers of such outdoor equipment. The term "three-season" presumably translates into "not for winter use in the Temperate Zones of the Northern and Southern hemispheres." I readily confess that I carefully disguised my initial ignorance of this expression when the young salesman first uttered it. His ensuing communication, expert and fluid, fell on deaf, inattentive ears as my diminishing, inferential thought process finally concluded that we were talking about spring, summer, and autumn. No other seasonal combination made sense.

I have never been a browser shopper via catalog or store and never intend to become one. When I need something, I go to a store, look at each option, make all appearances to understand what I am doing, ask an occasional question, take an extraordinary amount of time, and sometimes purchase an item. Patty and the salesperson usually get quite irritated with this technique. The young man would simply have to back up and repeat the parts of his sales pitch I had missed during my brief period of mental absence.

September and October had been purposefully chosen for this trip. The extremes of summer heat and winter cold would not have to be endured. Facilities would all be open for the annual tourist onslaught to view the approaching autumnal color display. I could reduce my pack weight significantly with the omission of heavier winter gear. There was nothing left to prove to myself in terms of winter adventure. I had experienced frozen water bottles at a younger age and had developed an unyielding resolve to never do so again.

Still, the selection of clothing necessarily had to accommodate the likely temperature range of twenty to eighty degrees Fahrenheit, variances in humidity, and the chilling effects of wind and rain. Its choice also had to be in full compliance with self-imposed Ground Rule #3: DO NOT GIVE THE APPEARANCE OF BEING A BUM. Rightly or wrongly, a bearded, dirty, disheveled man standing on an interstate access ramp with a backpack and a destination sign will likely have difficulty obtaining a ride. His chances of social interaction are vastly improved if the setting is a national park, and minus the sign, he just appears to be hiking. If I could further refine my image by avoiding a dirty, disheveled appearance and, to the extent possible, maintain a clean-shaven face, I hoped to maximize the potential for positive employee and visitor interactions. Bridled by a general disposition to rarely burst upon a stranger with my presence, a neat appearance would hopefully invite even the most cautious individual to initiate a conversation. My veteran fedora, expediently functional in its ability to offer protection from sun, rain, and heat loss and in masking the horror of a chronic case of "hat hair," would now be summoned to the higher calling of flying as an ensign of good will.

Although they are not the wisest choice during cold weather, rain, or both, I am most comfortable in full-length, loose-fitting, cotton trousers, supported by an adjustable drawstring. Their legs can be easily rolled up to the knees during the heat of the day, and the waist can be gradually adjusted as weight loss occurs. A pair of these, matched with a short-sleeved, buttoned shirt, synthetic undergarments, and sturdy boot socks would suffice for a few days. A single duplicate set of these items, with pants and shirt of different color, would be stowed inside a waterproof plastic bag, to be rotated with the set worn as laundry facilities became available. A red bandanna, carried in a rear pocket, would cool the sweaty brow and insulate the fingers from the heat of a boiling pot of water. Finally, a pair of cushioned boots, carefully selected for a specialized mission over pavement, would complete the basic wardrobe. Additional clothing accessories would include: a light pair of slippers for end-of-the-day foot relief and middle-of-the-night nature calls; a quilted, long-sleeved shirt, toboggan, and gloves for additional warmth (which could be supplemented with the rain gear if necessary); a cotton pullover shirt; and, as emergency contingencies, an extra pair of boot lacings and a needle and thread kit.

Proper attention to personal hygiene would boost the approachability factor but would be more critically important to health maintenance. This hike was not to be a five-day insult to the body, after which the blisters and strains could be doctored in the comfort of home with miraculous medical supplies. I needed to avoid injury and sickness at all costs for a sustained period of physical stress. Discomfort could and would be tolerated, but an infected blister could bring the trek to an embarrassing, premature conclusion. The last piece of equipment I wanted to use was my health insurance identification card, carefully hidden in a secret place along with photo identification in the form of a driver's license, a list of emergency telephone contacts, cash in the form of currency, and a credit card. I would not be robbed easily, but a meticulous investigator, under the worst of circumstances, would be able to find these items with a little effort.

A small but vital supply of personal hygiene items would be neatly stowed in the many zippered compartments of a fashionable, lightweight vinyl bag, trendily designed for the luxury of a hotel, yet ideal for the woods. A few ounces of baking soda would serve dual purposes of toothpaste and deodorant. Dental floss, carefully measured to a fifty-day supply in demonstration of a fanatic obsession with weight limitations, could substitute for strong thread, if necessary. Exactly fifty carefully counted, cotton-tipped ear swabs would satisfy another obsession, contrary to the advice once given by a medical doctor. The feeling of dirty ears ruins my day worse than tight underwear. A featherweight wash cloth, comb, toothbrush, and disposable razor would serve their obvious purposes, while a few ounces of all-purpose liquid soap would clean the hair, body, and kitchen or soften the whiskers enough for a minimally painful shave. A few adhesive bandages could patch either the body or the air mattress, while parts of the clean set of clothing could be sacrificed for larger bandaging, if needed. A daily multiple vitamin to supplement nutritionally deficient trail food, a few antacid tablets for the dinner gulped too quickly, a few acetaminophen tablets for an occasional headache, a few ibuprofen tablets for a strained muscle, and a few anti-diarrheal tablets for the dreaded curse would comprise the tiniest of medicine cabinets. Most importantly, a modest quantity of toilet paper, stored in a separate, waterproof bag, could be replenished through purchase or thievery along the way, depending on the desperation of the situation.

Self-imposed Ground Rule #4 would steer my selected menu clear of the wretched, rotten grape passed off by clever merchants as raisins. I missed an entire Saturday morning of cartoon shows as a little boy engaged in a stubborn standoff with my mother, who refused permission to leave the breakfast table until my oatmeal, cooked with raisins, was eaten. Cooked and still warm, they simply will not go down. Incorporated into cakes and cookies, they must be extracted prior to consumption. At inescapable social settings, they can be forced down in the interest of avoiding bruised feelings. Though a favorite and nutritious trail snack for many, they, along with dried banana slices, would not figure in my approximate initial load of forty pounds.

Dehydrated milk and an orange-flavored electrolyte replacement, however, would be considered, from tested experience, worth their weight in gold. Warm or cold, they would serve vital nutritional roles as beverages. Instant gelatin mix, served as a hot beverage instead of a cold blob, though lower in nutritional value, would warm the body and brighten the spirit in a variety of flavors. Water, most likely obtainable from safe taps on this trip, would be carried in two 900-millileter plastic bottles and a 500-millileter plastic mixing bottle. The weight consideration with all three of these containers completely filled might cause another veteran backpacker to cringe in agony, but this one never wanted his tongue to stick to the roof of his mouth again.

Modern grocery stores unwittingly cater to the most basic needs of a backpacker with their aisle-upon-aisle variety of lightweight, instant meals. "Add water and bring to a boil" are the directions of choice. Little packets of seasoning are now even conveniently included in the most basic of macaroni dinners. I appreciate their availability when I need them but pity the poor souls who make a steady diet of this fare. The cash and credit card carefully hidden away would be called upon frequently to supplement a fairly bland diet of trail food at every little restaurant or diner I might pass.

Trail habits evolve and are refined over time. Every trip I have taken, another handy tip has been learned from another hiker or through trial and error of my own. On rare occasions, usually when it is raining, I cook breakfast in bed, reaching just outside the tent door to manage a stove and pot of boiling water, still in the comfort of my sleeping bag. But accidental spillage and sudden, vicious bowel movements prompted by the starved body's first taste of food have taught important lessons. Getting dressed and packing away the tent and sleeping bag have proven superior first duties of the day. Breakfast, usually consisting of instant oatmeal or grits supplemented with dried fruit or available wild fruit, can then be prepared safely with no risk of burning down the tent or other unmentionable mishaps.

My brass, antique Svea 123 cookstove now occupies a sacred spot on the mantelpiece of our great room. Knowing it probably could have been repaired, I decided to retire it after a leaky seal constantly ignited a flame in a place that should not have been burning. Charming in appearance, it sounded like a jet engine in good repair and, in disrepair, it was a repeat Space Shuttle *Challenger* disaster on a smaller scale in the making. It had been replaced with a more efficient, awkward-appearing model that resembled a lunar landing contraption.

The inventor of this newer model cleverly designed it to collapse into a compact, distorted bundle, bearing close resemblance to the crushed spider in a *Garfield* cartoon. This wiry creature, along with a tiny stove repair tool, matches, and a flexible wind screen fashioned from space-age metal that will neither crack nor break, no matter how often it is folded, would all be carried conveniently in a little vinyl bag equipped with a handy drawstring. Fueled by regular, unleaded gasoline, easily obtainable and stored separately in a specially designed fuel bottle with a 650-millileter capacity, this little device would make breakfast and supper much more palatable.

For me, lunch is better defined as a succession of quick, uncooked snacks eaten throughout a hiking day rather than a midday event. Nuts, crackers, cereal, and dried fruit would be the usual fare, toted in one of three plastic bags segregating breakfast from lunch from supper. Cooking fuel, generally reserved for morning and evening meals, would occasionally be sacrificed for a hot cup of instant soup on a cold day.

Supper, the primary and celebrated culinary event of the day, is intended to please, fill, and load carbohydrates for the following day. About two hours before dark, I prefer to stop and enjoy this meal. The ideal spot, on a handy rock shelf with a panoramic view, near a water source, shielded from the wind, is rarely available at precisely the time it is needed. But several Parkway overlooks, as I remembered, fulfilled the spirit of these stringent criteria with an added bonus of a picnic table. On such, my entire kitchen, consisting of a 3½-pint aluminum cooking pot and lid, one plastic bowl, one heat-resistant plastic spoon, and a featherweight scouring pad and dishwashing cloth could be splayed. A plastic bag would be emptied, containing the ingredients to prepare a hearty dish of pasta in some form, spiked with instant cheese sauce and freeze-dried beef of superior cut. An occasional foil packet of chicken or tuna might substitute for the beef on some nights, along with an additional treat of rehydrated apple sauce or instant mashed potatoes. After carefully rotating the spoon into the breakfast bag for the next meal, the day would close with a relaxed walk in the sunset a mile or two farther, with the stomach replenished and an eye in search of the perfect camping spot.

In complete violation of my usual weight standards, but essential to this particular adventure, I would carry two notebooks and a lightweight camera on which to record thoughts and images. Three rolls of black and white film for a total of seventy-two exposures, a waterproof camera case, an ink pen, and an extra ink cartridge would support that process. Additionally, a watch, minus the wrist band, would be carried deep inside the backpack, more as a courtesy to Patty's schedule back home than as an essential item. About ten feet of twine could serve many purposes. The official map of the Blue Ridge Parkway would guide my estimation of distance to strategic points, particularly the next restaurant. A miniature flashlight and spare bulb would be used in only the worst of nocturnal circumstances. And a lightweight pocketknife, one-half inch longer than is permitted past the entrance door of my local county courthouse, I quite innocently and abruptly learned one day, would always be in the right-front trouser pocket. Old ranger habits never die. Consistently storing every piece of equipment in the same location could mean the difference in life or death under conditions of extreme stress, darkness, or injury.

Two adjustable straps would fasten two stuff bags containing the sleeping bag, tent, and air mattress to the bottom of an external-frame backpack. Not long ago, a new, dark green, so-called visually friendly backpack with many compartments had replaced my old model. Many years ago I had purchased the first Boy Scout model equipped with an aluminum frame, which had worn out beyond repair. Its bright red color had become, according to many, an affront to the wilderness landscape. Only earth tones were available when I replaced it, rendering its unwary transporter more easily mistaken for a trophy buck deer.

The inquiry and insistence of several well-meaning friends are solely responsible for the promulgation of self-imposed Ground Rules #5 and #6 — NO FIREARMS and NO CELL PHONES. Firstly, the possession of a loaded firearm is prohibited by Federal law on the Blue Ridge Parkway. I had strictly enforced this regulation for several years as a ranger and had no intention of violating it in letter or spirit at this point. A gun's additional weight would be no burden in comparison to the penalty of its discovery or use, no matter the justification. Secondly, I did not even own a cell phone but seriously considered the advantages of taking one. A close friend marketed a popular service and offered a tempting deal. But the additional weight, logistical complications related to recharging the little gizmo, questionable reception in mountainous terrain, and potentially exorbitant roaming charges led to a decision to simply memorize a personal identification number and use a phone card service. A passing motorist could be easily flagged down in the event of a true emergency and a known distribution of conventional telephones along the route seemed sufficient to keep Patty posted as to my whereabouts. My rejection of a cell phone would also serve as a silent protest to the proliferation of hideous towers across every scenic landscape in the world, especially to the fragile, threatened viewshed of the Parkway.

A nearly complete accounting of every item of equipment having thusly been made, at the estimable risk of boring the experienced backpacker, a final item stands deserving of honorable mention. My trusted walking stick and I had racked up about three hundred miles together on the Appalachian Trail. Its known history began as a child's garden hoe, found in an illegal marijuana patch around 1983. A tip from a local resident had led me to its discovery on land very near the Parkway in Franklin County, Virginia. The county authorities were promptly advised and made the decision to close the case by confiscating and destroying the few plants. In a despicably cocky mood that day, I left a business card and note in the trashed, vacant clearing with directions whereby its owner might claim the hoe. Needless to say, I never received a call.

For a few years, the hoe found legal employment in my own vegetable garden, until the weld holding the blade to the tongue broke. Idle for a season or two, the curved tongue was hammered straight, rendering it perfectly suitable to stake green beans. Two ragged nail holes would mar the beautiful grain of its strong hickory handle. One day I accidentally discovered it to be of perfect length and design for a walking stick. Harpoon-like in appearance with a steel tip, its utility as a defensive weapon against man and beast was duly perceived. Between my walking stick, pocketknife, and the heel of my boot, an attacker, lured into close proximity, would not fare well.

Despite, however, my lingering knowledge that mischief — even tragedy — could occur within its boundaries, the Blue Ridge Parkway, in all of its scenic grandeur, was deserving of more optimistic expectations. To the elements, to the critters, to its employees, and to its visitors I would come in peace.

6

Milepost Zero

"The land of our true selves is most surely reached by
walking."
— etched on an Appalachian Trail
shelter, author unknown

The first day of September had finally arrived — lately, relative to the surprise discovery of that waterfall of several years past and suddenly, relative to
my abrupt revelation not yet a month old. I could hardly get to sleep the night
before, mentally sorting through my checklist trying to determine which piece
of vital equipment I had forgotten. In the past few days I had purchased new
boots, rain gear, and a tent. The boots required no break-in period, and I had
carefully rehearsed the tent set-up procedure. What had I forgotten that a pro-
tracted hike of more than a few days, not ever before experienced, would have
taught me? Nothing came to mind as the repetition of check marks, like sheep
jumping over a fence, eventually put me to sleep.

Awake and excited at 5:30 A.M., I was not the least bit discouraged by
cloudy skies in north-central North Carolina. I knew the weather could change
dramatically along the approximately four-hour drive that would begin on gently rolling terrain at home, continue into the hillier foothills of south-central
Virginia, cross over the crest of the Blue Ridge Mountains near Roanoke, run
north up the Great Valley, and east once again to the crest of the Blue Ridge and
the starting point of the hike. The weather was of little concern, even though
the summer had brought record rainfall already to the region. Though I hoped
that the atypical drenching had subsided — fair weather being preferred for the
occasion — I nevertheless anticipated rain, fog, and even frozen precipitation.
Well understood was the difference between survival issues and comfort issues.
The backpack was equipped, and the mind was prepared for both. And the

walking stick, the only unattached appendage, had been strategically placed in the trunk of the car the night before to make certain it was not forgotten.

The first leg of the trip followed the same roller coaster ride along U.S. Route 220 we had taken to an earlier, blissful summer of seasonal employment at the Peaks of Otter. Near Boones Mill, Virginia, we noted the now-closed service station where we later turned in a rental truck following the move to full-time employment on the Blue Ridge Parkway. A few miles farther, our route intersected the Parkway. I knew this area well, having patrolled through it hundreds of times. Its proximity to a major city made this intersection a popular access point, and I had closed the snow gates and flipped the road closure signs at that location many times during winter storms. A noisy, dusty rock quarry, adjacent to the park boundary, still operated just barely out of view of the passing visitor. The stable where we had once boarded our skittish patrol steed, Freddie, now looked abandoned. Clearbrook Rescue Squad still stood nearby, ready for service. I had welcomed the approaching sound of their sirens and skilled hands many times myself during Parkway emergencies. In a nearby wooded area, a deputy sheriff, blinded by the setting sun, had drawn down on me with his revolver in the early, frantic minutes of a manhunt. The silhouette of my official Stetson, he nervously admitted afterwards, had saved me from being perforated.

I had estimated that I would reach this point on my trek in about twelve days and decided to experiment with an idea I had never before attempted — a supply cache. Not of vital necessity and more a notion of convenience, it would reduce the initial load and eliminate the need to resupply at least once. A #10 metal can was stuffed with a variety of consumable items, including a roll of toilet paper, the balance of a fifty-day supply of vitamins, matches, noodles, freeze-dried beef, and chocolate. The can was sealed with a plastic lid and reinforced with a generous wrap of duct tape. We drove a short distance down the Parkway, where I carefully selected a landmark I could not possibly forget. The can, tightly wrapped in a plastic bag, was then hung in a tree in such a manner that the most observant park ranger would not discover it. As stealthy as a robber hiding a loot of gold, I had secured the cache, and I was certain that no human had seen me hide it or would ever find it. The thought never occurred to me that an animal of another species might also enjoy its contents.

Preferring, for the moment, the faster route of the interstate highway system, we continued driving through the heart of Roanoke, Virginia, known locally as the "Star City of the South." Erected on the summit of Mill Mountain in 1949, a mammoth neon light, shaped in the form of a star, amplified the city's choice of its unique nickname. Former Parkway Superintendent Sam Weems called it "a perfect example of civic stupidity" and "an awful thing to happen to an innocent mountain." Standing underneath it in daylight, I would have to agree with Mr. Weems, but from a distance, it adds a charming quality to the night sky for a city already crippled aesthetically by the ugliness of a railroad hub. Within view of our drive through the city along Interstate 581, I could see two hospitals in whose emergency rooms I had conducted too many interviews of accident victims. Victory Stadium still stood along the banks of the Roanoke River, where our family had enjoyed many Fourth of July celebrations. We passed also the civic center, in whose large parking lot Sergeant Jobe had perilously taught the precision driving course when I attended basic law enforcement training at the Roanoke City Police Academy. Six years of memories had accumulated through this area.

Past the airport, we merged north onto Interstate 81 and meandered back and forth across the ancient trading path of Indians, which later became a migration route for Europeans in search of land and freedom. The names of many landmarks along our path — Tinker Mountain, Natural Bridge, Raphine, Steeles Tavern, Stuarts Draft — conjured up poetic images and added definition to the largely pastoral landscape. Washington and Lee University, along the route at Lexington, offered an appellative suggestion to a novice historian that two great men and possibly two American wars had influenced this region. Speculating that the town of Waynesboro offered the last known fast food restaurant before reaching our destination, I suggested an early lunch together so that Patty would not have to eat alone on her return trip home. Her wry smile proved certain manifestation that my thinly veiled offer had been exposed for its truer interpretation. This would be my last tasty meal for several days.

Rockfish Gap is a crossroads of many sorts. Topographically, a gap is defined as a low point of elevation along a ridge or mountain. To a hiker along the crest of such a formation, it generally dictates a descending approach and an ascending departure. Here, the Appalachian Trail dips in such manner along its Maine-to-Georgia course. Here also marks the southern terminus of the Skyline Drive of Shenandoah National Park and the northern terminus of the Blue Ridge Parkway as they both traverse the crest of the Blue Ridge. To a traveler attempting to cross such a formation perpendicularly, a gap generally represents the path of least resistance. Correspondingly, U.S. Route 250 and Interstate 64 have replaced the original wagon road across this gap in their easterly parallel race to Richmond. Playing tag with the Union Army, General Stonewall Jackson once sneaked his Confederate forces by railroad across this gap through a tunnel passing 513 feet below its surface.

Patty and I had already approached that awkward stage of goodbye when, following my usual assurance that I had "never been kil't yet," her eyes would moisten with a certainty that a horrible mishap would eventually validate the law of averages. Our fidgety farewell was sparingly interrupted by a nice lady who had driven up to the gap to walk her dog. Apparently honored by our request to take our picture by the large Parkway entrance sign, she proudly noted that four men had made the same request the last time she had come to walk her dog. Her eyes flew wide open with surprise when she learned of the journey on which I was about to embark. She became the first of many to make such inquiry and reaction. Meanwhile, we stood dwarfed and in awe of the massive, perfectly designed sign, thankful that an early proposal to name the Parkway "The Shenandoah-Great Smoky Mountains National Parks Parkway and Stabilization

The author and wife Patty at Rockfish Gap, elevation 1909 feet, at Milepost 0.0 on the Parkway in Virginia, September 1, 2003.

Project" had never been adopted. Signs and letterhead alike would have toppled from the sheer weight of so many letters.

Patty was more accustomed to a quick goodbye and watching me sprint down a soft footpath in an effort to immerse myself quickly into the solitude of wilderness. This trip, however, was very different from those previous escapes from a frenzied world. She seemed surprised, this time, that I would choose to linger. I needed to sit on a rock wall in the gap for a short while to feel its modern pulse and to imagine its bygone history.

The gap was alive with the roar of tires on pavement passing underneath the Parkway bridge in a mix of commercial and vacation weekend frenzy. The cadence of powerful diesel engines pulling heavy cargo changed dramatically in the gap, from the steady groan of raw horsepower and shifting gears coming up one side of the mountain, to the guttural sound of engine brakes going down its opposite side. Gone forever were the gaited sounds of horses' hooves and the clickety-clack of stagecoaches that had brought men such as Thomas Jefferson, James Madison, James Monroe, and others here in 1818 to the Mountain Top Tavern to choose nearby Charlottesville as the location for the University of Virginia. No resemblance to this quaint tavern remained today, having been replaced with more modern structures, some now closed and unbefitting the natural landscape. Quite an odd place it had become, with a convenience store now advertising gasoline at $1.59 per gallon and a tourist information office screaming it was open with a green and purple neon sign. Yet, today, as it has done through eons of time, the chicory bloomed its eternally beautiful blue, in superior contrast to flashy signs and in harmonious invitation at the boundary line to the most visited unit of the National Park Service.

The Blue Ridge Parkway could be described as a child of accidental conception, descending from the parentage of two previously established national parks. No scholarly investigation has yet definitively concluded the originator of the idea, but a conversation between three politically powerful men can certainly be given credit for propelling it toward fruition. President Franklin D. Roosevelt, Secretary of the Interior and Director of the Public Works Administration Harold L. Ickes, and Senator Harry F. Byrd of Virginia had met together in August 1933 for an inspection of a Civilian Conservation Corps camp located in Shenandoah National Park. While driving along its Skyline Drive, which was still under construction, Senator Byrd suggested that it be extended to the Great Smoky Mountains National Park. Instantly smitten with the idea, President Roosevelt excitedly rejoined that it should even be extended to the Canadian border! A subsequent, frosty reception to the northward extension by several New England governors had unwittingly saved me from several hundred miles of extra walking. More recently, in 1961, Congress had likewise saved me a few more steps when it formally transferred a nine-mile stretch of the Parkway between Rockfish Gap north to Jarman Gap over to Shenandoah National Park. This transfer of what was originally known as Parkway construction unit 1-A now provided a more logical entrance to both parks. Notwithstanding its intriguing history, the time had come to leave my stone perch and put Rockfish Gap and Milepost Zero behind me.

With half the light of day remaining, a backpack of appropriate weight was hoisted onto a fairly conditioned body about thirty pounds overweight. A yet unmentioned goal of this trip was to also trim the body down to an appropriate weight. The combination of a steady, uphill grade for the first three miles and warm, humid weather seemed determined to do just that, as perspiration quickly soaked my shirt and dripped from my nose onto journal notes. Technically, summer had not ended, and the humming chorus of cicadas emphasized no respite for the day. An elevation of slightly more than two thousand feet even failed to provide the usual relief of lower temperatures and cooling winds sought so desperately by flatlanders during this season of the year.

But a steady stream of automobiles and motorcycles on this busy Labor Day fanned a much appreciated breeze. As far as I was concerned, they had the right-of-way. It was for them that this park had been created, a scenic parkway, uncluttered by commercialism, to complement America's love affair with the automobile. Leisure driving was still one of the most popular and affordable forms of recreation, and everyone that passed seemed to be enjoying themselves. Determined to be their courteous guest, I stepped off the pavement onto the grass shoulder as each northbound vehicle passed. As a further expression of intended goodwill and peaceful coexistence, I made a point to wave at every oncoming vehicle with the right hand while steadying my gait with a firmly planted walking stick, held by the left hand, on a sometimes uneven shoulder. These waves were often reciprocated along with an occasional, friendly toot of a horn. I was confident that both pedestrian and motorist could simultaneously have a great day, provided that, at the point of our meeting, I stayed on the shoulder and they stayed on the pavement.

A surprise, late-summer snack of blackberries was soon followed by my first downhill glide. Due to the reflecting glare of sunlight from his windshield, I could not tell if a passing ranger had waved or scowled. The Labor Day holiday had ironically translated into a hectic day of work for him and, along this stretch of Parkway, I could have been easily mistaken for just another Appalachian Trail hiker, like the one I had just met trying to get shuttled to Rockfish Gap. Then, abruptly, I was reminded of a prediction I had made earlier that morning to Patty and the portentous reality that vehicles could not be trusted to keep their end of our bargain.

Upon rounding a sharp curve, the chalky residue of road flares, burned onto the pavement, first alerted me that something had gone tragically wrong there. Playing ranger once again, I carefully examined the aging evidence. Scuff marks on the pavement indicated that a northbound vehicle had entered a sharp, right-hand curve too fast to negotiate, and had run off the left side of the roadway. Dislodged earth and rocks indicated that the vehicle had impacted an embankment violently, which diverted its forward motion back onto the roadway. Two separate patterns of gouge marks on the pavement suggested that the vehicle might have tumbled. Finally, plowed grass and saplings, flattened and denuded of their bark on one side, indicated that the vehicle then went over an embankment on the right side of the road.

My prediction to Patty had been that I would either witness or come upon the scene of a motor vehicle accident not yet cleared at some point on the trip. Fortunately, this scene did not meet the precise criteria of my prediction, but it did punctuate a much too frequent reality for this park. Farther down the road, I found a black platform shoe along the road shoulder and successfully resisted every temptation to speculate on its origin.

Near midafternoon, I strolled into the jammed parking lot of the Humpback Rocks Visitor Center, pleased that I had lollygagged nearly six miles and pleased also to see so many visitors out enjoying themselves. I seemed to be the only person with a pace slow enough, though, to notice the showy, red display of the cardinal flower in a grove adjacent to the parking lot. Nor did anyone else quite appreciate, as much as I, the refreshment and resupply opportunity that tap water offered here. In a way, I pitied the difference in our circumstances; tomorrow they would return, for the most part, back to schools and jobs, while I would continue to enjoy this park for many days yet to come. It just did not seem "fair" to them, a word I have yet to find on any birth, marriage, or death certificate, and on the full spectrum of which we each have the opportunity to reside on more than one occasion throughout our lives.

The hurried frenzy and bumping of shoulders inside the crowded visitor center reminded me of a Saturday morning in a grocery store with snow in the forecast. Forfeiting closer study of its fine exhibits, I did manage to grab copies of the *Parkway Milepost* and *Blue Ridge Parkway Directory & Travel Planner* on the way out the door. Both publications would provide excellent reading material later, superseding any concern for the extra few ounces they added to my burden. The latter offered a wonderful advertising alternative to the clutter of commercial signage along the Parkway itself for nearby private establishments. Food, shower, and laundry services were already on my mind.

From the visitor center, a path meandered into and through a re-created pioneer homestead. Passing a log cabin, I caught the attention of an old gentleman sitting on the front porch, a living history volunteer. "How fer you totin' that thang mister?" he inquired. "Right at 469 miles," I replied to his puzzled astonishment, and without breaking stride added, "I'm hiking the whole Parkway." His lower jaw dropped like a hammer, suggesting that he considered my venture as farfetched as the man he was pretending to be probably thought of the first Parkway surveyor who chopped through that area. We could have swapped stories for the rest of the afternoon, but I was looking ahead at a rock formation high up the spine of Humpback Mountain. Our local newspaper had just run a feature story about Humpback Rocks and, having never climbed it, I was determined to do so that day.

About halfway up the steep, rocky trail, a summer shower offered a perfect opportunity to test my new pack cover. At the summit, I watched a thunderstorm a few miles south roar through another gap along the Blue Ridge, accompanied by a spectacular display of lightning. The climb with a full pack had been worth the view and fireworks, but it had taken its toll on a body more than a little out of shape. I was certain I would pay the price in sore leg muscles the next day. Descending back into Humpback Gap, I immediately employed an empty picnic table for a supine rest break for the back and then as a kitchen on which to prepare a dinner of noodles and chicken chunks. A kind gentleman stopped to talk and offered the surprise treat of a fresh tomato, which was consumed lastly as a dessert course.

As the day ebbed toward sunset, the land grew quieter as traffic on the Parkway gradually diminished in unison. Thistle and Queen Anne's lace bloomed in full maturity in a meadow near my table, oblivious to summer's approaching conclusion, their ranks now infiltrated with the emerging yellow blossoms of goldenrod hinting of cooler weather ahead. The passing of Labor Day likewise signaled a transition from the crowds of summer vacationers to a month-long lull before visitors would return in greater throngs, mostly on weekends, for the dazzling display of fall color. The brief respite comes as welcome relief to rangers who are behind on their paperwork and more than a bit weary of giving directions to the nearest restroom.

Rested and filled, I packed up and walked another two miles. More surprises and discoveries unfolded before darkness forced me to make camp for the night. A woolly mullein plant, sprouting in a crack in the pavement, would never attain its potential of one to five feet tall. Another old motor vehicle accident scene was studied. A ring-necked snake was ushered off the warm pavement on which his demise would have been certain. A wild turkey at roost in a tree decided to move to one deeper in the woods. A gushing pipe spring invited me for a drink. And a coyote, an animal I had never before seen in the wild, trotted onto the road ahead of me, stopped for a brief stare, then darted into the night. My quest for random encounters and discovery was already being realized and would increase in variety over the next forty days.

7

One Manpower

"Make an honest evaluation of your abilities before
beginning a bicycle trip on the Parkway."
— official Blue Ridge Parkway
Bicycling brochure, April 1988

Hampered by the grime and fatigue of a strenuous day, sleep on a back-packing trip never comes easily for me. Warm, humid weather now magnified this grungy feeling, and the combination of a single, pesky mosquito with the discordant rant of hundreds of katydids made falling asleep the first night a fretful, toss-and-turn experience lasting more than two hours. I probably should have pitched my tent but instead chose to sleep under the stars. Normally, I depended on the tranquilizing flames of a small campfire to induce sleep, but I had already resolved to deny myself that luxury on this trip. Nevertheless, sleep finally came. Sometime during the night I woke to a quieter woods, softened finally by a slight breeze, the faint hooting of a great horned owl on another mountain, and the sighting of a satellite racing silently across the sky. There was much about a night in the woods that I did love, and sleep returned more easily the second time.

I usually require only seven hours of sleep, and this night and all others to follow would find me awake again an hour or two before dawn, trying to ignore the beckoning pain of a full bladder, impatiently waiting for the first light of day. I confess it now: nights are too long for me when spent alone and out-of-doors. Newspaper reporters and park visitors would later ask what I missed the most. Patty and cold skim milk, in that order, would always be the answer.

Following a delicious breakfast of instant oatmeal, supplemented with dehydrated peaches and freshly picked blackberries, I set a deliberate course once again in a southerly direction at a cruise altitude of about three thousand feet.

The Parkway, as a road, is considered to run north and south in direction, and intersecting road access points are so marked. As a ranger, I was once humored by a visitor who complained that the signs did not agree with the compass director mounted on the dash of his car. He was advised to use it as a hat rack on his trip because the road would eventually point his car to every degree on his compass.

More accurately speaking, the Parkway geographically runs a northeast to southwest course, as does the entire Appalachian Mountain chain. The official Parkway map and brochure is almost four feet in length, with the map cleverly oriented to the northwest in order to fit it all on a single side. Sometimes referred to as a "strip map," its eleven folds divide it into twelve sections, folding accordion-style into a handy pocket guide. With only 460 miles left to travel, I would also reckon distance in terms of map folds. And in the interest of weight management, I had already begun the process of discarding pages of the travel directory that referenced locations I had already passed.

The natural vegetation was as lush as I had ever seen it, due to an over-abundance of rainfall which had prevailed during the current growing season. The absence of marked defoliation suggested that the devouring gypsy moth had likely been rained out for the year. Abnormally large growth rings on every tree would quietly document to foresters decades hence that the year 2003 was an unusually wet one. The mitten-shaped leaves of the sassafras tree could this year fit the hands of a giant. Wildflowers continued to bloom profusely in their season: sundrops, joe-pye-weed, the dainty virgin's bower, jewel weed in both the yellow and orange varieties, and purple aster. Two ravens nagged a third in flight over a piece of carrion. A tiger swallowtail butterfly chased another. The chickadee chattered in the bush, the towhee "che-winked" along the ground, and a pileated woodpecker "deet-deeted" high through the forest canopy. All of nature seemed to rejoice in robust health this morning. The three-sided concrete post, however, marking Milepost 13 stood injured.

Planted every mile along the western shoulder of the Parkway (referentially termed "Parkway Right" by the park staff), the mileposts are purposely designed to be unobtrusively noticeable to travelers going in either direction. The longer they weather, the more perfectly they blend into the landscape. Slightly out of plumb and missing a chunk of concrete, Unlucky 13 appeared to have taken a recent hit from a mower operator hurried by a summer of unrelenting fescue prosperity or another motor vehicle not keeping its end of our bargain.

Midday found me sprawled and resting under the shade of a large apple tree at a place known as Love Gap. Stories abound regarding the origins of its name. Of a certainty though, lovers of a bygone era once flocked to its now closed post office every February to mail valentines postmarked from Love, Virginia. I was certain that a Parkway ranger residence was located somewhere near here at one time, but the place now seemed strangely unfamiliar, perhaps the result of a fading memory or the changes wrought in a landscape I had not seen in over twenty years. Preferring my comfortable position over further exploration, I contented myself with one memory still vividly clear. A ranger who once lived here would occasionally crack up everyone within the sound of a Parkway radio. An inquiry regarding his "10-20," or whereabouts, would sometimes yield the response, "I'm in Love," in his best Southern drawl.

The afternoon was as hot and humid as the day before, and distant thunder warned that the day might become more interesting. A penny, found pressed into the tar of the road surface, was pried loose and became the first item of a collection of lucky charms. There was much to discover and contemplate along the way. A weathered arrangement of artificial flowers, tucked quietly into the wood's edge, memorialized what had to be the certain human victim of a very sharp curve. While furry chipmunks played chicken with passing cars, the fractured remains of a monarch butterfly and a flattened little snake bore further witness to the perils of a roadway. Most motorists would dodge animals large enough to see, and from my perspective, I saw no need to codify another ground rule that would restrict me from stepping on critters like the millipede and woollyworm. I considered them all my friends and had great sympathy for any animal traveling at a speed equal to or slower than my own.

My arrival at Twenty Minute Cliff Overlook brought a brief shower and a silent chuckle at myself. Having heard other rangers assigned to this area speak of this overlook many times, I errantly assumed that it had derived its name from a very high cliff from which a falling object would take twenty minutes to hit the ground. Wrong and very wrong I had been. An interpretive sign explained that it was used as a timepiece for people living deep in the valley below. During the summer months they know that the sun will set on the mountain twenty minutes after striking the face of the cliff. Still, it looked like a pretty long dropoff to me, and I moved along, mending a stung ego that my theory, though sharply inaccurate, had at least been colorfully dramatic.

This was only my second day out, and I was already experiencing an unexpected shortage of convenient water sources. Walking up a steep grade and down to the last two cups, my concentration became more focused on my looming predicament and how the road ahead might relieve it. Supper would require more water, and it was now in jeopardy of being canceled. Suddenly, with no warning, I had the bejabbers scared out of me.

People, in general, are frightened quite easily when surprised from behind. Add a few years of law enforcement experience to such victims to understand why sitting with their backs to the wall becomes a stubborn issue when being seated in a restaurant. So the sudden, uncomfortably close sound of a strained hello, uttered by a fatigued, southbound bicyclist passing me from behind, at a speed just barely greater than my own, created a massive short circuit of my fight-flight reflex. The analytical process that should have made an instantaneous determination that I had encountered either a friend or foe was delayed slightly beyond the normal few milliseconds when the rider and his vehicle came into full view. This fellow must have been pulling a hundred pounds of gear on a little two-wheeled cart attached to the rear of his bicycle. I had never seen anything quite like it, and by the time I was able to mutter a courteous, though unintelligible response, he was surely out of range to hear it. As he continued his painfully steady course up the mountain, I calmed a bruised psyche by congratulating myself on having chosen a safer, cheaper mode of transportation. My boots had only cost $19.95, and I could easily step off the road surface when a car approached. Two large motor homes meeting in a sharp curve could send this guy to the hospital or morgue and his conveyance to the landfill.

Having been temporarily electrified into a spiked style, my hair had not quite returned to its original, matted position when it was forced to stand at attention again. The thunderstorm I had been hearing in the distance all afternoon was suddenly upon me. Flawed science though it may be, I refuse to be attached to an aluminum-framed backpack on such occasions. So I stepped behind the protection of a sturdy, wooden guide rail, removed the pack, and placed the rain cover over it. Content to be cooled and cleansed by the downpour, I chose not to put any rain gear over myself. I had just moved to a safer position away from any large trees, the guide rail, and my pack when a loud sizzling sound was instantaneously followed by a blinding flash of light and a deafening crack. Lightning had struck just a few feet down the mountain below me. That was the closest I had ever been to a lightning strike, but I did not consider a front row seat for this outdoor show the least bit desirable. Three more close strikes followed as I crouched as low to the ground as I could get, helplessly hostage to whatever the sky might send, as each thunderclap shook the ground like an earthquake and echoed repeatedly off the mountains. As the storm lessened in intensity, I realized that the storm I had watched from Humpback Rocks the day before had just pounded the same location again. Then I remembered the story of an old ranger in Shenandoah National Park who had been struck by lightning several times and had survived in every case. We had never met, and this was not the day to go looking for him.

Almost a cup of water had graciously collected in a shallow pool on the top of my pack cover, which was carefully channeled into the spout of a nearly empty water bottle. Refreshed somewhat, I would still be forced to continue walking to a more abundant source. Six miles later and in a fading twilight, the sight of lights, visible from a residence high on a hill, led me to the kind hospitality of the caretaker of a research farm owned by Washington and Lee University and all the water I needed. Tuna and macaroni never tasted better after this seventeen-mile day. Twice I had been frightened to death, but now, with all apparent hazards of the day behind me, I could laugh at my follies and easily forgive everything that had sneaked up on me. I hoped that the trophy buck I had frightened a mile farther back could forgive me as easily.

Standing on the center line of the Parkway with his buddy, regally antlered as well but half his size, both were focused on a few does mingling among cattle in a nearby pasture when I first noticed them. At first, I stopped to watch them all and slowly began walking again toward the two bucks. The smaller one noticed me first but surprisingly offered no alarm, apparently waiting on a cue from his

Harold Peters of Lynchburg, Virginia, was headed north on September 3, 2003, near Milepost 29 on the Parkway in Virginia.

larger friend to run. I was no farther than thirty yards away when the big guy finally saw me, certainly disappointed that his wing man had failed him. Both looked like dogs trying to begin a sprint on a hardwood floor as their hooves scratched the pavement for traction. When they finally connected to sod, both sprang as gracefully over a fence as I had ever seen and thundered out of sight.

The next morning found me stopping to make an early courtesy call to Parkway personnel at the Montebello ranger station. Danny Myrtle reminded me that we had worked together on a forest fire in Montana a few years back and how the arrival of an early snowstorm had mocked our feeble efforts by snuffing out the inferno with ease. I finally got to meet the legendary Lester Roberts, whose singular, nasal monotone across the airwaves of the park radio still captured the humored attention of every listener. The district ranger would not be reporting to work that day, I was told. Lightning from the same storm that had danced around me the day before had fried nearly every electrical component in his home.

A former ranger residence now converted to an office, its bathroom facilities were offered for an unexpected bath and shave. Water bottles were filled, and my first call home brought relief that all had gone well with Patty's return trip home. Freshened once again in both body and spirit, I finally broke away from the heartwarming balm of old acquaintances.

Had I lingered five minutes longer, I would have missed him — a solo, northbound bicyclist approaching me head-on. Thankful this time for a visual connection to its silent approach, I stepped onto the shoulder to give the rider the entire uphill lane. Most bicyclists I had encountered on the Parkway seemed locked into their own private worlds, dressed in bright apparel, as if they were competing in the last leg of the Tour de France. My waves had been rarely acknowledged, as if I had been merely one of hundreds of spectators standing on the sidelines of their race course. Lance Armstrong's recent victories had certainly spawned a craze, and manufacturers of bicycles and their accessories all over the world had him to thank for millions of dollars in sales. For the most part, I seemed to be looked upon narrowly by this breed of visitor, pitifully or jealously I could never quite determine.

This particular rider, however, shattered the stereotypical mold so described. As he drew closer, the typically crouched posture converted to an upright one and the usually serious countenance blossomed into a happy smile as he jubilantly began asking, before even coming to a stop, if I was the former park ranger who was backpacking the Parkway. Puzzled slightly by his foreknowledge, I offered a hesitant affirmative reply, to which he rejoined with extended arm, "You are my hero, and I must shake your hand."

Harold Peters, age seventy-two and resident of nearby Lynchburg, also had a postretirement dream, its realization only thirty miles and a few hours away. Twelve days earlier he had begun a bicycle trip with his 21-speed machine at the opposite end of the Parkway. Excitedly, he recalled his murderous first day climbing away from Milepost 469 and warned me of a long tunnel in North Carolina in which he had become disoriented and crashed. Undeterred from his tunnel vertigo experience and flirtation with serious injury, he later enjoyed the hospitality of a winery in Virginia, where he read a newspaper article about my trip. We shared the frustration of a mutual problem, a dearth of legal camping opportunities for sojourners like us in the park. Harold's most memorable night had been spent in a freshly mowed field, tucked inconspicuously between two giant rolls of hay, with a full view of the heavens. Instantly, we became friends for life and could have talked the day away. Amid the busyness of tale swapping, picture taking, and exchange of address and telephone information, Mrs. Peters drove up and informed Harold that a local newspaper reporter was headed up to interview him. That was my cue to hit the road again and permit the real hero of the day his due recognition.

The Parkway had not been designed or intended to accommodate their mode of travel either. In most parts of the world, bicycles are generally considered a conveyance permitted on public highways, subject to the same traffic laws governing motorized vehicles. This mix, on a two-lane road such as the Parkway, wrought with a surplus of blind curves and frequented by large recreational vehicles, might inherently suggest a high frequency of disastrous collisions. But in all of my years of rangering, I could recall investigating only one collision between a bicycle and a motor vehicle. Fortunately, no one was injured in that unusual accident. The driver of one vehicle rear-ended her friend driving another vehicle who had come to a near stop in the road to gaze at a sunrise. Unfortunately, the two expensive bicycles mounted to the rear bumper of the lead car were demolished in the collision, and a planned day of riding had to be canceled. Still, I worried of their vulnerability and marveled at the inexplicable forces that seemed to protect them.

More likely to be encountered was the accidental spill. The hysterical screams of a woman, once found sitting in the road with a deep laceration to her head, remained a vivid memory I wished I could forget.

Even more disturbing was the discovery, near the conclusion of my hike, of sinister evidence apparently directed with malicious intent toward bicyclists, motorcyclists, or both. Someone had taken great pains to clip the individual barbs from a length of barbed wire and scatter them along several miles of the Parkway road surface. I shared my discovery and a sample with a local ranger, who had collected quite a few of the barbs himself from a parking lot. He was equally disturbed and astonished to learn that they had also been scattered along the roadway. How could anyone harm the likes of the five young men I had met a few days earlier — too young and happy to understand the dangers or to fit my unfair stereotype — who had finally answered my wave with five successive high-five slaps?

8

Boston Knob Overlook

"Here is a tranquil scene, restful and content to be happy rather than great."
—*Blue Ridge Parkway Guide*, by William G. Lord

The picnic table at Stillhouse Hollow Overlook looked like the perfect spot to don my rain gear and wait out a downpour. I was determined, as long as I could, to enjoy the all too temporary cleanliness that soap and warm water had afforded back at the ranger station three hours earlier. Exertion and humidity had a way of quickly erasing such comfortable freshness. Sitting in a hunkered mass, completely protected from the rain by those miraculous modern garments, I felt no particular contempt for the weather. Frequent rainfall was commonplace in the Southern Appalachians, and I was resolved to enjoy even it, to the extent possible.

The Parkway had by now plunged deeply into the George Washington National Forest, surrounded to an even greater degree by solitude and wildness. About a third of the Parkway had been routed through such lands, including also the Jefferson, Pisgah, and Nantahala National Forests, from which a visitor, no matter how conveyed, could experience something of remoteness and the illusion of an infinite succession of ancient mountains undulating into the horizon. These were the districts for which most rangers vigorously competed for duty; once obtained, only the force of retirement or involuntary reassignment could move some of them. What a splendid deal this had also been for the taxpayer — free right-of-way by virtue of the deeded transfer of land from one Federal agency to another. For the most part, the U.S. Forest Service had been most gracious and supportive of the Parkway project since its inception, and I had always found their employees a pleasure with whom to associate. Maintaining a good working relationship with them assured assistance and resources on fire and search and rescue operations and an endless supply of conservation trinkets their fatter budget always seemed to afford.

I was shaken from a peaceful, rain-induced trance by the sound of an approaching car, the driver of which seemed to have made a last-second decision to pull into the overlook. Overshooting the opportunity for a graceful entrance, the sedan braked hard, and with squalling tires, made an abrupt U-turn into the overlook, pulling right up in front of me with all the appearance of a poorly executed pit stop. I was hoping these folks were not expecting my sparse crew to provide a full tank of gasoline, four fresh tires, and refreshments in thirteen seconds flat. Seriously though, when the female passenger rolled down her window, I quite expected the usual inquiry for directions. Instead she asked, "Are you Tim Pegram?" Startled again, I instantly calculated that I had never before seen this lady. Fairly certain that there were no outstanding warrants for my arrest, the gaming side of my personality shot back, "Now that depends on who is looking for him."

I was perfectly content to stand in the rain to answer her questions, but Shannon Brennan, a reporter from *The News & Advance* out of Lynchburg, Virginia, and her daring driver-photographer insisted that I take shelter in the back seat of their car. Harold Peters had sent them looking for me, and a few weeks later I would enjoy reading her wonderful story about a hiker meeting a biker.

The third day of every backpacking trip I had ever taken always found me sluggish from muscles trying to wring themselves of soreness. Trail legs take a few days to develop, and this was not a day to rush for more than one reason. I was beginning to understand what the main character in the book *Joshua*, by Joseph F. Girzone, was trying to teach a medical doctor who had just witnessed a so-called miracle.

> A little thing like that stands out in your mind because you miss the much greater mysteries that take place continually every day. What happened the other day surprises you because it was unexpected. Look in the mirror when you go to your room tonight and you will see an evolution of wonders far more exciting than the healing of a broken bone and the revival of the spark of life. The whole course of each day is filled with endless wonder, which we take for granted because it all flows so smoothly as the ordinary course of life. But each tiny event, and each moment of time, is a miracle of creation.

The importance and place of every person I met, every tree that stood, every creature that crawled, and every step that I took became more clearly focused, yet I could not fathom the completeness of the picture due to its vastness. There was so much of life through which I had hurried and taken for granted.

The demands of fatigue rather than a compulsion for reflection dictated a midafternoon decision to cook supper at Yankee Horse Ridge Overlook. Good spring water seemed to gush from every crevice on this mountain in contrast to the previous day. My hydrologist friend would have to explain to me later why some mountains are dry and some are wet. The Appalachians are uncanny in that respect. About a mile back, I had spoken to a man and woman who were collecting salamanders as part of a contract study of the park's resource inventory program. The salamanders and I both were now quite happy with a plentiful supply of the good stuff so easily taken for granted in the "ordinary course of life."

The miracles of creation, I concluded, must also include the inventions of man, as I marveled at the ingenious design of the zipper on my rain jacket. Every item of clothing and gear I was carrying was the product of hundreds of thousands of inventions of people endowed with special abilities and curiosities. Clothing had progressed from animal hides to hand-woven, natural fibers to machine-woven, synthetic fibers and the ultralight, water-repellent jacket I was now wearing.

This Parkway also reflected a grand tribute to the successive inventions of man, from discovery of the wheel to the internal combustion engine and all of the devices on which they would roll. Crossing the Rocky Mountain Viaduct on foot, I further concluded that the Blue Ridge Parkway was truly a masterpiece of civil engineering and landscape architecture in every detail, visible and hidden. Crossing a deep, undisturbed ravine, the unaware motorist could never appreciate its hidden form and function and might easily mistake it for just another fine view. I kept a hand and knee close to the low stone wall retainer as I slowly walked across it, peeking at intervals over its perilous edge to view the seemingly scrawny, arched, stone piers that supported it. What brave men had constructed such a thing! And what a perfect marriage of an invention of man into the landscape! This was only the first of many viaducts, bridges, and stone walls from which I would gaze, rest, and cook breakfast upon.

I arrived at Boston Knob Overlook with about two hours of daylight remaining and realized that I had progressed farther than a tired and still overweight body had permitted me to imagine. Thirteen miles was a respectable distance and still, I had devoted an appropriate portion of the day to the attention of details and relationships that I might have otherwise whisked past in an earlier stage of life. I probably would have traveled even farther that day had I not met my first international visitors, a charming young couple from the Netherlands, who were cooking soup on a little cookstove at the picnic table. We became equally intrigued with each other's journey and accent, and the approaching darkness brought a premature conclusion to our cultural exchange. Before they drove into the night and I wandered a distance away to find an appropriate campsite, I offered them my copy of the *Parkway Milepost*, which contained a far better map of the Parkway than their road atlas provided. As the moon rose a short time later, coyote near and far howled all over the mountain. I was not afraid of them, but their recent migration into the Southern Appalachians had brought a new night sound to which my ears would need time to become accustomed.

Sprinkles of rain arrived with dawn the next morning, prompting a hasty dash out of bed to survey the sky. Clouds like the ones I saw never just pass over the mountains, and the race was on to get my gear packed and breakfast eaten before conditions worsened. The picnic table back at Boston Knob Overlook seemed to be the most logical place to cook it.

Not even William G. Lord, an early Parkway naturalist who wrote and published a wonderful guidebook still used by visitors today, offered a quaint story to explain how this overlook was named. Following my presumptuous debacle back at Twenty Minute Cliff Overlook, I dared not venture that it had any relationship to the city of Boston. But here, at this little nondescript wayside, would soon come an unexpected revelation.

I would have to rate overlooks as the signature design feature of the Parkway. Over 250 of them were incorporated into its lengthy course to afford the motoring visitor frequent locations at which to stop and park. Technically referred to as parking widenings, parking overlooks, and parking areas, all are uniquely sculpted into the terrain and assume many configurations. At least one was accidental in its creation — the result of a miscalculated overblast of explosives while cutting the road grade. Most of them offer panoramic views of mountain scenery, which prompted many local mountain people to initially refer to them as "balconies" in their own colorful vernacular. Some direct the attention of the visitor to a unique cultural or natural feature, supplemented with an interpretive sign at some locations. Most have been officially named and are so designated with sturdy, rustic signs that also denote their elevation. Many provide access to trails of varying lengths, and others invite a picnic with a table or grassy spot. Many of them become magical, favorite places for sentimental, repeat visits, and as a ranger, I stumbled more than once into the discreet ceremonies of unannounced weddings and unauthorized scatterings of cremation ashes.

Boston Knob Overlook was perched on a flattened knoll about a hundred yards off the Parkway, reached by a gently curved, ascending access road. With only a modest view into the Nettle Creek drainage, what it lacked in spectacle was made up for in serenity. Its short loop trail into the edge of a maturing hardwood forest epitomized the leg-stretcher intentions of its early designers, and there was no better place to read a book on a summer Sunday afternoon than along its neatly mowed fringes.

I hurried breakfast as the rain gradually increased in intensity and dense fog enveloped the mountain, stalling — even reversing at times— the normal, progressive candlepower offerings of a sun frustrated in its mission. Without the aid of this most basic time reference, a person could not tell if dawn was returning or twilight was approaching. Unbridled, this kind of weather could drag one's mood into its gloom, and I decided to avoid its tentacles by amusing myself with the details of my surroundings and the mental exercise of formulating the plot and title of this novel I would soon be writing. Taking notes in my journal had proven to be a difficult, if not impossible, exercise under these conditions. Here, at this picnic table, I would wait out the weather despite the subconscious tapping of experience on my shoulder reminding me that this cloud could last for hours or even days.

Tucked slightly into the dark edge of a hardwood forest still adorned in its leafy attire, the picnic table, my own Fort Defiance, held a commanding view of the overlook's six-car parking lot. The access road from the Parkway had now disappeared into the fog. The overhanging trees had initially provided a protective, umbrella effect but were now saturated with moisture, creating their own shower of larger drops and drenching bands when shaken by a gust of wind. An aluminum can, tossed by a careless visitor into the woods, played a single monotonous note as an occasional raindrop plunked against its hollowness. J. S. & A. S. had carved their initials into a tree within the outline of a heart. I wondered if they shared the same surname by virtue of marriage or only shared the first letter of different surnames while in courtship. Whatever the case, this overlook certainly held romantic significance for them. They now only needed special tutoring in conservation ethics. Autumn color was estimated to have advanced to a modest thirty percent, and a healthy sassafras tree was noted to be at least twelve inches dbh (diameter at breast height). The minutes turned to hours and my mind, as foggy as the weather, had made no progress on the literary objectives for the day.

The faint sound of a lone automobile, rolling invisibly down the Parkway through thick fog, finally brought a reassurance that humankind persisted in plurality. As it neared the overlook, the sound of its engine decelerating alerted my senses that it would emerge from the fog into the parking area momentarily. Suddenly, I was six years old again and excitedly clutched my imaginary machine gun and waited for the enemy to drive into my clever ambush. But, alas, it was not the enemy, but fellow comrades, limping and wounded.

An elderly man and woman pulled into a parking space only a few yards from my station but seemed to be quite unaware of my presence in the pouring rain. Apparently oblivious as well to their deflated left-rear tire, they sat for several minutes with the engine idling while they snacked and studied a road atlas. Fearing that their flat tire would later cause an accident, I felt compelled to warn them, but I was certain that my sudden approach in full rain attire would, for them, parallel an encounter with the Abominable Snowman. And it did, despite my best effort at friendly salutation. The balance of fear had unintentionally tipped in the opposite direction, as I recalled the lightning and the bicyclist that had spooked me. The gentleman's expression of horror faded to one of gratitude when he finally understood my hand gestures and accepted my offer to change their tire. They were visiting from Germany and I think understood enough English to follow my directions to the nearby town of Buena Vista for repair service. Boston Knob Overlook had certainly developed a flair for attracting the international visitor, in my estimation, but I was still not ready to suggest that Logan International Airport had anything to do with its naming.

As the German couple waved farewell and drove back into the fog, I suddenly realized the absurdity of writing a work of fiction. Why not mix the actual experiences of this trek with those I had experienced as a park ranger? They would probably be of more interest to a reader than anything my imagination could conjure. Decided. It would be my first publication. I stomped around the overlook searching for a title. Impatient with the self-imposed constraints I had blamed on the weather, I strapped on my backpack and struck stride, delighted that a book plan had finally crystallized. I was too eager to finish the story to wait out the rain. The title of the book would have to catch up with me.

I had walked less than a mile when the rain ceased and the sun broke through the clouds. Illumination of the body always follows illumination of the spirit. But the sun seemed at an odd angle in the sky and, for the first time on the trip, I dug into the deep recesses of my backpack to retrieve my watch. The day had already ticked away to 3:00 P.M.! Fog, I thought, could really distort time and sanity.

9

Spooked

"But what troubled me most was that I would run into the
Jersey Devil out there in the dark."
—*The Tracker*, by Tom Brown Jr.

The emergence of the sun, though late in the day, brought back the motorized visitor once again. Most had wisely avoided the fog earlier in the day. But their numbers were few, and in addition to waving at the cars I was meeting, I decided that those approaching from behind deserved the same courtesy as well. They likewise responded enthusiastically with toots of the horn and returned waves. There was something about the personality of this park that caused the goodness of people to bubble to the surface. Dr. Jolley's concern for all the people in the world who had never visited it, I think, was founded on an unspoken belief that the Parkway could change the world for the better, at least if visited on a sunny day. I, too, was now converted to that belief.

If overlooks prevail as the signature design feature of the Parkway, the diminutive, bothersome gnat would have to receive my vote as the signature insect of the Parkway. Their emergence in spring has long hailed the natural opening of trout season in the Appalachians, and native folk seem little annoyed by their persistent buzzing about the head and irritating bites. Wearing a hat and a long-sleeved shirt partially shields one from their perplexing intensity; the lack of same nearly caused me to cry out in agony as I once performed CPR on a heart attack victim for over an hour in the backcountry. Their presence in the park is far more responsible for rangers wearing the hot, stiff, summer flat hat than the strongly worded uniform compliance memorandum issued annually by the chief ranger.

Had I ripened that much since my bath only the day before, or were these critters just engaging in a final, late-summer feeding frenzy knowing that colder weather was approaching? Whatever the case, they seemed determined to make a meal of me until twilight beckoned them home. Grateful for their departure, I also settled into the night with seven miles under my belt and a calm assurance that the pesky mosquito, of no less importance in its own ecological role, dwelt not at that elevation.

The next morning I realized that I had progressed just past the second fold in my map and was comically delighted that I only had nine folds remaining. My inexorable march quickened on this cool, sunny morning with an increasing realization that the Otter Creek Restaurant was a viable supper option in lieu of trail fare that had already arrived at Bland Land. My walking stick seemed determined to convert me to left-handedness, as I preferred its soft, stable landing on the ground over its metallic tapping on the pavement. Mind, body, and walking stick meshed into a singleness of purpose that only the hunger for real food can explain. But all reasons to rush vanished with an approaching red pickup truck, which gingerly pulled onto the grass shoulder and parked in front of me.

Marvin Tucker, now retired, had been responsible for maintenance operations over the entire Virginia section of the Parkway during my ranger years, six of which we had shared work offices. When we finally recognized each other, Marvin walked right past my extended offer of a handshake and embraced me with tears in his eyes. He had read about my trip in the Lynchburg newspaper and was hoping to find me. Thank you, Shannon Brennan. He still lived near the Parkway down on Sheep Creek Hollow in Bedford County, my fantasy of heaven on earth. We spoke of times past and changes present, of colleagues still working, those retired, some deceased, and some dying. The Parkway had never looked finer or been a better place to work, we proudly agreed, than when our careers had rolled past its mileposts.

The enormity of his job had often been matched with budget shortfalls, and at least once, with my narrower perspective, I had failed to consider the stress under which he performed. I was attending an OSHA safety management course in Roanoke, and the instructor asked if any in the class, comprised entirely of Federal employees, knew of a facility whereby we might conduct a mock inspection. I helpfully suggested our local ranger and maintenance office and stupidly failed to obtain permission for the class exercise from all affected parties. Needless to say, the discovery of a dangerously wired drill press in the sign shop embarrassed Marvin enormously and tripped his ignition switch on my behalf.

Before departing, I asked Marvin to forgive me for any irritation I might have caused him during our years of working together. Time had faded his memory of this particular incident, and when reminded of it, he begged my forgiveness as well for his earlier, stress-induced temper. How cathartic is time and the burial of rusty hatchets and how painful the longing for a second undertaking.

The heat of the afternoon was softened by my hesitant entry into the coolness of Bluff Mountain Tunnel, the first of twenty-six tunnels along the Parkway through which I would venture and the only one along the entire Virginia section. Harold Peters' harrowing tale remained vivid, but clearance, not

The icy Lickstone Ridge Tunnel at Milepost 458.8 on the Parkway in North Carolina, circa 1985, where I had to smash huge icicles.

vertigo, was my primary concern. My earlier ventures into Parkway tunnels on foot had been for the sole purpose of smashing huge icicle formations that blocked passage of my patrol vehicle during winter months. A slight tap with a sledge hammer would bring down huge chunks of ice onto the pavement resulting in shattering explosions into millions of pieces. Such sport, of course, was always undertaken in sections of the Parkway which had been closed to traffic. This was my first attempt, then, to share one with traffic coming from both directions, and I was relieved to find adequate space for us all and grateful for their compliance with our agreement. Someday I would have to attempt the impossible task of describing with words the sound of footsteps in such places.

Not far past a safe exit from the tunnel, another little hazard presented itself a few feet in front of me. A stone about the size of a baseball had finally surrendered to erosion and gravity and tumbled onto the pavement from a scarred road cut. I kicked it into the ditch with a dance step, learned years ago, that was timed perfectly to avoid any damage to the toe of my boot. Rock slides are common along the Parkway, and they come in all sizes. Some, unfortunately, are large enough to require temporary closures and the use of explosives and hauling equipment. Smaller ones, I had discovered, could be manipulated out of the way with the emergency pry bar carried in the trunk of my patrol car. I had as many reasons to look up as I did down on this hike to dodge rock slides in whatever dimension fate might present them. What an ignominious death such would be to a backpacker.

By late afternoon I had descended into the lower elevation and flats of the Otter Creek drainage. Heat and thirst would be held responsible for memory lapses and resulting inaccurate notations discovered later in my journal. I had developed the habit of stopping periodically to record thoughts as well as the chronological passage of mileposts and overlooks. How could I have forgotten the poetically named Dancing Creek Overlook? As I approached a bridge crossing Otter Creek, a belted kingfisher, strafing the surface of the water at top speed, approached the bridge from upstream. To my amazement, it maintained its altitude and disappeared momentarily as it skirted right under the short bridge and out the other side, undeterred in its search for supper. I was as determined as well to reach the restaurant ahead of me before its suspected closing time of 6:00 P.M. A kind, old gentleman out for his daily bicycle ride, however, upon inquiry, voluntarily rode two miles out of his way to bring back the news that it did not close until 8:00 P.M. Yes!

I doubt that the manager of the Otter Creek Restaurant ever anticipated that any customer would take advantage of the free refill policy on milk by consuming four glasses. A generous tip was offered as a token of repentance for this misdeed and service of my inexplicable choice of a healthier salad, serving of cottage cheese, and beef and cheese hoagie over that of a juicy cheeseburger, fries, and soda. This restaurant had served me well during the summer of 1974 with the occasional purchase of supper just prior to inviting everyone in the campground to attend my campfire programs. On one such evening, I scrapped my planned program and invited a twelve-year-old boy from Pennsylvania, who was in the process of hiking the entire Appalachian Trail, to share his unfolding story. When asked by an adult in the audience how he could get excused from school for such a trip, usually requiring about six months, he replied that his teacher had told him he would learn far more on his journey than she could ever teach him in the classroom. Every kid from six to sixteen in the crowd could be seen tugging at their parents' arm for similar approval.

A noticeable increase of traffic along the Parkway the following morning signaled the certain arrival of the first day of the weekend. The fairly level, three-mile stretch from Otter Creek Campground to the James River was abuzz with visitors enjoying an array of water features. I chose the convenient access of Lower Otter Creek Overlook to wash out my socks and inspect a mild case of heat rash on the feet. Below the dam supporting Otter Lake, a father patiently baited the hooks and untangled the lines for his young son and daughter in their comically awkward attempts to catch a fish. I am sure that this father would have rather... no, I am certain that this father was doing precisely what he wanted to do that morning. When the son — who never left his line out for more than two seconds—caught a fish, I offered a congratulatory applause to them all from my elevated vantage point at road level. Somewhat startled from the unexpected accolade, they all curiously looked up my way and gleefully smiled. What a great dad those children had.

Otter Creek, which the Parkway had gracefully crisscrossed for the last few miles, quietly turned away and disappeared into the mighty James River near the lowest elevation point on the Parkway — 649 feet above sea level. I could not resist the temptation of a long delay to revisit a newer James River Visitor Center and its appurtenant interpretive features. A seasonal ranger of the current generation graciously permitted the storage of my burden at the visitor center while I rambled the grounds. I had enjoyed my earlier duties there, mingling with visitors along a walkway suspended from the Parkway bridge that accessed the restored Battery Creek Lock of the now defunct James River and Kanawha Canal. Two men fishing the shoreline in a johnboat drifted past in the gentle current, echoing silent declaration also that this day had been made for fishing. I took the time to read over thirty interpretive placards spaced along one of my favorite Parkway trails — the Trail of Trees. There, a patient visitor could learn that the princess tree was named to honor Russian Princess Anna Paulownia, and that the wood of the white ash is used to make baseball bats. A forgiving visitor might also feel compassion for the lovelorn lass who scratched "I Still ♥ You Jake" on the fringetree plate.

As I cooked a hearty lunch on a picnic table overlooking the river, I thought what a perfect location this would have been to comply with self-imposed Ground Rule #7 — NO HIKING ON SUNDAYS. Sunday, I had decided, would be my day of rest and meditation in harmony with a personal recognition of its sabbath designation. But I had arrived here one day too early. It was two o'clock in the afternoon before I finally crossed the long span of the James River bridge and saw in the distance the golf-ball-shaped radar dome high atop Apple Orchard Mountain. The Parkway ahead of me would climb from its lowest elevation at the river to its highest elevation in Virginia, 3,950 feet above sea level, near that dome. North or south of that dome, I could not remember — and my map did not denote — was a perfect place to spend a Sunday at a place called Sunset Field Overlook.

Neither the blank stares of very retired couples all driving the same make of automobile nor mufflerless motorcycles climbing the steep grade bugged me quite like the constant sound of a riding mower whose drone followed me for over an hour as I started up the mountain. An adjacent private landowner just trying to mow his lawn on a beautiful Saturday afternoon, though, could not be held accountable for my tardiness and the prospect of an unrelenting vertical climb of about 3,300 feet over the next thirteen miles that needed to be accomplished before midnight. He probably owned that property long before the Parkway was ever built.

Soon, however, I was refreshed by an unexpected visit from a colleague of the 1980s, Ranger Kathryn Brett, who took a break from her patrol to chat. Before departing, she donated her afternoon snack of a can of vegetable juice, which was slugged immediately, and a raisin cake. I toyed with the packaged cake until she left and then carefully peeled off all the raisins before inhaling the cake. The resultant sugar rush caused me to commit the unthinkable, and in a trembling fit in the interest of caloric economy, I swallowed all of the raisins at once like a spoonful of wretched medicine.

Daylight faded into darkness while fatigue and a nearly full moon triggered a succession of surreal events which began with coyote howling all over the crest of the dark ridge looming high to my right, mixed with the cries of bobcat. Was I hallucinating when I passed Arnold Valley Overlook for the second time or had I forgotten that two successive overlooks bore the same name? Rounding a curve, the radar dome suddenly appeared in the moonlight, and I felt like a displaced Lilliputian struggling through the fairway of another planet. An oval outline of lights flickering in the valley far below pinpointed not the cheers of a home team touchdown but the faint, incongruent buzz of Saturday night racing. In a patch of fog, Bedford County Deputy John Wilkes and I surprised each other. This was my first cognizant experience of being referred to as a "subject," as he cautiously advised his dispatcher of his "10-37" (checking a suspicious person) mission before chatting with me. Finally, almost two miles past the crest of the Parkway at Apple Orchard Mountain, I stumbled into Sunset Field Overlook and collapsed into a nearby campsite. For some reason it seemed important, before rolling out my sleeping bag under the stars, to expend a few of my last ounces of energy to find my watch. The time was exactly midnight.

I awoke the following morning early enough to enjoy the rising of the constellation Orion in the eastern sky just ahead of a beautiful sunrise. A stove failure during breakfast, though, threatened to tarnish the peace and rest I had hoped the day would bring. I should have never taken the risk of packing old fuel, and now it was clogging the narrow jet with soot. To complicate the situation, I had permitted the leg assembly to collapse apart in the repair process, and fitting it all back together again became a test of wits and dexterity. When the task was finally completed, only my sooty, black hands remained tarnished. But my spirit was soaring. I had walked 78 miles in six days — my longest trip of record — and I knew my trail legs had arrived.

Around noon, I moved down into the grassy open space of the overlook and began the lengthy process of inspecting, sorting, repairing, and drying all of my gear. What a wonderful atmosphere of sociality I found there, as curious rangers, bear hunters, and visitors from all walks of life approached to chat. My choice for a Sunday layover had proven superb, and by the end of the day, I was physically and spiritually recharged to the point of impatience for the arrival of Monday.

Sometime during the night I awoke to a sixth sensation that some being had intruded very close to my camp. I had only pitched my tent two of the past seven nights, preferring a closeness to the heavens and woods over the confines of a tent. But sleeping under the stars, as I had chosen to do this night, also left one exposed to an unexpected shower at the worst, a damp sleeping bag from dewfall at the least, the inevitable surprise of a harmless daddy-long-legs spider walking across your face, and, of course, the imaginary boogerman.

Had I been dreaming or had I been awakened by the actual sound of something sneaking up on me? Surely my ranger friends had better things to do on a Sunday night than to play spook. Lying motionless on my back, I listened carefully for the next sound that would certainly compromise its position, now gripping the security of my walking stick that had been carefully placed parallel to my sleeping bag for just such occasions. My stirring had either silenced the thing momentarily or it did not exist at all, as the passing seconds felt like minutes and my adrenalin flow vacillated with mixed signals. I would wait it out or fall back to sleep in the silly process.

Finally, the faint sound of breathing and the muffled thud of an animal shifting its weight very close to my head jerked me back into the reality that I was not alone. I slowly arched my neck to extend my peripheral vision behind me and came face-to-face with the inverted image of a fully grown doe deer not readily identifiable in the darkness. The dam of suppressed adrenalin burst as I exploded from a supine to an upright posture in a single motion and screamed an expletive never before uttered by man. Mrs. Doe calmly trotted away but returned to my camp several times throughout the night, whether enamored of my presence or annoyed that I had encroached on her favorite feeding grounds I never quite determined. The fact remained that *she* had sneaked up on *me*, and I wondered if the two bucks and the German couple I had frightened previously had conspired with her in exacting their revenge. The balance of fear would continue in seesaw comedy throughout the remainder of the trek as man and beast unwittingly invoked the element of surprise on each other.

Someone once asked me when I was a ranger if there was anything about working on the Parkway that scared me. Avoiding the truth of the matter, I quipped that I was indeed afraid of the blackberry canes I had once discovered while fighting a forest fire high on the devil's side (north slope) of Richland Balsam that were larger than my arm. Mac Dale, hired as the second Parkway ranger in 1938, offered a more genuine response to this issue in a 1980 interview:

> And everybody in Roanoke at every opportunity, told me what a dangerous section of the Blue Ridge I was being assigned to. And with due emphasis on the fact that they [the local people] liked nothing better than rangers for breakfast. And me being a constitutional practicing coward, I was really gun-shy about this, because I don't like to get et for breakfast.

Some of the more obvious, fear-provoking catalysts that I associated with the job included: arriving first on the scene of horrific car crashes; discovering murders and suicides; losing control of patrol vehicles on snow and ice along sections devoid of guide rails; high speed car chases; discovering that I was not the only person carrying loaded firearms; arresting angry people larger than myself; being attacked by dogs; and stepping near poisonous snakes and bear traps. Notwithstanding their relevant importance to heart and underwear life expectancy, some of their details remain postponed at this point in lieu of a few irregular scenarios herein worthy of preservation.

Lone Bald Overlook sits high on the Parkway at an elevation of 5,635 feet above sea level on the lower fringes of a spruce-fir forest. Surrounded by the wild, undeveloped lands of the Nantahala National Forest and the Waynesville (N.C.) watershed, it affords a magnificent view of the heavens on a clear night that is minimally diminished by artificial light. Alone, it can also be a very lonely place. Occasionally, I found gazing at the Milky Way and meteor showers from this location an acceptable diversion from an otherwise boring late-night patrol in the crisp clarity of a cold night. Lying across the warm hood of my patrol vehicle, I had discovered, could prolong the celestial experience beyond my usual comfort tolerance of the cold. One such night I reclined, marveling at the glorious expanse, with my hands folded underneath and supporting my head. I never saw it coming, but a large bird of some kind, perhaps an owl or a nighthawk, pounced violently against my chest as if I were some object of prey. Its talons were unable to clutch the slick, waterproof fabric of my winter jacket, and it retreated back into flight, its feathered wing brushing across my face. Was it my imagination or did I really hear the chief ranger laughing in the night thinking he had finally caught a ranger sleeping on the job? Never again did I view the stars from such a vulnerable position.

Some wrecker operators were more proficient than others when recovering vehicles that had plunged over the side of a mountain. Some could transform a $500 damage estimate into a total loss in the retrieval process and were usually summoned only as a last resort. But one particular operator was so skilled at his trade that I once remarked that a vehicle he recovered had less damage after he had pulled it up than when he started the job. It was his service that I summoned near the end of a June day to undertake an extraordinary task.

Two young women had stepped from their vehicle at an overlook to take some pictures. To their horror, it rolled through the overlook, jumped the stone curb, and plunged out of sight down the mountain despite the owner's insistence that she had pulled the emergency brake. It had tumbled beyond the available length of cable carried on the wrecker, and all parties agreed to postpone the recovery operation to the safer light of the following morning. As a courtesy to the distraught women, I dropped them off at a local motel after climbing down to their vehicle to lock it up for the night and to retrieve a few pieces of luggage. The emergency brake, I discovered, had not been pulled as so claimed.

Early the next morning I closed the overlook to traffic to permit the wrecker, now equipped with enough spliced cable, to complete the job safely. After hooking up all of the necessary chains and cables to the vehicle, the slow, winching process began. The linkage tightened and groaned as the vehicle began its long climb up the steep embankment over stumps and boulders. Metal creaked and strained. The owner of the service skillfully operated the levers at the rear of the wrecker as his young male assistant walked beside the vehicle, shouting up maneuvering directions. About half way up the embankment, something snagged the undercarriage of the car, bringing its upward motion to a halt. The front wheels of the wrecker lifted slightly off the ground. The young man opened the front door of the car and reached in, he said later, to check the emergency brake. At the very moment that he leaned his torso into the vehicle, something broke, and the car went crashing down the mountain with the sound of a freight train. I have never felt more helpless or panicked as I watched this tangle of man and machine disappear out of sight in front of a trail of dust, mangled vegetation, and a limp cable.

Fearing the worst, everyone in the overlook rushed down the mountain. Surprisingly, we found him alive, but the vehicle had come to rest on top of him, pinning the right-rear tire against his leg. The adrenalin was already surging but now kicked into high gear as we desperately struggled to free him while being pierced by his screams of pain. Two lightweight rangers, employing the leverage of a locust sapling, managed to lift the car just enough for his boss to pull him free. This hardy mountain boy, whose sweat shirt had been ripped from his back, rose to his feet, swatted the dust from his pants, and calmly uttered, "Well boys, let's finish the job. But I think I'd like to work the levers this go round." Only scratched and bruised, he refused any medical treatment beyond some light bandaging and completed the job.

I had just completed the basic law enforcement training that included a heavy dose of watching the "Shoot–Don't Shoot" video series and firing range exercises. Sergeant Rice was quite proud of the fact that not once had I shot the hearing-impaired teenager playing with a toy gun or the little old lady who stepped in the path of a fleeing bank robber.

On a late-night solo patrol, I pulled into the Roanoke River Overlook to find a vehicle parked with all four doors standing open, the radio playing and not a person in sight. Illuminating it with my handy remote-controlled spotlight, I called in the license tag to the dispatcher. With utmost confidence that I was doing everything correctly, I carefully adjusted my Stetson to a perfectly horizontal position and cautiously proceeded to step out of a borrowed patrol car to which I was not fully accustomed. Duty demanded an investigation, and despite my rookie jitters, I was determined to conduct one in proper uniform.

I never suspected an ambush from behind, as I took my first step away from the car and felt something slap against the back of my legs. The two-foot-long flashlight I was holding in my left hand connected only with air as I spun around while simultaneously reaching for my revolver with my right hand. There was nothing behind me. Then it slapped the back of my legs again. In the desperate struggle that followed, I realized that my handcuff case had snagged the dilapidated seat cushion upon which I had been sitting and had pulled it out of the car behind me. As I was stuffing this worthless piece of wire and plastic into a nearby trash can, two carefree couples, unaware that I had just slain my first foe, returned to their car from a brief walk down a trail. They seemed to be just as curious about my nervous presence as I had originally been of theirs. At this point in my career, I had yet to conquer my own Jersey Devil.

10

Ranger Bloopers

"You put your tongue on a pump handle when it's so bitterly cold, the spit freezes, you're stuck there. Then either they pull you away, ripping your tongue off, or else pitch a tent over you and wait for spring and hope for the best."
—*Lake Wobegon Days*, by Garrison Keillor

Eager to conclude a 32-hour layover in the vicinity of Sunset Field Overlook, I departed in a southerly direction only to discover a temptation worth an extension of the long delay. A short distance from the overlook and slightly over the eastern embankment (referentially termed "Parkway Left" by the park staff) stood a peach tree loaded with fruit only a day or two away from ripeness. Its fruit was as large and unblemished as any I had seen in a managed orchard. A seed tossed from a car window years ago and a mower operator with vision had made this anomaly possible, but another discoverer would have to enjoy its taste. Mrs. Doe had convinced me to blow this joint at first light, and my newfound trail legs begged for a workout.

My first distant view of the familiar peaks of Flat Top and Sharp Top Mountains assuaged an ominous soreness in the arch of my left foot that eighty-one miles of pavement had suddenly presented. While some rangers had been known to complain of the persistent visitor question, "How far is it to the Peaks of Otter?" and mocked its popularity with the fictional designation of "Peaks of Otter National Park," entering its portals always felt to me like coming back home again from the dark side of the moon. I had originally planned to enter the area in a roundabout manner by hiking a side trail over the summit of Flat Top Mountain instead of the Parkway. But the growing soreness in my foot compelled me to forfeit, at this point, any excursions not relevant to the distant goal of Milepost 469. A meal at the Peaks of Otter Restaurant and a courtesy call to

Ranger Gene Parker, however, remained my only mandatory indulgences on this particular pass through the area.

I arrived at the ranger office, another converted ranger residence, around noon only to find it locked. Drats! The prospect of a hot shower vanished as quickly as the thought had come to me. Still, I meticulously checked every door and window on the building in hopes of making a surreptitious entry, and in despair, remembered that "Superintendent" Parker indeed ran a tight ship. Discouraged further by the thought that he might not even be working that day, I walked up to a nearby maintenance office but found nobody there that I recognized. The employee family I had once known seemed to have disappeared from this now lonely place. What grand barbecues and Thanksgiving turkey shoots we and our families had once enjoyed together there.

I had hoisted the pack onto my back and was in the process of adjusting the waist strap when a four-wheel-drive ranger vehicle drove into the maintenance yard. Though we had stayed in touch with each other by telephone and Christmas cards, Gene and I had not seen each other in about fifteen years. We had literally walked through fire and bloodied our hands together as rangers. Within an hour, I was showered and had an invitation to spend the evening at his farmhouse in Bedford County. Agreeing to meet at the visitor center at 6:00 P.M., I headed to the restaurant while he finished his shift.

Rationalizing the necessity of comfort food came easily as I finally succumbed to the temptation of a cheeseburger, french fries, and multiple soda refills in the rustically elegant dining room with a window view of Abbott Lake and Sharp Top Mountain, once thought to be the tallest mountain in Virginia. A piece of stone from its summit had been incorporated into the construction of the Washington Monument. As I gazed upon its stony, rugged peak, forgotten thoughts and images of the area began to return.

There was a day when the sounds of huge water snakes plunging into the lake kept the rapt attention of the visitors on my guided walks along a less manicured shore lined with alder trees, grasses, and cattails. There was a day when Ranger Parker and I bumped into each other on the Harkening Hill Trail. His excuse had been that he was checking the mast crop. My excuse fell within the flimsy pretense of assigned roving contact duty but was actually a short escape from the crowd resulting in the discovery of the largest dewberries on earth in a meadow near its breezy crest. Another day, I was engaged in more dutiful roving contact among the Sunday afternoon throng in the picnic area when I heard a familiar female voice yell, "Hey, ranger. You missed a belt loop!" Turning first toward the sound of the voice, I was delighted to see my younger sister who had driven up for a surprise visit. Then, with a twisting motion that wrapped one hand all the way around to the small of my back, I discovered that, not only did I have a lot of shyness to overcome, I would probably also require daily assistance in getting properly dressed in the unfamiliarly complicated uniform I was wearing. Thus began a collection of ranger bloopers, both committed and observed, most mentionable, some not.

Wrecking a patrol car was never considered conducive to propelling a ranger career in an upward direction. In every reportable case, regardless of fault, the ranger was subjected to an extensive investigation, the rigorous review of a board of inquiry, and potential disciplinary action. At the worst, such accidents involved pain, suffering, and costs to all parties involved and a permanent stain on a ranger's record. At the least, they were just plain embarrassing and were to be avoided at all costs. Technically speaking, though, an incident involving a motor vehicle became a reportable accident only when personal injury, property damage, or both were sustained. Since most ranger accidents involved only minor body damage and no witnesses, a resourceful ranger with amateur repair skills, in confederacy with a can of spray paint of the proper color and perhaps a more talented ally sworn to secrecy, could save all concerned parties much bureaucratic hogwash.

Bud Carter held the unenviable responsibility of maintaining every piece of motorized equipment in the Roanoke Valley District. Front-end loaders, tractors, dump trucks, mowers, weed eaters, chain saws, snowmobiles, pickup trucks, and patrol cars all fell within the scope of his job description. I respected his ability to fix most things and his honesty in knowing when to send a job beyond his capacity to one better skilled. A local fellow of generally good cheer, he was a man that a smart ranger would have befriended anyway for practical purposes, but I found him most likeable in the purest sense of relationships. No matter how stressful the job for either of us, we always attempted to humor each other through a bad day. I always offered to stop at the auto parts store for him on any trips into town, and he always squeezed the service of my patrol car into his busy schedule when I needed it. We liked each other, and we trusted each other, despite my discovery of and encroachment on his long-held secret plum trees gone wild near Milepost 109.

One early December morning, I broke away from the tedium of report writing at my desk in the ranger office and headed to the break room in search of carbonated refreshment and any distraction preferable to sketching an accident diagram. The only interior access to the break room was straight through the garage, in which Bud had hoisted my patrol car high on a lift to perform its scheduled service. As I burst through the swinging door in the best swashbuckling style I could contrive, wearing a freshly starched winter uniform and leather polished to royal cordovan perfection, Bud fell within the range of my first candid outburst of the day.

"Do you know the true sign of a good mechanic?" I hollered at close range to his backside.

Startled enough to bump his head on the transmission of my patrol car, yet fond enough of my humor to overlook this crude invasion onto his turf, he shook off the pain forgivingly. In the throes of an oil change and lubrication, he stepped from underneath the car with grease gun in hand and suggested that he could service me in like manner if he so chose.

Only two hours into his workday, he had already degraded into the appearance for which he was best known — cap tilted to one side, sleeves rolled up to the elbows, shirt tucked half in and half out of baggy trousers, enough grease on his body and uniform to guarantee good marks on his next employee evaluation, and a smirky grin suggesting he knew something that I did not. Wiping the nozzle of the grease gun with an oily shop rag, he smiled at me with dropped jaw, unable to sort a response to my question, knowing he was about to fall victim to a clever punch line.

"He very seldom gets grease on himself," I finally answered for him.

Without even looking at his hands and arms, smeared with black to the elbows, Bud replied as if he believed the very words I had spoken. "They law, Tim. Then we're all in trouble." Little did I know that Bud had lured me into a trap of his own making.

"Tim. Did you realize that the front of your patrol car has hit something really hard?" he asked. I quickly re-examined the front bumper for damage that a previous clandestine inspection had apparently missed.

"Well, I don't see any damage to the bumper, Bud. How can you tell?"

He then proceeded to point out two obscure plastic rings that were slightly cracked, explaining that this particular bumper was equipped with two hydraulic shock absorbers. In order for these rings to become cracked, both shock absorbers had to have been compressed slightly past their maximum capacity as a result of a significant frontal collision. My turn had arrived to stand speechless with dropped jaw, as Bud finally rescued me from silent guilt with this grandfatherly advice: "I'd be careful loaning my car to some of these seasonal rangers around here in the future, Tim."

"I will, Bud. I will. Thanks," I muttered.

With hands carefully tucked in my back pockets to avoid the temptation of touching something that would dirty them, I took the opportunity to inspect the entire undercarriage of my patrol car. A few rocks in the road that I had ignorantly attempted to straddle, without sufficient clearance, had dented, but not penetrated, the oil pan. Tire wear appeared normal, with no indications of a bent frame that could have resulted from the collision to which Bud had alluded. Back again to a more thorough inspection of the front bumper assembly revealed nothing that could be technically classified as damage. The plastic rings, though cracked, functioned merely as indicators. I would have to give Bud more credit in the future for his sharp mechanical eye.

Attempting a graceful departure from Bud's work station, I offered to buy him a soda in sincere gratitude for his rendered services and, admittedly, in a cheap attempt to purchase his silence. He accepted my offer and, with wits to match, snickered to my departing backside, "And watch out for those grouse chicks crossing the Parkway, too!" With that statement, I knew that somehow Bud knew that which should have never been retold.

One humid summer evening I sought escape from the lower elevations of the Roanoke Valley with a patrol up Bent Mountain. Many local residents had done the same, enjoying the cooler, breezier heights among a sprinkling of over-looks along that section of the Parkway. Most were innocently engaged with enjoyment of the night air and sparkling lights in the valley below; the station-ary ones mostly marked places of residence, and the moving ones traced routes of roads. Most visitors were comfortable, even reassured of their safety, with my presence and offered a friendly word or nod upon my passing of their pleasant perch.

But darkness had already invited minor mischief into the early hours of its tranquility, and my eyes, ears, and nose were alert to the discovery of violations of park regulations. Any furtive movement made by a visitor usually belied the presence of innocent activity and most often involved alcohol, drugs, firearms, or disorderly conduct. The trunk of my patrol car already contained several cans of beer, for which some minors had received written warnings, and a small bag of marijuana and a smoking pipe, from which one unlucky visitor could not be excused. Two young lovers, in the advanced stages of undress, appeared obliv-ious to my passing headlights and were aptly reminded by word, in lieu of writ-ten documentation, that they were in a public park. Thus far the night had proven neither boring nor stressful.

The familiar voice of a ranger colleague from an adjacent district called suddenly on the radio with a quick, loud burst and a faint tone of panic. "What's your location, 222?" Its clarity and absence of a trailing repeater squelch indi-cated to me that the caller was transmitting on channel one and was either very close or we had a perfect, line-of-sight connection between distant points.

"On Bent Mountain," I quickly replied.

"Can you meet me at Read Mountain Overlook as soon as possible?"

"10-4. Is everything okay?"

"Not really."

"Is it an emergency?"

"Sort of."

"I'm on the way."

I had a twenty-mile drive to his requested location and just enough infor-mation to push my driving skills to the edge. His voice had become more nerv-ous with each transmission, accompanied by a curious reluctance to say any more over the radio than was absolutely necessary. Assuming the worst, and presuming he would do the same for me in a similar situation, I probably set a district land speed record for that stretch. Never did I drive that fast with a patrol car unless another ranger was in trouble.

As I rounded a final curve and descended into a straight stretch of road on the approach to Read Mountain Overlook, I glanced across a gently sloping cow pasture, expecting to see flashing red and blue lights. There were none. As I decelerated into the overlook, I was even more surprised to see no vehicles—not even a patrol car—parked in it. A momentary rush of panic slightly sub-sided when I finally saw my friend standing, apparently unharmed, holding a flashlight in one hand and a portable radio in the other. He had little to say to me at first, pointing only toward the sound of several cows, disturbed from their sleep, bellowing in the night. I shined my spotlight in their direction to discover what appeared to be the top of a patrol car buried in a tangle of weeds about a hundred yards below the overlook.

In a hasty exit from his patrol car to chase one of those suspicious furtive movements, a still undetermined human or mechanical malfunction had occurred. But the damage to the vehicle and the fence was minimal and, fortunately, no bovine casualties were incurred. I knew how my comrade felt, for I had been there, too.

Buried shall remain further details of blame and shame related to patrol vehicle bloopers, along with the case of the ranger who forgot he was driving within a gated area and woke up too late to avoid a gate; and the case of the game warden and ranger who turned off their headlights to sneak up on the same poacher and struck each other head-on; and the case of the...

Wit and a propensity for execution of the practical joke appears to be an inherited genetic trait along the Pegram line. My father quite often loads a humorous analogy with: "Do you know who that guy reminds me of?" I was too young to properly digest and appreciate most of Papaw Pegram's wit and humor, but tales later retold suggested a capacity bordering brilliance, even criminality. Beyond them, I can only speculate on the long trail of witty anecdotal history leading all the way back to Mother England and eventually to a medieval court jester yet to be discovered swinging on a limb of the family tree. We simply cannot help ourselves and often bore or embarrass our wives, children, and sometimes even the audience in the process.

I had the purest intentions in noticing the three modestly attractive, middle-aged teachers from the local high school who jogged together on the Parkway nearly every day. Understanding the concept of safety in numbers, they parked each of their vehicles en masse at the same overlook and jogged en masse as a trio, or they did not jog at all.

I jogged this section of the Parkway frequently myself and well understood the traffic perils they faced in this heavily traveled commuter zone. Our district incident files were also sprinkled with complaints of verbal harassment, games of "chicken," and thrown objects being directed at joggers from drivers and their passengers. Adding their female dimension to this troublesome equation, I felt certain that these ladies would eventually encounter some kook with less than noble intentions some day. So I quietly volunteered a little extra patrol presence when they were in the area and even managed to slow the traffic a bit for them with a radar gun.

My free services on their behalf did not go unnoticed, and one day they flagged me down after completing a run to thank me for the little extra protection. During our conversation, I jokingly suggested that they reminded me of the women in the television series, *Charlie's Angels*. Feeling perhaps a little more middle-aged at close range than from a distance, they laughingly disagreed with my analogy but thereafter addressed me as "Charlie."

At the conclusion of one long, hot workday, I pulled the patrol car into our driveway and noticed a vaguely familiar car parked at our quarters. Patty was always engaged in a host of enterprises, including tailored sewing, so I was not surprised to see a young girl, dressed in a wedding gown, standing on the round cocktail table in our living room. I stopped momentarily at the threshold of the doorway for some indication that entry was permissible. Patty, kneeling on the carpet and focused on a cumbersome hemline, glanced up with a smile and said, "Hi, honey. It's okay. Come on in." As I stepped into the room another female voice from a blind corner of the room also greeted me with, "Hi, Charlie. How are you?"

Unbeknownst to me, Patty had contracted with one of my "angels" to sew a wedding gown for her daughter. As my scrambled thoughts searched for the proper words of explanation, Patty, unable to verbalize normally due to all the pins she was now delicately holding in her mouth, squeaked with pursed lip, "Tarlie, huh."

Oops. Oops. Oops. I needed a shower and retreated in that direction.

Sometimes I found that the job of rangering could be performed too well and that a prying curiosity could sometimes bite my backside. I had begun to notice that a particular man, driving a particular sedan, parked at a particular overlook on a particular day of every week and never noticeably looked up from reading his newspaper. Nothing else about him appeared out of order other than his regularity. So, on a particularly uneventful day, I decided to run his license plate.

Dispatcher Joyce Pence seemed to be taking an inordinate length of time in returning the registration information, so I remained patient and continued my patrol, assuming that things had gotten busy on her end. She eventually responded with a request that I report to the nearest telephone immediately. I was only seconds from the pay telephone located at the Roanoke Mountain Campground. Joyce was known for a cranky sense of humor, and though mildly annoyed at her request, I waited for her call in great anticipation of some juicy information that could not be broadcast over the airwaves.

"Tim, a funny thing happened when I ran that plate for you," she began.

"Oh yeah. What?"

"Well, first of all, it came back not on file. And then your boss came in here bugging me about something, and I lost my train of thought and forgot to call you back. Then the phone rang, and a fellow from the FBI wanted to know why I had run that tag. I told him I would have to check with the ranger who had called it in. Then he said never mind the details, just tell your ranger to butt out."

No problem. I did not have to be told twice by the FBI. But I never saw the man again and never learned whether I had been responsible for accidentally blowing his cover or getting him in trouble for goofing off on the job.

The discovery of trail bike paths in the park was always a matter of mild concern. Sometimes they led straight to an illegal patch of marijuana or proved accessory to the burglary of private residences adjacent to park lands. The game of "cat and mouse" never seemed to end, but I rarely expended more than a meager amount of time and energy in playing it — until two teenage boys lunged from nowhere out of the woods on muddied machines directly into the path of my patrol car one day. Wearing no helmets and equipped with no license plates, they displayed first the wild-eyed fright of a near collision and then took on the look of stubborn determination to escape. Down the Parkway they chose to flee, with me in angry pursuit with lights flashing and siren blaring. The chase lasted only half a mile before they mockingly flipped a victorious hand gesture in my direction and turned down another path and disappeared down the mountain. I was steamed. This meant war. And I was determined to catch them on another day with a strategy that could not be defeated.

Their path up the side of Bent Mountain, though well worn, was easily concealed by thick undergrowth as it neared the Parkway, and it took some effort for me to find it. Following it a few yards down the mountain, I discovered that it connected to an old logging road and to a perfect trap. A huge chestnut log on one side of the road and a steep dropoff on the other side funneled the path directly into a manageable width of only six feet. In combination with the cover offered by a large rhododendron bush and a slight curve in the path, they could be stopped easily and even snatched from their bikes if they chose to flee in either direction. Fridays, after school, I theorized, would be prime time for the stakeout.

The first Friday of "Operation Gotcha" was interrupted by a dispatcher call that a visitor had locked his keys in his car. The second Friday ranked of boredom, as evidenced by a fair pile of wood shavings and sticks carved into a variety of abstract designs left scattered on the ground. The only thing I caught that day was the rare sight of a flying squirrel who had emerged prematurely from its sleep. Apparently curious of my presence, it peeked from the top of a hollowed stump of a tree broken off six feet above the ground. Paralyzed with fright, it stared at me, motionless, for several minutes before leaping from the stump. Stretching all four of its webbed limbs widely, it floated like a parachute down the mountain and out of sight. I never heard it land and have yet to this day to witness anything more graceful. The day had really not been wasted, I justified.

By the third Friday, I was beginning to think that the lights and siren had cured these boys from ever coming up that path again. But a noise high on the mountain above me jump-started my spirit with the prospect of catching an even more sinister ravager of the delicate resources of the park.

Ginseng, a scarce, endemic plant of the Appalachian mountains, has long supplemented the income of native folk with that little extra "Christmas money." Its roots, curative of many ailments in Chinese medicine, have traditionally brought a high price at even the first level of exchange. With proper permission under limited conditions, it can be harvested on private and some public lands. But it can never be lawfully gathered from a national park area, and its poachers are most difficult to catch in the act.

The distinct sound of at least three people slowly working their way down the mountain seemed to be heading in my direction. If they were speaking to each other in the process, it was being done in hushed whispers that I could not yet detect. Their shuffling, irregular walking pattern convinced me that ginseng poachers were in the park and were walking directly toward me. Only the targets of Operation Gotcha had changed; the tactics remained the same.

I crouched lengthwise behind the chestnut log I had been using for a bleacher seat in hopes of luring them as close as possible. The most solid case, with minimal search and seizure issues, could be made by witnessing the actual digging of a plant and then witnessing its placement into a sack where more were likely to be found. As they approached within certain sight of the log behind which I was hiding, I silently hoped, with diminishing patience, that any pistols they carried were loaded only with snake shot. Outnumbered at least three-to-one, I debated the merits of waiting out a perfect ginseng case over a surprise ambush that might compromise the more important interest of self-preservation.

Suddenly, the walking stopped a mere twenty feet from the log, and the sound of digging followed. The time had come to take my first peek at their activity. Slowly, ever so slowly, I eased my head around the corner of the log, my heart racing with excitement. To my surprised eyes, I stared face-to-face with — not three but — five of the fattest wild turkey hens I had ever beheld. Detection of movement being their keenest sense, I simultaneously relished victory with defeat by jumping wildly to my feet to witness the finest of Thanksgiving feasts launch furiously into the air. On the walk back to my patrol car, I concluded that I had developed some truly remarkable ranger skills for all the wrong reasons.

Bud Carter and I were exchanging pleasantries with each other again one day in his shop when one of our newest rangers drove briskly up to the edge of the bay door. With a broad grin, he motioned everyone within the sound of his voice to gather around the trunk of his patrol car for a surprise.

Now this was an educated, bright young man who was trying his best to learn the job. He had never hunted a day in his life and was barely past the infancy stage in his knowledge of wild game and ways of the hunter. This minor deficiency was excusable, of course, considering his proficiency in many other areas related to rangering.

Deriding the time and expense many in his company devoted to the art of turkey hunting, he boastfully exclaimed that his hunt had not even cost him the price of a hunting license and had been completed in a matter of seconds. To prove his catch, he opened the trunk of his patrol car and hoisted a clear plastic bag containing his "turkey" high into the air. He solemnly declared that his family would enjoy this barely mutilated road kill for their upcoming Thanksgiving dinner. We all stood in amazement, assessing his state of seriousness and sobriety.

"Should we tell him how to dress and cook it?" Bud whispered to me.

"I could never do that to that nice wife and daughter of his," I replied.

"Then somebody had better tell him before he takes it home."

"Not me, Bud. You tell him."

"They heck. I say just let him eat that old turkey vulture."

"The ranger division will never live this one down, will it Bud?"

"You got that right. That's the worst I've ever seen of one of you boys coming through here, and I've met a many of you. That's the honest to goodness truth, Tim."

Another case of performing the job too well is worthy of mention. A particular overlook in our district had become notorious for more serious mischief, to include drug deals, target shooting of trash cans, and even a suicide. Configured as a short loop road, its small parking area could not be seen from the Parkway, and in the time it took for a patrol vehicle to drive up its short access road, such activities could be easily whitewashed before they could be discovered. But a little knoll covered with thick briars, vines, and trees stood in the center of this loop and provided a perfect cover for stakeout operations. I was determined to reverse the reputation of this overlook with an unrelenting fusillade of arrests until the nonsense was halted.

Situated snugly a few feet up the slope of the knoll and well hidden, despite the fact that the leaves had dropped from the trees for winter, I patiently watched a man sitting in a parked vehicle one November afternoon. My vantage point was close enough to allow me to look directly into his rear window, through which I could see his fingers tapping on the console to the beat of a song playing on his radio. With the aid of a pair of binoculars, I could nearly identify the radio station to which he was listening. Perfectly innocent enjoyment of the park, it appeared.

In a few minutes, a woman drove into the overlook and parked next to him. With purse in hand, she exited her vehicle, looked nervously around the overlook, opened the right-front door of his car and seated herself in the front passenger seat. Following a brief conversation, without any doubt, I saw this man give her a handful of currency in exchange for a medicine bottle. The trap was sprung perfectly on them, artfully culminating in his consent to search his vehicle and her consent to search her purse.

A medicine bottle containing exactly twenty-one tablets was found in her purse, and a small bag also containing twenty-one of the same tablets was found on his seat. A bundle of currency in the amount of $32 was found on the right-front floorboard, and a loaded revolver was found under the driver's seat. All of the ingredients of a drug deal were present, but there was something about this case that gave me an uneasy feeling. The medicine bottle indicated that a local pharmacy had filled a prescription that day for forty-two metronidazole tablets for this man. I was not familiar with this drug and was not about to assume that the tablets I had confiscated were necessarily metronidazole. Both suspects were taken to our nearby ranger station and held until further investigation of the tablets could be made.

A telephone call to a regional DEA office quickly established that the tablets were not a controlled substance. Their description and markings, in fact, matched those of metronidazole, a prescription medication commonly used to treat a venereal disease. I was stunned. With no discrimination intended, I chose to interview the man first, in private. He shyly explained that he had contracted a disease from his lady friend, and due to the delicacy of the situation, his doctor had advised him to split the medicine with her to save them both further embarrassment. That was really more information than I wanted to hear.

We both returned to my office, whereupon I advised the lady that I really had no questions for her and told her she was free to leave. I hoped that she would leave quickly, and she did so. As for the unfortunate gentleman, all forty-two tablets were returned to him while his troubles were compounded with a firearms charge. It was the least I could do for us both.

Every profession reserves its most menial tasks for the new guy, the rookie, even the buck ranger. Regular inspection and maintenance of the district fire extinguishers and traffic counters were two of those duties that I accepted initially with utmost seriousness in the tradition of a long procession of rangers that had preceded me. I well understood the implications to my new career if a fire extinguisher, low of pressure, failed during a real emergency. I also understood the emphasis the park superintendent placed on counting every single vehicle that entered the park to maintain our position as the most visited unit of the National Park Service.

Policy only required fire extinguishers to be officially inspected and documented semiannually, but senior rangers, secretaries, janitors, and every jack-leg specialist on tour from headquarters took great pleasure in "assisting" me much more often with this duty when the least discrepancy was found. The traffic counters were an even greater nuisance, requiring daily recordings and service. Conversely, it was nearly impossible to get another employee to check them on days that I did not work, and I could have killed the maintenance employees who seemed to take sick pleasure in ripping up the rubber hoses with the blade of a snowplow.

Consequently, the trunk of my heavily laden patrol car was always equipped with a generous supply of rubber hose, clamps, masonry nails, batteries, and miscellaneous spare parts. Back in those days, unlike the invisible sensors buried in the pavement today, a length of rubber hose was stretched and secured across one lane of traffic. Assuming there were no leaks in the hose, the pressure of a tire rolling over it would force air within the hose through an external metal nozzle and into the guts of the counter itself. This mechanical force then somehow interacted with some little gizmo and, with an electrical assist from a battery, forced the movement of a mechanical counter. I never quite understood exactly how the thing worked, but soon I became quite skilled at making it work.

The two most common problems encountered with this ingenious invention — a tear in the hose or a dead battery — were quite simple to diagnose. If a sound stomp on the hose tripped the counter, everything was working fine. If it did not, the next logical procedure involved disconnecting the hose and blowing a puff of air through the metal nozzle. If the counter did not trip, the battery was dead. Otherwise, the hose usually was the problem.

Have you ever said or done something that, following its commission, you knew instantaneously had been a big mistake? Not long ago, Hershey, our loveable Siamese cat of twenty years, passed away. He had been a Christmas gift for Patty, who was a little more fond of his weirdness than I. His health had been failing for several months, and his passing was expected. Patty found him in the garage early one morning and shared the sad news with me with controlled emotion. It was a cold, rainy, winter morning, and I was already close to being late for work when she asked what we should do with his body. My impetuous observation that he had conveniently died on garbage pick-up day was countered with an icy stare that demanded immediate remedy. Why had I made such a stupid suggestion? We then found our sturdiest shoe box and a fitting cloth wrap in which to give him a proper burial on the highest point on our property.

On another even colder day, when weak batteries tend to die, I disconnected the rubber hose from a traffic counter and, without thinking again, placed my lips on its metal nozzle to check the battery. And there I stood, stuck to it like frost on a windshield, with only one unpleasant choice available to me. It hurt so much to leave so much of me on that nozzle.

11

Taking Flight

"It takes a lot more than just fancy flying."
— Kelly McGillis to Tom Cruise
in the movie *Top Gun*

My evening with the Parker family began with a hearty meal of venison tenderloin, gravy, green beans, mashed potatoes, sliced tomatoes, rolls, butter, salt, pepper, lemonade, cake, and ice cream. As a temporarily homeless creature, I developed an acute sensitivity to every kindness offered to me and, in matters of cuisine, developed a perfect memory of every detail, in fact, of every bite. I wondered if they ate like that every night or if my presence had generated a rare Monday night windfall for Gene.

Both daughters, now young adults, joined us for dinner in customarily late fashion for their ages. One seemed determined to be just like her father, and the other seemed just as determined to be the opposite. Julie, the ever-heroic Parkway wife, apparently sensed my growing need, perhaps strongly, to rotate into a fresh set of clothing and offered the use of their washer and dryer. Whether this offer was another simple act of kindness or an unspoken condition to me spending the night in her home, I never quite determined nor pursued. Nevertheless, it did become my first of five rotations into a complete set of clean clothes. Eight days on the trail had sufficiently ripened my first set.

Their border collie seemed indifferent regarding my state of grooming and romped like a child with me on the carpet in front of the television. This was a family, pets included, bound with a love and unity as strong as the oak beams that supported the farmhouse of many Parker generations.

Gene was a park ranger by profession and a farmer by upbringing. As we frittered the evening away exchanging news, he sadly spoke of the mandatory retirement he would have to take at the young age of fifty-seven in a few months.

But he still had the farm and the avocation of his third love of life — bear hunting — and the first love of his life — Julie.

I also began to wonder if they watched that same outdoor channel every night for three hours or if they thought it was my natural preference. I was heavily dosed on the Great Outdoors already and would have enjoyed a game show or a sitcom or a movie or some world news or some weather — anything, anything but... Sorry. Julie reminded me once again I was their guest when she rebuffed my offer to sleep on the living room floor and sent me to the softest bed on which I have ever slept.

Gene made it quite clear before retiring to bed that evening that my ride back to the Parkway would be leaving at six o'clock sharp the next morning. So I set my mental alarm clock for five o'clock and amazingly woke up near that hour in time to soak my left foot in a hot bath. Anatomically, I understood the implications of an inflamed arch to the point of serious worry. I would have to make some adjustment in walking or give it a rest, preferably the former.

I limped out the back door into the clear coldness of the darkest hour of the night in time to witness the ritual of watering and feeding a pack of twenty-six Walker hounds, six of whom were carefully selected to enjoy freedom from their pen for a few hours. Bear season had not yet arrived in that part of the country, but training season for the dogs was open, which permitted every element of a real hunt minus the actual taking of a bear. Every dog in the pen was eager to go but was strictly forbidden from howling for the opportunity. I did not understand the process completely and had no desire to own and feed that many dogs just for the thrill of a bear hunt. But Gene was the most legal hunter I knew, and if that was the thing he enjoyed doing, it was fine with me. I am sure he looked upon me just as narrowly for my love of backpacking and this silly hike I was taking.

As the chosen few dogs were loaded onto the truck, Julie arrived at the barn with a basket full of sausage biscuits and a jug of orange juice. Before the sun had risen, I was returned to the point of my last step in front of the visitor center and resumed my trek down the Parkway, quite honored that I had been welcomed into such a storybook home.

Before the Parkway and I were once again swallowed in the depths of the Jefferson National Forest, and in the faint light of early morning, I turned back for a final look at this magical place called the Peaks of Otter. Very little had changed about it over the nearly thirty years I had known it. My progeny and those of many others whose hearts had been captured by its spirit were counting on the National Park Service to keep it that way. In such places of permanence our souls find anchor in the ever-changing, troubled waters of this world.

Not too far into the day, an emboldened sun, filtered by the morning fog, began to warm the day and intensify the colors of autumn halfway to their peak. In the eeriness of the struggle between fog and light, the Maker of it all seemed to place his hand on my shoulder and walk beside me. Walking with me, too, it seemed, were the spirits of two men who would have visited this park in the same way. Henry David Thoreau would have done it quietly and meditatively over several months, while Edward Abbey would have forced all to walk it if they saw it at all and would have dispatched *The Monkey Wrench Gang* to destroy every rude encroachment that now threatened its beauty. Whether it was their combined company and endorsement, the soak in a hot bath, or a decision to cross over to the right shoulder through steeply superelevated left-hand curves I hesitate to judge. But the nagging pain in my left foot subsided and never became a real threat to ending the trek again.

At Upper Goose Creek Valley Overlook, I unexpectedly stumbled upon some of Gene's hunting companions with whom I had just shared breakfast. They were anxiously engaged in tracking the anointed dogs, equipped with radio collars, with a telemetry device. Baying in the distant valley below, the dogs had certainly "struck" on a bear scent and were hot on its trail. A familiar voice called his friends on the radio to advise that the bear chase had entered private property and that he was intercepting the dogs. That was Gene, legal and courteous in every respect with his hunt, and just in time to begin his ranger shift at noon.

The Blue Ridge Parkway roughly courses along its namesake for a little over 350 miles, from its beginning at Milepost Zero to about Mount Mitchell. Nowhere along that stretch does it do so in more dramatic fashion than over the next ten miles of my walk. Snaking the very spine of the Blue Ridge through this little stretch, it detours gracefully around an occasional bluff only to connect its contour again with the crest of the ridge. A plethora of breathtaking views both east and west begged the construction of numerous overlooks from which the scenery could be savored. But one early Parkway engineer, Bill Austin, concerned that this project should not duplicate the hundred-mile monotony of the Skyline Drive of Shenandoah National Park, to which this little section shows striking resemblance, suggested: "One could be gorged on scenery, and you can have too much ice cream and too much Beethoven." Stanley Abbott more poetically offered that "one panorama following right on another, thinking of that as *fortissimo*, doesn't make the interesting piece of music that *fortissimo* mixed with a little *pianissimo* provides." Abbott further explained the design philosophy of this massive project in a separate treatise:

> The Parkway does not exclusively follow the skyline, but assumes a changing position in the mountains. Like the movie cameraman who shoots his subjects from many angles to heighten the drama of his film, so the shifting position of the roadway unfolds a more interesting picture to the traveler. The sweeping view over the low country often holds the center of the stage, but seems to exit gracefully enough when the Parkway leaves the ridge for the more gentle slopes and the deeper forests.

While I was happily engaged in the partaking of this perfectly proportioned serving of "ice cream," a sedan deluxe enough to transport a respected dignitary, but bearing no official insignia, slowed and stopped. To my pleasant surprise, out stepped Dan Brown, whose ranger career had once brought him

I sat with Parkway Superintendent Dan Brown September 9, 2003, near Milepost 93 in Virginia.

through the Peaks of Otter and now back as the park superintendent. Dan had hired and supervised me on my initial ranger appointment, and we had much news to share. We sat together on a wooden guide rail and shared a good hour of time that I knew the fast clock of his day could rarely spare. As he departed, I thanked him for hiring me in 1978 and told him those had been the best years of my professional life. He replied that they had been for him, too.

Having previously memorized the name and sequence of nearly every overlook along this section of the Parkway, I hardly noticed the cleverly designed "Overlook Ahead" signs that also forewarned the attentive visitor to which side of the road each overlook was situated on. Sight of the one heralding Harvey's Knob Overlook quickened my pace, in anticipation of making conversation with a unique breed of visitor known to frequent it during that season of the year.

I chuckled with delight as the spectacle of two women and a man, close if not well into their eighties, each sitting comfortably in their favorite lounge chair, came into view. Dressed as if on some exotic safari, they were each outfitted with a pair of binoculars from which they occasionally gazed into the sky. Cured and sassy enough to share a strong opinion on every social, political, and religious issue of the day, but young enough to have escaped the traps of age, they were delightfully engaged in witnessing a natural cycle as old as the Blue Ridge itself.

In their annual southerly migration to warmer, winter temperatures, hawks and their kind tend to favor the long, parallel ridge formations along the Appalachian chain. Taking advantage of warm, vertical air currents flowing upslope from the valleys below, they tend to hug a ridge line for an almost effortless free ride. This particular overlook is strategically located in a blind spot, from which these birds can often be viewed in close proximity.

My new friends had only seen two broad-winged hawks all day but were vigilantly searching also for the eagle, osprey, red-tailed hawk, and others. Somewhat bored from the low count of the day, they eventually directed their attention my way, having plopped my backpack down in their midst and enjoying immensely their comical banter. I was offered a chocolate chip cookie on an equal basis with a deer who, nearly tamed from such unwise handouts, wandered unflinchingly nearby. I was just about to preach a little sermon about feeding wildlife to the elderly lady of charity, until she giggled to me that she had to keep her eye out for the park rangers, one of whom had reprimanded her the day before. Playing dumb like a fox, I made further inquiry into her encounter, and she described Gene Parker to the toenails. Incorrigible, I judged, and bid them farewell.

A mere eighty-three years had passed from the time Wilbur and Orville Wright launched their historic flight of man in a heavier-than-air, powered machine to the 1986 release of the movie *Top Gun.* In the possible lifetime of a human being, aviation had soared from the sands of Kill Devil Hill onto the bobbing deck of an aircraft carrier. Like many moviegoers of that time, I was captured by its aerial drama and have lost count of the number of times I have watched it.

It was not unusual to be startled by the sudden appearance and disappearance of a military jet darting past at a low elevation while on patrol. On at least one occasion, I am fairly certain that a mischievous pilot stalked me for entertainment. I was parked along the road shoulder near Milepost 419 running radar one day when I noticed an object streaking along the valley floor in my direction at a much lower elevation. In my fascination that I had actually spotted one of these guys before being frightened out of my wits, the forethought escaped me to turn the radar gun in his direction to lock on him first for a record reading. Before crashing into the mountain below me, he lifted up at the last possible second and streaked through the gap at treetop level, saluting me in passing. Whether the unexpected sight of Graveyard Ridge rising abruptly in front of him caused him to momentarily lose control or whether he was just strutting his skill, his plane appeared to spiral wildly out of control. Whatever the case, he was in Madison County by the time he leveled out the aircraft.

On another day, I watched six jets dogfight each other in the clear skies over Waterrock Knob. The aerial show was just like in the movie, vertical dives and all. Not too many years later, the skills of many of those same pilots would no doubt be employed in real combat over the Middle East. Unlike them, my direct involvement with aircraft as a ranger remained tame, with only the occasional securing of a landing sight for a rescue helicopter, an occasional overflight of park lands for marijuana detection, and assuring panicked hikers that the wreckage they had discovered just off park boundary on the backside of Browning Knob was from an old crash.

I had come to realize along my hike that wildlife, while tuned to the sound of approaching traffic, had little experience in detecting a traveler on foot and could be surprised quite easily. I had walked within a few feet of a great blue heron, fishing in a small seep just below me, when he spread his large wings to begin beating an escape. Startled myself, I froze. A dense thicket sealed his background and left him no choice but to fly in my direction and within my reach. I could have easily grabbed his dangling, gangling legs. As he climbed and turned south, my imagination flew away with him:

> Oh, for the lightness of a monarch,
> To butterfly piggyback for a time,
> O'er this wandering ribbon of a park
> To a much warmer clime.
> Past the illusion of suspension
> And downhills that up,
> I would coast to its end on the wind and the wend
>   — and fantasize for more.
>
> Now, as an eagle,
> I'd soar through the South,
> To the shores of the Gulf.
> What would Abbott do now?
> Bridge it, agreed,
> Put the stone masons to work.
> Connect to the Yucatan, yearning
> For the continuing journey.
> On through the isthmus this Parkway would snake,
> Soaring above to soon overtake —
>
> The equator. New divider. Another district realignment.
>
> Back to earth on these feet, still quite controversial,
> With seasons in complete reversal.
> Now high through the Andes,
> Pacific to west,
> Serpentine at its best,
> To Magellan's strait shore.
>
> The end? "Dare not," the dreamer declared.
> Waddle on to the ice land
> Where birds fly no more.

12

Stills and Fields

"Well, I might as well give you this [bag of marijuana] now."
— Parkway visitor (name withheld)
while complying with a request to
exit his vehicle

A fantasy trip down a Parkway extension to Antarctica, though dramatic, turned out to be the aberrant product of a wandering imagination, and I soon found my feet back on the reality of asphalt. But was I mistaken that President Roosevelt's original vision had taken it to the Canadian border or that, at least as recently as the 1960s, there was strong interest in extending it all the way to Cartersville, Georgia? Better it was, I thought, for what it had become than for what it had not.

By nightfall I had broken the triple-digit threshold of Milepost 100 and was well past the third fold of my map; only eight folds remained to be crossed. Serenaded to sleep by trains whistling through the community of Montvale in the valley below, I was awakened most unusually by the call of a whippoorwill at dawn. More commonly heard in the early night hours following dusk, this little nonsynchronous fellow could have been warning of the changing character of the park lying ahead of me.

As the Parkway began a long gradual descent into the Roanoke Valley, its narrow boundary eventually left the adjoining, protective embrace of the Jefferson National Forest to course, for the most part, adjacently through privately owned lands for about the next two hundred miles. Vast panoramas of forested wilderness yielded gradually, at first, to an occasional residence and hay field. The dramatic appearance of the twin, stone-faced, single-arch bridges carrying U.S. Route 460 over the Parkway abruptly marked a new landscape of gently rolling farmland mottled with the oozing finger paint of suburban sprawl.

In a somewhat unfair generalization, the visitor, too, changed from the carefree hawk watcher to the frenzied commuter.

Not only do these two bridges formalize a visual transition of the landscape, they seem to perpetually survive as an administrative line of demarcation between districts, sub-districts, or whatever units future Parkway reorganizations might term them. Stanley Abbott formally complained in 1943 to his superiors that, somewhere near this point, the Public Roads Administration insisted that the Parkway become a four-lane highway and a segment of a circumferential beltway around the city of Roanoke. Wiser planners of the National Park Service eventually prevailed in that battle. Nevertheless, the fifteen-mile stretch skirting the city to U.S. Route 220 still evolved into a pleasantly scenic shortcut for local traffic. Critics who allege that such areas along the Parkway grossly overinflate the count of "real visitors" have yet to convince me that a person using the Parkway on the way home from work on a Friday afternoon is not having a bona fide recreational experience. As a backpacker mingled with them, though, I would have to acknowledge their less than cheerful faces in the mornings on their way to work. Their sheer numbers at certain times of the day would necessitate either the constant support of my right arm in an improvised sling or a reduction in the number of passing vehicles to which I would wave.

By mid-afternoon I was coasting downhill on the final approach to what had been my first permanent duty station. The grade from Milepost 111 to Milepost 112 is deceptively steeper than it appears, I had learned and never forgotten one winter day.

The Parkway was closed to traffic due to a crippling ice storm that had coated the road surface at least an inch thick. Our family hooked two sleds together for what I had intended to be a long, fun ride. With little Laura on my back screaming with glee and Patty trailing behind us screaming with fright, I soon realized that we were skimming along at about 60 mph, or so it seemed, absolutely out of control. Somehow, someway, I managed to steer our family clear of eternity that day. But reminiscent terror was softened with a satisfying discovery that the Virginia pine seedlings I had helped an Eagle Scout candidate plant along that stretch had accomplished their intended purpose — to screen a residential subdivision that had been built directly adjacent to the Parkway in gross disharmony to its intended landscape. Like a campsite left in better condition than I had found it, my little legacy of healing trees made me rather proud.

The passage of time had dramatically altered the personality of what used to be the nerve center of activity for the entire Virginia section of the Parkway. The old Vinton ranger station had once housed a dispatch center and the offices of mid-level heads of administration, maintenance, interpretation, and ranger activities. Commingled also with their local district counterparts, this soup of many flavors had always bubbled with a small army of people working together, laughing together, and sometimes causing each other indigestion. Quite often, one had to wait his turn at the gasoline pump.

When I walked through the half-opened gate I noticed that the once busy gasoline pump had been removed, and I had to wander through the building a bit before finding anyone home. The place now felt like a ghost town, and it was a Wednesday afternoon! At least the place still had a working telephone, so I returned a call to Joel Turner, a local reporter with *The Vinton* (Va.) *Messenger*, who had left a message back home with Patty. One of the most pleasant journalists I have ever met, Joel dropped everything he was doing to meet me at the ranger station for an interview, and I gave him all the time he needed for his story. Intending only to say hello before passing through, I made another call to an old friend.

Harry Farley is the sort of man one would want to be near if the earth was suddenly thrown out of kilter. A native of West Virginia, he had turned a few acres of poor mountain land in nearby Stewartsville into a self-sustaining paradise. Patching together an old sawmill he had salvaged, he milled every stud and joist that went into a home built with his own hands from timber growing on his property. He had cleverly boxed a natural spring from which his home and small farm was well supplied with good water. He even had the foresight to survey and properly record in the Bedford County courthouse a small parcel of his land for a future family cemetery. Not to be mistaken for a whacky survivalist, Harry and his family could survive anything. Unrelated to our professions, we had become acquainted through an organization that served others, and I learned from him that there was at least one man on this earth with no guile in his heart.

Like the Parkers, the Farleys insisted that I spend the evening with them, and I again surrendered peacefully to the invitation. Instead of dining in, though, we dined out, but not before attending to the necessary farm chores of literally milking the cow, feeding the chickens, and slopping the hogs. Harry seemed determined to kill me by taking me to one of those chain steakhouse restaurants with unlimited buffet access to meat, salad, vegetable, and dessert bars. I believe that I partook quite civilly right up to the point when I discovered their famous butter and yeast rolls. By about midnight, the pain had worn off sufficiently enough to enjoy a good quart of farm-fresh buttermilk before, freshly showered, I turned in to the comfort of another unexpected bed. The most prized of possessions such friends had become.

For some reason I felt a little guilty taking another shower so soon the following morning, but there it was across the hallway. And so I did. Equipped with a fresh bottle of fuel, which cured my cookstove woes, and a few items of food purchased at a local grocery, I was ready to continue, and Harry was kind enough to drive me back to the ranger station.

I had only walked a few feet down the Parkway when the faint sight of an overgrown roadway leading back into the woods brought back a forgotten memory. The path led back into what we once called a "boneyard" or a place where dirt, stone, brush, and other materials could be dumped and stored out of sight. This particular boneyard had been mysteriously graced with a cluster of daffodils

"I walked past Milepost 112 and the place we had once called home for six years." This photo was taken about 1984.

that bloomed each spring, by which I had buried Smoky, another pet cat. Smoky was the only cat I have ever known that would fearlessly chase both cars and horses, quickly burning up his nine lives at a young age. I found him lying on the Parkway one day, the presumed victim of a moving car. I could not find the now overgrown daffodils but paid my respects to Smoky in their general area nonetheless.

A few feet farther down the Parkway, I walked past Milepost 112 and the place we had once called home for six years. At the crest of the hill above me still stood our ranger quarters. Gone was the beautiful split rail fence upon which Laura and I had once sat and joyfully played the game of guessing the color of the next car to come down the Parkway. How I missed that breezy day and her childish giggles and 85 percent of the Parkway's original fences and vistas now overgrown and shocked corn on agricultural leases and Parkway neighbors like Fletcher Wimmer and... I had to move on.

I was soon shocked back into my senses by the slight brush of a motorcyclist passing a car from my blind side and the discovery of something lying in the road I had never before seen on the Parkway — a used syringe. Treating it like a booby trap ready to detonate, I gave a wide berth to it, certain that no diabetic would be that careless with a used needle. Rangering had provided me with more than enough experience with beer, wine, liquor, marijuana, and the occasional pill or quart of moonshine — but never with heroin and other substances abused by injection.

When Mac Dale reported for duty in 1938 as the second park ranger hired on the Parkway, rangers were required to purchase their own uniforms. Their salary began at $1,860 per year, with no embellishment of overtime or hazardous duty pay. Sidearms were authorized to be carried in the glove compartments of their patrol cars, but they could not be worn.

Construction of the Parkway was cutting through the heart of the moonshine industry, where outdoor operations in hidden coves with pure supplies of spring water and the cover of fog were plentiful. Today, Stillhouse Hollow Overlook memorializes one of the early challenges faced by park rangers, told most colorfully in the words of Ranger Dale himself:

> It got to be sort of a game. And it was amazing to me the people who were not just casually interested, but personally and intensely interested in discovering whether or not I was a revenuer. Their approach to this, the innuendo and the nicety of their little sidestepping tactics in leading up to and never quite asking, but letting you know precisely what it was they wanted to know. And it got to be a game to me to be unaware, you see, of what it was that they were really after. So that, it was fun, kind of a thrust and parry bit, you see, a witless bit of wit to discover on their part — they didn't know anybody that knew whether I was a revenuer or not. So we finally resolved this to everybody's satisfaction, without me ever saying that I was or wasn't. The answer to what came to be almost a question was that, look, we are not — this is the real answer, this isn't what we said to them, but we are not revenuers per se. As long as you operate off of the Blue Ridge and don't try to use the Parkway as a route to market with the product, we'll get along fine. And what you do is up to you, as long as you don't do it on the Parkway. As a sort of verification of this, there was a time, this a bit later, when a ranger went to Sam Weems [an early Parkway superintendent] and said, "Mr. Weems, there is a still down on Rennet Bag Creek. And what should I do about it?" And Sam said, "Well, tell you what, right opposite Smart View Park — and this is where Rennet Bag Creek is — there is a little snuff shop, a store, country store. Go over and sit down and drink a Coca-Cola and talk to the man that runs the store. And about the time you get ready to leave, you say, oh, by the way, I saw Mr. Weems or Sam Weems — don't say Mister because they don't know anything about Mister Weems, but they do know Sam Weems. I saw Sam Weems and he asked me to see if I couldn't get word to whoever it is that has that still down on Rennet Bag, and ask them to please get it off. And you go on out, and that's all you need to say. And I think that the still will disappear. If it doesn't, let me know." So the ranger did just about as instructed. He was back at the store perhaps a week later, and when he got ready to leave, the storekeeper said, "Oh, by the way, if you happen to see Sam Weems, tell him that his old friend that had that bucket down on Rennet Bag said he only got about three more days of running before he finishes up, then he'll take it off right away and won't bring it back no more."

Granville Liles, who later became a Parkway superintendent, also began his work on the Parkway in 1938, but as a landscape technician. He soon became interested in becoming a ranger and expressed his interest in a most unusual way. Aware that Sam Weems, the assistant superintendent at the time, would be making an inspection tour of a particular section of the Parkway one day, he blocked the road with split rails. Says Liles: "Upon his arrival at the blockade he was visibly upset. Quickly approaching his car, I apologized for the delay and advised him of my interest in a ranger post.... Calming down, he then advised me to get an appointment through his office for an interview."

His unorthodox tactic apparently worked with Mr. Weems, and by the spring of 1940, he became the first ranger to express a genuine interest in law enforcement and was sent to the FBI Academy for training. While Ranger Liles well understood the necessity to pussyfoot around the moonshine issue outside of the park boundary to avoid "having the whole countryside burned over and all the rangers shot," he proved to be no slouch when the issue was forced upon him, as he recounted with this story:

And I on this particular occasion was traveling over my district and I saw three men off in the woods with a truck, and I stopped to visit them, and they were all drinking moonshine liquor at that time and I proceeded to confiscate the liquor and tell them that they were going to have to be on their way. And one of the fellows told me that I wasn't going to have the liquor and they did not intend to move. And I said, "Well, I'm going to have to arrest you," and he said, "You know you aren't going to be able to handle all three of us," so I said, "Well, I'll take you one at a time." So I proceeded to put one of them under arrest, and I had in my car in the glove pocket a forty-five, and lo and behold, I started to take him to the car and he jerked around with a pocket knife and said he was going to cut my [deleted] throat if I didn't turn him loose. Well, momentarily I did until I could dash and get my forty-five and I came back, and in the meantime all three of them headed for the brush. And so I tried to catch the fellow that tried to knife me and I had no luck, so I immediately went down to North Wilkesboro [North Carolina] to the nearest United States marshal and got him and the State troopers from nearby, and it took us three days to find this fellow. And I found out that he was an escaped convict and had been put in jail for killing a Federal officer about two years before. And of course I felt pretty fortunate to have escaped getting pretty badly wounded. And we found him hiding in a barn. We had an informer there, one of the natives, who knew where he was hiding in an old barn, and we went in one night — the United States marshal and some of the local police, and we caught him and the marshals took him to jail and a few days later the United States judge had a special trial and charged him with attempting to assault a Federal officer with a deadly weapon. And he was sentenced to three years in prison, and his two pardners were sentenced to one year each. And this was one of the finest examples of law enforcement as far as its effect on the neighborhood. The courthouse in North Wilkesboro was filled with those mountain people, and this was the first time a park ranger had ever been in the court in that district. And the judge delivered one of the finest sermons to all those people about abiding by the law and recognizing the National Park Service that I have ever heard.

In a strangely familiar Biblical sense, I reported to my first ranger duty station in 1978, forty years following the first arrivals of Rangers Wallace Barlow, Mac Dale, and Bernard Campbell. Beginning ranger salaries had skyrocketed to a whopping $9,959 per year, supplemented by a modest allowance just shy of a complete uniform. Rangers had only recently been permitted to wear sidearms, but their sight was strictly forbidden in Parkway offices, visitor centers, and concession facilities. How well I remember a fair scolding from an assistant superintendent for wearing my sidearm for a few brief seconds as I replenished a brochure rack at a roadside information station. In sad testimony to the grave dangers they face today, rangers now have convenient access to cleverly concealed automatic weapons.

By the time I arrived on the scene, most moonshine operations had been moved indoors, hidden in barns, and were fired with bottled gas. A long succession of rangers preceding me had successfully drawn the line without getting the park burned down in the process. Though I never went looking for it, I always sensed its closeness. I became aware that State and Federal agents and local sheriffs were forever sneaking about looking for it. I knew men who had served prison time over it. But prison had not stopped them — it had just made them more careful. Had I not been a known teetotaler myself, I am certain arrangements could have been made for me to "accidentally" find a quart of my own brew hidden in a secret culvert. It was close, always close. I could feel, almost smell pure peach brandy. One day I thought I had gotten too close to it.

The park boundary had not been inspected and cleared below Pine Spur, I had been told, since the original survey had been made. Corners were still marked with iron pins instead of the more recognizable cylindrical, cement posts. Quite a few hundred acres had been purchased for a recreation area in this vicinity that had sputtered from the drawing board into abandonment, and sources were telling us that ginseng poachers were cleaning us out every summer. Determined to "find" and reclaim this forgotten acreage, I set out one winter morning with the standard tools of such trade: maps, bearings, compass, bush axe, boundary signs, hammer, nails, water, and lunch.

I was working a line which extended almost a mile from pin to pin. It was difficult to follow, but faint scars chipped on line trees were still visible. An occasional corner of an old metal boundary sign could be found peeking above the duff, which had eventually popped loose from its moorings by the unstoppable expansion in girth of the tree to which it had been nailed. With the exception of the stubborn American beech, whose brown leaves would continue to cling to the trees until spring, winter had rendered this predominately deciduous forest fairly barren from the ground up, making these little clues easier to find. As I walked back and forth and up and down this line, against the grain of parallel lateral ridges separated by deep drainages, my thoughts grew less and less complimentary of the Parkway staff who had preceded me for allowing this stretch of boundary to become so neglected. Why had the iron pins not been replaced with the standard markers? Soon the job of finding the line went from difficult and frustrating to seemingly impossible.

I could clearly see where it entered a thick and nearly impervious rhododendron thicket. Mountain people sometimes refer to such places as "laurel hells" because they are so difficult through which to maneuver. Scouting around its uphill perimeter, the line appeared to run through it about a hundred yards before emerging into open woods again. But I could not find a trace of the line on the other side of it, and I was certain that it did not make a turn inside it. The only option I had remaining was to go back to the line's point of entry and attempt to negotiate through the thicket with a compass.

A few yards into the tangle, I realized the impossibility of following a straight line through such a mess, and I was not about to chop a path through its uncertainty. With every twist, turn, and crawl, I realized that the bearing I was trying to maintain was becoming less accurate with each step. Perhaps the inaccuracies would all average out to the discovery of a boundary tree right at the point of exit, I hoped.

Nearly halfway through the thicket, I suddenly and awkwardly stumbled out of its grasp into a small clearing — right into the middle of an abandoned moonshine still situated next to a little gurgling spring. Had it been in current operation, my noisy approach would have resulted in my ambush at the worst, and at the best, would have resulted in a considerable drop in my standing in some circles within the local community. Some clandestine act of violence would also have been directed at park resources for a certainty. But it appeared from the scattered remains of barrels pierced with axes and broken glass jars that the revenuers had found this one years before I had stumbled upon it. With regard to the boundary line running through or near it, a surveyor with proper instruments would have to come back and find that line on another day. Drats, I would have to be more careful in the future!

While the heyday of ranger interaction involving the actual manufacture of moonshine had probably passed into oblivion, it and its legal counterparts were ever present in the park. Encountering alcohol violations such as driving under the influence, public intoxication, underage possession, and possession of an open container in a motor vehicle were about as frequent as breathing. The plumbing and septic systems in our ranger stations were often tested to their limits on evidence-destruction days to the delight of every aquatic organism downstream. On occasion, though, the routine details of so many cases developed peculiar and sometimes humorous twists.

Perhaps it was my imagination, but the consumption of moonshine seemed to have a more deleterious effect on some people than the legal stuff. One man I arrested had hauntingly concentric grey circles in both pupils of his eyes. Another would not cease speaking fluent Spanish all the way to jail. When I complimented him on his bilingual talent the next morning just before his hearing, he glared at me with disbelief and swore that he had never spoken a single word of Spanish in his life!

Beer, by far, was the most common alcoholic beverage I encountered, and the most common response from anyone being asked how much they had consumed was, "Only two beers, officer." One day I stopped a pickup truck on a suspicion that the young driver was intoxicated. Whether his occasional crossing of the center line was from the effects of alcohol or mere nervousness from me following him was yet to be determined. When I approached his door, I noticed that the bed of his truck contained a healthy load of empty beer cans. A true conservationist, I thought, as the antennae came to attention. Noticing next that his eyes were a little bloodshot, I asked, "How many of these beers back here have you had today?"

"Only one, sir. About twenty minutes ago when you drove past that last overlook."

"Would you mind stepping out of your truck for a minute?" I asked, opening the door slowly myself to assist him in making the right decision.

As the door opened, a freshly opened can of beer, which he had hidden on the floorboard between the door and the seat, fell onto my foot, soaking my trousers and the shoes and socks on both of my feet with the frothy liquid. As I jumped back from the truck, he looked at me with the most pitiful, pleading, puppy-dog eyes and asked, "Could I change that to two beers, sir?"

The dispatcher with the local sheriff department rousted me out of bed about four o'clock one morning to let me know that it had begun snowing on Bent Mountain and that the roads were becoming hazardous. A skeleton crew of ranger staff during the winter months prohibited routine night patrols, and this cooperative arrangement was helpful in getting a head start on closing the affected sections in the district. The ideal scenario was to sweep a section clear of traffic and get the snow gates locked before problems had a chance to develop. So there was some urgency about the matter that demanded swift but safely executed action. On this particular morning, I had the time of day in my favor, or so I thought.

As I swung the southbound half of the gate at the U.S. Route 220 intersection, snow had already accumulated to a depth of about two inches on the roadway, and it was snowing heavily. This could get tricky with a two-wheel-drive sedan, I thought, knowing that I would be ascending about 1,200 feet over the next fifteen miles to the next gate at Adney Gap. What troubled me more was the wobbly set of tire tracks headed up the mountain in front of me.

The tire tracks I was following became more erratic, running completely off and back onto the roadway in two places before I finally found the car six miles later. The third time it ran off the roadway it went over a slight embankment and made a soft landing in a thicket of honeysuckle vine. The driver had left the keys in the ignition, the emergency lights flashing, and the windshield wipers flapping wildly at their highest speed. A single set of footprints continued up the mountain and closely resembled the weaving pattern of the tire tracks I had been following earlier.

About a mile later, the tracks led to a young man sitting on a wooden guide rail, uninjured, tired, cold, and very drunk. My patience had always been particularly thin for people whose abuse of alcohol in the park hurt themselves and others and created work for me that I rather not preferred. And now this fellow had sucked me into his own sorry predicament at the worst possible time. Softened somewhat by his grateful and cooperative demeanor, I nevertheless concluded that the most efficient way to dispose of our problem was to arrest him for public intoxication and take him straight to jail. Within an hour, a record time for the Roanoke City jail, he was processed and incarcerated, and I returned to the Parkway in time to finish closing it before anybody else was able to slide off the road.

A few days later this man appeared in court and pleaded guilty to the charge. Following my brief summary of the facts of the case to the United States magistrate, he was permitted to make a statement before being sentenced with a fair fine. To my astonished surprise and with all sincerity, he turned in my direction and thanked me for arresting him and saving his life. I wish the girl who jumped on my back one night, whose boyfriend was being arrested for driving under the influence, had felt the same way.

Parkway problems with alcohol were not necessarily confined to just the visiting public, as Sam Weems once recalled:

> Now, I got caught in this thing, from the operations standpoint. I was ordered to construct fee collection stations; I was ordered to employ personnel to man these stations. Now let me tell you a funny incident: I built these stations and I had them all in place, and I had personnel signed up and I had even gone so far as to have them put into uniforms, when that telegram came that you mentioned. And it came one afternoon, the afternoon before we were going to start collecting fees the next morning. My men were all ready in uniform. About 11:00 that night I had a telephone call from the Roanoke jail. "Mr. Weems, we have one of your rangers in jail for drunk and disorderly." I said, "Just a minute. You must be mistaken. I don't have any rangers like that." And he said, "Well, he has got on a National Park Service uniform." And I says, "I will be down there in a few minutes." I went down to the jail and here was one of my fee collectors who, when he got fired just before he was to go on duty the next morning, went out and got drunk, wearing the uniform. That is how close we came to starting the fee collecting system.

Rangers Danny Drye, left, and Jeff Swortzel with a crop of marijuana found on Parkway land on August 5, 1981, near Milepost 143 in Franklin County, Virginia.

The more modern and lucrative business of cultivating marijuana raised its ugly head one day when a rather large crop of it was found on a Parkway agricultural lease, cleverly mixed into a patch of sorghum cane. I had been unknowingly patrolling past it every day. More plots were found in nearby wooded areas. This was the Parkway's Pearl Harbor of the Drug War as far as I was concerned.

The moonshine industry had evolved into quaint folklore, and though illegal, in reality it only violated the quality control and taxation standards of an otherwise legal substance. Marijuana, however, was a Schedule I controlled substance and would forever remain so under the terms of international treaties. This meant war, and I was determined to work with every local, state, and federal authority who would give me the time of day to find any of it growing on or near the Parkway. Besides, flying in helicopters, developing informants who were willing to draw maps to patches, and exploring every nook and cranny of the park made an otherwise adventurous job, well, even more adventurous.

Meanwhile, cases involving possession of marijuana and its related paraphernalia rang up on the arrest log like groceries at the supermarket checkout counter. Though not encountered as frequently as alcohol violations, they were easy to make and also gave evidence-destruction days a special charm, as pipes and clips in every form were mutilated, and the flying insects and birds downwind of a burn enjoyed a most pleasant flight. I worry still about the health of the individuals from whom were seized one pipe fashioned from a plastic disinfectant bottle and another fashioned from a ⁹⁄₁₆-inch socket wrench. The individual who swallowed the nasty contents of his ashtray to avoid prosecution, I suppose, should be commended for bravery, though I gave fleeting thought to obtaining a search warrant to have his stomach pumped. Better punishment, I thought, left to his own designs.

They were easy to make, I say, because the distinct smell of burning marijuana cannot be easily ventilated from the interior of a car or removed from clothing. One particular ranger loved to preface his postshift search and seizure tales with the line, "I detected the stinking odor of marijuana emanating from the vehicle," done so with a most comically disgusting scrunch of his nose. He accidentally repeated that line in court one day, to which the defense attorney fired a quick objection. Correcting himself, he then offered that he had meant to say, "the distinct odor of marijuana." A second objection finally resulted in the acceptable testimony of "an odor resembling that of marijuana."

That "distinct" odor was not always marijuana, I learned one day, when the catalytic converter on my patrol car caught the grass on fire underneath me while I wrote a speeding citation. Another time, I almost arrested a hitchhiker for smoking a perfectly legal blend of rosemary and thyme. Thank goodness for those little chemical field test kits.

Perhaps the most devious tactic we ever employed using the sense of smell involved the supplemental use of an infrared night scope. One ranger, disguised as a visitor in an unmarked car, would scan the vehicles parked in an overlook for the telltale sign of two or more people passing a "cigarette" back and forth to each other. A second ranger in a marked car would be summoned to the overlook to offer a friendly, "How are you folks doing tonight?" If the smell and other factors were present, probable cause was usually sufficient at that point to search the vehicle for marijuana.

I considered the element of surprise, by far, the most manpower-efficient and fair tactic available in developing possession cases. Ask the man who, using a Frisbee to centrifuge the seeds from a wad of marijuana, distracted also by the music from his car radio, looked up to see me parked next to him in a monstrous four-wheel-drive patrol vehicle. Another man, doing the same thing with the lid of a cooler, would also agree and stepped from his vehicle so flustered that he was still holding a bag of marijuana and a slip of rolling paper in his hand. Another guy, unable to hide all the evidence before I could see it, could only say, "I knew when you drove up I was busted."

13

Ranger Mischief

"And I about made up my mind to pray, and see if I couldn't try to quit being the kind of boy I was and be better."
—*The Adventures of Huckleberry Finn*,
by Mark Twain

Not too far past the fresh syringe, a terrifying and disappointing memory rushed back. Scars on the trunk of a very large oak tree remained at points twelve and fifteen feet above its base, caused by the impact of an airborne motor vehicle out of control. This was the tree that had finally brought the stray missile to a stop, under which it came to rest upside down. Before hitting this tree, the speeding vehicle lost traction while attempting to negotiate a moderately sharp, right-hand curve. All four tires left rolling scuff marks on the pavement before it skidded off the left side of the road. Before becoming airborne, it scattered seven large boulders and completely uprooted and carried with it an ailanthus tree seven inches thick at its base. After becoming airborne, it sheared one poplar tree about seven feet above its base at a diameter of five inches and another poplar tree eight feet above its base at a diameter of four inches. With the exception of two vent windows, every window was completely shattered from the vehicle, and every body panel was heavily damaged. Colorful wrapping paper, ribbons, and bows were found scattered and eerily hanging in tree branches high above the ground. Miraculously, all three occupants were treated and released at a local hospital, though they suffered terribly from the pain of lacerations, broken bones, and severe contusions. Some would call them lucky.

What I remember most about this accident was that it was reported to me at 12:15 on Christmas morning. Santa Claus had just visited our home and was enjoying the milk and cookies left for him under the sparkling lights of our Christmas tree when the telephone rang. For the next several hours, which occu-

In the 1982 accident, the vehicle sheared one poplar tree about seven feet above its base at a diameter of five inches and another poplar tree eight feet above its base at a diameter of four inches. The location is near the Roanoke River bridge in Virginia.

pied most of Christmas Day, I was not only pressed with the routine details of a serious accident investigation, but also with the added complexity that two of the three occupants were absent without leave from the U.S. Navy. That the enjoyment of a cozy Christmas by the fire with my family was lost that year would be a fair statement to make.

The same type of loss would also occur on an Easter Sunday, when duty called to a forest fire near the headwaters of Wilson Creek below Grandfather Mountain. Beginning our task on Saturday, we worked through the night and were denied even a woodsy sunrise service early the next morning by snow flurries. Another similar loss would also occur on a Thanksgiving Day when, after working the full day, I finally sat down to a lovingly prepared turkey dinner only to be called back out because a bear hunter had torn down one of our snow gates to get to his dogs. Oh, the romantic life of a park ranger, the womenfolk and children might not say.

Not quite a half-mile past the scene of this Christmas Eve crash, I stepped onto the Roanoke River bridge, from which the driver of that car must have launched at a speed well over the limit of 45 mph. Mistakenly thinking the speed limit to be 55 mph, he had admitted to a suspiciously precise 52 mph at the point he lost control of the car. Almost an exact quarter-mile, straight and level, this bridge seemed to invite speed and had a history of use for illegal drag racing by the local youth. But this was not a bridge on which to play, and it still gave me the willies walking across its expanse high above the Roanoke River Gorge.

The small delegation of dignitaries and spectators that gathered on it to dedicate the completion of the 217-mile Virginia section of the Parkway on July 17, 1965, probably never envisioned the mischief it would invite. National Park Service Associate Director A. Clark Stratton, the keynote speaker, probably did not predict, on this historic occasion, that drag racing across it would become a temptation. United States Senator A. Willis Robertson most certainly did not offer in his address a medal of courage to the first vandal foolish enough to perilously walk the lower flange of its supporting I-beams around several vertical stiffeners to spray "LED ZEPPELIN" in red, six-foot-high letters across its highest point. United States Congressman Richard H. Poff surely did not mention in his remarks that a ranger would someday "accidentally" coax a man with suicidal tendencies from its heights by trickery. And former National Park Service Director Conrad L. Wirth, as much as he may have wanted to, dared not disrupt the dignity of the occasion by spitting over the rail to see if he could hit the river 160 feet below.

As I worked my way across it, I timidly walked the precarious line between the passing traffic and the low, metal rail. About halfway across it, with no one around to embarrass but myself, the suppressed little boy inside me returned. In just the proper volume and synchronized with a perfect snap of the head, a wad of spittle was ejected in a graceful arch over the rail. Kneeling carefully next to the rail to avoid any possibility that the top heaviness rendered by my pack would propel me over with it, I leaned over the rail to watch the projectile fall. Down, down, down it fell toward the target. Splat! A direct hit at midstream! Surely it had caught the attention of a large striped bass that had wandered up from nearby Smith Mountain Lake. It only took a few minutes to make the astute determination, based upon the crude scientific sample of a half dozen attempts, that it took exactly ten seconds for a wad of spittle to reach the river.

There is absolutely no physiological necessity for spitting, unless some repulsive object, such as a bug or tobacco juice, has entered the mouth and a deliberate decision is made not to swallow it. Though I never partook of the habit, I marveled at the skill at which my uncles spat tobacco juice while pitching horseshoes by the old barn. Papaw Pegram had even perfected the art to a usually direct hit into a tin can placed on the living room floor. Any misses could always be blamed on a rogue splash, at least whenever Mamaw was not looking.

And so began the emulation process for me at a very young age. As crucial as the mechanical process itself, the proper time and place of its execution had also to be learned, as does any nonsensical act perpetrated wholly for its intended pleasure or hilarity. Too, a proper defense would have to be formulated against the scorn of a daughter and wife that was sure to come upon discovery that I had taught my grandchildren, at the age of passage for each, the proper time, place, and manner of spitting. In some matters, many of us will forever remain children.

A fellow ranger, neat and meticulous in all respects, had furloughed during two winter months and was soon due back on the job. A few of his colleagues decided to welcome his return with some gifts and a reorganization of his desk. Overwhelmed by the attention bestowed upon him on the first day of his return, he took the time to document the occasion on a Case Incident Record Form 10–343. The "Nature of Incident" category was coded, "Vandalism of Government Property." The "Involved Persons" category stated, "Unable to prove, but known." Never submitted through the chain of command but widely distributed throughout the office, it read precisely as follows:

> On 3/7/82, at 0900 hrs. I began my initial tour of duty after a lengthy but quiet furlough. Having taken great pains to ensure that my first days back on duty would be as smooth and hassle-free as possible by leaving everything in and around my office desk in a state of utmost order before I left, I was bubbling over with new found enthusiasm and confidence as I began the new day. All of my hopes and dreams of sanity returning to the Vinton office vanished when, much to my shock and horror, I observed that my desk had been unscrupulously and irrevetribly [we think he was trying to say irretrievably] vandalized. Everything which I had worked so hard to leave in order was undone, as was I. The space above the desk was cluttered with what may have been used toilet tissue (the state lab in Roanoke has assured me that wonders can be performed using evidence such as this!). Devious little notes were sprinkled liberally over the desk top, and a set of foreign made tools (most likely stolen) was found wrapped in plain white paper, probably an attempt to obliterate fingerprints. A warning note was found directing me to cautiously open the center drawer, which, after consulting with the Va. State Police Bomb Squad, I did. Therein I did find subversive literature unfit for human consumption, particularly one with a pregnant wife! It is my honest opinion that those responsible for these activities are sick and in need of much care, particularly when it is noted that that [a rare stutter by this individual] such actions are appreciated, although much time and energy was expended on an individual whose presence or absence has never before prompted such an act of violence.

The Federal Communications Commission enforced some fairly stiff rules regarding radio traffic, and misuse of the park radio system could bring disciplinary action to the miscreant employee. Since being reprimanded or fired did not interface with the Individual Development Plan for most career-minded employees, the rare infraction was more likely accidental rather than intentional.

A borderline incident occurred one night when I stopped a vehicle bearing a Virginia license that began with the letters "KKX" and ended with three numerals. The seasonal ranger riding with me, experienced but in no way career-minded, had never become proficient with either the military or police phonetic alphabets. As he called in the license number to the dispatcher while I maneuvered the stop, the letter "X" gave him no problem. With both alphabets, "X-ray" was used to denote "X." But neither "Kilo" nor "King" seemed to register in his head that night as he haltingly delivered, "We are stopping Virginia license... uh... uh... uh... Ku-Klux-X-ray." I could have killed him, and our boss nearly did after summoning us immediately back to the ranger station.

An even more serious incident occurred one day when an unidentified male voice began transmitting rambling statements over the radio, which eventually deteriorated into obscenities. When the shenanigans began, it sounded like a sloppy employee had left a microphone in a place where it could unknowingly become keyed. Such accidents could easily occur if a microphone was not hung back on a vehicle's dash mount and was left to wander over a cluttered front seat. (My, how our conversations would be different if we knew the entire world was listening!) We soon learned that this fellow was transmitting on the park-wide channel when a far-away telephone call from headquarters delivered a terse message to track this guy down and stop him. At this point we knew his mischief was intentional. He had insulted the superintendent.

Telephone calls were quickly made to every ranger office and residence to check all microphones. A hasty inventory of all portable radios was begun. Every available ranger was quietly dispatched to check park vehicles at work sites scattered over the 469-mile length of the Parkway. In the meantime, strong warnings to this person, via radio transmission from the dispatcher and chief ranger, only worsened his language.

As I drove into the one-way tent loop of the Roanoke Mountain Campground, I noticed a man sitting in the passenger seat of a Parkway maintenance truck parked on the far side of the loop near a restroom. Apparently he did not see me drive into the campground due to light fog and a slight drizzle. Disappearing from his view as I drove through the loop, I never imagined, when the truck reappeared, that I would see him raise the microphone to his mouth at the very moment another crude transmission came across the air. Parking my patrol car, I approached the rear of the truck, careful to avoid being detected in its side mirrors. Standing only a few inches from his door when he made his final transmission, I whispered into my portable radio, "Put the microphone down. Now."

Shaken terribly, to the point of tears, this bored young employee of the Young Adult Conservation Corps had been left unsupervised. On the ride back to the ranger station he apologized profusely for his mischief, speculating that his career prospects on the Parkway had been tarnished. I silently agreed with him, reserving any statements or questions I had for him to be made in the presence of witnesses. Before the day ended though, he was judiciously and unequivocally fired from his position by an authority much higher than myself. That sort of mischief was neither funny nor acceptable.

The occasional toddler who managed to maneuver a stool within reach of a radio located at a ranger residence, however, was always excused. Provided that their conversation was of short duration and that no emergency traffic was interrupted, they could, in fact, be downright entertaining. You just could not blame a little tyke who recognized her father's voice on the radio and wanted to say hello. There were times also when their chatter seemed to scold unnecessarily verbose radio traffic that was disrupting a favorite cartoon show.

Rangers, too, had developed their own little technique of expressing ridicule or disdain through use of the radio system that bordered on misuse but guaranteed anonymity. It worked something like this. In theory, a transmission over channel two would activate only the repeaters located in either Virginia or North Carolina. A transmission over channel three would activate every repeater on the entire system. When the key on the microphone was depressed and released, a backwash squelch noise could be generated from the affected repeaters. If several rangers engaged in such folly in close succession to one another, the resulting sound mimicked the scolding sound of a blue jay.

One particular ranger provoked the maneuver, generally reserved for the most egregious of radio bloopers, more often than most. Blaming a rather deficient vocabulary on a mythical speech impediment, he could repeatedly corrupt the simplest of words. Smart View Overlook, known for its "right smart view," was referred to as "Smart's View Overlook," as if it had been named after

Bandy Road, which intersected the Parkway at Milepost 118.6 near Roanoke, Virginia, was referred to as "Bambi Road." This photo was taken about 1984.

a fellow with the surname of Smart. Bandy Road, which intersected the Parkway near Roanoke, Va., was referred to as "Bambi Road." Come to think of it, a few deer did cross the road in that vicinity. Norfolk & Western Railroad Overlook was referred to as "Norfolk & Westward Overlook," as if some pioneer wagon train had passed through the valley rather than a railroad. "Westward, ho! Chi-duh-chi-duh-chi-duh-chi-duh!"

Becoming a lightning rod for such electric laughter never implied honor, but the attention bestowed was sometimes reassuring. About two o'clock one morning, my patrol car ran out of fuel at Haywood-Jackson Overlook as I was returning to the Balsam Gap ranger station. Of all the many nuisances that irritated rangers, visitors who had locked themselves out of their vehicles or who had run out of fuel ranked near the top of the list. So, in the quietest voice I could muster, I attempted to awaken an off-duty ranger located at Mount Pisgah on channel one. Since I supervised him, I felt fairly certain that my little predicament would remain unpublished. Following several tries, his sleepy voice finally answered on channel one, and he agreed to bring me five gallons of gasoline. Apparently, my location at a little over six thousand feet in elevation, assisted by just the proper atmospheric conditions, propelled my transmissions much farther into the night than our radio technician considered possible. "Chi-duh-chi-duh-chi-duh-chi-duh," came the acknowledgment that I had been heard as far north as Virginia. Thanks for being there for me when I needed you, folks. And why would so many rangers be awake at that hour? More mischief, I supposed.

Without the vigilant efforts of the maintenance division, Mother Nature would quickly swallow up the Blue Ridge Parkway. Within a year, fallen trees, rock slides, and washouts would make most of it impassable to motor vehicles. Within five years most of its open areas could not be easily walked, choked by thickets of thorny locust trees and blackberry canes on dryer ground and lush jewelweed on the wetter ground. The freeze and thaw cycle of hard winters would heave and crack the pavement. Expanding wedges of ice would pry the cracks wider, until eventually the roots of trees would join in disintegrating the beautiful puzzle. Within fifty years the Parkway would resemble no more than an old logging road by which only hunters and hikers would tread. It is the maintenance employees who represent the proverbial finger in the dike and keep the mansion dusted.

For the most part, they are local stock, bringing to their jobs the skills and ingenuity of generations of mountain dwellers. Outsiders are generally welcomed and tolerated, especially when their differences become a source of entertainment. On this premise was founded our relationship and that of most rangers. I liked them, and they liked me, for the most part. How well I understood also that I needed them on the job far more than they needed me. So I stretched the parameters of the "Other Duties As Assigned" category of my position description to provide them with all the entertainment I could muster.

Mower operators were especially vulnerable to the frenzied attack of a swarm of yellow jackets whose home had just been ravaged by twirling blades. When a local physician offered an additional certification to administer epinephrine to the EMT refresher course I was taking in Bryson City, N.C., I was delighted. I had already experienced the futility of treating one emergency case of anaphylactic shock from a bee sting without the proper tools, and the panic was not pleasant. I was certain that a female motorcyclist would die in the arms of her partner in the back seat of my patrol car before I could get her to medical treatment. But the certification process required each student to administer, as well as receive, a small dose. Muttering rebellious thoughts about how nursing students were allowed to practice on oranges, I cringed at both ends of the needle but somehow passed the test and promptly filled my prescription to obtain my own injection kit.

At monthly employee safety meetings in the spring and throughout the summer, I brashly displayed the little red kit and its contents therein. Removing the syringe from the kit for everyone's closer inspection, I explained how the two adult doses would be administered. Hard, seasoned mountain men could be seen wringing their hands and easing their chairs backward a few inches. "I aim to please if you ever need it, boys," I would tease. Driving slowly past their work sites, I would flash the kit, only to be shooed away like I was just another pesky yellow jacket. They were fortunate, in many respects, that I was never called upon to sting them with it.

While all were humored by the way I could mimic the sound of a galloping horse with repetitious clicks made by keying the microphone of the public address unit on my patrol car, only a few appreciated the humor I associated with the "Slow — Men Working Ahead" signs they placed at both ends of their work sites. When asked where I could find the "slow men," Ernest Bryson would tell me, in all sincerity, that I was looking at them. When asked where I could find the "working men," he would somehow cut a 360-degree pirouette with his large frame and suggest that I look in the next district.

Charlie Norman thought he had evened the score with me at lunch one cold, winter day. Seated by the woodstove in the break room, he intentionally dropped his guard on the contents of his lunch pail, knowing I would snatch what appeared to be a piece of fried rabbit. As I munched away on this delicious cut of meat, everyone in the room started laughing at me. "This *is* rabbit, right?" I asked. To my relief, someone finally told me I was eating groundhog. At least it was not opossum, an animal of which I presumed Charlie was quite capable of partaking. "Good stuff. It's actually better than rabbit," I casually replied, offering them no visible sign of distress. "You know they only eat grass. Hey, somebody set up the checkerboard. I feel lucky today."

While the maintenance division prevented the Parkway from falling from the edge of the earth, the administrative employees were credited with circulating the life blood of the whole organization — the money. Without their patient adherence to strict procurement rules and regulations and its voluminous paperwork requirements, the tools of our trade could not be obtained. More importantly, without their payroll expertise, none of us would get paid. We were all dependent, to the point of servitude at times, upon their services. Victims also we became of their own brand of practical joke.

Wes Earnest was a career administrative employee of the Parkway and a collector of those humorous posters you see shabbily hung around the personal work zones of every profession. Some of them slam members of the opposite sex, others offer fair warning to worrisome pests and others are just plain funny, like the list of "HOW YOU CAN TELL WHEN IT'S GOING TO BE A ROTTEN DAY." Wes had such a proclivity for wit I would venture to guess that he masterminded at least a few of those hundreds in his collection.

Arriving at the office early one morning, I had just enough time to gather a bundle of evidence from my storage locker and quickly review the cases on which I would offer sworn testimony in a couple of hours. While I was thus busily engaged, Wes stuck his head in my office to let me know that a visitor had brought in a stray dog that had been found on the Parkway. I was the only ranger on duty and really did not have time for this distraction. "I tied him to the back gate and gave him a dish of water," Wes offered apologetically, sensing my growing irritation. Hoping this was a poorly timed joke, I charged out to the gate, only to find the mutt happily wagging his tail and showing an especial fondness for Wes, who had wandered out behind me. Because the dog was wearing no identification collar, I would have to complete a report, summon the county animal control officer, and wait for his arrival to sign the release papers.

With all these details finally accomplished, I jumped in the patrol car with no time to spare, much less prepared to give sworn testimony in court than one should have been. As I was wheeling out of the yard, Bud Carter stepped out of his shop and flagged me down. "Hey, Tim. What's the deal with that dog?" he asked.

"Wes said it was a stray. Visitor brought it in. Animal control took it. Got to run."

"Oh, really?" he replied as if he did not believe me.

"What is it, Bud?" I had seen that smile before and hesitated momentarily for the punch line.

"I'm not for sure, Tim. But it seems Wes had a dog once that looked a lot like that one. Told me the other day he was tired of feeding it and was thinking about giving it away."

After court that day, as I often did, I walked down to the Federal employees health unit to get a blood pressure check and scout for any other free services they had to offer. "You are borderline high again," the nurse reported with lowered chin while peering accusingly over the top of her glasses at me. Offering a means of escape from her indicting gaze, she suggested that I get it checked one day before court rather than afterward. "If we had done that today, you probably would have rushed me straight to the hospital," I answered. "And you would only laugh if I told you why."

The Rocky Knob ranger station was only a couple of miles outside of my district, and I quite enjoyed slipping down that way as often as I could to escape the bustle of the Roanoke Valley. It was a friendly, scenic place, and I would often meet the rangers in that area for lunch, at which time we swapped tales and news. One of the rangers from that area and I had just been issued new patrol vehicles of the same make, and he offered to show me how to increase its horsepower. Popping the hood of my patrol car, he removed the air filter and began tinkering with the guts of the carburetor. In a few seconds, he handed me some metal parts that he called metering rods. "You can just throw these things away," he assured me, before we took it out for a test spin. Even though I trusted his mechanical ability in these matters far above my own, I just did not feel comfortable in discarding them. Like a pack rat, I later transferred them from my trouser pocket to a small plastic evidence bag and tucked them into the glove compartment, just in case I needed them again someday.

What a remarkable difference this modification made in my car's performance! Faster acceleration and higher top speed dramatically reduced the number of escapees from the radar gun. One fanciful ranger went so far as to submit an official report coded "Reckless Driving" that read, in part: "While on routine patrol I observed that an unknown vehicle drove recklessly as evidenced by lengthy skid marks on the Parkway at MP 121.6, 123.3, 124.5, and 136.0 sometime during the past evening. The skid marks gave the appearance of someone practicing power turns." I always contended that a unit of the Virginia State Police had been responsible for this artwork. Still, I agreed with the advice once given to me by a wise, seasoned ranger that "you need to know what your patrol car will do before you ever try to do it."

The thought never crossed my mind that an increasing number of grass fires started by my catalytic converter was in any way correlated to the removal of those metering rods. Though easy to extinguish with a few stomps of the boots, they were, nevertheless, bothersome and embarrassing, not to mention the potential risk of the vehicle going up in flames. Then, one day, my souped-up car just sputtered to a stop and would not restart.

Bud Carter drove out to my stranded location and looked at it briefly, and like a good old doctor whose intuitive diagnostic skills had been outpaced by technology, he referred it on to a specialist. Towed to a local garage known for its honesty and fair prices, it remained hospitalized for several days.

When the owner of the garage finally called with the news that it had been repaired, I was there to pick it up in minutes. Borrowing other patrol cars had been inconvenient for all concerned, and I was ready to get back into a car in which I knew where to find spare handcuffs and road flares. Every ranger had their own unique system of storage or lack thereof.

The bill was much larger than I had expected it to be, and as the mechanic began to explain the repair, I noticed a suspicious entry on the parts list. There was a charge for metering rods!

"After the engine cooled, your car cranked right up," the mechanic began to explain. "I took it out for a test drive, brought it back in and put it up on the rack, and the catalytic converter was glowing like a light bulb. It's a wonder this car didn't burn up on you."

Noticing on the bill that a new catalytic converter had also been installed, I asked, "So, what do metering rods have to do with any of that?"

"That's the funny thing about it, Tim. Apparently the metering rods didn't get installed in the carburetor at the factory. And way too much unburned fuel overloaded and eventually burned up the catalytic converter. Too bad it's not still on warranty."

"Yeah," I agreed, paying the bill and getting out of there before he had a chance to speculate otherwise. Needless to say, the little bag secreted in my glove compartment mysteriously disappeared. To this day, I am still not sure whether I was the victim of another practical joke or a maverick mechanic who knew not what he was doing.

Employee barbecues held at the Vinton ranger station were fun affairs. Any strains within the supervisory hierarchy were usually checked at the door, as families of rangers, clerks, mower operators, interpreters, sign makers, and brass gathered for an evening of good food and pleasant sociality. Despite a natural inclination toward posturing and bickering at the periphery, usually at the spousal level, these occasions formed a sincere, happy Parkway family.

About midsummer one particular year, when the seasonal staff swelled the employee ranks to its highest level, we threw such an affair on a Saturday night. One employee convinced the other members of his Wheat Valley Gospel and Bluegrass Band to play free of charge for the sheer gluttony and fun of it. We deliberately staged the event in Bud Carter's garage area to force him to give it a good cleaning. The bay doors were raised to provide ventilation to relieve a warm night. Chicken, venison, hamburgers, hot dogs, and covered dishes of every make filled our stomachs. Children played on the fire truck. Menfolk told tales. Spouses chummed up to their partners' bosses. Everyone sipped something from a paper cup. Life was good. And the string band played on.

Dressed in a bear costume, a seasonal ranger surprised the children with a special appearance, and all had to have their picture made with him. As the evening progressed, the Bear degraded to camera poses with fully grown women sitting on his lap, while he smoked a cigar and drank an unidentified liquid straight from a bottle. The band sounded better the louder it got, playing mostly bluegrass numbers, but its members probably sensed that gospel music would eventually be required to call this crowd to repentance. When the Parkway dispatcher signed off at midnight and came back to enjoy the fun, only the very youngest and the very oldest had wandered home.

Sometime later, the telephone in the dispatch office began to ring off the hook. When I finally realized that every ranger in the district was still enjoying the party and not at home, I decided to answer the phone, just in case a cooperating agency was trying to report an emergency.

"Blue Ridge Parkway. Ranger Pegram speaking," I answered.

"Ranger who?" an elderly lady barked at the other end of the line.

"Ranger Pegram, Tim Pegram."

"So, you're down there, too. I thought better of you, Tim."

I was puzzled. "Who's calling, please?"

"Don't you know who I am? This is Mrs. Hannabass. Your neighbor. I live right down the street from you right behind that blasted ranger station. Now I don't mind you people having a party every once in a while, but this is ridiculous. Do you realize what time it is? And do you realize how loud you are? I can't go to sleep, and I'm calling the sheriff."

Stunned, I poked my head out the side door and — sure enough — her front porch light was burning. Perhaps we should have invited her to the party, even though she had no employee connection. She was a very nice lady and a good neighbor, and I felt terribly that we had ruined her peace. Even though her call seemed very out of character, I silently agreed that we should not have done this to her.

"Oh, please don't call the sheriff, Mrs. Hannabass," I begged. "I'll take care of this," I profusely apologized until I was reasonably certain that she would not make the call.

I burst through the swinging door into the shop area and stopped the band in the middle of a number. At least two tipsy people continued their flatfoot shuffle on a cement floor, which had been sprinkled with a dusting of sand, in spite of a silenced band. I told everyone about the call we had just received, and a decision was made to lower the bay doors on the complaining side of the building. With the loss of ventilation, however, the building warmed to the point of discomfort, and the party quickly disintegrated.

On Monday morning, Edith Garst, an administrative clerk, walked into my office to ask me what time the party had ended on Saturday night. She and her husband had been in attendance but had left around midnight. "About one o'clock, I suppose. Probably would have lasted longer had we not received that call from Mrs. Hannabass," I answered.

"Oh, really. Tell me what happened," she begged, making herself comfortable in a nearby chair. The day's work would have to wait for this story, and I held her rapt attention with every detail of the call. Prim and proper in many respects, but by no means a dour personality, Edith had a great sense of humor and reveled in the story. Too much. Too many questions. Too much smiling. Too much laughter. This was *not* a funny story. Near its conclusion, I finally realized that she had executed the perfect practical joke. Edith had made that call from her home, impersonating a perfectly innocent woman. It would take me weeks to restore the good name of Mrs. Hannabass with the disappointed party goers.

"You'll pay for this Edith. I promise. You will pay. And soon," I hollered down the hallway as she cackled and scurried back to her office. I should have known. Wes Earnest was her supervisor.

So, what is the first thing most office workers do when they return from lunch? They extend their lunch break, of course, by placing a personal telephone call. On such habit my revenge depended, as Edith rushed past my desk upon her return from lunch. During her absence, I had taped an urgent message onto the receiver of her telephone with instructions to call a particular number immediately.

"Did you realize that your patrol car is idling out here by the gas pump?" she tauntingly asked in passing, hardly waiting for an answer.

"Yeah. I'm getting ready to leave."

As she entered her office, all hands quietly gathered in the hallway outside her door in time to hear her mutter, "Uh, oh." She quickly dialed the number. The brief silence nearly caused us to burst. "The what... say that again... the Rape Hotline... but I had an urgent message to call you... no... no... no! I have *not* been raped!" she finally screamed and slammed down the phone.

The sudden, annoying squeaking sound of all four wheels, all in dire need of oil, on her vintage swivel chair was my cue for a hasty exit. "I'll kill him," were the last words I heard Edith yell as I jumped into my steely steed and peeled out for an afternoon patrol.

14

Beware of Dog

> "I've also always wanted to write a story that included a dog."
> — Author's Note to *The Guardian*, by
> Nicholas Sparks

Not even the temptation of a rustic wooden bench could lure me into the parking area located just south of the Roanoke River bridge. Every memory I could conjure up about the place reminded me of my own vulnerability to mischief and the fact that I had once nicknamed it "Big Trouble Overlook." As a ranger, I had always looked for trouble there. This day, I did not want it to come looking for me.

Although a short trail leads to spectacular views of the river and the underside of the six-span, structural steel bridge, for some reason, this location always seemed to also attract more than an equitable share of vandalism, drugs, alcohol, disorderly conduct, and thefts from unattended vehicles. Excusing all innocent fishermen, the combination of rivers and bridges everywhere seems to generate a similar magnetism.

I would still, however, recommend it to potential visitors as a safe place to explore, provided that they remain alert to their surroundings and conceal their valuables in a locked car. It is the same advice I would give to anyone, whether they were visiting a shopping mall or any other location on the Parkway.

My caution and bias thus expelled, confession that this parking area was also the scene of my aforementioned battle with a ruthless seat cushion is duly noted. Furthermore, the fact that I had squandered away enough of the morning conducting gravitational studies from the bridge prompted a rapid flyby more so than any danger that could be lurking about on a sleepy Thursday morning.

Milepost 115 had always been my turnaround point for daily, six-mile jogs from our ranger residence. "That was back in the days when I could run like a deer," I told a friend many years later, who curiously peered at an old photograph of me in uniform hanging in our hallway. As I approached the marker, the morning grew more interesting. The loud sound of the sudden acceleration of a motorcycle behind me caused me to turn and look in its direction as it passed a car on a double-yellow line on the bridge. I had been brushed by one passing a car the day before and was not interested in a repeat performance. I waved at both of them as they drove past and started up a hill. Suddenly, a wild turkey emerged from the woods and ran across the road between the car and motorcycle. The driver of the car slammed on the brakes while the motorcyclist sped away, apparently unaware just how close he had come to a catastrophic collision.

As I approached the unmarked turkey crossing, the warming sun had already stirred the stench from the carcass of another animal whose crossing had not been quite as successful — a yearling deer. Up to this point, I had been keeping a road kill count in my head, which surprisingly had amounted to only six snakes for the first 115 miles. The time had now come, with the sad observation of this unfortunate creature, to devote a page of my journal to a memorial road kill log for whatever pseudo-scientific purpose or mental exercise it would serve. Perusers might later be stunned by its magnitude and diversity.

The day grew uncomfortably warmer and the traffic heavier and faster as I inched my way through the heart of the Roanoke Valley section of the Parkway. I must have dropped my backpack a hundred times that day to furiously record the flood of memories triggered by the sight of this curve and that bridge and yonder horse crossing. So many patrols, so many law enforcement incidents, and far too many fatal motor vehicle accidents remained invisibly overlaid across this still beautiful canvas of rolling hills, hay fields, and suburban Roanoke. The top of my backpack became an improvised desk as I developed a proficiency in kneeling on a single knee to record thoughts and images in the journal stowed in its uppermost pouch. Curious passersby who might have assumed me to be in the attitude of praying during such exercises, were not wholly mistaken; I was quite concerned that not all motorists would keep their part of our bargain. So I gave wide berth to their haste and stumbled cautiously along an uneven shoulder. Where were the rangers? These folks were running interstate highway speeds.

A detour up the four-mile loop road to the crest of Roanoke Mountain would probably have provided the adventure story of the day and perhaps a chance to watch a hang glider launch from its summit. But its steep grade, the blind curves on its narrow, one-way course, and the heat of the day easily justified a decision to deny myself its dangers, pains, and pleasures.

Instead, I turned down the Mill Mountain Spur Road for a detour out to the Roanoke Mountain Campground. There I took advantage of the last known source of tap water at a Parkway facility for the next thirty-five miles and the last known telephone at a Parkway facility for the next forty-eight miles. Too, it was a good place for a civilized sponge bath and an early supper prepared upon the luxury of a picnic table in a quiet corner of the RV loop. Such a calm, peaceful place this little loop was, though technically within the city limits of Roanoke, and I could not recall a single law enforcement incident that I had encountered within it. Only one site had so far been claimed for the evening, and I chatted briefly with a retired couple from Florida who were taking the same journey as I, only they in a motorized camper.

Refreshed now, I headed back toward the Parkway with a good three hours of daylight remaining. The discovery of a little yellow birch sapling, which had rooted and was growing from the top of a wooden guide rail on the spur road, caused me to chuckle. Defying the manicured tendencies of man, this little soldier of aromatic stems bore mute testimony to Stanley Abbott's prophecy that future Parkway challenges would include "too little money for proper upkeep." Too, it stood ready, with its companion elements, to gobble up and recover its invaded habitat with a zeal so masterfully described in Robert Frost's poem "The Birthplace."

Within site of the Parkway, I stopped at Gum Spring Overlook for a brief respite from an uphill pull carrying fully loaded water bottles. Leaning against the overlook sign, I noticed that it was made from — no — yes, plastic! My 1979 employee suggestion to discontinue the use of redwood due to cost and conservation considerations, in lieu of another suitable wood, had been taken way too far! But, from a distance, it looked so much like wood and was surely more durable. How many of these had I passed in the last 120 miles? Then I remembered that the sign marking this overlook had been unusually prone to theft. Those with catchy names and others to which sentimental value had been quietly attached always disappeared more frequently. Perhaps another suggestion that they be commercially produced for sale in Parkway visitor centers, both in full size and in miniature, would relieve the park of replacement costs and provide a legal avenue for obtaining a souvenir coffee table or key chain trinket. Perhaps one of the Parkway's cooperative support organizations could capitalize on that idea and use the proceeds to further protect and promote this treasured Parkway. Easy does it, I thought. I needed to get back in the saddle and finish this hike before becoming too lofty and flying off to Antarctica again.

This particular day, I noted, was September the eleventh, an infamous date in modern American history. Another September the eleventh, of a happier and more memorable bygone year, I would discover farther down the Parkway. Eleven days prior, Patty and I had passed underneath the Parkway bridge spanning U.S. Route 220. With 121 miles behind me, I had averaged exactly eleven miles in eleven days, arriving at this juncture the eleventh day of the month. Eerie, this number eleven on this particular day. Intrigued less by any superstitious interpretation and more by its coincidence, I rejoicingly crossed the bridge, stepping out of the worst of the commuter zone worries and into the more tranquil prelude of the Parkway's run up Bent Mountain. The supply cache I had carefully hidden eleven days earlier was just ahead.

As I approached my secret supply point, I quietly congratulated myself on how well it had been hidden. It could not be seen at all from the roadway. As I angled into the woods and peered upward in the direction of the tree from which it had been hung, my heart stopped at the sight of a fat gray squirrel scampering from its vicinity. How could I have made such a strategic mistake? Notwithstanding an amateur command of the ways of the natural world, I had failed to consider the squirrel, the raccoon, the bobcat, the bear, and all other climbing and aerial creatures capable of easily penetrating the plastic lid and duct tape to access the contents of the #10 can.

In the few seconds it took to visually locate the cache, I offered silent forgiveness to any creature who had robbed my toilet paper for nesting material. I could make other arrangements. Matches, too, could be spared for whatever sick use a wild animal might have for them. I had plenty. And vitamins I could sacrifice for a shinier coat of fur. My own hair was beginning to thin and vitamins were not going to reverse the process. But please, please, not my freeze-dried beef and chocolate. But I found the cache intact and gratefully added its weight to my load in exchange for a few cashew nuts left for the inopportunely tardy squirrel. Just ahead, near the Buck Mountain Road underpass, lay buried the tale of another once wild critter, one *Canis familiaris,* better known locally as "Dawg."

While on patrol one day, my subconscious camera shutter opened for a millisecond, exposing the subliminal message that something was out of order in the woods on Parkway Left. The slightest disruption to the memorized landscape was always worthy of investigation. A fresh scuff mark on the pavement, a broken sapling at wood's edge, or a trail of litter along the shoulder often led to the discovery of a motor vehicle accident or the discarded contents of a woman's purse that had been stolen from a vehicle parked at a trail head. Duty bound one to check the obvious signs. Boredom often prompted the curious pursuit of the more subtle signs. Had I foreseen the pile of a story into which I was stepping, I would have continued on in the comfort of an air-conditioned car enjoying Gordon Lightfoot singing "Carefree Highway" on the radio.

Instead, I grabbed a portable radio and walked into the woods to discover a most unusual sight — something that a little boy might do whose parents had refused him permission to take in a stray dog. A well built, shingled doghouse had been placed within the park boundary. Worse than the doghouse, though, was the enormous amount of litter scattered around it: pieces of cardboard, empty cans and bags of dog food, and rubber toys. Someone had made considerable effort to provide and conceal a home for an obviously special pet, nowhere to be found. But, wait. There he was, in the distant woods, watching my every move. When I attempted to call him, though, he turned and ran out of sight.

Assuming the most innocent of circumstances, as mysteriously justifiable as they might have been, the doghouse still needed to be removed from park lands and, more importantly, from the view of the Parkway. So I tacked a note onto it requesting its owner to so comply and left my name and telephone number in hopes that I might learn the whole story about this shy dog.

I stopped to check the doghouse over the next couple of days, always spotting the wary animal staring at me from a distance in the woods. No amount of coaxing would bring him closer than fifty yards. To whom did he belong and who was feeding him? Then, one day, the doghouse and its associated scatterings disappeared.

I was completing an investigative report late one afternoon at the office when I received a telephone call from a man affiliated with a local newspaper, *The Roanoke Times & World-News.* He wanted to verify that I had left the note on this doghouse but was too hurried to listen to any further details I tried to offer. The next morning I learned why. He was apparently trying to meet a deadline for a story.

I could not believe my eyes when I saw the headline, "<u>Evicted</u>— Abandoned dog loses his home on Blue Ridge Parkway." The article, accompanied by a sad photo of "Dawg," detailed a warm story of how some local residents had adopted the shy stray. The part of the story that really steamed me was the insinuation that Parkway rangers had stolen the doghouse. I had already developed a less than appreciative attitude of the press in my young career due to their avalanche of inquiries every time they heard the rescue squad dispatched to the Parkway over their scanners. And this unfair story was not improving their status per my estimation.

Assistant Superintendent Dick Stokes summoned me to his office in downtown Roanoke before noon and demanded the details. Feeling like a defendant forced to testify at his own trial, I provided them in the solemn style of sworn testimony. To my relief, Mr. Stokes rocked back in his stately swivel chair and laughed hilariously as his secretary, Pinky Dayton, peeked around the corner of his open doorway for a sanity check. "Now, you go back and put everything you just told me in a report, and don't worry about any of this. I'll take care of it from here on out," he reassured me. Whew, at least he believed me.

A few days later, another article appeared in the same newspaper with the headline reading, "And now Dawg has disappeared." Had I now been accused of killing the story by disposing of Dawg? No, I learned after a careful reading. Dawg had mysteriously disappeared, and this staff writer moved up one rung on my ladder with this recantation: "For the record, the dog house ... wasn't stolen. It was moved farther into the woods off parkway property on the advice of a ranger." Once again, I became a happy ranger.

A few weeks later, however, it became apparent that Mr. Stokes was not fully satisfied that this newspaper had completely atoned for its hasty, if not sloppy, portrayal of ranger activities. "Tim, I've made arrangements for you to take a reporter and a photographer out with you tomorrow night. Same ones that did your infamous Dawg story," he joked over the telephone. "Show them everything you rangers do. And be sure to show them that load of junk you carry in your trunk."

I protested immediately, momentarily blurring the distinction between his professional position and the fact that, as friends and next door neighbors, I was only permitted to argue with him over the proper time to plant corn and green beans. "You know how badly they mangled the Dawg story. Can you imagine what they'll write if the least little thing goes wrong?" I pleaded.

"This will be good medicine for both of you. You'll do fine."

A few days later, in the Sunday edition, a most comprehensive and complimentary article detailing the duties of a Parkway ranger appeared. Dawg, most likely an angel in disguise, had performed a miracle among men.

An instructor at the Horace M. Albright Training Center, located at Grand Canyon National Park, had warned our young Ranger Skills class of 1980 about dogs. "You will become involved in more altercations with park visitors enforcing the six-foot leash law than any other regulation," he prophesied. Those of us representing larger parks did not take his remark seriously and quietly gossiped, during the break following his presentation, that his field experience must have been very limited. We had duties far more important than dealing with such trivial matters. Did he ever prove us wrong.

On the Parkway, I soon learned that dog dealings came in two varieties—one in which adjacent landowners or hunters permitted their dogs to wander into the park and the other in which dogs were deliberately brought into the park by their owners, as temporary visitors like themselves. In either case, owners generally, despite their own culpability, expected the rangers to find, retrieve, and provide care for their lost pets as if they were lost children. One had to be diplomatic in dealing with a hunter who unquestionably loved his bear dogs more than his wife and sensitive to the urban couple who had chosen canine adoption over having children of their own. Sometimes, it seemed, there were more legs in the park representing these four-legged, domesticated visitors than there were of *Homo sapiens.*

One November afternoon found me inspecting a section of the park boundary on the backside of Roanoke Mountain. It was the perfect time of the year to be in the woods, with cooler temperatures and a little autumn color remaining. The particular line I was running emerged into the edge of the back lawn of a private residence located in a fairly populated suburban area of the county. Before proceeding around the property, I waited momentarily for the sight or sound of any activity suggested by a "Beware of Dog" sign posted on a tree. There was none, and nobody appeared to be at home.

As I angled down an embankment along the line, a fully grown German shepherd came trotting around a corner of the house, growling and baring his teeth. No amount of yelling at him interrupted his steady, determined advance. As his trot broke into a run in my direction, I frantically looked about for a rock or stick to throw at him, but none were handy. When he launched into midair a few feet in front of me, I fired a single shot into the air with my revolver. He landed at my feet with all four of his legs sprawled in a spread-eagle posture, peering up at me with pitiful eyes that seemed to beg for mercy. "Get on," I yelled, aiming now for his head in the event he decided to continue his attack. He seemed to understand and whimpered back around the corner of the house, shaken. Shaken more so myself, I waited a few minutes for his owner to emerge from the house so I could explain the disturbance. Nobody appeared, and I was probably spared another attack of a different sort.

Both the dog and I had only done what we had been trained to do. His owner, who had flagrantly chosen to ignore a county ordinance, had almost become responsible for a tragedy.

I could see a couple sitting at the edge of the woods on an embankment above the overlook when I drove in to check their unattended car. They quickly leashed their German shepherd as I climbed up the embankment to talk to them. Before I could reach their location, they hurried past me en route back to their vehicle, muttering more a hasty farewell than a pleasant greeting. Something did not feel right about this encounter, and I continued climbing up to the spot where they had been sitting.

My hunch was validated. A smell of burned marijuana remained in the air, and I found an empty bottle of prescription cough medicine tossed into the brush. The couple had almost reached their car when I yelled for them to stop. "What's the problem?" the man yelled back.

"I just want to talk to you," I answered, as I hid the bottle in my pocket and started back down the embankment. Not wanting the incident to escalate into a car chase, I hurried down to their car, hoping to stop them before they could get inside the vehicle. As I approached them in the parking lot, the woman, who was holding the dog close to her side with about fifteen feet of leather leash coiled in her hand, dropped the coil and permitted the animal to charge me. In an instant, the dog clamped down on my right thigh.

"Pull him off or I'll shoot him," I demanded with an intensity that convinced her I was not bluffing. The dog, whose teeth never penetrated the skin, released his grip on me with one tug of the leash. Her partner, more under the influence of a narcotic drug than sound reasoning, flew into a rage and informed me that he also had a gun in his car that he would likewise use on me. Needless to say, this was another instance when the dog was only doing what he had been trained to do. And when my ranger backup unit arrived a few minutes later, we also did what we had been trained to do.

At one point on my trek, I was getting somewhat low on water and decided to take a detour down a dirt road to a nearby farmhouse to see if I could get resupplied. In all my years of backpacking, I had never known anyone to turn down a humble request for water. As soon as I turned down the road, an old hound came charging toward me from the house, cutting through Parkway land leased for pasture use. As I approached the house, I began to plant my handy walking stick a little farther away from my body than normal to keep the barking, snapping canine away from my feet. I had nearly made the decision to retreat back to the Parkway, figuring my need for water was not worth the risk, when a man nearly broke the screen door from its hinges coming out onto his front porch.

"You had better *not* hit my dog with that stick," he fumed.

Grateful that he was not backing up his strong words with a visible firearm, I replied, "I've not hit your dog. I'm just trying to keep him off me." At this point, I had not even walked onto his property, but was still standing in the road. "I'm backpacking down the Parkway and was wondering if you could spare me some water?"

Satisfied that he had not heard his dog yelp from a blow and that I appeared harmless, he calmed the dog and permitted me to fill my water bottles from a spigot near his front porch. I introduced myself and told him I had once worked in that area as a ranger, to which he simply grunted. Though the dog and I warmed up to each other's company, no amount of conversation or courtesy to this man left me with any impression that I had been added to his Christmas card list. Beware of dog? Better said, beware of owner.

15

Gone Awry

"Inman looked at the lights in the big houses at night ... and it made him sick."
—*Cold Mountain*, by Charles Frazier

Approaching darkness and the foreboding wail of sirens originating from the nearby Clearbrook Rescue Squad station prompted a quickened pace from the scene of the infamous "Dawg" case to a prospective campsite for the night. Much of this low country at the base of Bent Mountain was thickly wooded and clogged with a nearly impenetrable mesh of honeysuckle vine. These were the backwoods and backwash of rural Roanoke County, where even the air remained stagnant due to faulty circulation. A sewage treatment plant, not quite visible from the Parkway, was still close enough to prick the olfactory nerve when the air did choose to move in a certain direction. Until someone informed me of its existence, I had quietly and harshly judged Ranger Jim Keller. For months, I thought he had surreptitiously gassed me one night as we rode together on one of my first patrols through that area. Less civilized rangers had been known to initiate rookie rangers by consuming vast quantities of pickled boiled eggs and trapping them in a patrol car with the heater running full blast. Yes, scenic values and property values had bypassed this part of the earth and so would I, as far as camping was concerned.

As I pressed forward into absolute darkness, the tunnel of growth through which I walked blocked any visual assistance the afterglow or a rising, nearly full moon had to offer. To worsen matters, the occasional headlights of a passing vehicle shattered the night vision of eyes that had surely performed better in their earlier years under similar conditions. It was so dark that, in the absence of traffic, I walked the center line of the roadway to avoid a misstep and a twisted ankle along its edge. Conserving the batteries in my flashlight for more pressing circumstances, I tried not to think about the silent copperhead that might be intent on warming itself on the pavement. Manipulating the game of rationale, I concluded that, if we considered too seriously the dangers of snakes, we would never step out of our cars. If we considered too seriously the dangers of driving, we would never leave the safety of our homes. If we considered too seriously the dangers of spiders, we would draw up into a ball in our bedrooms and never go to sleep. And then what?

A tired body that had successfully dodged cars over fifteen hot miles, in concert with a thought process that was deteriorating rapidly toward faulty logic, needed to stop for the day. Soon. Backpackers know they are most prone to injury when they become either fatigued or hurried or both. I was both.

Relief from this bothersome day finally appeared as the Parkway emerged from its dark hollow into the open expanse of a starry night. Ascending vistas of open pasture land on both sides of the Parkway appeared to offer a perfect place to camp. Like the calculated shot of a pinball, though, the sight of what I viewed high to my right steered me quickly to the left.

I had climbed over many barbed wire fences in my life and well understood the fundamental process and the inherent dangers. It is a fine art worthy of every young boy's mastery, tricky under even the best of circumstances and most easily executed on flat terrain over a fence in good repair. But the combined ingredients of darkness, a rickety, vine-infested fence, a landing a foot lower than the launch, fatigue, a less familiar center of gravity wrought by a backpack, and the sudden appearance of blinding headlights at the critical juncture of crossover spelled a recipe for certain disaster.

As the tension on the top strand of wire slipped, my forward momentum could not be reversed, and a barb hooked and stung the inside of my right thigh. Determined to minimize whatever damage I was about to incur, I grabbed the top strand of wire with both hands in hopes of at least riding to a soft landing. One hand had begun the climb in a safe place; the other blindly grabbed onto a barb in desperation. Except for a burning sensation in both hands and the sound of ripping fabric very close to my groin, the ride and landing was about as pleasant as any I had taken from the top of a birch tree.

Postponing an immediate diagnostic assessment (I was too afraid to look), I clambered up through the pasture, hoping now to avoid prickly thistle and fresh manure. An odd sensation of airiness prompted brief downward glances at the moonlit, fluttering remnants of my trousers. At some point on the trek, I had recorded in the margin of my journal: "I must experience adventure in my life; if it does not occur through the natural course, then I create it." This was not the sort of adventure for which I had bargained, and one would have to be a male to understand the potential ramifications.

Finding a suitable, level spot on a bench of the hillside just outside the park boundary, I dropped my gear and determined it to be a proper time to break out the flashlight. To my surprise and great relief, except for a shallow cut on one hand, there were no lacerations, only minor abrasions. A single barb, though, had ripped the trousers thirteen inches vertically and six inches horizontally. Their time-consuming repair was possible with my needle and thread kit but would necessarily be delayed for another time. This had been a long, difficult day, and I needed time to rest and ponder the monstrosity facing me on the opposite ridge.

When this section of the Parkway was completed in 1960, and after its construction scars had healed, the scene was as perfect as could be ever be sculpted. As far as the eye could see, which was less than a mile in either direction due to the Parkway's lowland course among rolling hills, a visitor was graced with a pristine, pastoral scene. Guaranteed only fractionally by fee simple ownership of a narrow strip of Parkway land, most of what could be viewed remained vulnerable to the uncontrollable whims of adjacent private ownership.

Like Michelangelo's statue of David, every inch of the Parkway, upon the day of its completion, was as perfect as it would ever become. But the passage of time and the effect of the elements would inevitably tarnish it microscopically. Vandals would hammer away at its toes. Rioters in the street would break one of its arms. Even those conservators entrusted with its preservation would attempt to clean it with hydrochloric acid.

Here, the finger paint had squirted, rather than oozed onto the canvas. Here, rioters had broken an arm from the statue. Here, the masterpiece had sustained irreparable damage. Strung in a line across the opposing ridge, I stared in disbelief at the backside of about two dozen, two-story homes punched from the same cookie cutter. The developer had neither the foresight nor the courtesy to present their architecturally better side in the direction of the most scenic highway in America. Decks, propane grills, boats, lawn mowers, swing sets, storage sheds, and every other contrivance any respectable homeowner would hide from the frontal view of his mansion had replaced a gentle scene of cattle grazing in a pasture. Their curtains were not even pulled closed. Figures moved past lit windows in the distance. Their bedtimes could have all been documented as the lights were successively extinguished, and had I been wrought with the peeping disease and equipped with a cheap pair of binoculars, I could have verily peered into their oblivious souls. Vegetative screening would require fifty years of growth to hide this thoughtless, blatant, in-your-face stain on the landscape.

Ironically, I would meet one of these homeowners a few months later shopping for a new home in my own neighborhood in North Carolina. "Borrow to the hilt, spend to the hilt, and declare bankruptcy when death appears imminent" was the arrogant philosophy he proudly spouted from his luxurious SUV. It made me sick.

The popularity of the Blue Ridge Parkway appears to be its worst enemy. People desire to own a home near it to buffer their own property from undesirable encroachment. Real estate advertisements offer "borders Parkway" or "within view of Parkway" as positive selling points. Business owners likewise clamor for the attention of the passing tourist by locating their establishments and signage as close to the Parkway as possible.

Bobbing in this sea of free enterprise and rights of ownership ideals, the battle to preserve the scenic quality of the Parkway began at its inception. How much land to purchase for its right-of-way and viewshed became a troublesome issue. In his book, *The Blue Ridge Parkway*, Harley E. Jolley illustrates the earliest of problems:

> To provide ample room for the cuts and fills on the steep slopes of the scenic highway, the Park Service and the Bureau of Public Roads decided to ask the two states to procure a fee simple right-of-way that would average one hundred acres per mile and an additional fifty acres per mile of scenic easement. North Carolina readily accepted the proposal, but Virginia was reluctant to do so because of previous difficulty experienced in obtaining scenic easement. As late as 1948, the supervisory landscape architect for the Parkway was reporting that "Virginia has never officially accepted the 100 acres per mile in fee simple. There was a gentleman's agreement between the Governor and the Secretary [of the Interior] that the State would acquire 400 feet of scenic easement on either side in addition to the 200 foot right of way." The gentleman's agreement obviously did not solve the problem satisfactorily: "North Carolina has always been most cooperative and generous in trying to acquire all the right-of-way requested. In Virginia the attitude has been quite different.... They never accepted the 100 acres per mile standard.... At times the impression has almost been that official Richmond was doing the Government a big favor by allowing the Parkway to be built through the State."

Additionally, many tracts of land that Virginia did purchase were so encumbered with road access easements that intersected the Parkway that Secretary Ickes finally refused to accept any more of them. Many such tracts that already had been accepted eventually evolved into enormous challenges for future park managers.

Although Stanley Abbott managed to steer the Parkway clear of the "hot dog and gasoline shanties" of his day, he nevertheless predicted: "There will be adverse forces later, never doubt." Some of the forces now seem uncontrollable. Mother Nature herself has ravished the Parkway's forests of chestnut, Fraser fir, hemlock, and dogwood trees. While she cleverly heals or hides her own wounds, it is the man-made forces that more forcefully and more permanently shock the aesthetic senses.

Shame on all those responsible for the erection of a municipal water storage tank a few feet from the park boundary. Shame on all those responsible for allowing a construction company to cheaply advertise itself on an Adopt-A-Highway sign a few feet from the edge of the Parkway road. Shame on all those responsible for hurtling The Orchards Overlook into obsolescence. Once interpreting one of the largest apple orchards in North Carolina, it now offers a superb view of another residential subdivision. I saw it all, slowly and closely.

Yet, hurrah to every individual, interest group, agency, and government who has stepped into the path of the madman who would attack the sculpture with a hammer. Hurrah to the U.S. Forest Service for its more sensitive approach to harvesting timber within view of the Parkway. Hurrah to North Carolina for its passage of the Mountain Ridge Protection Act. Hurrah to the Asheville City Council for granting a conservation easement on its 20,000-acre watershed. Hurrah, hurrah, these efforts must not stop! Unlike the statue of David, the Blue Ridge Parkway can neither be copied nor can it be moved indoors from the plaza to the Galleria dell'Accademia. Let it not be chipped away into oblivion before it even marks its centennial. Let not another page be torn from its story.

    Exhausted and hopeful that clear skies would not succumb to precipitation during the night, I canceled my reservation with my tent and spread my sleeping bag directly underneath the stars. I laid next to my beloved park; we both had been ripped asunder. Sleep finally came but was interrupted sometime during the night by a pack of coyote whose sudden barking and yipping frenzy ceased as abruptly as it had begun. Perhaps a mother had given a final lesson on killing to her litter of pups, whose time had come to leave her care and establish their own territory. Perhaps a loose confederation of their kind was merely welcoming another member into their temporary fold. I do not know. I could not see them. In the other direction, though, a few lights still stubbornly shone, probably of those addicted to the late-night talk show. Again, I drifted back to sleep, awakened near dawn this time by the lonesome hooting of a great horned owl. Orion had risen and was now chasing Pleiades across the sky. Something, too, was chasing a rabbit through the pasture, whose bouncing cottontail came within inches of my toboggan-draped head. I rose quickly from the disturbance to see what I could see. Its predator, alerted, had diverted and disappeared. And in the faint, hazy light of a new morning, I discovered that the heavens had wept great drops of dew on us all.

16

Disorderly Conduct

"It is hoped that word of the fines imposed will get around
and help us put a stop to such activities."
— Superintendent Sam Weems,
"Monthly Narrative Report —
September 1945"

My little accident crossing the fence the previous night necessitated a premature change into a partial set of new clothing. Ground Rule #3, as I recalled, had something to do with looking like a bum, and even though mismatched clothing did not fall precisely within its purview, I still did not want to look goofy. Switching the green and yellow plaid shirt out with the torn green trousers for my clean pair of beige trousers and matching blue plaid shirt, however, totally disrupted my laundry schedule. Continuing to wear the same socks and underwear according to my original plan, I quizzed myself unmercifully over what I would wear while both sets of trousers and shirts were spinning in the next available washing machine. Forming the simple solution of wearing my rain gear at my next laundry stop finally brought a pleasant relief to my quandary. Such are the stresses of backpackers ridiculously engaged in the thrifty enterprise of extreme weight management.

A clean shirt and pair of trousers also helped to reorder my disposition, as I turned my attention from the things that had disturbed me the night before and focused ahead on the second long climb of the trip. The ascent up Bent Mountain would require about a 1,500-foot vertical climb over the next seven miles. A cool, overcast day, combined now with strong trail legs, would render it a cinch. But how many motorists had I assisted whose machines had blown a water hose or a transmission seal pulling its grade? And how many deaths and injuries had I investigated of those who had attempted to ride it downhill too quickly?

A first order of business for the day was to make a quick inspection of one of my secret stashes of transplanted ginseng. One of the Federal magistrates who tried many of our cases was quite fond of the park and was a conservationist at heart. If a large, freshly dug quantity of ginseng was seized from a defendant, he accepted a single root and a photograph of the entire seizure as sufficient evidence to prove the case. This allowance permitted the replanting and hopeful recovery of the bulk of the catch, and no amount of torture could force a ranger to divulge the whereabouts of his patches. The two patches I had begun were carefully located in places near landmarks that I could never forget and in abnormal habitat that a ginseng poacher would never suspect. I had not checked my patch on Bent Mountain in over twenty years and had visions of finding it in succulent health and now worth thousands of dollars.

The struggle to reach it was taxing. I should have hidden my backpack near the edge of the road instead of carrying it with me up the steep, rocky side of the mountain. Its burden was my lifeline, as important as the arm that carried my walking stick, and I rarely permitted it far from my sight. But this old mountain had been ravaged by a hot fire, deer had overgrazed its foliage, and wild turkey had scratched its surface until it bled. There was no sign of my ginseng or any other healthy vegetation at ground level. Disappointed, I hoped that their roots still retained a spark of life to send forth healthy shoots in better, future times.

About halfway up the mountain, one particular curve gave me cause for mild consternation. Outside a funeral home, it was the place where I had seen my first dead body. Near the time of this occurrence, I recorded the following in my personal journal: "Worked my first fatality ... when a boy went through the guide rail.... We searched for him in 15° weather, 30 mph [wind] and 3 AM. An experience I'll never forget."

This curve was also the scene of a mid-morning crash involving a drunk driver who strayed across the center line and collided head-on with an elderly couple. In a reversal of the usual circumstance, the drunk driver was severely injured and died a short time after pleading guilty to the charge, while the innocent couple was treated and released, their vacation nonetheless ruined.

Here also, the driving skills of Ranger Keller precipitated my first and only self-doubt that I was a suitable candidate for the job of rangering. I had been hired only a few days prior when Jim asked me to accompany him one night to close that section of the Parkway. After giving me a glimpse of eternity over the mountain from the passenger side of his patrol car, Jim gracefully spun it into a ditch on the "safe" side of the roadway in a blinding snowstorm. A two-wheel-drive sedan, it would move neither forward nor backward, requiring us to jack up the vehicle on a superelevated slope in order to mount chains on the rear tires.

As a little boy, I had watched my dad do the same thing in our driveway and worried that I would ever be able to do such adult things. And the cold. How could he withstand handling those cold, heavy chains and kneeling on the frozen ground? Not one to allow a little snow to prevent him from going to work in order to provide for his family, he was my hero. Now, I was staring that childhood phobia and challenge to prove my own mettle directly in the face, under much worse circumstances.

Contributing equally to the task, we finally freed the car from the ditch and resumed our tricky journey, spinning and weaving up the steep grade. I could not avoid the telltale impulse to lower my head between my legs when a sudden feeling of lightheadedness and nausea struck. I had never before been stricken with motion sickness. "You okay, Tim?" Jim asked.

"Yeah, I think so. Must have been something I ate," I answered less than truthfully while snapping back to an upright position, hoping he would not mistake my condition for a weakness. As Jim joked about the perils of winter driving on the Parkway, I, that night, swallowed whatever was ailing me and never experienced that feeling again. In fact, driving on snow and ice eventually developed into adventurous fun for me, while I also took sick pleasure in scaring the living daylights out of every passenger willing to ride with me. Jim knew exactly what he had done.

Before I topped out on the crest of the mountain, the couple from Florida I had met in the campground the day before refreshed my body with a breeze and my spirit with a toot of their horn as they passed me in their motor home. I had gotten a good head start on them that morning, and based on their proven inclination to loiter in camp, I speculated that I had a fair chance of beating them to Milepost 469. They were definitely retired in the strictest sense of the word.

The curvy flats beyond the crest of the mountain came as welcome relief as I bored into the afternoon with my brain operating fairly in neutral. It is in those hazy moments of mental fibrillation that I become most startled, and the discovery of a huge copperhead lying in the grass near my path made my backpack instantly lighter. I knew I was back up in timber rattlesnake country, for I had seen many of them in this area warming themselves at night on the pavement while on patrols. Even though he was still within his elevation range, I was not expecting to find his kind. There was always something creepy about his species' silence and disguise that frightened me worse than the more potent venom of a rattlesnake. A history of numerous close calls, highlighted by a single encounter of having once stepped upon the head of a copperhead, had crystallized such fear and respect.

But this specimen showed no signs of life, and a closer inspection with the aid of my walking stick revealed that it was a road kill. A disturbing trend was now beginning to formulate in my road kill log — snakes were outnumbering every other species and were widening the gap between the runner-up salamanders.

That old serpent of Garden of Eden times was also well represented in many other ways along the Parkway. The road itself slithered along in undulating, serpentine rhythm in seeming disregard of any obstacles in its path. Snake rail fences zigzagged in many places along its way. Names of features hinted of his presence: Devil's Courthouse Tunnel, Rattlesnake Mountain Tunnel, Purgatory Mountain Overlook, Devil's Backbone Overlook, Devil's Garden Overlook, and Devil's Courthouse Overlook. Later in the hike, I would be amused by a bumper sticker reading, "Eve Was Framed." I always thought Adam had been, too. Even William G. Lord, in his *Blue Ridge Parkway Guide*, had scattered at least three sketches of timber rattlesnakes throughout his book and provided these chilling words:

> The heavy body glides forward in slow, tight curves pushing the raised head peering hypnotically just above the grass. Sensor tongue flicks into the air for taste of prey or danger. A movement is caught by the searching eyes. Taut, with rattle raised and ready to strike, the snake pauses. The dark stare turns slowly to and fro. Nothing there. The head dips down and guides the body, quietly vanishing into the thicket. No one follows. But we remember the times we walked through grass and thicket too dense for our eyes to see our feet.

My concern about stepping on a copperhead the night before had just been proven well-founded. Better to not dwell on the matter, I resolved, lest I find myself drawn up into a ball in the middle of my bed one night, unable to sleep.

My enjoyment of walking into the vast, open expanse of Adney Gap was coupled with the prospect of finding a pint of cold, skim milk and a telephone at a little store just off the Parkway. I had patronized it hundreds of times and was once again hungry for its offerings. The next known stop for such services was another thirty miles down the Parkway. My pace quickened, as I thoroughly enjoyed a wonderful scene of open pasture and crop land situated in what had to be one of the windiest, coldest places on the Parkway during the winter. Perhaps later, I would locate and petition the custodians for permission to be buried in the quaint, private cemetery located in that beautiful place.

My half-mile detour off the Parkway proved to be a waste of energy upon the discovery that my oasis had vanished — torn down and hauled away. For the first time on my trek, I felt very lonely and dejected. I had really wanted to chat with Patty. Too many negative thoughts and occurrences had transpired over the past twenty-four hours, and I was in dire need of encouragement. Short on water as well, I employed my water purification pump for the first and only time of the trip to pull water from a nearby stream, plopped down in the middle of a freshly dug potato patch, and cooked my supper. A few passersby gave me curious looks, as well they should have. No rangers were still in sight to investigate.

Soon, I was well into the land of the beautiful white pine. The wind sliding through its thin needles produced a sound of uncontrollable loneliness. As the day drew near its end, I could not even find an uplifting location for a campsite and settled for one in an overgrown pasture. Snake country, I thought, as I pitched my tent, determined to psychologically protect myself within the confines of its paper-thin walls. Perhaps those old movies had been a bit overly dramatic with scenes of rattlesnakes crawling into the bedrolls of sleeping cowboys. But my senses had been rattled to the point that I would not spend another

The quaint, private Shaver Family Cemetery at Adney Gap, elev. 2690 feet, at Milepost 135.6 on the Parkway in Virginia. Photo taken about 1984.

night under the stars, except for one, for the remainder of the trek. Spooked? Yes. Deterred? Never. Despite firsthand knowledge that the old serpent had and still lurked about the Parkway, he would not steer me off course.

Maintenance supervisor Whitt Sutphin used to poke his head into my office and announce that he was "headed down to one end." At least that is what I thought he was telling me in that high-pitched voice of his that in no way matched his tall, barrel-chested frame. Whitt also farmed and lived near the Parkway in Floyd County, and I just assumed that his southerly direction from the Vinton ranger station was just his favorite inclination. "Why not head up to the other end, for a change?" I replied one day to his icy, bewildered stare. There was also a twist of his mouth that later caused me to wonder if he had mistaken my attempt to humor him for smart aleck behavior. One day I accidentally discovered my error of interpretation and the cause of his fidgety body language.

Every wise ranger carried a working set of land use maps for his district in his patrol car. They were critically useful in establishing jurisdiction with their precise, detailed scaled drawings delineating the park boundary and county lines. Summoning the wrong county medical examiner or charging someone with poaching on private land could result in embarrassing and disastrous consequences. Too, they showed elevation contours, deeded accesses to private land

and springs, cemeteries, original landscape intentions, and all sorts of information that a map lover like myself would relish. I spent hours poring over their enlightening details.

The motor road itself was precisely drawn to scale on these maps, metered in hundred-foot stations, which was extremely useful in diagramming motor vehicle accidents. The "location of accident" field on Form 10–413 was considered complete when it included the milepost number to the nearest tenth of a mile, the land use map section and sheet number, and the station number.

In consultation with one such map and tormented by the minutiae such forms required, I one day typed "Section 1-N" onto such a form. This accident had occurred within the section that the original Parkway designers had designated as construction unit 1-N, between U.S. Route 220 and Adney Gap. (Sections 1-A through 1-W in Virginia were designated in alphabetical order from north to south. Sections 2-A through 2-Z in North Carolina were likewise designated. The letters "I" and "O" were not employed in this identification system for either state in order to avoid confusion.) I cracked a smile when I suddenly realized that Whitt had not been telling me he "was headed down to one end" all this time. He was "headed down to 1-N"!

Whitt's radio transmission was barely audible one summer day when he requested assistance "down on one end" near Milepost 125. Not one prone to frequently inject himself into law enforcement situations, everyone was surprised to hear words to the effect that he might have apprehended someone. His location was proceeded to posthaste.

Whitt and his men had captured a young man who had chosen to "streak" across the Parkway in front of the wrong vehicle. "We caught one. We finally caught one," they proudly exclaimed. Ray Stevens's hit song of 1974, "The Streak," had popularized the prank beyond college campuses onto sports arenas and even an occasional naked body running through an open field along the Parkway. The poor man was found sitting in their pickup truck, surrounded by a group of grinning men just daring him to attempt an escape. They had kindly given him a clear plastic trash bag with which to cover his nakedness, for which the investigating ranger was extremely grateful. These fine men in green and gray had performed admirably. Denying them the reward of their blood lust might have jeopardized their willingness to assist the rangers in the future. So the man was appropriately "rewarded" for his cute prank, shooed in the direction of his nearby residence, and told he was more than welcome to keep the trash bag.

When Parkway Superintendent Sam Weems noted in his "Monthly Narrative Report–September 1945" that "disorderly behavior in Cumberland Knob and along the Parkway in that vicinity reached an all-time high during the month," he was probably referring to rowdiness and fighting. A listing of people charged and the disposition of their cases in the same report suggests that drunkenness and disorderly conduct were companion charges, evoking images of less than peaceful, romantic activities.

By the time I emerged onto the Parkway scene as an enforcement ranger, that sort of behavior, along with the placement of moonshine stills within the park, had been fairly stymied through vigorous enforcement. Disorderly conduct, for my generation, was more frequently associated with persons in various stages of undress, engaged in activities in view of the public that they, as my dad used to say, "ort not a been doin'." Any mention of a disorderly conduct case around the office usually prompted a coaxing of every lurid detail that an arresting ranger was willing to provide. While the innocently immature streaker was regarded more as entertaining than shocking and was usually more fleet of foot than was worth chasing, an occasional disgusting joker would slither into the park who warranted capture by even the laziest of rangers.

One day I drove into an overlook to assist a gentleman from Ohio who had run out of gasoline. He had forgotten to neutralize the international distress signal of the raised hood on his car and advised me that another visitor who had stopped to assist him would be returning shortly. I had no other pressing duties at the time and chose to linger a while until his gasoline arrived. During the course of our conversation, this man quite shocked me with a nonchalant inquiry. "Tell me something. Is it normal for people in this part of the country to stand on the side of the road and expose themselves to passing cars?" he asked.

Dumbfounded by the question, I replied, "Of course not. Why?" He went on to explain that, before I had driven into the overlook, a man had been doing that very thing from the top of an embankment just around the curve from where we were parked. The gentleman did not seem offended by this behavior, but it angered me that any visitor to this beautiful place would have his visit so marred and think that this kook represented "normal" in Southern Appalachia. I formulated a hasty plan by which to catch him.

When the gasoline arrived momentarily, I shared my plan with the man and asked him to drive out of the overlook and continue his trip as if he had never noticed the mischief. I drove my patrol car in the opposite direction, parked it out of sight, and walked the ditch line back to the point just underneath the alleged suspect's location. When the next car drove past, I stepped out onto the Parkway and looked upward. Near the top of the steep, thirty-foot cliff stood a man doing something I wished I could forget and would rather not describe. "Halt or I'll shoot," I bluffed. Ignoring my command, he jerked his trousers up from his ankles and began scrambling toward the top of the cliff, sending a cascade of loose rock in my direction as I began the climb after him. Fearing the possibility that he might be waiting to give me a swift kick to the face, I proceeded cautiously over the lip of the cliff, only to discover that he had disappeared. Instead, I found myself staring at a small family cemetery at the end of a dirt road.

I had not yet studied my land use map for this area and was surprised that such a thing could exist so close to yet so invisible from the Parkway. My man had vanished, but in the absence of dust in the air and the sound of a fleeing vehicle, I was certain that he must have lived nearby. A little detective work, some discreet surveillance, the back-up presence of a deputy sheriff, and an angry wife forced this man to his front door a few days later. Cutting his hair and shaving his beard had altered his appearance but could not prevent a positive identification. As a matter of public record, he was charged with and convicted of disorderly conduct, for which he paid a modest fine.

On another day, another man would attempt the same stunt in a picnic area within the view of two outraged woman. When he outran me back to our vehicles in the parking lot, his apprehension turned into a high-speed car chase over several miles. In the absence, at that time, of clear chase and roadblock policies, a ranger ahead of us presented him with the limited choices of stopping or driving into a river, a rock cliff, or a patrol car. He wisely stopped. Initially attempting to hide behind the cloak of an ordained minister, this man eventually told me he was on State probation for a similar offense. As a matter of public record, this man was also charged with disorderly conduct and, upon conviction, was sentenced to six months active jail time and mandatory psychiatric treatment.

Mindful of my rude interruption of the important work of the FBI at another overlook, I did not hesitate in giving foot chase to a young man in possession of a pair of binoculars one day who, upon seeing me drive into an overlook, darted into the woods. I and other rangers had previously observed this man parked in and wandering about this overlook with a pair of binoculars. Amateur ornithologists engage in the same activity but never "rabbit" at the site of a ranger. This one I managed to capture on the run, and he nervously confessed that he had been watching visitors, in and out of their cars, doing things they also "ort not a been doin'" within the public view. After I warned him that he was placing his own safety in jeopardy while invading the privacy of other visitors, he slithered out of the park and was never seen again. Harmful only to himself, I supposed.

A reunion of former Parkway rangers would inevitably degrade into a contest of retelling salacious disorderly conduct tales as voluminous and bizarre as the imagination might conjecture. Privacy issues aside, blinking at any form of disorderly conduct, day or night, carried with it the horrible risk of overlooking a possible sexual assault in progress. And every prudent ranger, in the course of such investigations, was also, like it or not, bound to get an eyeful.

I would have rather not caught a prominent politician in a compromising position one afternoon in one of our boneyards. Panicked that my patrol car had blocked his exit, he rammed a tree trying to drive past me, operating a vehicle with an expired license.

I would have rather not interrupted the naked couple who thought they were concealed behind their jeep parked up on an embankment when, in fact, they were clearly visible to every man, woman, and child driving past. When I walked up to their location and cleared my throat to get their attention, the man casually told me, "I'll be with you in a minute," and continued his frolic. "The heck. You'll be with me right now," I tersely shot back. Angered to the brink of fisticuffs, he informed me that he would do anything with his wife that he wanted to on the Parkway. She thought the entire situation was hilarious and calmed her husband to a point that the matter could be peacefully concluded.

I would have rather not noticed the three bags of litter lying along the shoulder of the Parkway, from which an unknown vehicle had made a quick retreat, as evidenced by spin marks on the grass and pavement. Two of the bags contained pornographic magazines of the X-rated variety from which numerous pictures had been clipped. The contents of the third bag were carefully inventoried in my report: one empty beer can, one empty pack of cigarettes, one half-full bag of cheese popcorn, one ticket stub to a local X-rated drive-in theater, one package carton for a pair of scissors, one pair of scissors, one roll of common adhesive tape (all of which had been dispensed), one package carton for a pair of utility gloves (gloves missing), and one partially full bottle of baby oil. It was the leftover cheese popcorn that puzzled me the most.

Neither bounties, fines, nor jail time could ever completely eradicate from the Parkway that old serpent, the devil himself.

17

Clocking Butterflies
and Bumblebees

"Some wonderful things to observe: the mountains, the
trees, the flowers, the curves, the traffic, and the 45 mph
speed limit."
— Official Blue Ridge Parkway
Safety Poster

The cattle in whose territory I had trespassed were restless most of the night.
They stomped and bellowed and a few times broke out into stampedes of short
lengths and durations but never came closer than fifty yards to my camp, for
which I was grateful.

Having camped many nights among cattle at the old Gentry farm as a Boy
Scout, I knew them to be mostly harmless. In the daylight, they always maintained a safe distance. At night, only their clumsy curiosity lured them close
enough to cause us any great alarm. The sound of their big, clumsy hooves stepping on pots and pans left scattered around camp rudely woke us from our sleep
and broadcasted our untidiness. "A Scout is [or should be] clean," they noisily
reminded us of the eleventh point of the Scout Law. Their ghastly shadows, distorted further within the angular architecture of our large wall tents, unsettled
the tenderfoot and at least one adult leader on moonlit nights. We never worried that they would bite or eat us. But getting stepped upon was another matter. Only when they got close enough to trip on the guy ropes, which violently
jerked the tent, sometimes bringing it crashing down upon us, did we rise up
and attack them with righteous indignation.

The cattle on this night were definitely more frightened of me than I was
of them. My little blue and white tent might have resembled, to them, a motor-

cycle that had crashed unnoticed through the barbed wire fence from the Parkway. Perhaps they were spooked by the old serpent, too, or coyote on the prowl for easy prey. Whatever the case, their caretaker's visit sometime after midnight in a rickety old pickup truck only temporarily calmed their fuss. My tent was well hidden and not discovered, and I chose not to look for trouble at that time of the night with an explanatory appearance. To all residual parties who deemed their rest that night fitful, I extended my sincerest apologies upon departing the next morning. To those not in attendance, I do so now.

With two national forests, one urban area and four folds of the Parkway map behind me, I had advanced well into a new landscape that would remain fairly constant for the next hundred miles, all the way to the North Carolina border and a little beyond it. Stanley Abbott described it as "a managed museum of the American countryside." Small family farms, many of original settlement, are spread like a quilt upon the landscape with their patchwork mix of hayfields, pastures, orchards, gardens, and wood lots. While fences often noticeably delineate the private property lines between adjacent landowners, the Parkway's agricultural lease program dovetails so beautifully into this scene that it is nearly impossible for a passing visitor to notice where the park ends and where these farms begin in many places. Split rail fences in their many styles, a grist mill, a springhouse, a mill pond, and other quaint features of a bygone era have been thoughtfully preserved on park lands throughout this area.

Topographically, the Parkway skirts the eastern edge of an elevated peneplain through this section, offering views eastward over the edge of an escarpment into the lower elevations of the piedmont area. Averaging between two and three thousand feet in elevation, it is just high enough to provide pleasant summers and interesting winters. Winds, unchecked by any significant obstructions to the immediate west, form snowdrifts several feet deep in most peculiar patterns, while bumper crops of tomatoes, cabbage, and potatoes testify of gentle, definitive summers. Local men I had known, like Seth Poff, reflected the character of the winters in their hardened faces and hands while their eyes sparkled with the kindness and charity of a summer bounty. This was a goodly land through which I was about to walk.

In my immediate path, the Parkway crisscrossed the Floyd-Franklin County line, defined as the water divide between eastward and westward flowing streams, numerous times. A resourceful ranger with a full bladder could bypass consultation with the land use map and quite accurately and quickly determine in which county he stood. Such demarcation of county lines prevailed along other sections of the Parkway as well.

No paved roads existed in Floyd County when construction began on the Parkway. Bypassed for the most part by industry and services, it still retains most of its original rural character, which has attracted a small invasion of summer residents and seekers of a simpler, more peaceful lifestyle. In the county but not of the county, they are quietly accepted by the native folk, but few of these newcomers choose or are welcomed into final rest in the stone-fenced ceme-

The Parkway's agricultural lease program dovetails so beautifully into this scene that it is nearly impossible for a passing visitor to notice where the park ends and where these farms begin in many places. This farm is adjacent to the Parkway near Milepost 163 in Floyd County, Virginia. The photo was taken about 1984.

teries of quaint, country churches. It is a cultural mix worthy of academic, investigative study.

The day was Saturday; late summer was the season. Though not as fatigued as I was at the end of my first week on the trek, I nevertheless was looking forward to a day of rest and some time to test my sewing skills. If the day progressed as planned, I would be positioned for my Sunday layover near the spacious Smart View picnic area, where I could make wise use of its porcelain bathroom fixtures and its plentiful supply of tap water.

The sound of chirping crickets and the smell of tall weeds curing in an overgrown field reminded me of home when, as a young boy, we tunneled through such places, avoiding the large webs of the dreaded writing spiders. More properly classified as the black and yellow argiope, such spiders spin conspicuous, zigzag bands within their geometric webs, and we had been told that if they ever wrote your name, you would become the next person to die. Just coming abruptly face-to-face with such a critter while crawling along the ground was enough to frighten a young boy to death.

Large chunks of bark, freshly missing from the base of a large tree on Parkway Left, testified that southbound travelers were still attempting to negotiate a particular curve too fast. But a newly designed wooden guide rail near this same location virtually guaranteed that rangers would never again have to investigate a motor vehicle accident quite like the one I had once done in that very spot.

A compact car was demolished after wandering slightly off the roadway and colliding head-on with the blunt end of a ten-inch by ten-inch timber guide rail. Although the driver of this car was technically at fault through inattention, I quickly recognized an easily correctable design flaw. Citing safety concerns and the fact that most State and Federal highway systems had already adopted such a design, I attached an employee suggestion form to this accident report, recommending that terminal rails on guide rail sections be tapered into the ground. That suggestion was eventually adopted and was still, I sadly observed, slow in its implementation, appearing coincidental to repaving contracts. Not only are the newer twelve-inch by twelve-inch timber rails stronger, safer, and in equal harmony with the landscape, but I found them to be perfect devices on which to stretch a sore back and take a carefully balanced nap, hoping not to be impacted in the process.

Looking behind me is something I rarely do on a hike, but I wanted to be certain it was the right spot. Yes, I concluded. Here, I had occasionally operated a radar gun in the stationary mode in hopes of reducing the carnage of motor vehicle accidents.

I considered it "fair" territory. Speeders could not blame their excesses on a downgrade; the road was level. My patrol car was openly visible to drivers approaching from either direction, though I must confess that I took advantage of the partial camouflage afforded by any available shade on a hot day. Dangerous curves ahead, in both directions, justified strict enforcement of the 45 mph speed limit at that location. And for me, it was about as pleasant a place as any to cool my jets, munch on a packed lunch, and solve the problems of the world.

One lazy summer afternoon I beamed a radar gun down this open, straight stretch of the Parkway adjacent to a field of clover mixed with an assortment of native wildflowers. With no apparent vehicles in sight, my catnap was continually interrupted by the radar's audible alarm, which emitted brief, unusual zipping and fluttering noises. I was puzzled by these sounds, and my attention was further drawn to the digital display window, which burped intermittent speeds as high as 16 mph. My curiosity was piqued. Training had warned me to beware of ghost readings. But these were not ghosts, I finally realized. I was clocking the random flights of butterflies and bumblebees, none of which were fast enough to trigger the radar to lock on a preset speed of 55 mph. It was definitely a slow day on the Parkway.

The pressures that World War II placed on the resources of the nation affected the Parkway in a most unusual way. In the December 1941-January 1942 edition of the *Blue Ridge Parkway News*, Parkway officials wrote:

At the order of the Secretary of the Interior we will open in the spring under a forty miles per hour top speed limit. This goes for all national parks and parkways during the present emergency need for saving rubber. We could add some remarks about how the reduced speed will doubtless also save in bumped fenders and in injury to persons. In any event we are sure that this timely suggestion of the Secretary's will meet with popular support and full cooperation. Even though portions of the Parkway may be safely driven at higher speeds, we hope in fact that the *temporary 40-mile limit* may become something of a *permanent habit* where the Parkway is concerned.

Any "hope" that such a speed limit would become a "permanent habit" vanished at war's end, and the maximum speed limit returned to and remained at 45 mph, along with an increased propensity to exceed it. Enforcing it became a test of will and discretionary fairness for every ranger.

Rarely did a driver, whose speed had been determined by the pacing method, ever contest the charge or become belligerent with me. Its unobtrusive character apparently rang of fairness. In order to prove such a case in court, the speeder had to be followed from a fairly constant distance for more than just a few seconds using a speedometer whose accuracy had been certified. Acknowledging its crudeness and limitations, I avoided employment of the pacing method as a matter of routine. No sober or sensible person would exceed the speed limit while being followed anyway, and the cover of darkness or access to an unmarked patrol car were not often available.

But bathe an independent American with silent, invisible radio waves to determine speed with pinpoint accuracy and the cries of unfairness reverberated loudly throughout the mountains. They began with accusations that the radar gun must have malfunctioned and then quickly deteriorated into every imaginable excuse to justify speeds that could no longer be denied.

One of the worst verbal beatings I ever received came from a motorcyclist who was driving a very expensive machine and was decked in the finest leather money could buy. When I asked for his driver's license, he handed me a business card that indicated he was a minister. Silly, silly me thought it was an invitation to visit his church and placed it in my pocket to avoid any suggestion of discourtesy. When this gentleman was presented with a speeding citation, the tirade that followed shattered the hospitable characteristic his Southern stereotype and choice of profession should have displayed. Conversely, much praise I now give to the New Yorker who swallowed his medicine with dignity and calmly admitted that he had been doing a "good bit over" the speed limit and deserved the citation.

In recognition of every conceivable factor that might cause a driver to exceed the speed limit and on the assumption that a driver was merely in the process of enjoying a bona fide recreational experience, I usually did not even stop a vehicle traveling between 46 and 54 mph. If I was in the mood, a vehicle traveling between 55 and 59 mph was stopped and the driver was often given a nauseatingly diplomatic written warning known as a "Courtesy Tag." Genuinely dangerous speeds of 60 mph and higher almost always tripped the citation switch. Those were my own general rules of fairness to which I remained untethered in the event of extenuating circumstances.

For instance, one day I clocked a vehicle on the Mill Mountain Spur Road traveling 70 mph in a 35 mph zone. As I approached this vehicle, there was no doubt in my mind that the driver was going to be issued a citation. When the driver arrogantly refused to show me his driver's license, I advised him in no uncertain terms that he was very close to being arrested and taken forthwith before a Federal magistrate. A few seconds of hesitation on his part prompted a command to exit his vehicle, following which he quickly handed me his license and burst into tears and apologies. This poor man, I was able to confirm, was a doctor in residency at a local hospital and had just completed a 36-hour shift in an emergency room. I released him with a written warning, for which I was later mildly reprimanded by my immediate supervisor.

But getting into trouble for being too lenient with a speeder never bothered me as much as criticism from higher levels of management that I was writing too many speeding citations. While I was hustling on the job trying to keep visitors out of the hospitals and morgues, statisticians at headquarters were keeping score and developing faulty conclusions. One day I was driving a particular critic through my district, and the conversation evolved into a discussion on speeding tickets. Our opinions differed widely on the matter, and I ever so slightly began to increase my speed. By the time our conversation reached the point he wanted to make with the discussion (I was writing more speeding tickets than any other ranger on the Parkway), I was cruising at a steady 60 mph. I had a steering wheel on which to cling, as the tires cried loudly through sharp curves in spite of fifty pounds of pressure. Despite the constraint of his seat belt and shoulder harness, he, however, was being slung wildly about the right-front passenger seat. Gripping the dash with his right hand and the console with his left hand, his half of our conversation became choppier, while I calmly continued to talk and maintain a speed of 60 mph. Exasperated, he was finally forced to blurt out the obvious question. "Pegram, why are you driving so fast?"

"Fast?" I replied. "I just wanted you to experience the minimum speed at which I *begin* to write speeding tickets." We never discussed the subject again.

The instructor of our Ranger Skills class failed to mention that, second to enforcing the six-foot leash regulation, running radar would get a ranger in more trouble than any other enforcement activity. Its mere placement on the dash of my patrol car seemed to invite trouble from my boss, Bud Carter, headquarters, and, worst of all, my own self.

I thought I had blown an engine one day when I made a U-turn in the road to pursue a speeder I had met traveling in the opposite direction. Accelerating hard, I was almost close enough to read the license plate when I heard a pop. What I thought was white smoke appeared in the rear view mirror, at which point my car began to fishtail as if I had been driving on ice. I released the pressure on the accelerator enough to regain control, and when I depressed it again, the engine seemed to retain its full power. I continued driving and managed to stop the vehicle I was pursuing just as the temperature gauge began to climb upward. I had blown a freeze plug out of the engine block and dumped every drop of antifreeze onto the exhaust system and rear tires. The second time this happened to me, Bud cussingly replaced every original zinc freeze plug on the car with stronger ones made of brass. "Tim. This car can't take what you're givin' it," he lamented, shaking his head in disgust. I was quickly depleting his annual budget allotment for antifreeze. It was the same car from which the metering rods had been removed, but I honestly cannot remember the sequence in which these events occurred. Factory defects, those freeze plugs surely must have been.

Ranger Keller was riding shotgun with me when I took my maiden voyage with the radar. He had trained me well, and I had watched his skillful technique dozens of times. We were operating in the moving mode. A speeding target came out of a curve in front of us. The audible alarm screamed, and the digital display locked onto a dangerous speed. I could not make a U-turn safely at that location and proceeded a little farther around the curve. I bungled the turn and wasted precious seconds spinning in the grass. We never saw the vehicle again. I banged on the steering wheel, upset that my first speeding case had escaped. Ranger Keller just laughed and wisely counseled me to be patient. "Many more will get away, and some you should let," he cautioned.

I remembered those words on another day, when I executed a perfect turn and began a powerful acceleration toward the target. As the distance between us began to shrink, I reached for the microphone and glanced at my radio to switch to another channel. In that brief second of inattention, my right-front tire dropped off the shoulder of the road, and I began a frightening ride I will never forget. Neither I nor my patrol car sustained any damage, but I cleaned out the ditches that day on each side of the road for about a hundred yards. And another lesson was learned that required no repetition.

One morning, a week before Christmas, the radar locked on a vehicle traveling 57 mph. My first inclination was to ignore it, but the morning had been uneventful, and the two young male occupants, it seemed, should have been in school instead of sightseeing. Better stop them, I thought, and at least issue the driver a warning. I caught up with the vehicle, called in the license plate, and activated my blue and red lights less than a mile from an access ramp to a state highway. Much to my surprise, the driver accelerated and turned onto the ramp. Surely he did not think that I could not continue pursuit off the Parkway. Time for the siren had arrived.

When he blew past the stop sign at the intersection and nearly struck another vehicle, I realized the seriousness of his desire to escape and entered that zone where sound is muffled and everything seems to move in slow motion. Why would he do such a thing to a nice ranger desiring only to warn him? I marked "10-80" (chase in progress) with the dispatcher and requested back-up from the Virginia State Police, as the movie in which I had surely not been cast unfolded in front of me. As customary, the Parkway dispatcher advised all units to cease radio transmissions during the emergency while Patty, unbeknownst to me, fretted nervously by the radio at our residence.

His speed must have exceeded 100 mph on the narrow, two-lane road. I refused to run that speed, recalling the cautious words of Ranger Keller, but managed to keep him in sight. Suddenly, he braked and turned onto a dirt road and into territory unfamiliar to me. A chilling message returned from the dispatcher that all State units in that county were "tied up in court," as I frantically tried to read and report the tiny road numbers on signposts at every turn we made. In addition to all of the help unavailable to me, I silently cursed the local weatherman for not predicting the snowstorm that could have closed that section of the Parkway and prevented the moment.

Had he continued down the paved road, I would have soon discontinued the chase at those speeds. He was exceeding my nerve, and I did not want to become a secondary cause of death or injury to innocent parties. But he made a right turn, and his decision to continue the chase on dirt and gravel roads played right into my hand. While his nerve might have exceeded mine on an open highway, I had him trumped on precision driving skills and closed the distance on him, just short of being blinded by his trail of dust. It looked like a scene right out of an episode of *The Dukes of Hazzard* minus any resemblance to humor or a pretty country girl. The inevitable outcome finally occurred.

His driving skills on gravel were so poor that it was difficult for me to tell if he actually attempted to turn into a driveway or if he just lost control of the car. In either case, the car in front of me bounced slightly into the air and disappeared in a swirling cloud of dust. As the dust settled enough to see the car again, I could see both front doors standing open and a man running behind a nearby mobile home. The hood of the car had been peeled back against the windshield, as a result of a collision with a mailbox made from an old plow. Assuming that both men were now inside the mobile home, I cautiously approached the car and was shocked to find a handgun lying on the front seat and an empty bank money bag lying on the floorboard. The sudden urge to just drive back home and take my wife and daughter to the mall to do some Christmas shopping nearly overwhelmed me.

The belated cavalry I had needed earlier was finally mustered into action, and I patiently watched the mobile home, waiting for the arrival of State and County authorities before proceeding further. I could not tell if I was shaking from the excitement or from the numbing cold of a winter day. But the sound of the fourteen-year-old passenger sneaking up behind me in the woods answered the question. His turn then came to shake, and he quickly found himself in custody. When the first trooper arrived, he recalled seeing a young man without a coat hitchhiking on a nearby road and soon returned with the seventeen-year-old driver in custody. The car was full of stolen property, and the authorities in the boys' county of residence eventually closed numerous home burglaries with information gleaned from the case. The story and photographs made the front page of a small town newspaper that could rarely find a story more sensational than the current price of pork bellies. These boys should have stayed in school and opted for fame in their yearbook, and I seriously considered never placing that radar gun in my car again.

Runners always had a reason for running. On another December day, in another year, another seventeen-year-old driver was clocked on radar doing 66 mph. He chose to flee lights and siren as well at a steady speed of 85 mph until a long upgrade slowed him down and better senses whispered him to a stop. Following advisement of his rights, he answered a request for his driver's license with, "I don't have one." When asked to whom the vehicle belonged, he replied, "I don't know." He further stated that he had stolen the vehicle, brought it up to the Parkway to see how fast it would run, and unfortunately learned that it would not exceed 85 mph in the process of trying to outrun me.

Was he truthful? Yes. Was his sentence light? No. Did anyone ever say that I slept with the radar gun? Yes. Did I ever say that I enjoyed running radar? No.

For final judgment of the entire, controversial matter, I offer a few excerpts from my very own fan mail club. One accusatory gentleman wrote:

> Please advise how an officer can accurately read radar, when he cannot distinguish the difference between a 2 door vehicle and a 4 door sedan. Was I really traveling at 64 mph? Enclosed is my check for $50.00.

Another gentleman, who bungled grammar and my name far worse than I estimated the particular shade of white with which his car was painted, wrote:

> Officer Tom Ryan #601 listed my car as a *white* Lincoln and I don't have one. Though very courteous, Tom evidently is color blind and I question his ability to read the scope! I had followed a gawking tourist from Fla. who was going very slowly for miles. So when we came to the 45 mile zone I went around him quickly so as not to endanger myself or anyone I might meet and Officer Tom was parked off the road to sight down that straitaway. I have traveled the Parkway for over 30 years and I wonder if Officer Tom doesn't sit at that point to pick off vehickles doing the same as I was.
> Sincerely yours, [name withheld]

One lady paid the fine but refused to admit guilt, invoking the Almighty on behalf of us both:

I not only plead not guilty to the charge — I am not guilty. Your fine is less expensive to me than a days wages. It is a shame the beauty of the park is colored by less than true & pure law practices. In all sincerety before you & God — [name withheld]

Another concerned lady suggested a new fine structure that bore a familiar resemblance to that of the Federal income tax. My boss was so moved by this letter that he scribbled onto it, "Tim, shame on you!" before giving it to me. She wrote:

I'm sure this letter will do no good but perhaps it may help. When I received my ticket I was upset as most Americans would be. Here I had spent my savings on a new car (one day old) and not being used to it's pepiness exceeded the speed limited for a short time. I thought how unfair, forty dollars where will I get it here after Xmas etc. Then I thought about all the wealthy citizens that $40.00 wouldn't mean anything to and then I thought about those poorer than me that $40.00 would mean no groceries this month or no new coats for the children. I deserve my ticket for not watching my speedometer more closely since I wasn't use to the car but some poor people out there don't deserve a $40.00 ticket and some deserve a $70.00 or more dollar ticket for the same offense. Isn't there some way with all the intelligence we have today to regulate traffic tickets according to income. Maybe this is done & I'm not aware. If it isn't please do what is necessary to bring this to the attention of a committee who would right this unjust means of penalizing those who break the traffic laws. The policeman who stopped me said, "All we care about is your welfare." That was nice of him but I don't think I was in that much danger not as much anyway as some infant in a cold home where mother paid $40.00 for going 15 mph over the speed limit and therefore can't pay the electric or fuel bill this month. Thank you for your time, [name withheld]

But it was the rare author of another tone of letter that made every anxious moment on the job worth the trouble. A mother wrote:

Dear Ranger Pegram,
    Again I want to thank you for your tact, understanding and gentleness in handling our son's wreck on the Parkway last Thursday morning. Our greatest relief is that he and the other boy weren't hurt and our second concern was the dire circumstances he could be facing. All of us know you gave him a break and I truly believe he and the other boys have a much greater respect for cars, speed limits and for those in authority to enforce the laws. You made quite an impression on all of us. Our deep and grateful thanks. [name withheld]

Dear Mom of Fortunate Son: Thank you for that thoughtful letter. Someone once gave me a break, and I turned out to be a better boy, too. Sincerely and belatedly, Ranger Pegram.

18

Not of This Earth

"In a narrow country we suffer no more ... but we prefer the wide one of pain."
—*Better a Dinner of Herbs*, by
Byron Herbert Reece

The weather could not decide if it wanted to rain or not, as I continued walking past the field of clover where nary a flying insect ever exceeded the speed limit. I only had one pair of wearable trousers, and they needed to be kept dry until the other pair could be repaired. So every little shower prompted a donning of the rain gear, and every respite from it prompted its divestiture. An alien being, unfamiliar with our kind's relationship to the elements, might have falsely concluded from my antics that wearing rain gear actually *cleared* the skies and that its removal triggered precipitation. Such tag with the weather can become a frustrating and tiresome exercise with backpackers.

The afternoon played out into a succession of unrelated events as choppy and changeable as the weather itself. An inspection showed that the second patch of ginseng I had secreted in the park had also vanished. But neither deer browse nor turkey scratch, in this case, appeared to have been a factor in its demise. Perhaps the very landmark I had chosen by which to remember its location in conjunction with a secret bearing and distance had attracted the wrong kind of attention. Thieves of another sort had apparently plundered another one of my buried treasures in the park.

Ninety years following his death, someone had still remembered and honored the life of George A. King with a fresh, miniature Confederate flag placed by his tombstone. His grave, close enough to the Parkway to feel the vibration of traffic, lies virtually invisible in a quiet woods within a stone's throw of every passing visitor. I was aware of its presence only because I had once been assigned to seek out many of the owners and caretakers of such places within the park and offer them the maintenance services of the Blue Ridge Parkway. I had always been intrigued with the inscription that noted his birth year as 1813 and his death year as 1913. Had he lived to see his hundredth birthday? Even if he had fallen a few days or months short of that benchmark, he was still a survivor, having served, according to the stone, in Company 1 of the 54th Virginia Infantry of the Confederate States of America. As I stood by his grave and unsuccessfully attempted to imagine the story of his life and time, it began to rain again so on I moved.

Another beautiful farm scene, perhaps the best along this section of the Parkway, had been marred with the construction of a new private road, which appeared to lead to a large castle in the background. A park employee would later tell me it was a monastery. As the rain poured harder, I bid sad farewell to the quaint log cabin which once stood by a pond in pleasant pasture. This robbery hurt worse than that of my secret ginseng.

A park maintenance employee stopped to chat and shared the same disappointment that the little store back at Adney Gap no longer existed. The rangers complained the most, she said, for a dearth of refreshments along that section of the Parkway. In a memorandum dated June 27, 1939, Stanley Abbott proposed an idea to establish "rest areas" or "outdoor living rooms" along the Parkway. They were to be equipped with "furniture" more comfortable than an ordinary bench — "chairs with arms and backs constructed probably of a log base and slabs for the seat, back, and arms." They were to be located in a "nice setting among shade trees, with a view if possible." The most appealing element of this proposal was his idea to send vendors down the Parkway in "passenger cars into the back of which could be installed a refrigerator which could be used as a source of supply from which to carry drinks in small quantities." Had his idea been implemented, rangers and strange backpackers would have, along this section, displaced the intended patrons like an occupational force in a hostile, foreign land.

Before my day and second week on the trail ended with finding a camp near the Smart View picnic area, I was rewarded with the sighting of a pair of American goldfinches feeding furiously on wild thistle and my first observation of a red eft on the trek. My favorite among the salamanders because of its colorfully orange appearance in its land form stage, its sighting was unfortunately in the form of a road kill. Salamanders, in fact, surged temporarily into first place on the road kill log as I discovered an unusually dense population of the red eft, including sixteen casualties, in the short distance between Milepost 149.9 and 150.0. Herpetologist census takers would have to work overtime in that little township.

I spent the morning at my camp, resting and tediously stitching my pants back together. The repair job was large for a very inexperienced tailor, and the process consumed nearly all of my emergency thread and patience. I had never before tackled such a project and rather surprised myself upon its successful completion. The stitches were strong and tight and were well concealed on the inside of the pants. They shortened the length, however, of the right leg about one size and gave them a puckered look that later drew curious glances, but never a comment. If mistaken for a bum thereafter, I at least hoped to be considered one resourceful and self-styled.

Sunday afternoon found me sprawled and sunning on top of a picnic table, surrounded by the joyful activities of two large family reunions and a variety of other small groups, families, and couples. The skies had cleared, and everyone within sight was happy and enjoying the Smart View picnic facilities in every way that its planners had envisioned. No one seemed to mind that I had chosen a little spot near the far end of the loop, out of their way, on which to spread my gear to dry and nap away the day. The table I had chosen was close enough to enjoy their pleasant company and laughter, but private enough that my weekly inspection and maintenance of gear and toenails would not offend anyone.

A nearby restroom, which might have been regarded by a more cultured tourist as rustic — even primitive — due to its lack of electricity and hot water, served me luxuriously. I took full advantage of its porcelain fixtures and, in the quite adequate illumination of its skylight, managed a fairly thorough and accurate shave in the reflection of a real mirror. What a clever, introspective device this invention was by which to loathe or love oneself. This day I was just content with its utility and reassuring revelation that my face did not appear nearly as yucky as it felt. While I was slowly becoming more accustomed to shaves, shampoos, and sponge baths with clear, cold mountain water, no amount of outdoor living could make me grow fonder of dirtiness. In a climactic conquest of cleanliness over filth, I carefully twisted a cotton swab in both ears, brushed and flossed my teeth, and exited the building.

Around the corner, on the women's side, another man once attempted to use this facility in a way for which it had not been designed.

The message that three men from West Virginia had camped in the picnic area overnight and were thought to be digging ginseng in the area came to me far too loudly over the park radio. Everyone in at least two states who owned a scanner also received the same message. It was the kind of blunder that could kill a case, and ginseng poachers were hard enough to catch. But the report came from a kind, well-intentioned maintenance employee who lovingly cleaned and manicured Smart View picnic area as if it was his own private property. Though I trembled and shook like Jimmy Dugan, played by Tom Hanks in the movie *A League of Their Own*, I, too, corked my fury and chose not to make this good man cry, squeaking back in the most polite voice I could muster for him to leave the area and say no more over the air. Another ranger and I rendezvoused at Smart View Overlook, well out of sight of the location of these men, and formulated a simple plan. He would remain with the patrol cars as a back-up, and I would sneak in on foot for a peek at the action.

The Smart View trail system had been built largely by conscientious objectors attached to one of three Civilian Public Service camps assigned to the Parkway during World War II. I doubt they would have approved of me slithering down a section of trail they had constructed toting a firearm. But I was sworn and duty-bound to protect the resources of the park, and my short-term plans did not include getting "et for breakfast" by three West Virginians.

Stepping from the path of the trail into the tangle and cover of thick woods, I moved quietly within sight of the suspect vehicle. I had seen it, parked and unattended at the same location, on a patrol through the area the previous afternoon. But now, two men were hurriedly packing their cookstove and other gear into their truck. Something had spooked them to the point of leaving, and I could blame no one but myself for not having detected the obvious clues the day before. Surely, I thought, a payload of ginseng, dug from the park, was about to drive away before my very eyes, and only a long shot at a consent search of the truck could stop it. Perhaps they would just move to another location on the Parkway, and we could follow them into the woods. But if they turned north leaving the picnic area, they would drive right past two patrol cars parked at the overlook. Even if I radioed the back-up ranger to exit the area, they would still drive past one unattended, glaringly suspicious patrol car and would likely scurry back to West Virginia. Drats. Drats. Drats. My thoughts banged and collided into each other like rattletraps in a demolition derby in search of some salvaged conclusion to the steamy mess.

At the point they appeared to be packed and ready to leave, another thought crashed head-on into the fray. Where was the third man? Had they posted him as a lookout? I scanned the area but could not detect any unnatural colors or movements. The two men then whispered briefly to each other and, instead of getting into the truck, began walking away from each other in opposite directions. One walked toward an open picnic shelter and down an embankment and the other walked straight in my direction.

Fortunately, I had chosen a large red oak tree for cover. The man entered the edge of the woods and continued in my direction. As I stood and eased my body around the girth of the tree to remain hidden, he walked right past me and stooped at the base of another tree just a few feet away from me. Digging through the leaves, he retrieved a small mattock and a blue denim bag and began walking back toward the truck.

"Park ranger. Halt!" I blurted, startling even myself at the impulsive decision to take some action in lieu of just watching him walk away with the suspected loot. Severely frightened by my sudden announcement and appearance behind him, he dropped the mattock and bag onto the pavement of the loop road onto which he had just stepped. Whether he had fumbled or dropped these items deliberately mattered little. The important thing was that he was now separated from the mattock, and freshly dug ginseng spilled out of the bag into plain view onto the pavement! My search and seizure dilemma was solved, and I now had a wedge with which to further pry. As I hastily called the back-up ranger on my portable radio and requested that he get in there as fast as he could, I noticed the missing third man, his morning constitution apparently interrupted by the commotion, peek around the corner of the restroom and duck back out of sight.

The back-up ranger, an inexperienced seasonal employee eager to shine, arrived in seconds, and I requested that he retrieve the good gentleman from the restroom. "He's not in here," he yelled back to me from the doorway of the men's section.

"Check the women's side."

He hesitated.

"It's okay. Just knock first," I reassured him. Mystery Man #3 was found standing on the commode inside a locked stall, a victim of his own making. We had apparently watched the same cop movies.

Another head slowly raised into view from the direction in which the man had walked over the embankment. With my left arm extended, I only had to curl my index finger twice in my direction to convince him to step out of the brush.

"Take this ranger down in there and show him your stash of ginseng," I bluffed. He complied and returned with two mattocks and two additional bags of ginseng!

A consent search of their vehicle yielded two more bags! What had begun as a comedy of errors by every involved player turned out to be the largest ginseng case of my career with the seizure of 316 roots. And a statement that one of the men made after advisement of rights — that they had planned to hunt ginseng all the way up the Parkway into Shenandoah National Park — did not play well with the Federal magistrate when I repeated it in sworn testimony. Thank goodness they had not flown away on me like those five turkey hens I had once mistaken for ginseng poachers!

A second restroom in the picnic area, located closer to the main entrance, had also played a material role in another crime-related comedy of errors.

I had already worked past the end of my designated shift and still had an hour's drive back to the ranger station when I whizzed past the entrance to the Smart View picnic area. The days of early March were still short, and light fog and drizzle were determined to bring the day to an even earlier close. The picnic area was closed and gated for the winter, but a small parking area just outside the gate remained open to the public for access to the trail system. Blinded by the corner of a hill, my momentum had already carried me past the turn into this parking area when I noticed two vehicles parked in it, side by side. Their sudden appearance in the growing darkness prompted an automatic reflex to brake the car for a closer look. But there was some now-forgotten function calling me homeward that evening, and I continued driving. Any other time I would have returned for a closer inspection. The circumstances begged for one. No. Every vehicle parked at an odd time in an odd place in the park did not constitute trouble, I rationalized, remembering the jogger I had once tracked through the snow, suspecting him to be hunting squirrel in the same closed picnic area.

The following morning I received a telephone call from an officer with the Franklin County Sheriff Department. We had developed a good working relationship with each other, finding and plundering more than one patch of marijuana together. "Was that you who drove past Smart View yesterday just before dark?" he asked.

"Yeah. Why?"

"We were in the process of making an undercover purchase of marijuana from a college student when you drove by. I saw you hit your brakes, and I appreciate you not stopping. It would have blown the whole deal."

I was flabbergasted that he had chosen the Parkway on which to conduct such business and even more disappointed that he had left me out of the loop. Understanding the inherent dangers and the necessity for secrecy in such matters, I swallowed all thoughts of criticism that foamed in my mouth. I did not want to say the wrong thing and jeopardize our alliance. Nor did I want to see a visitor or a park employee, especially myself, stumble unknowingly into the potential crossfire of an undercover drug deal. Somehow, I found the middle ground.

"Oh, yeah? Thanks for finally telling me! Had I known it was you, I would have stopped and taken the whole bunch of you in! By the way, you guys were parked dangerously close to the county line. Exactly where did the deal go down?"

"What do you mean?"

"The county line. Yeah. It runs at an odd angle right through the middle of that parking lot. Are you sure you were within your jurisdiction?"

"I'm pretty sure we were on our side of the water divide."

"You know the water divide was altered when they graded the parking lot during its construction, don't you?" A few seconds of dead silence followed.

"Tim. Could you meet me up there this afternoon with your handy-dandy land use map? By the way, we plan to do one last big deal there in a few days. Would you like to participate?"

"Yes!" I silently screamed inside. "Probably so. Let me run it past my superiors, and I'll let you know," I calmly replied, though, to him.

Two weeks later, I found myself at the designated meeting point, in the company of the undercover officer (UC), another ranger, four unmarked Franklin County Sheriff Department units, three unmarked Virginia State Police units, and a dog and handler from the Virginia Department of Corrections. The target could escape only with the aid of a helicopter, and we doubted that a college student could be that well connected.

Darkness had fallen. The UC was nervous. This was to be his third buy from the same target at the entrance to the Smart View picnic area and involved a considerable amount of marijuana and a large sum of cash. The buy-bust was supposed to have gone down during the afternoon in daylight but had been postponed. Drug dealers have notoriously bad reputations for punctuality, and this one was typically nervous and careful.

The plan was solid and simple. The UC, wearing a body transmitter, would exit his vehicle and seat himself inside the target vehicle upon its arrival. Their conversation would be monitored by a receiving unit, positioned a short distance away inside the lower restroom building located in the picnic area. When the money count reached a certain point, all units would storm into the parking area and effect the arrest of everyone in the vehicle. My primary function in this plan was to lead in the pack driving the only marked vehicle, park behind the target vehicle to prevent its escape, flood its interior with light, and generally shock the daylights out of the target with speed, lights, and siren.

With the UC parked and waiting, the plan began to skew dangerously out of control. A panicked call came from the restroom that the receiving unit had failed just as the target drove into the parking area. The UC, already jittery and unaware, could not be monitored. To make matters worse, the target had arrived as a passenger in an unfamiliar car driven by an unknown companion.

"Give me the frequency. I have a programmable scanner in my car," I blurted across the airwaves. I quickly punched it in, but a tall hill blocked the weak signal. I looked in my rear view mirror at the long string of unmarked cruisers parked behind me along the shoulder of the Parkway, their occupants nervous and eager to strike. We had to move forward a little to pick up the signal. As we inched our way closer, just out of view of the parking area, the scanner finally picked up the conversation.

"One hundred, two hundred..." came the words followed eventually by the cue. The excitement was over in a matter of seconds, and the lives of two young college students changed instantly and dramatically. Their eyes opened wider with disbelief and fright when I simulated the arrest of the UC, seized his hidden handgun, and announced that he was "going Federal" as I hustled him away from the area. This, they learned, was serious business in which they were engaged. The primary target realized that even more when he was eventually convicted on four felony counts of distribution, for which he received a ten-year prison sentence.

Smart View picnic area, having witnessed it all, yawned and once again returned to its sleepy peace.

I had given little thought to what I would cook for Sunday supper, but it would be a treat, concocted from the tastiest ingredients available in my backpack. I was keenly aware that dozens of people surrounding me were enjoying fried chicken, sliced tomatoes, deviled eggs, grilled hamburgers, and every other delicacy associated with a picnic. But, strangely, I was not overwhelmed with covetousness, probably because I was located barely outside the perimeter of the punishing sights and smells that would have otherwise reduced me to a pitiful beggar. Just being in the presence of lovely, peaceful people and within the reach of any passing conversationalist was watermelon enough for me. I was beginning to appreciate good company as much as I did good food.

I was setting up my cookstove in preparation for Sunday's best when I noticed a man and woman walk away from a dwindling family reunion in my direction. A few hours earlier I had chatted with some members of this gathering when I walked into the picnic area.

"It's leftovers and it's not much, but we want you to have it," said Denver and Virginia Atkins of Ferrum, Virginia. "And good luck on your trip."

These were not the kind of people whose inclination toward charity hinged on vain accolades, and they almost seemed embarrassed by my repeated thanks. Before I could learn hardly more than their names, they excused themselves and left a feast: two slices of ham as large as my hands, broccoli casserole, squash casserole, rolls, cherry cobbler, and a two-liter bottle of soda, every drop and morsel of which was consumed at one sitting. But it was the special touch of a spoon, fork, napkins, and a large cup of ice that really touched me. Ice, of all things! Such acts of human kindness, bestowed on my behalf, were beginning to supersede what I thought would be the dominating theme of my trek — an adventuresome immersion in the world of nature.

From the old days, Ranger Mac Dale recalled:

> The big thing while I was chief ranger, the thing that used to make Sam Weems real unhappy, real unhappy — would be for somebody to come in to the office and they had come up from Asheville or down from Washington, and say, "You know, I've been all the way down the parkway, or up the parkway, to here, and I haven't seen a ranger!" And this made Sam so unhappy he didn't know what to do....
> They got to know that this bothered Sam, and word got around, so they'd do it I think whether they had seen one or not.

That observation continued to pester Parkway managers, at least through my years of rangering, and its fallout generally rolled downhill in the form of complaints that we spent too much time in the office. "Read your mail in an overlook." "Write your reports in the field." "Be seen, be visible," came the hue and cry from the heights above.

I had walked five days over a distance of fifty-five miles since I had seen the last ranger. One I met on the trek complained to me that the park no longer employed a seasonal staff of protection rangers. Another complained that the existing staff spent all of their time at refresher training trying to maintain their credentials, many of them required. Budget constraints. Firefighting and homeland security details in other parks. The reasons appeared numerous and valid.

I had just finished my feast and was beginning to repack all the gear I had strewn on the picnic table and the grass around it. A sun near setting and the workaday call of Monday morning had nearly emptied the picnic area. Only a few scattered couples, some with their heads drawing closer together, defied the close of day, as a ranger surprisingly appeared and patrolled slowly through the loop. He drove past, behind and around me and appeared to be unconcerned that I was not associated with a parked vehicle. A good one would have at least stopped and played the role of friendly ranger under the guise of making a closer inspection and some inquiry regarding my camping plans for the night.

This one proved to be no slouch, though, as he circled back for a second pass through the loop and parked in the slip a genuine picnicker would have chosen for my table. We watched each other with suspicious determination as he called in his location to his dispatcher and carefully adjusted his flat hat. This was the second time I had overheard myself being referred to as a "subject," and I hated the sound of it. "Are you Mr. Pegram?" he asked, stepping from his vehicle.

"Now that depends on what he is wanted for," I shot back. "And you don't have to wear that flat hat on my account if you don't want to," I joked, quite under the influence of too much food and drink, hoping to meet a matching sense of humor.

He hesitated momentarily and dropped the hat back in his car. As complete as they make a ranger, they are uncomfortable to wear and unwieldy in a wind or fray. "You don't remember me, do you?" he asked, as he walked slowly in my direction, relieved of the necessity of formality.

"Put your hand over your name tag, and come on over here. It will take me a second, but I think I know you."

The passage of almost twenty years and its effect on hair color could not disguise the unmistakably erect posture and wide smile of Pete Schula. His circuitous ranger career had begun as a seasonal employee at the Peaks of Otter, taken him to several other parks, and had landed him back on the Parkway. It was good to see him again. We had worked together some. He had a level head and, in my opinion, fit the image of what a park ranger should be.

We swapped histories and stories to the brink of darkness. I challenged Pete to get the commercial signs removed that had been erected on park land at the intersection of the Parkway access ramp and U.S. Route 221 back at Adney Gap. He was surprised to learn that the park owned land on the west side of U.S. Route 221. "Check your land use map," I told him. "Parkway planners went to a lot of trouble to purchase that frontage property. Go forth now and impress your boss with this new knowledge."

Pete reciprocated with some useful information for me — a Category 5 hurricane was predicted to hit the coastline somewhere between North Carolina and New Jersey within the next five days. Great. I had dodged the bullet of Hurricane Fabian, an earlier threat that had clobbered Bermuda on September the fifth with Category 3 intensity, which then changed its trajectory northeastward and fizzled out at sea. I had always enjoyed watching great storms bend trees to the ground in the mountains from the safety of a patrol car. But the thought of getting ripped to shreds with that kind of wind and rain did not sound appealing; it was a road down which I would have chosen not to walk. Perhaps I could dodge another bullet.

Courteously avoiding any investigative inquiries, Pete eventually drove off into the prime of his career, and I evaporated to my campsite of the previous night. But sleep did not come easily. Bizarre images and memories inexplicably began to flash through my head like bolts of lightning.

An old woman stared at me from the second-story window of an ancient wooden house that had never known paint. Snow covered the stark, winter landscape, but the roads were passable as I explored one of the many dirt roads that crossed and paralleled the Parkway in Floyd County. I waved to her through the window of my patrol car, but she returned only that sad stare, imprisoned, perhaps, in her own mind. There, but not there, she seemed. That stricken image of her staring from the window still haunted me.

The weather was cold and foggy about 9:30 one night when I located the reported young man — barefoot — wearing only jeans and a long-sleeved thermal shirt. He was sitting on a bench along a trail, in the dark.

"What's your name?" I asked.

"Hercules," he responded with no hesitation, appearing agitated by my presence and the piercing light of my flashlight.

"Okaaay. Where are you from?"

"I am not of this earth." Hmm. This could get tricky, I thought. Be careful with this guy.

I gently coaxed him to the warmth of my patrol car, which seemed to calm his mood. This was not the time to test the volume of my radio with the squelch button. Once, I had nearly launched a poor drunk into a delirium tremens orbit, forgetting I had cranked up the volume for the external speaker. This was not a man that I wanted to further agitate. Somehow, during his meanderings between reality and Greek mythology, I managed to learn his name, the names of his parents, and their address and telephone number.

The dispatcher successfully made telephone contact with his parents, who lived in another state. They demonstrated no willingness to further assist their twenty-three-year-old son but warned that he was prone to abuse PCP (also known as angel dust), suffered from schizophrenia, and was potentially violent. Another ranger, whose patrol car was equipped with a protective cage between the front and rear seats, was requested to assist me in transporting him to a medical facility for evaluation.

Before we could begin the transport, I received a report of a motor vehicle accident involving injuries. It happened more often than one would suppose in a deceptively tranquil park setting — one crisis stacked on top of another. One understaffed year, after having worked a day shift, I was called out just past midnight to investigate a motor vehicle accident. For the next thirty-six hours, I responded to a rolling succession of four more serious accidents, and it took about two weeks to complete the paperwork and regain some semblance of a normal sleep pattern. This night, at least, there were two of us on duty to share the stresses.

The man was examined and released from a local hospital and eventually taken to a Salvation Army shelter for the night. I called his parole officer the next morning and learned that he had been convicted of assault and battery on his father and that a warrant would be issued for his arrest for leaving his state of residence. Hercules, to my knowledge, was never seen on the Parkway again.

The weird zone sometimes encompassed official government correspondence in the form of memoranda. One grammar-challenged supervisor wrote:

> Let me remind you that when you eat lunch, go to the lounge and eat, not in the office. Since the trash containers are not emptied until Monday morning the office has a tendency to smell like [three restaurants are named]. I don't think we should advertise for the different fast food chains especially since we make quite a few visitors contact in this office. The only person authorized to eat in the office are the dispatchers.

Employees finding themselves in higher positions of temporary acting authority sometimes took liberties that their designator might not have done. One acting superintendent, either a victim himself, or perhaps sensing victimization within the organization, had this to say to all Parkway employees, and I commend him for his bravery:

> Gossip almost always does more harm than good! A message from the Director about "the snake that poisons everybody" is included on the reverse side of this memorandum for your consideration when next you are beset with the urge to pass on some spicy bit of information.

But the most hilarious and serious of all memoranda cannot match the one that scared me the most, issued during my rookie year. The subject of Informational Memorandum No. 78–25 was, "Nationwide Post-Attack Registration of Federal Employees," and read, in part:

> If you are prevented from going to your regular place of work or prevented from reporting to an emergency location because of an enemy attack, go to the nearest post office, ask for a Federal Employee Emergency Registration Card (CSC Form 600), fill it out, address and mail it. The Postal Service will attempt to deliver the registration card to us or our representative.... You should obtain and complete the registration card as soon after enemy attack as possible but not until you are reasonably sure where you will be staying for a few days. If you change your address after you have sent in a card, get a new one and send it in.

I shall opine no further on this subject other than to thank the Postal Service for always being there for me.

Late one night, I was patrolling along a section of the Parkway known to be frequented by deer. After ten years of rangering, the only reportable damage I had inflicted on a patrol car resulted from collisions with two unlikely objects.

The first collision was with a malfunctioning electric door, which crushed the bar light and spotlight mounted on the roof of my patrol car as I attempted to drive into the basement of a Federal building. That story ended happily when the General Services Administration agreed to pay for the damages.

The second collision involved poultry and destroyed my grill and a head-light. The report of a motor vehicle accident on the Parkway came to me while making a courtesy visit to the Maggie Valley (N.C.) Police Department. I had always wanted to blow through that little tourist town with lights and siren, and the opportunity had finally presented itself. Just past the point where I merged into a single lane to begin the steep climb up U.S. Route 19 to Soco Gap, I slowed a bit at the sight of a woman walking toward her mailbox. A flock of chickens was following her, and one bold rooster made a fatal decision to take flight and cross the road in front of me. Bam. He disintegrated in an explosion of feathers, and I continued driving, justifying the emergency in front of me over the stern reflection of a woman shaking her fist at me in the rear view mirror. For several days, the chief ranger playfully threatened to bring me before a board of inquiry and, thereafter, often asked me to retell the story of the infamous "Rooster Wreck."

Somehow, though, I had never hit a deer but had left a plentiful number of skid marks on the pavement trying to avoid them. On one particular night, the sight of three large does standing ahead on a grassy embankment was true cause to decelerate. In the confusion of headlights, their movements were always unpredictable. As I approached, two of them darted into the woods, as they should have. But one of them ran toward the road and paralleled my course until I came to a complete stop. Then, in one gigantic leap, this magnificent lady tried to jump over the top of the patrol car and landed on her belly sprawled across the hood. I could not believe my eyes, as she kicked and flailed and snorted and finally rolled off the front of the car, collapsing but not breaking the spring-loaded hood ornament.

I just sat there and stared in disbelief. Without a video camera, nobody would ever believe what caused the damage I was sure had been sustained. Fortunately there was none, only smears of saliva mixed with hair sullied the shiny white paint. The chief ranger would have surely bitten his smoking pipe in half had I proposed the preposterous tale of the "Disoriented Deer" to explain more dollars out of his tight budget.

The message had been brief and clear from the assistant superintendent. A woman from the regional office was flying up from Atlanta on a commercial flight. I was to meet her at the local airport, receive from her a sealed package, take it directly to the office of an attorney in Salem, Virginia, open it in the presence of the attorney, give its contents to the attorney, and obtain a signed receipt for the contents. I was specifically instructed not to open the package until the attorney was present. Sounded like exciting James Bond stuff to me. My ego was inflated to be entrusted with such a solemn mission. I only had two questions.

"Who is this person I am supposed to meet, and how will I recognize her?"

"Never mind that," came his reply. "She'll have no trouble finding you with that uniform you're wearing. But she should be wearing a black pantsuit."

At the appointed arrival time of her flight, I was standing near the gate, my image as an international spy rudely tarnished from being repeatedly mistaken for airport security by a steady procession of travelers asking me for directions to the baggage claim area. As forecast, a woman wearing a black pantsuit, carrying a package, walked pertly up to me, shook my hand, and said, "I have no idea what this is all about, but I am supposed to give this to a ranger named Tim Pegram. And it appears from your name tag that is you."

What I had not been told was that this lady was drop-dead gorgeous, just like in the James Bond movies. My cover already blown, I fumbled for appropriate words. "Do you need some lunch or need to be taken somewhere?"

"No, I have to get back to Atlanta. Thanks anyway." And as quickly as she had appeared, she turned and disappeared back onto the same plane that had brought her to Roanoke while I stood there stunned and emasculated.

The mysterious package, I later discovered at the attorney's office, contained a government check in the amount of $125,640 that was payment for some land the Parkway had purchased. When I delivered the receipt back to Mr. Stokes, I questioned the secrecy of the whole matter. "Because at your salary, I wanted to make sure you didn't run off with all that money," he answered with a wagging finger and a glint in his eye, insinuating less emphasis on the money. For a rookie ranger, at least, it beat the heck out of inspecting fire extinguishers and servicing traffic counters for the day.

Incident codes had been developed for every conceivable circumstance and there existed many which I neither hoped nor planned to use. But out of sheer boredom I decided one day to run a sleep check on headquarters and document what I truly thought to be a unique observation. Incident Code 80–20–03 (Resource Management Incident-Monitoring-Wildlife) was employed, and I quote from my report:

> At approximately 1030 hours on 1-7-88 I observed an immature herring gull (*Larus argentatus*) perched on the interpretive easel at Pounding Mill OL. Weather conditions at the time were heavy snowfall and temperature of 10° F. This ranger had never observed a gull in the district and the sighting appeared to be unusual considering the usual habitat of this species.

I honestly, honestly did not discover the following account until the year 2004, given by my much-earlier predecessor, Ranger Mac Dale:

Eloise and I were coming up to the last Ranger conference, Blue Ridge Parkway type, that I attended before going in the service early in [World] war two. As we drove across Rocky Knob it had snowed just ahead of us so that there was complete coverage and we were the first car over this. And it's well that I remembered the road sufficiently or I'd have had trouble. And it was in fog. And here was a seagull alongside of the road. He got off, and circled away and came back again. I couldn't believe it, but here he was, a seagull in a foggy snowstorm on the mountain[!]

19

Weathering Isabel

"And everybody knows ... the big fish won't bite on a
bluebird day."
—*Ava's Man*, by Rick Bragg

Becky Lee, a reporter with the *Kernersville* (N.C.) *News*, headlined her concluding story of my trek as "a walk through memory lane." My fifteenth day on
the trail, except for the discovery of two sets of keys along the side of the road,
would have been written off as uneventful had it not been sprinkled with pleasant memories of other days—here a pond, there a stream in which I had once
stocked brook trout; a little craft shop, whose owner once told me he made more
money operating it on weekends than he could make all year teaching school; a
secret place near the park where, each year, to the delight of Patty, I gathered a
branch or two of mountain winterberry for the Christmas mantle; a pottery
shop whose owner never locked the door and was rarely seen on the premises,
but used an honor system of payment to inspire the better nature of his patrons;
and a log cabin and Christmas tree farm that I dreamed of owning someday.

By the time the morning fog had burned off, leaving in its wake a still muggy,
late summer day, the Parkway and I had left Franklin County behind and were
now playing hopscotch with Floyd County's extended border with Patrick
County, the ancestral home of my mother's side of the family. In the lower
foothills region to the east stand hundreds of mailboxes and tombstones—monuments to the living and the dead — bearing the surnames of Corn, Smith, Doss,
Cunningham, Hall, Shelton, and Mays. The Blue Ridge, like a gigantic, purple
wall, seemed to have abruptly halted the westward migration of my people. Only
Great-Aunt Maggie Dell Smith and her family are known to have breached this
elevation barrier into Floyd County, where they lived only a short time in poverty
before migrating to Pennsylvania. Grateful for the genetic aberration responsi-

ble for causing me to become a lover of higher places, I straddled "home" on both sides of the center line.

Monday's walk was through a section of Parkway fairly devoid of any significant landmarks. Only two overlooks had been constructed in an eleven-mile stretch between Smart View picnic area and Tuggle Gap. A quiet land of peaceful farms and neighbors, it was patrolled less frequently, being situated at the southern tip of what was once known as the Roanoke Valley District. I always had to make a conscious effort to note the passage of every milepost marker while on patrol in that area, just in case my exact location suddenly became a critical issue. Other rangers, wrecker operators, and EMS response units were generally not pleased with a margin of error of plus or minus two miles whenever they were trying to find my location in a hurry. But one particular landmark emerged as a center-of-the-earth point of reference, at least for seasonal ranger Jeff Swortzel and myself.

The maintenance employees who once operated out of the Rocky Knob ranger station were led by a man self-sworn to the highest standards of park maintenance. The facilities in his district were always immaculately clean. Guide rails were always neatly trimmed. Beautiful, stone-lined ditches were never clogged with leaves and sediment. Fencing never sagged. In his district, I would have guessed the old-timers to have coined the name "The Scenic" before the Blue Ridge Parkway was given its official name. L.T. Nolen was his name.

L.T. was no landmark of a man, standing short in stature and mild-mannered in disposition, at least over the radio. But he was not a man to be riled face-to-face, and any man venturing a horse trade with him would have been well advised to have employed the services of a shrewd agent. His mother lived in a modest farmhouse along that sleepy, aforementioned stretch of Parkway. I never knew her name. She was just L.T. Nolen's mother to me, and that was all I really needed to know. Ranger Swortzel, if I remember correctly, first began the practice of using L.T. Nolen's mother's house as a point of reference when trying to tell me where he had seen this buck deer cross the road or where that motorcycle had crashed. This practice proved quite useful, but in our youthful delight with the job and each other's company, we took our orientation device way beyond practicality. Soon, directions to places as far away as the capital city of Denmark were prefaced with the line, "Do you know where L.T. Nolen's mother lives?" Nobody in our presence could ever keep a straight face when we did it, and we laughed hilariously at its every execution. My, how those days of really loving a job sped by so quickly.

As I slowly walked past her house again, I tipped my hat in her direction. But there was no car in the driveway. The boxwood bushes in front of the house were overgrown, forming a nearly impenetrable barrier that blocked the step up to the front porch. The house looked empty. How would rangers of the future ever find their way, I thought, if she were gone?

I stepped into the shelter of a little restaurant near the Parkway, just as a stormy gale blew through Tuggle Gap. The young waitress gave me an odd look, as I clutched unyieldingly to the menu after ordering only a house salad and a soda. "I'll need to order in stages, to see how much my stomach can handle," I explained. The imagined capacity for consumption, I had previously learned, never quite matched the limits of a shrunken stomach.

She and the cook, both of whom kept peeking around the corner for a look at me, eventually understood, I think, my mission and process and politely accommodated my gluttonous progression to a "Big G Burger" (named after nearby Rock Castle Gorge), a grilled cheese sandwich, and one final soda. I had not enjoyed such misery in several days—hold the pickles next time, please. My waitress bore such a striking resemblance to Scarlett Johanssen of *The Horse Whisperer* fame that I had to ask if she had seen the movie. She had not, and I hoped the generous tip sufficiently compensated for all of my trouble and the compliment inspired her to see the movie. Like "Grace MacLean," eighteen-year-old Megan Spangler seemed also to be standing at an important crossroads in her life.

When I stepped back up onto the Parkway, the skies were clearing to a brilliant blue. The storm had blown out the warm, stagnant air, replacing it with a brisk wind and at least a fifteen degree drop in temperature. I chose a place to camp that night that I quickly rated the most panoramic to date and randomly preset an early bedtime to coincide with the appearance of the eighth star in the afterglow. Instead, I continued to watch the eternities unfold and sparkle through the airy windows of my tent and finally fell asleep with their count somewhere in the hundreds. Neither my sleepy eyes nor my meager intellect could fathom their billions.

I was awake before dawn, gazing into a new, twinkling sky, whose players had migrated from east to west in a timeless repetition of earth's rotation and revolution. I watched them, every single one, until they all disappeared, snuffed by the emerging dawn, until our own fiery sun broke its first rays on yonder ridge. I timed my visit to the Rocky Knob ranger station perfectly to visit a few old colleagues before their work day was old enough to scatter them in every direction. The news was varied and voluminous, most heartwarming of which was the assurance that L.T. Nolen's mother was still living in the same house. She had finally permitted her son to install some modern conveniences in it to make her life more comfortable. The time was 11:15 A.M. before I realized that I was standing in the way of important government business and hit the road, minus the weight of two sets of keys.

The sky was clear enough to have spent the day in its entirety at the Saddle Overlook. Two hawk watchers were setting up lounge chairs to do that very thing, as an invisible force bucked me from its lazy, lofty perch.

"You had your eight seconds on another day," she neighed, rearing on her hind legs in angry defiance. Bruised and dusty, I picked myself up and hobbled away. In a ditch, I found a shoe which had been thrown by the chestnut mare. Forgivingly, I hung it, round and shiny, adorned with chrome and spokes, on a fence post and continued walking, a little broken myself. The minutes rolled into years and then one day, while still wandering, I felt the touch of warm velvet on the back of my arm. The chestnut mare had caught up with me and nudged me with her nose. "Your ride is not over. Let me help with the story," she whinnied gently and, with lowered head, invited me once again upon her back. Promising to never buck or spur each other again, together we now reverently rode.

If the lowly gnat is to be distinguished as the signature insect of the Parkway, the groundhog is certainly deserving of the title of signature mammal. Some voters might disagree with that choice and select the black bear, who appears and disappears about as quickly as one of those low-flying fighter jets, piloted by mavericks bent on scaring the daylights out of park rangers. Other voters might select the white-tailed deer, whose population has certainly risen dramatically in some areas of the park. But the groundhog stands at attention along every mile of the Parkway, munching grass and nodding at every passing vehicle. Unflinchingly dutiful in their unofficial role as welcoming ambassadors, they rarely budge from their positions, inches away from large, rolling vehicles. But slow down that behemoth of plastic and steel to take their picture and they, along with their transparent bravery, vanish instantly into a nearby secret burrow.

Every farmer attempting to rid his property of this wary critter knows it is best stalked with a rifle equipped with a good scope; its eyesight is comparable to that of a wild turkey. Removing the sense of smell from the equation, one has a better chance of seeing a bear on foot than a groundhog. I had walked 170 miles down the Parkway and had seen neither.

But there he sat, sunning on a rock ledge, less than six feet from me as I quietly rounded a sharp curve. He reminded me of a bobcat I once surprised while patrolling within a gated section of the Parkway. A soft snow had muffled the sound of my approach, as I surprised him standing in the middle of the road. In both cases, these animals attempted inescapable retreats up steep, rocky slopes. Because the groundhog had scared me as much as I had him, I gave him all the room he required when he found the uphill door closed and reversed his escape back in my direction in a rippling flurry of dust and fur. The bobcat, however, had trapped himself on a rock ledge about twelve feet above me. Safe within the confines of my patrol car, I teasingly drove underneath him and rolled down the window. Screaming a hissing cry of defeat, he descended to the ground in a single leap and bolted over the embankment on the opposite side of the road.

Slightly past midday, I stopped to chat with two mower operators who were eating their lunch. Isabel, they said, was the name of the hurricane about which Ranger Schula had warned me.

I would have never sidetracked a good mile off my route to visit the Rocky Knob Cabins had they not advertised a "centrally located bath house" in the Parkway's travel directory I was toting. Though I had no plans to spend the night there, and having learned that all things in life are negotiable, I at least hoped to purchase the service of a shower and laundry, of both of which I was in dire need.

Stanley Abbott intended the cabins, constructed in the early 1940s, to be a pilot project for more "rough-it" camps that would provide accommodations to hikers along an "extensive trail system paralleling the Parkway." His vision to build such a system never materialized, and the Rocky Knob Cabins were eventually upgraded enough to be rented as vacation cabins to the public through a concessionaire. But hurrah to the fact that almost 75 percent of the Parkway was now closely paralleled by either the Appalachian Trail or North Carolina's Mountains-to-Sea Trail! I at least owed Mr. Abbott a courtesy visit to the focal point of his vision for thinking about guys like me.

I concluded a $2.00 transaction with the manager of the Rocky Knob Cabins for the purchase of a hot shower that included a surprise bonus of a wash rag and a bar of soap. But the laundry facilities, she explained, were not available to the public.

This was not the rustic cow town of the Old West that it appeared to be, and I was no longer the handsome, mysterious cowboy who had ridden into town from yesteryear. A young boy running from the livery stable would not take the reins of my horse before I could tie her to the hitching post. Crusty women with raspy voices, wearing long, frilly dresses, would not pour buckets of hot water into my tub, while I sank embarrassedly deeper into the soapy bubbles upon their every entry, still wearing my hat. The barber would lock his door before I could ask for a shave and a haircut. The crowd in the saloon would ignore my presence when I stepped through the doorway, and the bartender would refuse me a cold sarsaparilla. And no amount of negotiation, money, or name-dropping would coax the proprietor of this establishment into the use of her laundry. Polite in defeat, I accepted the cold, hard fact that my long detour would yield a clean body, but that I would ride out of this hard town still wearing dirty clothes. Before I could tip my hat to the place, a simple, single event uncannily rolled in and rewrote the script.

As I stepped from the doorway of the tiny office, a car drove into the small parking area. The plastic spoiler underneath the front of the car had broken loose and was dragging the ground, utterly destroying an otherwise peaceful afternoon. It was a make of vehicle that I had promised myself never to purchase because it looked "too retired," and the elderly couple riding in it fit the stereotype perfectly. As the noisy car approached the office and parked right in front of me, I realized that I was probably the youngest, most capable, and certainly the dirtiest choice of the whole bunch to help them with their problem. I asked the manager, who had stepped outside to check on the commotion, if I could borrow a screwdriver. I had no idea that the Rocky Knob Cabins had been a favorite getaway destination for several years for the Paynes from Gastonia, North Carolina, as I crawled underneath their car. The job was simple enough to make a poor mechanic appear gifted, and after its completion, I was more interested in receiving a shower than the couple's grateful thanks.

As I slung my pack over one shoulder and turned in the direction of the bathhouse, the manager, bearing a much sunnier countenance, stepped my way and whispered, "Listen. Since you used to be a park ranger, and since you know Pete Schula, that's good enough for me. Let me walk up here and show you how to use the washer and dryer. No charge." Like General George Pickett, who later supposed to an inquirer that the Union Army had something to do with his failed charge at Gettysburg, I, too, supposed that the mere act of helping these loyal customers, obviously, had something to do with a kindness boomeranged.

An hour later found me clean, wearing my rain pants and rain coat, sitting on the front stoop of a rustic service building, waiting for both sets of my clothes to complete the spin cycle. I was writing in my journal when Mrs. Payne walked past and thanked me again for helping repair their car. She insisted that I occupy a third rocking chair on the front porch of their cabin while my clothes tumbled in the dryer.

The Paynes and I shared bits of our lives with each other. Mr. Payne was a retired school teacher and Wesleyan minister. Both were thrilled to learn that I had worked as a park ranger a few short months at Crowders Mountain State Park, located near their home. Mrs. Payne, like many mothers I met on my trek, could not wait to tell her son what I was doing. Mr. Payne, upon learning of my dinner plans at the Mabry Mill Restaurant, informed me that I would never make their closing time of six o'clock and invited me to join them for dinner at a local inn. I was as delighted to continue our pleasant conversation over dinner as I was to avoid the hard climb back out to the Parkway. For a brief time, the differences in our ages and circumstances permitted me to become their adopted son and they my adopted parents. Childhood and adolescence passed in less than four hours, and in the tradition of the ages, I once again experienced the thrill of striking out on my own and they the anguish of watching me leave. This time, though, I knew how they felt.

I stepped into the lobby of the inn to make a call home to Patty. There, displayed in bold colors on the giant screen of a television set, was a map of the eastern half of the United States. A large, red, squiggly-looking symbol denoted the current location of Hurricane Isabel, just off the coast of North Carolina. Behind it was a solid red line, from whence it had come. A dotted red line ahead of it marked its projected course — straight in my direction.

I was standing at the front door of the Mabry Mill Restaurant the next morning, forty-five minutes before it opened, wearing my gloves for the first time on the trip. The temperature felt like it had dropped within a degree of the first frost of the season, and I was excited by the prospect of cooler weather and

more colorful scenery. Before the doors of the restaurant opened, I was joined
by a small army of elderly people who, by all indications of their nervous excitement and conversation, were about to experience the apparent highlight of their
day — a hearty breakfast. The combined smells of every breakfast delicacy imaginable, leaking from its locked interior into the cold, morning air, could have
easily provoked a less civilized crowd of shivering, impatient customers to riot
and force an early opening.

A pure miracle had made it possible that the restored gristmill, sawmill, and
blacksmith shop of Ed and Lizzie Mabry still stood quietly nearby, arguably the
most photographed feature along the entire Parkway. Sam Weems recounted
the story of its near demise in the early days:

> I give Mac Dale, my first chief ranger, credit for saving that mill. We had an
> agreement with the States of Virginia and North Carolina that they would clear
> all buildings off the right-of-way before they would deliver it. Anyway it was
> their responsibility to get rid of all buildings on the right-of-way. Well, Mac Dale
> went by one day and here were some people beginning to tear down the mill.
> And Mac got on the radio real quick and called in and he said, "They are about
> to tear the Mabry Mill down," and I said, "What in the world are they doing?"
> And he said, "They said they are hired by the Highway Department." And I said,
> "Tell them to stop this minute," and I got on the phone and called Richmond,
> and they said, "We are following what you told us to do—clear the right-of-
> way." And I said, "Well, for gosh sake, don't clear this one. We have got to leave
> this." Well, this kind of thing — I could probably cite other instances, but it is
> about the same all over and I said, "Will you give me authority to pull them off
> it?" So he did, and so we saved the mill, but it was just about gone. Had it not
> been for Mac Dale coming along there at the right time with the right interest,
> we would have lost it.

Somehow I survived the stampede of humanity when the doors of the
restaurant were finally opened. The breakfast menu combinations were dazzling, and I made the typical mistake of ordering more than I could eat — one
scrambled egg, three pancakes, two patties of sausage, a slice of orange, and a
cold glass of milk. Taking a breather from the feast, I checked the Parkway map
and realized that I had crossed its fifth fold and was about sixteen miles ahead
of my initially projected mileage. My waitress stopped abruptly at my table,
eyed my backpack, placed her hands on her hips, and asked, "Are you the guy I
read about in the *Floyd Press* who is hiking the whole Parkway?" Upon hearing
my answer and in a way that only a lady named Loretta can do, she announced
to everyone within earshot, "Hey, everybody. Guess what this fella…"

I could not escape quickly enough and wrapped a leftover pancake and
sausage patty in a napkin. It was too early in the morning to answer that many
"Have you seen a bear?" questions proffered by that many people looking for
cheap entertainment. Back onto the more tranquil safety of the Parkway, I felt
confident and refreshed. Every stitch of clothing I was wearing or carrying was
clean. I was freshly showered and had spoiled myself by eating three restaurant
meals within the last ten miles. Being homeless, I thought, was not too bad if

one were properly equipped with credit and phone cards and a knack for finding proper shower and laundry facilities.

The skies were perfectly clear, but strong crosswinds from the east were already beginning to make passage through some of the exposed gaps a tricky game of remaining in contact with my hat. I wondered, too, how much this wind would have swayed the imaginary suspension bridge that was never built 750 feet above the Dan River and if I would have had the nerve to venture across its 1,000-foot length in such conditions. At this point, the Parkway would have offered a stupendous view into the deep Dan River Gorge, where it forms a nearly complete loop around two oddly-shaped spires known as the Pinnacles of Dan. At a planning hearing held in 1934 at Baltimore, Maryland, where the proposed route of the Parkway was being debated, Kyle Weeks of Floyd, Virginia, referred to this area as "possibly the most outstanding scenic spot in the eastern part of the United States." R.E. Cox, a member of the American Society of Engineers, stated, "It is the opinion of one traveler who has seen the Swiss Alps, the Peruvian Andes, and the Rockies of our own United States, that the view of this gorge and the Pinnacles from this point is the most impressive he has ever seen." Whether or not these assessments had been overstated I would never know. The powers interested in damming the river for hydroelectric development unbelievably prevailed over those interested in its preservation, and the Parkway was routed a mile away, the tragedy quietly hidden from view.

The Paynes, en route to their home back in flatter lands, stopped to say hello. Like my own good mother did when I was a boy, she had worried about me sleeping out in the cold, telling me they had been forced to turn on the heater in their cabin that morning. Sometime during the afternoon, a large hayfield on Parkway Left opened an expansive view into the lower regions of my literal motherland of Patrick County. The shape of a distant cluster of smaller mountains to the east almost went unnoticed, until I gradually realized that I was looking across an invisible border into North Carolina — at Hanging Rock State Park! A few miles beyond it lay the land of my birth, upbringing, and a large lawn and vegetable garden that Patty had agreed to mow and tend for a few weeks.

The facilities at Groundhog Mountain seemed the perfect location to cook supper. A plentiful supply of tap water was available from a little comfort station and picnic area. A steady trickle of visitors stopping to view an assorted display of rail fence designs would keep me company. And for the umpteenth time a mother would tell me she could not wait to tell her son what I was doing.

The lee side of an observation tower, perched on the crest of the mountain, proved to be an excellent barrier to a steady wind and became my makeshift, outdoor kitchen. The addition of the leftover sausage patty from breakfast converted my standard macaroni and cheese mush into a gourmet dinner. Or so I pretended.

The sudden, explosive ignition of a diesel engine just below the crest of the mountain and barely out of sight of the tower launched me from a post-dinner snooze on the grass and sent startled visitors scurrying back to their cars. None of them lingered for my explanatory theory that the Parkway's signature mammal, whom I had so rudely disturbed from his sleep the day before, had exacted his revenge on me at his namesake of Groundhog Mountain. Unaware of my turnabout game of fear with some of the Parkway's animals, they probably just assumed that a sensor switch had started an engine that pumped water to a remote day-use area at the top of a mountain. Silly, silly visitors. I had never been surprised that so many of them required assistance after running out of fuel or locking their keys in their cars.

The sky was still sunny, but an ominous wall of clouds was forming in the eastern sky, as I shook off the scary groundhog and continued the daily quest for the perfect camp for the night. Just past Pilot Mountain Overlook, I found it. I was now close enough to Hanging Rock State Park to recognize, with the naked eye, its rocky namesake feature and Moore's Wall. To the south, within the same frame, stood another jewel of the North Carolina state park system — Pilot Mountain State Park — with its ancient, distinguishable dome. Between both of these parks stood Sauratown Mountain, from whose back I had scratched clusters of precious quartz crystals — diamonds, we had called them as Boy Scouts. From all of their heights I had gazed upon the Blue Ridge upon which I now camped — as a boy and as a man — and had dreamed. Now, from my own dream, I gazed back at *them* and slept well that night.

Early the next morning, I was reading an interpretive display by the restored cabin of Orelena Hawks Puckett when a few Parkway maintenance men stopped to talk. Her incredible life began in 1837 and ended in 1939. None of her own twenty-four children had lived beyond infancy. But as a midwife, she had delivered over one thousand babies after the age of fifty! The Parkway had been built so close to her cabin that it could have served as her driveway. Like a determined young boy walking a compass bearing straight to the Hanging Rock, I felt a little guilty intruding across the curtilage of her once private property, somewhere between an imaginary clothesline and a garden plot. Still, I was thankful that her story, and those of many other hardy natives of the Blue Ridge, would be retold to millions and never forgotten.

The men told me that Hurricane Isabel was moving at 14 mph and was about to hit Ocracoke Island along the coast of North Carolina with 105 mph winds. It was then expected to move inland and head straight for Roanoke. I could already see the edge of the swirling mass of clouds off to the east. To the south, the skies remained blue, offering an optimistic illusion that I just might be able to scoot around the thing if I kept walking in that direction. But the winds grew stronger, and the clouds drew closer.

A southbound bicyclist flew past me, only to return in a few minutes to tell me that the crosswinds at Orchard Gap were too strong for him to maneuver through it. He also mentioned that a gas station and sandwich shop was located there, just off the Parkway. There was no turning back for me; I was pretty sure I could fight my way to some more real food.

I watched, with some bewilderment, the hurried, worried customers as they made last-minute purchases in preparation for the storm. A man with a ham radio stopped long enough to tell me that Virginia Beach had just been pounded and was without power and that five inches of rain was predicted in our immediate area. While he filled every five-gallon can that he owned with gasoline, I calmly munched on a hot ham and cheese sandwich and sipped on a soda. A lady from the lower lands of Tobaccoville, N.C. told me that the schools back home had closed for the day and that she and her husband had driven up on the mountain to ride out the hurricane with her elderly father. I finished a bag of potato chips, saved a mint for later consumption, and began working on a thick, chocolate ice cream bar. My only immediate worry was walking past a long row of colorfully painted whirligig ducks planted in the grass between me and the Parkway. Their wooden wings were now spinning so furiously in the high wind that I joked to the owner of the place that we would all be killed if just one of them actually took flight. I must have looked like a war correspondent calmly taking notes in the midst of a major battle.

Just before reaching Fancy Gap, I stopped to take a picture of cloud formations I had never seen before. The winds were now coming out of the northwest, dragging concentric bands of stormy clouds in long, swirling arcs across a now completely cloudy sky. At the Parkway maintenance building in the gap, Lester Wood, in the tradition of L.T. Nolen, was diligently preparing his men and equipment for the worst scenario. Trucks were being readied. Chain saws were being sharpened. And the skies were growing darker.

The wind speed increased dramatically when the rain began, and I used the shelter of their facility to carefully zip, snap, button, and secure every protection my rain gear had to offer. Rick Baker, an old ranger colleague who had converted to the maintenance division, stopped to chat earlier in the day and offered me the shelter of his home for the evening. But it was located fifty miles in the wrong direction and, at that point, I thought I could outrun the storm and declined the invitation. As I stepped out into the horizontal rain, I wondered if that decision had been a mistake.

The wind blows through Fancy Gap when it blows nowhere else on the earth, and by the time I reached the Interstate 77 overpass, I was being battered by rain and wind speeds that I had never before experienced. To the truck drivers passing underneath I must have looked like a drunk crawling his way back home, crouched as low to the pavement as I could bend, holding on to my hat like it was my last earthly possession. Safely across it, I decided to disregard the "don't try this at home" warning and attempted something I had seen on television. With my backpack still attached to me, I faced the wind, extended my arms to each side and tried to fall forward. I could not. Without a wind gauge to measure it, I could not be sure of its speed, but I felt like I was seventeen again, standing in the seat of my convertible MG Midget doing 70 mph.

Things began to get a little scary when the wind ripped off my tightly secured pack cover, sending me tumbling through a hayfield trying to catch it. At every breach in the forest thereafter, where an open field or pasture permitted the wind to gust the heaviest, I kept a cautious eye to the northwest for flying pigs and chickens.

As dusk approached, I began a mental debate on whether it would be safer to pitch my tent in an open area or in a more protected, wooded area. The lack of six more hands to pitch it ruled out the former, and the danger of falling trees ruled out the latter. A vacant, summer cabin within sight of the Parkway tempted me enough to stop and seriously consider breaking into it for the night. Although it would have livened up the story with another chapter, I did not relish the thought of having to call Patty from the Carroll County jail for her assistance in helping me post bail. I had walked five miles south of Fancy Gap when darkness finally forced me to make a decision.

None of the trees above me appeared dead or broken. A sturdy stand of timber north and west of me broke the wind somewhat at ground level, but the canopy above me roared and swayed like an angry ocean. Forfeiting a cooked supper, I made a meal out of a handful of cashews and dried apples. Tucked within the dry walls of my tent, I was surprised to find that so much of my clothing and gear had remained dry. Despite the din, overwhelming fatigue and a special prayer for safety brought sleep sooner than normal.

Sometime during the night, I was jolted from my sleep by an aftershock that caused my head to bounce up off my improvised pillow made from a stuff bag filled with clothing. Something very large had landed very near my tent. With the storm still raging, I opted to save an inspection until daylight.

Sometime around three o'clock in the morning, I woke again. The wind and rain had stopped. Peace had returned to the mountain, and I drifted back to sleep again. The sound of a chain saw buzzing in the distance woke me a third time at daybreak. As I poked my head through the unzipped vestibule of my tent into the calm of a clear, blue day, I discovered the top of a tree lying a foot from the head wall of my tent.

Thank you, Isabel, for a most interesting date. You sort of reminded me of a girl I dated only once during high school. Like her, we will not be seeing each other again.

20

Crossing Paths

"Sometimes he thought he heard voices in the distance, but
they were faint and might have been imagination, as when
one sleeps near a river and all night thinks he hears conversation pitched too low for understanding."
—*Cold Mountain*, by Charles Frazier

The calm had been worth the storm, a myopic observer might have concluded at my makeshift breakfast table near Milepost 205, where clearing skies
set another sublimity record and breezy eddies lingered in the wake of Isabel.
How many times in my life had I commented to someone that I had never seen
the skies more beautiful than following the passage of a mighty storm?

But her winds had stripped the trees of most of their leafy foliage, denying
them the opportunity to flutter in brilliance at the upcoming annual color parade.
Enough pine needles had been plucked from their resinous footings and crushed
on the roadway to remind one of either an aromatic candle shop or a liquid disinfectant cleanser, depending upon one's position on the couth-crude meter.
The needle rocked wildly back and forth trying to gauge my own reaction. Broken limbs and branches of every size were scattered all over the ground. The
wind had broken out the top halves of trees more so than leveling entire trees
themselves. South of me, I only encountered one that had actually fallen across
the Parkway, a huge white pine. Lester Wood's top-notch crew, whose chain saws
were probably responsible for my early morning wake-up call, had already
removed it. But I would later learn that Isabel's winds had found many more
weak trees along the Parkway north of me and had so ravished the Shenandoah
National Park that it had to be closed temporarily. Hurricanes, usually down-
graded to tropical storms by the time they reach the mountains, never bring
good news to the Appalachian region, sometimes triggering a secondary punch

of deadly mud and rock slides on steep slopes and flash floods in narrow valleys. Isabel, for the most part, had just made a big mess.

By noon, I had crossed the sixth fold of my map and was well into a warm, sunny afternoon when a mare and her colt took an interest in me and strolled up to the fence next to the Parkway. Both were spoiled with a good rubdown and greener grass from my side of the fence.

A freshly mowed hayfield near the entrance to the Parkway's developing Blue Ridge Music Center proved to be a perfect place to spread and dry my gear. But the hot sun and an annoying battalion of nervous grasshoppers cut short a nap that would have otherwise lasted much longer.

I had moved into territory less familiar and could not remember any details of an upcoming intersection with a major highway. The prospect of finding an ice cream sandwich within a reasonable walking distance of the Parkway seemed a proper reward for a man who had just spent the night with a hurricane. I had used similar logic back in college. If I scored well on an examination, I congratulated myself with a chocolate sundae at the student center. If I scored poorly, I soothed the pain with — yes — a chocolate sundae. On any day that I did not receive a test result, well, I often found some other reason to treat myself to a chocolate sundae. The imagined taste of an ice cream sandwich could not be shaken.

When I reached the intersection of the Parkway and Va. Route 89, I strained my eyes and ears in both directions, detecting no visible sign of nearby refreshments. The State of Virginia had secured enough right-of-way in this area to preserve the natural scenery as far as I could see, and steep grades in both directions stymied any thoughts of striking out on a detour of unknown length.

The bridge carrying this road over the Parkway was deserving of such protection. It was the only double-arch bridge constructed on its entire length and, like so many others, had been constructed by the skilled hands of gifted Italian and Spanish masons using native stone. National Park Service historian Richard Quin echoed the sentiments of most observers that "the most distinctive architectural features of the Blue Ridge Parkway are its outstanding collection of bridges." I was in the process of enjoying every single one of them at a pace they so richly deserved.

The Parkway must have crossed Chestnut Creek a half-dozen times before I realized I was walking past several opportunities to take a full-blown bath. I was less than a mile from the Virginia–North Carolina border, and it only felt appropriate to enter "home" clean and shaven. I felt like a Mormon pioneer taking a bath in the Platte River along the plains of Nebraska. It was to be my only complete immersion into a cold, mountain stream on the entire trek. Discreetly hidden from the public view under one of the Parkway bridges, I still worried about womenfolk stopping to take a picture, trout fishermen bent on mischief, and park rangers with a twisted definition of disorderly conduct. But the clean feeling that followed this outdoor bath in the wild was worth every bit of the risk and goose bumps the size of my fist.

On September 19, 2003, I reached the state line and celebrated the occasion by taking my usual self-portrait. The location is at Milepost 216.9.

I reached the state line at 4:30 P.M. and celebrated the occasion by taking my usual self-portrait — backpack propped against the Parkway sign, walking stick stuck in the ground beside it, and fedora, hung like a balanced saucer in an old variety show, on top of it. My camera was not equipped with a timer, so I had to be creative in the absence of other visitors.

In 1749, Peter Jefferson had crossed my path at this very location while surveying the boundary line between these two states. Nineteen days earlier, I had crossed paths with his son, Thomas, at Milepost Zero. Behind me I had crossed paths with many people of past and present, common and famous. Ahead, I would cross the paths of many more.

At a restaurant in Glendale Springs, N.C., I would meet a young waiter by the name of Jared Yelton, who had just completed a bicycle trip across the United States. Two years earlier, he had backpacked the entire Appalachian Trail and offered me several logical reasons why I should not, as I intended to soon do, walk it from north to south.

At another restaurant, near Benge Gap, I would meet Athishdam and Meena Tharmaratnam — he a native of Sri Lanka and recently retired from the World Bank and she a native of India. I was as fascinated in meeting them as they were with me, and we could not take enough pictures of each other — trophies of each other's own exotic safari. Their plan to drive all the way up the Parkway and on to their home near Washington, D.C., that same day concerned me. "Spend a night at the Peaks of Otter Lodge," I urged them, and proceeded to describe to them in words what an actual visit could only tell. As we departed each other's company, I hoped I had convinced this lovely couple to make the right decision.

Near Milepost 285 I would cross paths with the legendary Daniel Boone and the Wilderness Road he blazed from his home in Yadkin County, N.C., over the Blue Ridge, into the wild frontier of Kentucky.

At Gillespie Gap, I would cross paths with a mustered force of 1,100 riled mountain men who did not take kindly to the threats of British commander Major Patrick Ferguson, who threatened to invade and pilfer their region if they continued to support the American Revolution. Passing through this gap in 1780, they joined other forces and tracked down Ferguson at Kings Mountain in South Carolina, defeating his forces and mortally wounding him in the process.

At Balsam Gap, I would cross paths with the 2,400-man army of General Griffith Rutherford who, in 1776, marched into the region to punish the Cherokee Indians for raiding white settlers.

At Mills River Valley Overlook, I would meet eighty-two-year-old Ruth Black from Fort Lauderdale, Florida. In 1984, at the age of sixty-three, she had walked the entire length of the Appalachian Trail using the trail name "Geritol Lady." And here I was thinking I was in the process of accomplishing something unique in the world of backpacking!

21

Death of a Chorus

"There have been no serious accidents anywhere on the
Parkway since the opening of the tourist season on April
15. So good a record should not go unsung and we sing.
Should it hold through the year, you may be sure we'd lift
the chorus."

—*Blue Ridge Parkway News*, Volume IV,
July-August 1941

The fact that I was stepping into North Carolina and would remain within
her borders for the remainder of my trek was not one to be dismissed with a ho-
hum attitude for its historical significance. The location of Shenandoah National
Park virtually guaranteed that a good two hundred miles of the Parkway would
be located in Virginia. But the length of the Great Smoky Mountains National
Park was bisected by the North Carolina-Tennessee line, and how the Parkway
would connect to it became a subject of heated political debate between those
two states. In a gross oversimplification of the issue, Tennessee favored a connection on her side of the border at Gatlinburg, while North Carolina favored
a connection on her side of the border at Cherokee. Of paramount importance
to each of these parties was the short-term influx of construction dollars and
the perpetual flow of tourism dollars that would surely roll into their respective
state and local economies from such a grand undertaking.

In the words of early Parkway landscape architect Edward Abbuehl, the
National Park Service "never had a monster like this in their backyard." The
agency found itself in the paradoxical predicament of endorsing a route that
would complement the scenic vigor already established with the Skyline Drive
in Virginia, without compromising its preservation mandate by marring some
of the most pristine areas of the Southern Appalachians. In the purest sense of

the word, the National Park Service struggled to do the "right" thing within a swarm of self-interests.

At the vortex of this firestorm stood Secretary of the Interior Harold L. Ickes, once described as a "crusty old gentleman." Only a personality of his own strength and resolve could have withstood the political forces he would endure, and his own pen would ultimately settle the whole matter.

Early in the fray, North Carolina assumed a stubborn position, arguing that its superior scenery was justification enough for routing the southern half of the Parkway entirely within its borders and along the general route it eventually coursed. At a hearing held in Baltimore in February 1934, Senator Kenneth D. McKellar of Tennessee, a top-ranking member of the Senate appropriations committee, tainted an otherwise gentlemanly process with veiled threats of withholding funding if Tennessee did not get at least half the route south of the Virginia border. North Carolina, fearing that any compromise which bypassed the city of Asheville would shoot an arrow through the heart of tourism in the region, fired every gun it possessed in its lobby arsenal.

Governor J.C.B. Ehringhaus and others personally presented a special photo album of North Carolina mountain scenery to President Roosevelt. Native son Josephus Daniels, serving at the time as the U.S. Ambassador to Mexico, employed his influence with the President and Secretary Ickes, both of whom were close political friends. Ambassador Daniels hosted Mrs. Ickes on her much desired visit to the Cherokee Indian Reservation, timed perfectly for her to become an honored guest at the annual Rhododendron Ball in Asheville. Lower rungs on the political food chain were courted with invitations to bear hunts and fishing trips in western North Carolina. Every person thought to have any influence in the decision-making process was deluged with urgings from politicians, civic leaders, and ordinary citizens to approve the North Carolina route. And an hour before the final hearing on the matter was to begin on September 18, 1934, every seat and much of the standing room in the auditorium of the Department of the Interior Building in Washington, D.C., was already occupied by a huge North Carolina delegation wearing large white badges well before the first Tennessee delegates arrived. The Tarheels came well-organized and firmly entrenched for the final battle.

A month prior to the hearing, Robert Marshall, Director of Forestry for the Department of the Interior, conducted the closest exercise comparable to what we would today call an environmental-economic impact assessment. At the request of Ickes, he conducted a five-day reconnaissance tour of the route proposed by North Carolina versus one quietly endorsed by an internal departmental committee — a route which would descend down the Blue Ridge from Virginia to Linville, N.C., then veer into Tennessee, avoiding the rugged wilderness of the Black, Craggy, Balsam, and Plott Balsam mountain ranges of North Carolina, terminating with forked entrances into Gatlinburg and Cherokee as it approached the Smokies. His eyeball assessment, a graphically crude method by today's standards, favored the route proposed by North Carolina by "a hair's breadth."

In his precise, fair style, Ickes began the hearing at the appointed hour, granted each state exactly an hour and a half to present their respective arguments, and tossed a coin to determine which state would proceed first. Both sides presented such convincing arguments that a neutral observer might have called the contest a draw — until Senator McKellar, making another unforgettable appearance, fired a strategic shot into the bull's-eye of the Tarheel cause. Someone had leaked to him a copy of the Tennessee route proposal, which he read into the record, after which he demanded that Ickes approve the recommendation of his own internal committee. At the conclusion of the hearing, Ickes humorously illustrated the enormous stress endured by leaders in positions requiring enormous decisions with this statement: "I shall take my head between my hands and after wrapping a wet towel around said head shall try to be fair and just.... If any one here envies my task I'll be glad to resign and let them have the job."

Ickes was struggling with more than one serving of unseasoned broccoli on his plate during this period of time. A short article on the front page of the November 13, 1934, edition of *The Asheville* (N.C.) *Citizen* newspaper quoted him as saying he could "see no reason for the Arizona governor's calling out troops in the Parker dam controversy." In a dispute over power rights, the governor had proclaimed martial law and dispatched national guardsmen, armed with machine guns, to halt construction of a dam! On the same page, an even shorter article entitled, "France Alarmed At Rapid Growth Of German Fleet," warned of trouble brewing in other parts of the world. But the dominating story of the day was proclaimed in bold print across the top of the page — ICKES' DECISION PLACING ROUTE FOR PARKWAY IN N.C. HAILED AS GREAT VICTORY FOR ENTIRE STATE. North Carolina had swept the table!

The passage of time had silenced the steady rustle of Peter Jefferson's survey crew chopping out brush, as I stepped into the sleepy woods of my home state. Quiet too was the hue and cry of a fumbling, mumbling, democratic process that, in my prejudiced opinion, somehow proceeded in the "right" direction. Current environmental laws, coupled with our modern litigious tendencies, would likely halt the progress of such a project today. Nearsighted lovers of wilderness such as I, in that day, would have much preferred a trail instead of a roadway over the likes of Craggy Gardens and Richland Balsam. But skilled landscape architects and engineers of the visionary genre of Michelangelo, assisted by the healing powers of Mother Nature, had crafted a marvelous paved path along which the spirit of any age or condition could soar. The Parkway, through a coincidental process of time and politics, became our handicapped access into wilderness, and in some twisted mutation of my own outdoor philosophy, I had come to love it more than any through which I had walked.

Just a few steps into North Carolina, I passed a state historic marker commemorating a September the eleventh of a happier day. On that day in 1935, construction of the Parkway began with ground being broken on what had once been a piece of the Pack Murphy farm.

A little farther down the road, at the Cumberland Knob recreation area, I walked into the memory of the Parkway's golden anniversary celebration. I was present for that occasion on the eleventh day of September 1985, in uniform but out of sight and sound of the ceremony, trying to manage an off-site parking plan doomed to failure because not enough shuttle buses had been ordered to handle the large crowd.

The visitor center had closed for the day, and I chose a picnic table with a commanding view of the grounds on which to prepare supper. For a late Friday afternoon, the visitors seemed to flock to the area in unusually large numbers. If they had come there to view the damage from Hurricane Isabel, there was none. A couple from Huntersville, N.C., shared some pretzel sticks and trail bars with me. A threesome from Galax, Va., apparently overlooked a beautiful sunset when they surprisingly told me that our conversation had made their trip up the mountain worthwhile.

At that very moment, in that immortally historic and friendly place, I resolved, if still living, to attend and enjoy the Parkway's centennial celebration in the year 2035. I was only eight years old at the passing of the Parkway's twenty-fifth anniversary and then had not an inkling of its existence. I had quietly noted its sixty-eighth anniversary back at Milepost 121 on the eleventh day of my trek. With the same resolve I had formed to complete this walk, I would crawl, if necessary, to attend the Parkway's hundredth birthday celebration at the ripe old age of eighty-four. No terrorist would steal this date from my heart and woe, I thought, to any force of man—foreign or domestic—that ever attempted to wrench this treasure from the citizens of this free land.

Saturday morning found me in a reverent, meditative mood, trying to imagine the scene of sweaty men in coveralls whose rough hands had set one stone upon another to form, without the use of mortar, beautiful lengths of stone wall. For decades now, they had not budged from their points of placement, silent monuments to their Maker and makers. Hand-laid stone walls speak such visceral volumes of man's relationship to the earth and each other. I had already observed some, on Humpback Mountain, that had been built by force of slavery to contain hogs. The one I walked past that morning, not far south of Cumberland Knob, had been built by meager wages in destitute times. Functionally, it quietly begged vehicles to stay on the Parkway in exchange for a pleasing contribution to the landscape.

I was looking down more than up this last day of my walking week, less from fatigue than from the pure enjoyment of gazing introspectively here and there upon stands of delicate species growing close to the ground—beds of shiny galax, whose peculiar odor never fails to transport me spiritually back to Hanging Rock; nodding clusters of saprophytic Indian pipes, whose solemn presence always reminds me of the natural web of interdependency; and a robust crop of teaberry, whose sweet aroma of crushed leaves inevitably creates a time warp in which I am stranded at Linville Falls, happily fidgeting between sixteen years of schooling and a career, chewing my favorite brand of gum.

The sign at Greenstone Overlook at Milepost 8.8 in Virginia tells the story behind the hand-laid stone walls found on Humpback Mountain.

I was walking through a fairly flat, wooded section where the Parkway again seemed to crisscross the same stream several times. A key chain, adorned with a safety message in the form of a miniature roadway caution sign, dangled from a zipper on my backpack. I had publicly displayed it in this manner since receiving it as a gift from Ranger Brett fourteen days earlier, along with the can of vegetable juice and raisin cake. I adhered to its simple warning—"ENJOY THE VIEW. WATCH THE ROAD."—and hoped every motorist driving past me would do the same. It was a clever idea, along with numerous posters that I had seen in campgrounds and visitor centers. Bearing catchy safety messages, one of my favorites read: "Do you know what a descending radius curve is? Don't find out the hard way." Each poster also warned that rangers responded to 450 serious accidents annually. A tanker truck from a local volunteer fire department, in no particular hurry, fanned me with a nice breeze. It must be out on a training run, I thought, absent flashing red lights and wailing siren.

A short distance farther, I noticed several vehicles, mostly pickup trucks, parked along the shoulder of the road. Many appeared to be of the four-wheel-drive variety, and as the distance between us diminished, certain clues suggested that

The carnage that occurs in this park as a result of motor vehicle accidents is absolutely senseless.

I had stumbled upon a flock of local trout fishermen who had become privy to a recent stocking. Their owners were nowhere in sight. All of the license plates I could see were from North Carolina. Though many were tagged with NRA decals and other traditional symbols of masculinity, only scattered fishing tackle, visible through a few rear windows, could be seen hanging from otherwise empty gun racks. A small sign tacked to a tree declared a nearby stream to be "Hatchery Supported." I decided to take a rest behind the caboose of this long, good-old-boy train and wait for the chance to see a fine stringer of fish headed for the frying pan.

But two, grim-faced young men with muddied trousers and no fishing gear eventually returned to their vehicle and wrecked my faulty conclusion with sad news. Sometime during the night, just ahead, a vehicle had missed a curve, traveled a short distance through the woods, jumped the stream, and crashed violently into the opposite embankment. The accident had not been discovered until daybreak. The driver and sole occupant of the vehicle had sustained severe head injuries but was still alive and had just been airlifted to a hospital. Had I walked about five more miles the previous day, my campsite would have been very near the scene of this crash. Despite all of my hopes otherwise, the prediction I had made to Patty twenty days earlier had sadly come to pass.

There are no sadder sounds along the Parkway than the sighing sobs of the mourning dove by day and the wailing cries of the screech owl by night. Let the legend begin that they perpetually weep for the absolutely senseless carnage that occurs in this park as a result of motor vehicle accidents. Little white crosses would dot its entire length —clustered in places— if one were placed at every scene of death or serious injury.

To this day, I still cannot distinguish between the smell of antifreeze, alcohol, and blood. When my telephone rings after midnight, I still jump from my sleep, my heart racing, and reach for a uniform that no longer hangs on the bedpost. Of all the images that still flash intermittently across the big screen in my mind, the one of a three-year-old girl shaking uncontrollably on an emergency room table rattles me the most. It was the only time this superficially strong ranger lost control of his emotions during such an investigation; a nurse thoughtfully offered me the privacy of another room to regain my composure. Would that visitors and Parkway rangers alike could experience just one year without having to endure such suffering so again the chorus could sing.

22

Finding, at Last,
the Wild Asparagus

"Why go fishing for mountain trout when codfish fillets are
for sale in any supermarket?"
—*Stalking the Wild Asparagus*, by
Euell Gibbons

The first drops of a light rain hastened a premature conclusion of my Monday morning breakfast and prompted me to hurriedly pack my gear and prepare myself for a dreary day. Fog had rolled in with the rain at precisely the same time and in the same manner that I had experienced back at Boston Knob Overlook. With a full day's rest behind me, I had neither the desire nor intention to wait out another precipitation event of indeterminate length, not with a restaurant and a possible laundry facility eight miles ahead of me at the Doughton Park recreation area. I was only one hurricane and six days overdue a clean set of clothes and a real meal.

As I scurried to get my tent and sleeping bag stowed and under the protection of my pack cover, hindsight berated my earlier decision to spend my third Sunday near Stone Mountain Overlook, which gave a commanding view of the massive geologic feature for which another premier North Carolina state park was named. I had envisioned it, upon my arrival near sunset on Saturday evening, to be the perfect place to relax and enjoy the company of visitors for an entire day. In all respects, it seemed to offer the same potential for human interaction that I had experienced my first Sunday at Sunset Field Overlook. For reasons I still cannot explain, though, it failed my expectation miserably. Despite its splendid perch at 3,200 feet, tempting picnic table, and grassy blanket, visitors mostly made it a stop-and-go experience, stepping from their vehicles only for a quick look-see and camera shot before dashing off again. Most of them only glanced at me from the corners of their eyes, as if I had been a mere vagabond interrupting their hasty attempts to use the overlook as a makeshift restroom. More disappointingly, not a single ranger patrolled through the area during the entire day.

Had I only walked eight more miles into Saturday night, I could have enjoyed the airy, open highlands of one of the most popular recreation areas on the Parkway, I argued with myself. Its campground, lodge, picnic area, restaurant, trails, scenic vistas, historic Brinegar Cabin, and hosts of delighted people enjoying the same would have guaranteed me an uplifting Sunday experience. Had I been too content to rest on my laurels, having reached the psychological halfway mark of my trek at the state line and only two miles short of the actual point at Milepost 234.5? Had I squandered an entire day, bereft of any meaningful conversation, reading a *Parkway Milepost* that I had nearly memorized? I was beginning to crave fresh literature and music as much as cold, skim milk. Now it was raining, and I would have to forgo some of the best views along the Parkway and be very careful not to walk right past the Bluffs Restaurant in this soupy fog.

But no sense of urgency had propelled me to walk until midnight as it had done that first Saturday night on the trail. A tired body and the little voice inside my head had simply prompted me to stop where I did. Still, I silently cursed the weather and my decision. As I jerked my backpack from the ground to hoist it upon my back, I immediately remembered an axiom of this sport and most every other endeavor in life — anger increases the probability of injury. My trail legs had been long developed, and I had become a fit walking machine. Now, only an occasional back muscle ever got sore, and I had to be careful not to pull one. As I stepped into the fog and began a long, uphill climb, I calmed myself and repented again of my now less frequent, destructive habit of second-guessing my circumstance. In the days, weeks, months, and years that would follow I would grow increasingly grateful for the succession of random experiences triggered by that eight-mile delay. Oh, how different this song would have played just a few hours off-key.

Milepost 234 faintly appeared on the opposite side of the road, a notable observation considering the heavy rainfall and thick fog through which I was walking. I had already noted in my journal the absence of seventeen milepost markers, and I was beginning to suspect that I had walked right past most of them, blinded by darkness, fog, or the trancelike daze in which I often caught myself walking on sunny afternoons. Another half mile and I would officially reach the midpoint of my trip.

This was the kind of day that used to give me a royal headache as a ranger, when patrolling through such thickness caused the eyes to constantly refocus on imaginary obstacles that never quite came into view. It was also the kind of day that, due to distortion of time and space, caused me to scrawl in the margin of my journal: "Living a day in the fog is as if you didn't live it at all." Like an uninvited guest crashing a grand party, it sneaks in and snuffs out the lights, hiding the decorated hall, the costumed finery, and the banquet feast staged on silver linings, while those properly invited snarl entangled and grope for the exit door. If scientifically polled, visitors would surely vote fog to be the signature weather feature of the Parkway for less than noble reasons.

About halfway up the mountain, at a welcome break in the fog, District Ranger Brent Pennington stopped to chat. Though we had never met, his name rang vaguely familiar. As we became cordially acquainted, he gently reminded me that I had not selected him for a ranger position for which he had applied when I was the district ranger at Balsam Gap. His name slowly began to come into focus on an old roster of best qualified candidates, and a memory I had conveniently suppressed returned. Apologetically, I confessed that I could not remember if he had been my first or second choice but that the powers above me had selected my third choice. Understanding well the politics of such matters himself, Brent explained that, like my eight-mile delay, his little career delay had eventually worked in his favor, and he, too, was quite happy with his current circumstance. In the hereafter, I hope to meet Albert Einstein for a more understandable explanation of this time, space, and coincidence stuff.

Even though I was somewhat familiar with the area, I could hardly find the Bluffs Lodge, located a few hundred feet up a spur road from the Parkway. Visibility was about as bad as it had been one night when I had to hold the door open on my patrol car and use a flashlight to follow the center line on the road. When I finally found the office, my shadowy reflection in a window pane displayed the figure of a man very close to violating one of his own ground rules. No matter how dapper the attire, an unshaven man, walking in fog and rain, looks like a bum, and I quite startled my own self. My dripping, bedraggled appearance in the quaintly elegant lobby should have sent little children scurrying for the security of their parents' knees and the desk clerk reaching for the telephone to summon security.

But I was received with grace and courtesy, enough at least, for Sparky, the manager, to allow me the use of his own office telephone to call home. Pay telephones, I was beginning to discover, were slowly disappearing from that part of the country due to the proliferation of cellular phones. Laundry facilities were not available, I was told again, and showers were available only with the purchase of a room. Where were the Paynes and Ranger Schula when I needed them?

Patty was not home, so I left a message on the answering machine. I never liked talking to myself, and it seemed I had been doing so for days. Dejected, yet determined to profit in some way from my detour, uphill to boot, I called my daughter in Rhode Island and instantly recharged my spirit with the lively chatter of grandchildren Emily and Cameron. Solomon of the Old Testament was right. Children's children truly are the crown on an old man. For a few brief moments, at least in my mind, the rain ceased and the sun appeared, as I slowly inched my way back down to the Parkway, having an easier time finding the Bluffs Restaurant with my nose than with my eyes.

I was too embarrassed to ask my waitress if the helpings were always that plentiful or if the cooking staff just felt sorry for me. Sparky himself might have ordered the staff to heap my plate high after finally remembering a name and a face that had purchased many a hamburger from him in 1975 when he managed the Crabtree Meadows Restaurant during my tenure in that area as a seasonal ranger. Or perhaps all of the scant few customers who were foolish enough to travel in such weather were being especially rewarded that day for even finding the place. Whatever the case, I gorged myself on more salad, fried flounder, green beans, and french fries than I should have eaten.

A group of motorcyclists, looking a fraction more soaked than myself, were seated at a table near me and shared the dismal news that rain and fog persisted all the way to Boone. I stared through the window at the fog and, for the first time on the trek, gave serious consideration to violating Ground Rule #1 and renting a room for the night. I needed a shower more than I needed a comfortable bed, and I would at least be able to wash out my clothes in the bathtub.

But I dismissed the thought as quickly as it formed. This was not a survival issue with which I was dealing. It was a comfort issue, and it was only two o'clock in the afternoon. I could not help the fact that I might have looked like a bum, but willful commission of one cardinal sin, I was afraid, might lead to another. If not careful, I thought, I would soon be eating raisins and building fires in suspicious places. Besides, my little travel directory advertised a private campground, located near the Parkway a few miles ahead, that offered shower and laundry facilities. Decided. I would at least complete a respectable fourteen miles for the day with a fair chance of attending to some pressing hygienic needs, minus the necessity for sincere repentance and a nagging temptation to repeat the sorry sin again. I rewarded my valiant decision with a bowl of chocolate ice cream while my gracious waitress, sensing an imminent departure and judging, perhaps, that my stomach was approaching its maximum capacity, offered to package two enormous biscuits I had not yet touched.

Drunkenly overfed and carbonated, I staggered back out into the fog and drizzle, grateful that the grade ahead of me turned downward rather than upward. I knocked the legs out of gear and jubilantly coasted past Ice Rock Cliffs, with a cautious eye scanning its massive face for any rocks, loosened by the rain, that might tumble my way.

Suddenly, without warning, a formidable creature appeared on the foggy roadway and halted me in mid step. A little crayfish, mistaking me perhaps for an unmerciful rain god, stood in my path and, with both pincers held high in the air in the attack mode, defiantly dared me to step past him. Amused and grateful that the scale of our dimensions was not reversed, I admired his bravery and offered him the satisfaction of winning the standoff for a few minutes. But I was determined to reach my goal before nightfall and had no interest in sidestepping the issue and permitting a less understanding party to make road kill gravy of this little soldier who had obviously been out in the field too long. So I gently offered the metal tip of my walking stick for his closer inspection and permitted him a wise, honorable retreat onto the safety of the grass shoulder.

A newspaper deliveryman for the *Winston-Salem* (N.C.) *Journal* had no idea that the little white bundle he accidentally dropped that morning would fall into the most yearning of hands. I found it near the foot of the mountain, where the Parkway leveled out near its intersection with another road. It had been thoughtfully tied inside a plastic bag and was dry, and I was happy and determined to soon find a dry place in which to read it. About a mile farther down the Parkway, peeking through the fog, I found, like an oasis on the horizon, the campground and services I had been seeking. And more. Much, much more. First impressions could be deceiving, the experience would soon reiterate.

By the time I reached the campground office, the sky was raining buckets. Edgar, the owner of the place, threw in a free cup of laundry detergent in exchange for the hot shower I had just purchased for the very modest price of three dollars. "Don't forget to turn off the water in the shower," he surprisingly implored, as I stepped toward the door in the direction of a torturous walk up a steep hill to the bathhouse and an unrelenting, unauthorized, totally unnecessary, torrential baptism which gave all appearances of extending into the night. I asked what he would charge to pitch my tent somewhere on the premises. Since I was backpacking and writing a book, he said, there would be no charge. His wife, Jean, I would later learn, had also done some writing of her own.

Edgar looked old enough to have been a young boy when the Parkway was constructed through that area. Age had slowed him considerably, but he doggedly ran the facility as if he were still a young man. Like most of the men I had met who were native to the lands through which the Parkway coursed, he had a gentle nature, hands that could make or fix anything, and eyes unable to hide an inner strength capable of withstanding harsh winters as courageously as hard times. Instinctively, I accepted his comment about the water as an expression of frugality rather than one of ill will. Edgar appeared to be perfectly content to spend every day of his life in harmonious consortium with his fellow beings, making an honest living rather than a killing off of them.

Before I could take the first step up the hill, a golf cart rolled up to the front door, driven with the finesse of an overweight, weekend golfer who used eighteen holes as an excuse to hang out at the clubhouse. Katlyn, Edgar and Jean's little nine-year-old granddaughter, grinned like a sixteen-year-old who had just passed her driver's license exam and offered me a ride up the hill. Money, I thought, could never purchase this kind of service, as I delightedly clambered on board and struggled to fit a backpack onto a conveyance better designed for golf clubs. On the way up to the bathhouse, I spotted a grassy place beside a pond, well out of the way of a looming assortment of motor homes and travel trailers, that might later suffice as a soggy campsite for the night. Soon, in the comfort of a steamy, hot shower, I escaped an inevitable future and imagined myself in a warm, dry clime.

Only a few minutes remained before the dryer, at the conclusion of its fifty-cent cycle, would force me back out into the rain. Edgar had told me the office would not close until nine o'clock that night, but, having obtained all of the services I had been seeking, I really did not want to be remembered as a pathetic loiterer and seriously considered hiking a little farther in the remaining two hours of daylight.

The hypnotic drone of the dryer had nearly put me to sleep when the sound of a car, stopping very close to the door, startled me. A car door slammed, and a young boy, a good five years shy of the legal driving age, stepped into the dim laundry room and asked, "Grandpa wants to know how much longer you will be?"

Sensing that my assumed welcome was approaching its expiration (Edgar *had* warned a grown man to shut off the water), I began to gather up the newspaper I had scavenged earlier that afternoon and replied, "As soon as the dryer stops I'll be heading back down to the Parkway." The decision on whether to continue walking seemed to have been made for me.

Cody, Katlyn's older brother, shuffled his feet and finally broke the awkward silence that followed with a surprising announcement. "But Grandpa sent me up here to give you a ride back down to the office. Lots of the campers gather there after supper, and we'd love for you to join us."

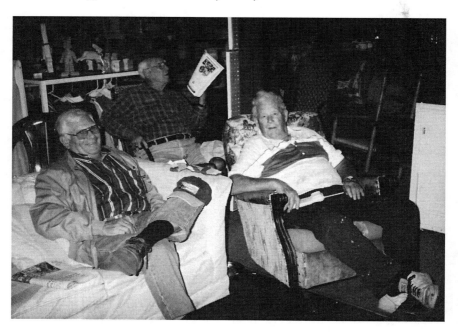

Camper Lowry Russell from Sharon, South Carolina, left, camper George Foy from Cullman, Alabama, center, and campground co-owner Edgar Miller are seated in the camp store of a privately owned campground near Milepost 247 in North Carolina, September 22, 2003.

When the dryer stopped, I quickly repacked my gear and nixed all thoughts of walking anymore that day. Cody and I jumped in his car, and to make him feel a little older, I slouched in the front seat somewhat to match his limited view over the dash, as he rather proficiently drove the thing back down to the office. Thank goodness there were still grandpas like Edgar left in the world willing to take a chance on kids and strangers.

When I stepped back into the dry refuge of the campground office the second time, I felt like I was attending a family reunion. Several camping guests had gathered for what had become a nightly tradition of sociality, quietly officiated, of course, by the proprietors. In one corner of the room, surrounded by snacks, crafts, postcards, and everything else one would expect to find in a quaint camp store, all the men were watching *Wheel of Fortune* by the warmth of an old wood stove. Edgar sat in a chair that most folks would have already tossed into the dumpster, an old recliner that had been reupholstered — piecemeal — at least three times. The quorum over which he presided, consisting mostly of veteran customers about his same age, sat around him just as comfortably in rocking chairs and on a large sofa of the same generation as the recliner.

The wives of these men sat around a table on the opposite side of the room, playing an intense game of Rummikub, not the least bit concerned that their well-seasoned husbands showed more interest in Vanna White than in solving the puzzle. I, too, became dazzled somewhat by all the glittering sequins. Upon my entry, Edgar immediately rose from his throne, introduced me to his customers and asked me to share the story of my trip with them. Before taking a seat on the sofa, I grabbed a can of cold soda from one of those old coolers you have to reach down into to get your drink and nodded to Edgar to start my tab. Between the company, the fire, and the television, I now felt welcome enough to gab and imbibe until closing time.

In a few minutes, I felt a bump against my right shoulder and turned to discover a heaping plate of food staring me in the face. Cody, whose hands extended it in my direction, smiled and, in his matter-of-fact manner, said, "Grandma fixed this for you. Take it." I was overcome by the hospitality and this family's unconditional trust in a total stranger. A deep plate of baked ham, corn on the cob, green beans, corn bread, tomatoes, and cucumbers required another soda, to which Edgar nodded in quiet acknowledgement. No Christmas or Thanksgiving had ever come close to the amount of food I ate on that twenty-second day of September.

The conclusion of *Jeopardy* seemed to trigger an intermission from the television set, and Edgar said he had something he wanted me to see upstairs. Careful to show me all the light switches along the way, we walked up a flight of stairs and into an open banquet room occupied by empty tables. Edgar insisted that I spend the night up there and not out in the rain. At that point, I decided it was time to pay for the two sodas with a ten dollar bill and walk away from the change. Edgar refused to accept it. "Then give it to Jean to buy something for

Campground co-owner Jean Miller is shown at the Rummikub table, September 22, 2003.

herself," I insisted. Still, he refused. "Then split it as a tip between those two grandchildren for the taxi service they provided me today," to which Edgar hesitatingly replied, "I'll see that they get it."

As nine o'clock approached, the crowd dwindled, and the leftover men merged with the womenfolk at the game table. Too tired to learn a game I had never played before in my life, I wandered back to the sofa and slowly melted into a horizontal position by the fire and television.

Sometime during the night, I woke up on that same sofa and found myself covered with a brightly patterned, handmade afghan. Except for a row of tiny red lights chasing each other on what had to be the first radio scanner ever produced, the room was dark, empty, and closed for business. The wood stove tinged occasionally as it continued to cool. Edgar and Jean had chosen not to wake me before closing for the night, and in a dream-like state of half-consciousness, I surrendered to the fantasy that I had landed either in heaven or the North Pole and went back to sleep.

It was not the first rays of sun on a clear, crisp morning that woke me, but a quiet, familiar voice. "This is the Blue Ridge Parkway radio dispatch center...," came the words of Dispatcher Mary Cook over the scanner. I had heard neither her voice nor that official sign-on jingle since 1990. For a startling moment, until I could wipe the sleep from my eyes, I thought I had awakened in the old ranger cabin at Soco Gap; the place was that quaint. Not wanting Jean to feel obliged to serve me breakfast, too, I hurriedly packed my gear, left a thank-you note by the cash register, and stepped into a chilly morning as pure and fresh as the good people I had just met.

A cold front had blown out the clouds during the night, and only a steady breeze had stifled the formation of frost on a landscape I could now clearly see. I had entered the enchanting wonderland of scattered Christmas tree farms, through which the Parkway and I would wander for the next several days. Evenly spaced in perfectly straight rows, privately owned plots of Fraser fir trees wrapped themselves over distant, irregular terrain like dark patches of cloth distributed randomly over an unmade bed.

Along the Parkway, the wind sifted smoothly through the thin needles of stately white pine trees like cold, spring water through a finely meshed sieve. I had always loved that sound, to which ears, not words, could only do justice. I thought it uncanny how that same sound could produce such a sense of loneliness near the conclusion of a day, as I had experienced back at Adney Gap a few days earlier. A patch of sunlight, warming a rock wall at the south end of the Laurel Fork Viaduct, invited me to stop for breakfast. The day was already developing into a struggle with my jacket, as I tried to decide if I was hot or cold, moving across overlapping gradients of calm and breeze, sunshine and shade, uphill exertion and downhill ease.

In the sun and out of the breeze, I shed my jacket and rummaged through my backpack in search of a white paper bag that would spare me the bother of firing up my cookstove. It would be a quick and simple meal that would make wise use of leftovers from my feast the previous day at the Bluffs Restaurant. As I reached inside the bag for a cold biscuit, I was stunned by the attention to details my waitress had paid in its preparation. Back in the kitchen, out of my sight, she had lovingly emptied the blueberry preserves, which I had also not touched, from a glass bowl into a disposable cup. A lid had been placed on the cup and the entire container had been carefully wrapped with cellophane to prevent any possible leakage. Four packets of butter, a plastic spoon, and a napkin (!) completed the care package. Had I truly discovered the Land of Kindness or had the novelty of the trek, a slower pace of living, and a mild state of deprivation only brought into better focus that which occurs so familiarly, so rapidly, and so abundantly back in The Other World? Some of all three, I concluded, as I enjoyed one large biscuit and fixings and saved the remainder for lunch.

The next highlight of my morning occurred at Alder Gap, where I encountered a stubborn cow who had escaped the confines of a nearby pasture and was wandering dangerously along the Parkway. Not a cattleman by birth, I had, nevertheless, developed some expertise in handling such matters during my rangering years and strutted into this scene with the confidence of a Blue Ridge cowboy.

My self-training experiences with cattle, as a buck ranger, had been simultaneously amusing and frustrating. The owners of such beasts could rarely be located when needed, and until I mastered the fine art of cow whispering, I more than once considered my shotgun as a potential fix for such problems. Eventually, though, I learned how to find or create a break in the fence, nudge them toward the fence line with a bump of the siren, and gently herd them, with the aid of my patrol car, in the direction of the break. Few collars ever matched the feeling of accomplishment offered by the successful capture of a wayward cow.

But Miss Alder Gap 2003 was not in a cooperative mood that morning and displayed the temperament of an animal that had been traumatized by coyote or feral dogs during the previous night. Spooked further by slowing traffic, she refused to walk the fence line for me and finally bolted into thick woods and thundered out of sight down the mountain. Satisfied that I had at least temporarily eliminated her as a traffic hazard, I hoisted my burden once again upon my back, as a man and woman rode past on bicycles. A few feet past me, the woman stopped, turned in my direction and asked, "Aren't you the guy from Lynchburg (Va.) hiking the whole Parkway?"

"Well, I am hiking the Parkway, but I live in North Carolina. You must be confusing me with Harold Peters, the bicyclist from Lynchburg," I answered.

She had read Shannon Brennan's article in *The News & Advance* and was herself a resident of Lynchburg. She and her husband had just begun a 270-mile bike trip along the Parkway themselves. As we talked, the mysteries of time, space, and coincidence I had pondered only the previous day resurfaced. She and I had grown up within a mile of each other and had graduated from the same high school. But the psychological barrier of Muddy Creek between our neighborhoods and a six-year difference in our ages had, until now, separated us into two different worlds. And a chance meeting between a hiker and a biker had prompted a chance meeting with a reporter whose article prompted a chance meeting with a reader who had a chance meeting with a hiker who had a chance meeting with a cow because he had stopped eight miles short of Doughton Park on a Saturday night, finding himself in the rain and fog on Monday morning and... Albert, we need to talk. Soon.

By midafternoon I was well past the seventh fold of my map (only four remained) and thought, perchance, that I had caught my first glimpse of Grandfather Mountain in the distance. The wild apple crop, to which I had been looking forward as a tasty supplement to my trail diet, had thus far disappointed me. Passing another milepost marker, I finally found the first one after a 257-mile search. It presented itself as a lone specimen on the shoulder of the road, the only survivor, thanks to the grace of gravity, of ravenous deer, who had plundered its every brother and sister within reach from the mother tree located on the opposite side of the road. Unsure of its variety, I noted in my journal that it was the tastiest apple I had ever eaten.

During my earliest years as an amateur naturalist, trying to learn the names, characteristics, and habits of every wild plant and animal around me, I developed an intense fascination with those species that were edible and became an avid student of Euell Gibbons. His books, *Stalking the Wild Asparagus* and *Stalking the Healthful Herbs*, became my field guides for a season. Using the fruit of the smooth sumac tree to make "pink lemonade" and acorns from the white oak tree to make "oatmeal cookies" best describes the depth and extent to which I studied his works. Such knowledge and expertise, I figured, was as good as having a pantry stocked with food. But he described some species that I could never find, such as wild asparagus, and some uses, such as ingesting the leaves of poison ivy as a means of self-immunization, with which I never quite developed the nerve to experiment.

With the passage of time, my interest in this hobby faded, but my books never lost their position on my bookshelf as a valuable survival guide in every way as important as my emergency supply of wheat, dehydrated milk, and home-canned green beans. Now, I had become more of a recreational gatherer, content to partake of Mother Nature's delicacies more on a random, accidental basis rather than as a deliberate pursuit. Too late in the season to enjoy morel mushrooms and too early for mayapples that taste like a cross between a lemon and a banana, I had still enjoyed — at no inconvenience — blackberries, blueberries, and elderberries along my path. Farther down the Parkway, I would even enjoy a handful of late-variety strawberries that someone had planted underneath the new Parkway headquarters entrance sign. Ranger Parker had floored me with the suggestion that, when he retired, he might even walk the entire length of the Parkway, surviving only on the land in the process! Nuts not edible, many might speak of us both.

The day was drawing to a close as I resumed a sunset walk down the Parkway following a brief stop at the Northwest Trading Post and a detour into the nearby community of Glendale Springs. A recently deceased friend had often urged me to visit the locally famous Holy Trinity Church of the Frescoes to see the beautiful depiction of *The Last Supper* painted on an interior wall. In the process of honoring his memory, I stumbled also onto a restaurant and a meal served far more elegantly than its reasonable cost would have suggested. A disposable camera appeared along the shoulder, cracked and broken, its film probably ruined. Like the hubcap I had imaginarily mistaken for a horseshoe back near the Saddle Overlook, I placed it on a nearby fence post. A man on a motorcycle back at the visitor center had just two hours earlier been looking for it. A few feet away, growing along the split rail fence, a lacy plant caught my eye. Captured by its novelty, I stepped closer to examine its delicate finery and discovered, for the first time in my life, asparagus growing in the wild — right there along the edge of the Parkway!

23

Pure Harmony

"There had to be a good deal of wandering away from the shortest distance between two points."
—"Finding a Route for the Blue Ridge Parkway," by S. Herbert Evison, *National Parks Magazine*, September 1969

I was now in the heart of what is known as the northwest mountain region of North Carolina. Nearly every child who grows up in the Triad region of central North Carolina dreams, at some point, between kindergarten and twelfth grade, of living in those higher elevations of Alleghany, Ashe, and Watauga counties. Their dreams become more vivid and desperate on winter nights preceding the due date of a term paper or a scheduled test for which adequate preparation has not been made. Why? Because the local meteorologists associated with radio and television stations, based in the cities of Greensboro, High Point, and Winston-Salem, constantly remind them that they are not getting their fair share of snow and resultant school cancellations enjoyed by their higher, northwestern counterparts. Most of them eventually mature out of the notion that poor grades can be blamed on their parents' choice of domicile, discontinue their search for the word "fair" on their birth certificates, and go on to repeat the disregardful process with their own children.

I was approaching the southern boundary of my own personal Parkway "wilderness"—an approximately seventy-five-mile stretch between Fancy Gap and Deep Gap. Except for a handful of special details, I had done little ranger-ing through this area and could, in fact, count the number of times I had even driven over it on my fingers and toes. Its unfamiliarity came as a chef's surprise to an otherwise delicious five-course feast, and I reveled in the discovery and consumption of poetic places I had once heard bantered over the park radio as mere points of reference: Pipers Gap, The Lump, Fox Hunter's Paradise, Air Bellows Gap, and Betsy's Rock Falls. Why had no one ever before thought to visit the Parkway in such manner? I was having the adventure of a lifetime.

By now, I had become a master of efficiency with respect to my gear, having memorized the location and idiosyncrasies of every item. Except for the obvious hazards associated with cooking and the confounded zipper on my rain jacket, whose contrary personality always surfaced at its most critical time of need, I could maneuver my way around most of my equipment with my eyes closed. My flashlight was now rarely summoned to duty, even on nights as dark as the one previous, in which I had pitched my tent without its use. Protectively tucked under the gigantic, drooping boughs of a white pine tree, with an open window to a clear, western sky, I had parked for the night to make dessert of the original Milky Way, courtesy of an invisible moon lost somewhere out there in its new phase. As penance for my recent overindulgence in real food, I settled for a meager serving of instant grits for breakfast, packed my gear in record time, and began another walking day.

Three miles later, an open window on a nearby farmhouse reminded me how much I had also been missing music. It was not the brand I would have selected, given a choice, but it was music, and it played loud enough for me to detect the distinct, nasal sound of Randy Travis and a smattering of lyrics unfamiliar to me. Once a loather of any form of country music, I had been instantly converted, rather late in life, by Rosanne Cash and her "Runaway Train" to some of its sounds and many of its words. Ballads especially. I jotted down enough of the words in my journal to later determine that I was listening to "An Old Pair of Shoes."

This was a sad-sounding song with clever wordplay, drifting on the morning air through the natural amphitheater of a quiet, mountain dell. There was an eerie absence of humanity about the property from which it cried, and the depression-riddled words almost prompted me to make an emergency detour to check the rafters inside the barn. Instead, I made a quick inspection of the tread of my hiking boots and recalled another day when I finally realized that the constant, twisting motion I made getting in and out of a patrol car was responsible for grinding a hole in the sole of my left dress shoe when the right one looked hardly worn. With uplifted chin and resolute gait, I pulled myself from the quicksand of that place and proceeded into a day that would bring wondrous views of Mount Jefferson State Park to the west and closer glimpses of Grandfather Mountain ahead.

Backpacking experience had taught me to be wary of trails crossing through anything named Deep Gap. Along with Brushy Mountain, there must be dozens of them so named along the Appalachian chain. They usually imply murderously steep descents and ascents in and out of them. The Parkway itself crossed through four of them, and the one I found myself walking into near the end of the day fit the dreaded profile.

Parkway engineers had limited themselves to building a roadway with max-

The Parkway offered no more than a dozen level strides over U.S. Route 421 before ascending just as steeply up the other side at Deep Gap, elevation 3142 feet, at Milepost 276.4 in North Carolina. Photo taken September 24, 2003.

imum grades of 6–8 percent and curves with an absolute minimum radius of two hundred feet. In rugged mountain terrain, such parameters required lots of snaking along the contour and a little tunnel building. All told, these self-imposed limits added about 160 extra miles to an otherwise straight, level distance between Milepost Zero and Milepost 469.

The southbound grade into this particular Deep Gap must have approached the maximum stated limit over most of its distance, as I descended almost a thousand feet in a little over three miles, with gelatinized knees and ankles screaming their age and burning hotly. By no means the longest, steepest descent I had ever made carrying a full backpack, it nevertheless reminded me that I much preferred a steep ascent over a steep descent, especially on pavement. My wish was promptly granted as the Parkway offered no more than a dozen level strides over U.S. Route 421 before ascending just as steeply up the other side of the gap. Before tackling my preferred choice of pain, I rested briefly on the magnificent stone bridge, a veritable western gateway to the favored Land of More Snow and ski resorts. To the east lived all the snow-deprived children and their dream-deprived parents.

The ascent out of Deep Gap was difficult, and I glared and snorted like a perturbed draft horse at a brass marijuana pipe found lying on the road surface, leaving it for cars to grind and pulverize into more useful dust of the earth. With my "wilderness" and 276 miles behind me, I struggled between two conflicting motivations. Part of me wanted to lengthen my stride into the more familiar territory of many pleasant employment memories and the completion of my goal. Another part of me wanted to procrastinate the conclusion of this wonderful experience.

The climb mercifully lasted only a mile before topping out to an orange sunset, filtered through the dark, clean understory of a mature stand of white pine. A wonderfully peculiar feeling stopped me in my tracks, as my imagination added a nervous horse, a gentle breeze, and falling snow to the scene. For a moment, I transcendentally became the protagonist in Robert Frost's poem "Stopping by Woods on a Snowy Evening," and settled my inner struggle with his last verse. So many times had I, too, been tempted to permanently escape the demands and troubles of life by plunging headlong into the shelter of a quiet woods. But temporary excursions had taught me that I would eventually become cold and hungry and lonely. More importantly, the lives of others, too, depended upon me staying the higher course of purposeful human existence.

Upon finding a suitable campsite for the evening, I escaped the spell of an artist of words only to surrender again to the spell of an artist of colors and watched the Big Dipper pour itself over the horizon on a truly *Starry Night* before falling into a deep, comfortable sleep. Nights have such a wonderful way of softening a day.

Only three miles into Thursday morning, I met Parkway mower operator Bill Hall, who shut down his whirring machine to offer a kind hello and give me directions to a nearby diner. Using the noble excuse that I needed to telephone Patty, I justified the inhalation of a cheeseburger at ten o'clock in the morning as due compensation for dodging monstrous trucks along a dangerously busy state highway with hardly a shoulder on which to walk.

The news back home proved quite interesting. The neighbors were righteously alarmed over the discovery of a family of copperheads that had allegedly spawned from the pine island on the corner of our property. "Watch your step and sleep in a tent," were my immediate thoughts of caution. How treacherous could be those dandelion-free subdivisions boasting 24–7 termite protection! An even better chuckle came when I paid my bill and noticed a sign on a window by the cash register designating it the "Window of Shame," on which were taped numerous bounced checks. I was beginning to feel like a Charles Kuralt on foot and soon emptied the first cartridge of my ink pen.

The day continued to pan the spectrum of strangeness, somewhat out of sync with the harmonious track on which I had coasted since Hurricane Isabel. A bumper sticker was observed that read, "I Hate Normal People." Another used syringe was found lying on the road. What would the next generation of Parkway rangers have to face? But it was the unscheduled meeting of another reporter, near an oddly named place called Aho Gap, whose name derivation I dared not venture to guess, that nearly sucked me down the drain of a day gone weird.

An approaching car topped the crest of the hill in front of me and, while quickly decelerating, pulled onto the grass shoulder, head-on in my direction. I had investigated many accidents in which a vehicle, having dropped the two right tires onto a surface with a much lower coefficient of friction, never made a successful recovery back onto the roadway. Before I could decide whether to dart blindly onto the pavement, jump over the embankment, or take my chances by leaping into the air at the last second to hopefully bounce off the windshield, the vehicle came to a stop just a few feet in front of me.

My first thought was that John O'Dowd, a reporter for the *Watauga Democrat* (Boone, N.C.), might have once been associated with the military police when he jumped from his car before it hardly came to a stop and blurted, "If you're the guy hiking the Parkway, just drop your pack and get comfortable for a while. My editor sent me up here to find you, and you're not leaving until I get your story."

I surrendered peacefully to his arresting demeanor, and despite another interview in which the same old questions were beginning to grow stale, I was rather surprised and entertained by a jolly, witty style that belied my first impression of him. I began to like the guy but could not tell if he was enjoying the assignment or was just trying to get his boss off his back. And, in my dreamy fatigue near the end of another walking day, I forgot he was a reporter looking for a sensational story, taking notes on every word I uttered.

"Has anyone threatened to harm you on your trip?" came the quite appropriate question leading to an innocent reply which eventually meandered awry.

"Absolutely not," I replied truthfully without hesitation, unfairly and impatiently placing the question, whose answer was obvious to me but not to him, in the same category as the oft-repeated one regarding how many bears I had seen on the trip. In defense of every good, law-abiding visitor I had met, I continued.

"Actually, everyone I have met has been friendly, and many have offered good conversation, food, drinks, and other kind acts. I try to wave at everyone who drives past me, and most wave back."

Had I concluded my reply at this point, an honorable answer would have been given to a legitimate question. But, no. In a fatigue-induced lapse of sensibility, I blundered into a statement as absurd as the one made by President Harry Truman at a press conference on November 30, 1950, when he unintentionally and inaccurately suggested that the United States was considering use of the atomic bomb in Korea.

"But I *have* noticed that no one from Georgia waves back. They must all be from Atlanta," I added with the last unnecessary tap of a hammer on a nail already flush. Intending no offense, I just assumed that this reporter understood the comment to be a lighthearted observation of the effects of population density on human behavior. I had lived in Atlanta for five years and knew what a daily, ninety-minute commute in stop-and-go traffic would do to a soul. I understood Atlantans and had already forgiven them for what one inexperienced in such matters might consider a character flaw. I was just trying to explain them and quickly forgot that I had even made the statement. Two days later my memory would be surprisingly refreshed.

Friday morning began in the usual manner, with me wide awake before dawn. As with my gear, the heavens and I had reached a state of harmonious consanguinity, and Pleiades had become my designated timepiece on cloudless nights. When it rose on the eastern horizon, I knew it was near midnight; at its zenith, I knew it was about to fade into the light of a new day. It was the same little cluster of seven stars, also known as the Seven Sisters (the seven daughters of Atlas and Pleione in Greek mythology), that I had mistakenly thought, as a young boy, to be the Little Dipper.

I sat upright, still in my sleeping bag, to watch it peak in the sky above me and concluded that shepherds of ancient times probably had the lowest turnover rate of any profession in the history of mankind. As the stars faded and my surroundings began to reflect form, I realized that the campsite I had selected, in total darkness the previous night, was within a stone's throw of a large family cemetery. If my snoring had disturbed anyone during the night, no one felt it important enough to complain. When enough light made it possible to study my map, I also discovered that I had camped precisely on its eighth fold. Only three folds remained, and the most anticipated section of the trek would be walked that day.

Before the sun had risen very far in the clear, morning sky, I was enjoying the peaceful motion of a rocking chair on the front porch of what had once been the three-season (remember the rating of my sleeping bag and tent) retreat of the Moses and Bertha Cone family. Flat Top Manor was not the quaint American dream of a little mountain cabin on five acres of land. Rather, it was a 23-room, frame mansion, constructed in the Beaux-Arts style, perched high on a 3,500-acre-plus tract of land sprawled over Flat Top and Rich Mountains.

Cone had already amassed a fortune from investments in the textile business when his lofty getaway was completed in 1900, thirty-three years before Senator Byrd's historic suggestion of a parkway to President Roosevelt at Shenandoah National Park. But unbeknownst to Moses, even at his passing in 1908, Flat Top Manor was on a collision course with the eventual route of the Parkway. Bertha, however, enjoyed the estate many more seasons until her death in 1947 but anguished over the prospect of the Parkway coursing near or through the lovely property adorned with orchards, vegetable gardens, ponds, lakes, natural plantings, and several miles of carriage roads and hiking trails. Three years following her death, the Cone heirs donated the property to the National Park Service for its use as a "park and pleasuring ground in perpetuity."

I had already decided that, if it was raining when I arrived at Flat Top Manor, I would claim a rocking chair and not budge from it until the skies cleared. Whether that took two hours or two days would be inconsequential;

the rangers would just have to deal with me, at which time it would then become, experience assured me, a true matter of consequence.

The morning, however, was beautiful, and I basked in the warmth of a new day, pardoned before convicted, knowing I had soon better walk it away than rock it away. Joggers and walkers and lovers of horses were already about the grounds, enjoying them in the same way that the benevolent Cone family had opened them to the local community in their time. I wondered if any of my ancestors along the Leonard line had ever enjoyed the view from one of these rocking chairs. The census records of 1900 and 1910 indicate that many of them worked in the cotton mills established by Cone over a hundred miles away in Greensboro, N.C. The death certificate of poor Eli Clem Leonard states that, at the age of seventy-three, he was mangled under the wheels of a freight car while working as a watchman at the Revolution Cotton Mill. Before finally rising from the comfort of my rocker, I silently thanked both Moses and Eli for their sacrificial contributions, equal in their own right, that had made my enjoyment of denim fabric and that moment possible.

Not long after the acquisition of the Cone estate, Superintendent Sam Weems was pressured by his regional director to move Parkway headquarters from its location in Roanoke, Va., to Flat Top Manor. Chilled by the thoughts of cold winters with deep snows, Weems scrambled to "find something for this house before [he got] moved into it." Appalachian crafts became the permanent quick-fix for his dilemma.

Feeling a bit underdressed wearing my hand-stitched trousers, hiking boots, and felt hat, I stepped through the same front door that wealthy members of the Cone family had so often done themselves in times past into what had evolved into a showcase for the Southern Highland Craft Guild. The elegant display of traditional and contemporary crafts of Appalachia was stunning, and I felt like I was walking through a fine museum.

Another visitor kept glancing my way, whose presumptive expression seemed to have mistaken me for a skilled artisan just arrived to begin one of many craft demonstrations offered at the center. I suppose I could have passed for the part with the outfit I was wearing and hands now worn and weathered. But I could neither weave nor throw a pot, and I had literally taken years to carve from wood my own self-portrait — a miniature hiking boot which became a "left" quite accidentally. Sensing I was about to be commissioned to complete some great work for which I would have had much appreciation but was sorely lacking in the skills necessary to create, I eased into a room less intimidating and the company of closer friends — books.

Thus far, I had managed to time my arrival at every visitor center I had encountered along the Parkway to their respective hours of operation. One convenient room on the ground floor of Flat Top Manor had been converted to such purpose. Eastern National, a not-for-profit cooperating association, had done much over the years to improve and assist such facilities along the Parkway, and I introduced myself to one of their associates who was working at the counter. Soon I was perusing the bookshelves stocked with themes and quality carefully selected to interpret the Parkway and enhance the experience of its visitors.

Two women near me debated nervously over which compact disc to purchase from a small selection of recorded music. Any of the choices would have been worthy replacement to the hardest of earned wages, but I feared they were perilously close to an oblivious mistake. Unable to restrain myself any longer, I pointed to one whose cover could have been a view from any number of overlooks along the Parkway. "They are all good," I interrupted. "But this one is the best. I have been backpacking the Parkway for the last twenty-six days and have heard every sound on that disc."

Apparently grateful that the difficult decision had been made for them, they purchased my recommendation and left the building. I resumed my study of titles and authors and, for the first time in my life, the companies who had published them. Fascinated with a new book detailing the hiking trails of North Carolina, I almost lost track of time and space as I delved into its pages. I had walked many of them, and I always found it entertaining to read another's opinion regarding their features and difficulty.

Then I heard it — a familiar sound whose first note caused me to look up from my book to make sure I had not just finished a seafood dinner at the Peaks of Otter Restaurant. This time "The Morning Sun" did not bring moistened eyes, but a smile. This time I was home for more than just a few hours.

I turned around slowly in search of the source of the music that interpreted the heart and soul of the Parkway. I was the only visitor in the room. The lady behind the counter looked up from her work and smiled. "Thanks," I replied and stepped back onto the Parkway.

By noon, the spacious picnic ground located in the Julian Price Memorial Park presented itself as a logical place for a thorough sponge bath and rest stop before my afternoon assault on Grandfather Mountain. By all appearances, every elementary school student in Watauga County seemed to be enjoying a field trip at the same location.

Rightfully joyous of their Friday freedom from the confining walls of structured classrooms, they chased butterflies through open fields and threw rocks into the waters of Boone Fork. Time would tell if what they had been taught the day before would ever be remembered. Their day in the park, though, would never be forgotten, and many would live to tell their own children of that wonderful day in September. At least one of them, smitten by the experience, might even dream of becoming a park ranger someday.

I rather enjoyed their playful chatter from an appropriate distance while my tent, wet from several nights of unusually heavy dewfall, dried in the sun. Lugging unnecessary weight made no sense whatsoever.

If true, Ranger Hope Powers never told me that a suspicious man had been reported loitering in the picnic grounds when he patrolled through the area just as I was leaving. I was beginning to develop a history of bumping into rangers in such places and could understand any misperceptions. I would have investigated myself had I still been a ranger — thoroughly and completely, especially considering my location and proximity to little children. But Ranger Powers and I had briefly met each other the previous day, and our less-hurried reunion immediately evolved into a friendly swap of war stories and Parkway news.

In addition to my camping dilemma, with which I had been grappling over the entire trip, another problem had been nagging me for almost three hundred miles. No sooner had the Linn Cove Viaduct been opened for traffic in 1987, than the photographers, bungee jumpers, climbers, and all other manner of sightseers and daredevils had forced park officials to close it to pedestrians.

I had no desire to violate either the letter or spirit of any park regulation, but this prohibition doggedly presented a serious impediment to someone attempting to backpack the entire length of the Parkway. I had still not formulated a solution to my predicament, and this barrier, only eight miles ahead, sat waiting for me like a mousetrap on the shoulder of Grandfather Mountain.

I was seriously considering disregarding a sign that stated, if memory served correctly, "Pedestrians Not Permitted on Viaduct." Dare I venture onto the famous S-and-one-half curve, and hope, for a length of 1,240 feet, that the rangers were busy elsewhere? Should I further reduce the likelihood of an embarrassing trial in Federal court by delaying its passage until three o'clock in the morning, when all good rangers should be asleep? Dare I even discuss the matter with Ranger Powers and risk a surveillance trap?

"Sure. Go ahead and walk across the thing," came his quick reply. "It's in my district. We only enforce that regulation when somebody creates a traffic hazard."

"I really appreciate that. Say, does your district still end just the other side of the viaduct?"

"Yep. Sure does."

Still concerned, I continued. "So. If I step into the sights of a hungry buck ranger waiting for me on the far end of it, you'll vouch for me?"

"Sure will."

With an admission ticket as good as in my back pocket, I quickened my pace in the direction of the most prominent engineering feature on the Parkway. In retrospect, part of me wished I had not blown right past Price Lake, the largest water feature along the Parkway, and had walked its shoreline trail. But that little diversion would have disrupted and disordered the tale not yet concluded.

Soon I began a gentle climb over the last 7½-mile section of the Parkway to be constructed. Which route it would take over the delicate features of the tallest mountain along the Blue Ridge proper and perhaps the oldest mountain in North America had been disputed for decades. The National Park Service had argued for a route higher up the mountain. The owner of the mountain had stubbornly held out for a lower route. When the fussing and cussing ceased and

"By the time I reached the Linn Cove Viaduct, I knew I had just taken the grandest walk of my life." Photo taken September 26, 2003.

a compromise was reached, pure harmony prevailed, and stepping over the underpass at Holloway Mountain Road was like crossing a threshold into the reverence of a massive cathedral around which every curve I entered another grand hall.

As the stairway ascended, I soon found myself in the regal company of the silent remnants of a once colder climate. Strong and prickly "he-balsams" stood guard in every cove. Soft and dainty "she-balsams" curtsied quietly above and below. How much better they looked scattered randomly by nature than planted in rows. To know the difference between red spruce and Fraser fir, one only had to accept their extended handshake. I wanted to meet them all, even the nodding ladies' tresses on the embankments only inches tall.

Autumn had arrived as scheduled on the mountain, and the deciduous trees fluttered in color amidst the green permanence of conifers and ageless hues of gray on enormous boulders. Carefully dodging the heavy traffic of weekend motorists arrived early, I peeked over bridges spanning rushing waters and deep chasms. In the coolness of elevation, I reached for a jacket.

By the time I reached the Linn Cove Viaduct, I knew I had just taken the grandest walk of my life, having spent more time looking up, down, and behind than ahead of me. Sometime between the sunset and afterglow, when all the cars had gone home, I crossed the viaduct and recalled the grandest day the Parkway had ever seen. I know. I was there.

The day was September 11, 1987. The occasion was the fifty-second anniversary of the day construction began on the Parkway. The last and most expensive section of the Parkway had just been completed, and the proper day and venue had arrived for its dedication. The distraction of the Korean conflict had snuffed the first attempt to dedicate it prematurely in 1950.

Banners flew. Music played. Dignitaries arrived. Among them beamed Gary Everhardt, the current Parkway superintendent; former superintendents Sam Weems, Granville Liles, and Joe Brown; National Park Service Director William P. Mott Jr.; and U.S. Secretary of Transportation Elizabeth Dole. Even the U.S. Postal Service joined the occasion and offered a special, one-day cancellation for the temporary post office of "Grandfather Station, Linville, NC 28646." Not only had my Patty designed the cachet, but collectors of such memorabilia would have to look hard to notice her initials "ptp" camouflaged carefully on the stylized drawing of the Linn Cove Viaduct printed on the limited edition of envelopes sold that day.

But it was the "Parade of Years on Wheels" that made the show. Led by a 1935 Studebaker, a motorcade of mostly convertible motor vehicles, representing every year of manufacture through 1987, transported the honorable guests to the focal point of the occasion. Neither a bomb threat, the fog, nor the stern look of the former commander of U.S. forces in Vietnam, General William Westmoreland, riding in a 1944 Willys Jeep, could dampen the celebration at the ribbon-cutting ceremony at the Linn Cove Viaduct.

Had that really been its grandest day, or had I just walked it?

24

Derailed in Avery County

"For I was an hungred, and ye gave me meat: I was thirsty,
and ye gave me drink: I was a stranger, and ye took me in."
— Matthew 25:35, King James Version
of *The Holy Bible*

Though exhilarating, the climb over the shoulder of old Grandfather Mountain had drained me for the week, my fat reserves having been depleted to the point that my caloric intake now controlled more directly how long my engine could run. Had I consorted with automobiles for so long that I had metamorphosed into one of them? For breakfast on Saturday morning I would have much preferred a tank of premium-grade, butter pecan ice cream over a regular cup of instant grits. Aside from the false notion that it could propel me faster and farther down the Parkway, ice cream would have more effectively assuaged a mild depression wrought by a few things recently come unraveled.

My choice of campsite the previous night had not been a stellar decision. In the daily chore of attempting to find a suitable location that was safe and legal, I had pushed myself once again into abject darkness and the inability to take an accurate reading on the surrounding terrain. Despite having to fight through the wretched tangle of a mountain laurel thicket, my little flashlight of limited range eventually found a spot level and clear enough to qualify as a temporary home. As the night progressed, however, and the long-awaited light of day finally arrived, I realized that I had camped in a dry wash between the Parkway and a state highway. What little traffic that had come through that night felt uncomfortably close, and by morning I was grateful that nobody had fallen asleep at the wheel in my vicinity. Though it could happen following the most meticulous of ground inspections, the location I had chosen on which to pitch my tent probably played a contributing role in creating another aggravation.

My air mattress had developed a slow leak during the night, rendering it useful only as an expensive ground cloth halfway to dawn, and my hips and shoulders felt as if they had assumed the same rutty complexion as the surface on which they had rested. Repairing the leak, though, would not be a difficult challenge — just an uncomfortable one. My veteran mattress was already scarred with wounds patched from previous battles, and I possessed the means by which another could be healed. But finding the nearly microscopic puncture would require submersing it, inflated, in a body of water to locate the telltale sign of tiny spurting bubbles. And I was not looking forward to wrestling this beast, prone to fight like a panicked drowning victim, in an icy cold mountain stream in late September. The simple bathtub, my battlefield of preference, had now found itself on my own list of endangered species.

A leak of another sort, created by my own negligence, had nearly cost me the use of my cookstove and could have caused me serious injury. My failure to snugly tighten the pump assembly into the fuel tank before pressurizing it caused a small fire to erupt in the wrong place when I lit a match to preheat the stove. Slapping and flailing the fiery contraption, first with my bare hands to distance it from my cross-legged lap, and finally with my bandanna, which had fortunately already been laid out for use as a pot holder, I managed to extinguish the blaze. Though my fingers and ego sustained only first degree burns, the plastic parts of the pump assembly suffered those of the second and third degree but remained miraculously functional.

Despite these minor stumbling blocks, more psychological in nature than physical, I looked brightly upon the day ahead of me and ingested my cup of grits like a man. I had plenty enough fuel to coast eleven miles on a gentle, thousand-foot descent into Sunday and my fourth day of rest at a place where I had spent the most glorious season of my life — Linville Falls.

The prospect of an easy day of walking tempted me early in the morning to detour onto the Flat Rock Loop Trail, one of my favorites. Patty and I had spent entire days frolicking on the broad, exposed, quartzite beds along the western flank of Grandmother Mountain. Enjoying its perpetual breeze on warm, summer days, we watched hang gliders, launched from nearby Grandfather Mountain, float into the valley below. He-mountain and she-mountain made the perfect couple and stood as ancient examples to what young, married couples like us could someday become.

A botanical paradise spotted with islands of vegetation, the Flat Rock had become my amateur outdoor university for the study of pioneer plant species, wildflowers, snakes, and skinks. Between naps, daydreams of our future, fried chicken, and wild blueberries, we handily employed the cheapest field guides our meager wages could afford at the time — the *Golden Nature Guide* series.

One particular day, while hiking the woodland path from the Parkway out to the Flat Rock, we found a thick, hard-bound book worth at least its weight in freshly dug ginseng. It was the *Manual of the Vascular Flora of the Carolinas*! I was elated. Any serious botanist who could afford one owned one. If turned in through the park's lost and found system, I knew it could soon be mine if no one claimed it. With a little more study of botanical terminology, I could "key out" just about any plant native to North Carolina with its descending lists of diminishing characteristics.

As I gloated in my newfound discovery and imminent good fortune, an image began to prick my conscience. A few days earlier, over thirty miles away, a gentleman camped at Crabtree Meadows had been toting one of those books on a guided walk I was conducting. I quickly checked the inside cover of the book and found no name inscribed on it. Yes! Its owner would have to be very specific about where it had been lost to make a valid claim on it.

On my next trip to Crabtree Meadows, I was surprised to find the aforementioned man still camped there. In a gutsy gesture designed to clear my conscience, I feigned the need of his book to identify a wildflower that had stumped me. Dejectedly, he replied that he had lost it — no, no, no— somewhere on the Flat Rock Trail. Stunned, I took a seat at his picnic table to grieve with him and began to ask meaningless, inconsequential questions such as, "Exactly which day were you up there?"

Until the last reserve of honesty from parts previously unknown to me prevailed, the rescuing angels of heaven and the tormented spirits of hell nearly ripped the skinny limbs from my torso in a vicious game of tug-of-war unfit for little children to behold. When I returned from my car with his book, one would have thought, based on his jubilant celebration, that a precious, once-lost wedding ring had been miraculously recovered from the floor of a vast ocean. Eventually I felt better, but the closest I ever came to owning this book was years later when, as a district ranger, I convinced headquarters to purchase a copy for the Balsam Gap reference library.

"He thought, that, if waked up from a trance ... he could tell by the plants what time of year it was within two days," Ralph Waldo Emerson said of Henry David Thoreau at his funeral. Bright, orange-red clusters of berry-like fruit waving high on the mountain ash and shy, purple petals nodding lowly on the closed gentian were the indicators I chose to employ on my jaunt that Saturday morning. Plus or minus two weeks on each side of the twenty-seventh day of September would have been my own crude calculation based on much less sophisticated study and experience. For a former Parkway ranger, though, the steady flow of leaf lookers was the giveaway indicator, far more accurate than any of the natural signs, that the month of October was right around the corner.

A northbound vehicle slowed to a stop in the middle of the road, and with traffic already heavy, I could foresee an unsafe traffic jam rapidly beginning to develop. Probably an inconsiderate camera jockey from the flatlands acting on a sudden urge to take a picture, I prejudged.

"Are you Tim, the guy hiking the Parkway?" asked an elderly lady at the wheel, leaning across the lap of an older, frail man in the front passenger seat. Both appeared to be aged well into their eighties and, from the looks of their vehicle and dress, were of limited means. There was something about their smiles, though, that instantly told me I was talking to good, humble mountain people whose advanced years had somewhat diminished their ability to discern approaching danger.

"Yes ma'am," I replied nervously through the man's lowered window. As traffic that had backed up behind them tried to maneuver around them, oncoming traffic braked hard to dodge them all. Without the protection of air bags and steel-reinforced doors, I suddenly felt like a slice of bologna about to become the featured ingredient of a multi-vehicle sandwich.

"We've been driving up and down the Parkway all morning looking for you. We read about you in the newspaper yesterday and want to talk to you," she implored and, with a cheerful glint in her eye added, "I also have a little surprise for you."

My diversion out to the Flat Rock flashed guiltily through my mind as I realized that I had been the cause of their wasted gasoline. Not wanting us to be the cause of an accident, I glanced around for some place for her to pull off the road. Lost Cove Cliffs Overlook, situated a short distance down the Parkway, appeared to be the perfect refuge where our conversation could continue. I had wanted to stop there anyway to rest and make some detailed notes in my journal. It was a locally famous observation point from which could be viewed the mysterious, legendary lights that dance some nights across Brown Mountain in the distance. I had seen them myself on a few occasions from that overlook and had often invited visitors, following my campfire programs at nearby Linville Falls, to join me there via car caravan for a rare opportunity to see them. Straining to look back in the direction I was pointing, she agreed to meet me in the overlook and proceeded to make a dangerous U-turn in the middle of the road. As I walked onward, I cringed at the sounds of annoyed traffic behind me and prayed to be spared the sound of crunching metal.

I was not able to read the article until I returned home, but it was apparent that reporter John O'Dowd of the *Watauga Democrat* had not only pleased his editor by finding me, but he had written a piece that inspired local residents Bunnie and Russell Richards to do an extraordinary thing. I would have talked to them the entire day in appreciation of their efforts to meet me, but Bunnie was a practical woman and soon decided it was time for me to walk again. I asked to take their picture by the overlook sign. Russell was so feeble he could hardly walk with a cane. I was humbled. Then I melted.

"It's not much, but we want you to have it," came the words behind extended arms that presented a small paper bag folded neatly across the top. I looked inside the bag. It was filled with cheese and crackers, a large, homegrown tomato, and a packet of salt fashioned from a piece of aluminum foil. I looked at them. I looked at their car. I thought of a beatitude related to the meek people of the earth. I thought of the story of the poor widow who cast two mites (all that she had) into the treasury. I thought of another passage from the book *Joshua*: "The poor never have enough for themselves ... but always have enough to give away."

Bunnie and Russell Richards of Boone, North Carolina, met me at Lost Cove Cliffs Overlook at Milepost 310.0 in North Carolina. Photo taken September 27, 2003.

I thought about the official slogan of the Boy Scouts of America — Do a Good Turn Daily — and imagined a world changed by this simple precept.

This had not been my first experience on the trek with charity in its purest form. On my sixth day, Michelle Spinner, a seasonal Parkway maintenance worker, drove into an overlook where I was washing out my socks in Otter Creek. Her last name sounded awfully familiar, and I finally asked if any of her relatives had ever worked on the Parkway. She proudly told me that Jewel Spinner was her uncle and that he had recently chosen retirement in lieu of being forced to obtain a commercial driver's license (CDL) to do the same job he had been doing for years. "Just did not want to take the DMV exams," she said of his decision. That definitely sounded like the Jewel Spinner with whom I had done a little firefighting — a forget-the-paperwork, get-the-job-done kind of a man. I could empathize with him; just a few months earlier I had obtained a CDL, and the exams were no cakewalk.

Michelle, I learned during the course of our conversation, had been struggling for seven years as a seasonal worker in hopes of getting a full-time position on the Parkway. During the winter months she worked part-time for the U.S. Postal Service. I had walked a few miles in her shoes myself, and sensing that her youthful optimism was beginning to fade, I encouraged her to persist with her dreams.

About an hour later, I ran into her again at Otter Lake Overlook, where she handed me a paper bag filled with two cans of vegetable beef stew, two packs of crackers, two meat sticks, and a candy bar. She refused to accept any money for what she had purchased with her own meager funds from a nearby store I had planned to visit anyway. "It's not much," she also said.

Neither had this been my first experience in life with charity in its purest form. I thought about the cold winter morning when I pulled into a rest area along an interstate highway, and due to a failing alternator, my battery was too weak to restart the car. As I displayed the universal distress signal — raised hood adorned with pleading jumper cables — a shiny, expensive car soon pulled into the parking space next to me. The man driving it appeared to ignore my silent request, and as he began to walk toward the restroom, I asked if he could help me jump start my car. "No, I don't have time," came his short, hurried reply. Surprised, I sat back inside my car, whose interior was rapidly reaching a state of equilibrium with the subfreezing, ambient temperature. When the man returned to his car, he refused to even make eye contact with me and sped away.

A few minutes later, an old man from West Virginia, driving a dilapidated pickup truck with two of its wheels already in the junkyard, filled the parking space left vacant by the hurried man. He was pulling a small trailer loaded with another truck that appeared to already have all four of its wheels in the junkyard. Unaffected by the impatient horn-blowing launched by drivers whose egress from the rest area was temporarily impeded by his trailer, his only purpose in parking next to me had been to loan me a charge from his battery. He had already made his bathroom stop and was exiting the rest area when he recognized my plight and drove inconveniently out of his way to assist me.

Bunnie and Russell reminded me so much of that humble man, who also refused any payment for his kindness. I made a meal out of their fresh tomato and two large slices of cheddar cheese at the picnic table in the overlook. There was no need to carry that kind of weight on my back when I could carry it in my stomach. I had done the same thing with the two cans of stew Michelle had given me — cooked and eaten them immediately. Meat sticks I would have never purchased, but what a spicy addition crumbled bits of them made to bland grits, I later discovered.

I thought also of the man of Middle Eastern descent, driving a car with New York license plates, who had stopped and offered me a ride and the ranger who had given me a banana and all the people who had offered me the use of their cell phones and all the people who had offered to call, write, or e-mail Patty to report my location and condition... and *I thought that waterfalls, scenic views, sunsets, and wildlife would be the meat of this hike.* Human kindness had usurped their ability to leave the most indelible impressions; I had certainly stumbled upon the perfect hike.

Prior accidents involving motorcycles are easy to discern along the Parkway, especially by someone walking. Short, narrow skidmarks memorialize the final, frightful moments before the driver lost control of the machine. Painfully ugly, irregularly shaped gouge marks on the pavement indicate where metal twisted and ground into the asphalt. Intermittent spaces between gouge marks suggest that the motorcycle flipped and tumbled. Small pieces of broken mirror glass, flecks of chrome finish, shreds of torn denim and leather, and traces of medical supply packaging are never completely cleansed from the scene.

Ouch. Not far past my tomato treat I discovered a fairly recent scene where a motorcycle had gone into a curve too fast and struck a wooden guide rail. Although the rail did not fail, three sections of it were grotesquely bent out of shape at the point of greatest impact, and it appeared that the motorcycle peeled down its splintery surface for a good two hundred feet. I noted in my journal that the driver, if not dead, probably wished that he was, considering the injuries he must have sustained.

Not far into the afternoon, I took a gamble that a Parkway access ramp to another highway might lead to some type of refreshments within a reasonable walking distance. As the intersection came into view, so also did a little country store and a sign advertising — I could not believe it — ICE CREAM! Last stop for premium grade fuel, I imagined, and recklessly blew past the stop sign into oncoming traffic as the newest unnamed, untitled, unregistered, uninsured, unrecognizable make of motor vehicle on the road.

Only in Avery County can a total stranger, carrying a backpack, walk into such an establishment and instantly become an accepted member of the community. A sandwich deli and the welcome I received when I stepped through the front door caused me to temporarily forget why I had stopped. "Just put on it whatever you think I might like," were my only instructions to Janine Hughes, the designated master builder of fine sandwiches. "But no pickles or black olives," I quickly recanted before moving on to a corner of the store where a small group of men offered me a chair.

Lee Dale, a respected Saturday regular, rightfully occupied the throne. An oxygen tank connected to a snaky delivery apparatus provided him enough breath to note and solve every problem in the world. I silently nicknamed him "Governor" and nodded and agreed with everything he had to say. You just do not argue with someone that age in that condition.

Duke King, a seasonal lunch regular, could have easily played Robert Redford's role in the movie *The Horse Whisperer*. A confirmed snowbird from Florida, he spent the warmer months in the mountains of western North Carolina training thoroughbred horses. Tall, lanky, and handsomely attired in western style, he had a quietly sophisticated manner of speaking that soon rescued me from the good but dull sense Governor Dale was making. Just as I was about to conclude that I had finally met a smooth talker with a genuine honest streak, a lady leaned over behind me and whispered, "Says he is married, but we have yet to meet his wife," in an accusatory sort of way.

No man in the house, including the Duke, could match the attention George Strait commandeered of every female in the place each time his image appeared in the movie *Pure Country*, playing on a television set perched high in the corner of the room. Grown women stood frozen and silent, with jaws dropped and hands tucked in the rear pockets of their blue jeans every time he walked across the screen. Sidelined temporarily, a signed photograph of Garth Brooks smiled jealously on a nearby wall, while another of President George W. Bush firmly established the political persuasions of owners Sam and Christa Poore.

Travis Proctor was the most reserved member of the lunch-corner triumvirate. A wiry, mustached, weather-worn man recently retired from the local telephone company, he took an immediate, curious interest in my trek. Claiming to know the editors of two local newspapers, he soon had me writing a short bio and hoisting on my backpack for pictures made with his digital camera. "You walked right past the road that goes down to my cabin two miles back up the Parkway. Next time you're up this way you've got to stop by and see it," he said with eyes revealing as much pride in what he was trying to describe as genuine hospitality. "I'll come back to visit," I promised.

It was beginning to feel like the kind of place I could spend the better part of the afternoon, especially when a thunderous storm burst across the mountain, bringing a steady rain that showed no sign of leaving in a hurry. An impromptu string band, which formed one member at a time on the front porch, further cemented me to a wooden bench where Moses (Sam and Christa's dog) and I shared equal halves of a large bag of chips.

Unlike a boring convenience store, where a security monitor would have replaced the movie on the television set and customers would not have been welcome beyond the point of purchase, the owners of this store encouraged folks to loiter. Christa spent more time wandering through the store talking to an equal mix of tourists and members of the local community than she did ringing up their purchases. Horseshoe tracks painted on the floor invited one to wander through aisles stocked with such novelties as red pepper jelly and pumpkin butter and more practical items like "Big Strike" floating fish food for ponds and "Dionne" udder balm. I was tempted to purchase some dry skin lotion sold as "Cowboy Magic" that was "formulated for outdoor people," but settled for a spare pair of triple "A" batteries for my flashlight and — I almost forgot — a heaping dish of ice cream. Colder weather was bound to kill my original batteries soon.

Sam seemed to maintain a detached presence around the store while Christa and her cousin, Janine, clearly managed things. But he always seemed to be available just about the time a customer needed help loading rolls of barbed wire or fifty-pound bags of "12 Legends" textured horse feed. Known formerly as "Yosemite Sam" during his days of monster truck fame, he had settled in to the tamer life of an independent feed and seed dealer and Christmas tree farmer. "Where do you plan to spend the night?" he suddenly asked me with a seemingly suspicious curiosity.

"Down at the Linville Falls Campground. It's only about five more miles down the Parkway and I really should get going," I answered, reaching for the rain gear in my backpack.

"You know, it's supposed to rain until midnight, and then a cold front is moving in behind it," he cautioned.

"That's okay. Rain and I have become well acquainted on this trip, and I'm sort of looking forward to colder weather. I'll be fine."

"Before you leave, come around back. I want to show you something."

Proud of his newly constructed barn, Sam pointed out a loft filled with fresh hay. "You're welcome to spend the night up here. Jacob [his donkey] and Abraham [his mule] might make a little fuss during the night, but pay them no mind," he beamed.

I have never spent a cozier night, stretched out over bales of comfortable, summer-scented hay underneath the softer keyboard of a tin roof played by millions of tiny fingers of rain. Just as Sam had forecast, the rain ceased around midnight, and Jacob brayed intermittently throughout the night as if in the throes of a bad dream or severe gas pains. Once during the night, I heard a soft thump on the wooden floor and shined my flashlight in the direction of the sound. Horton, their barn cat, was so frightened by my wild hair and suddenly illuminated appearance, half in and half out of my sleeping bag, that I neither saw nor heard him the remainder of the night.

According to a thermometer hanging on the barn, Sunday morning began at a cool forty degrees, and the sky was clear. Cousin Janine (I now felt like part of the family) had mentioned to me the previous day that she managed a cafe about a mile up the road and encouraged me to partake of their breakfast buffet. I detested the thought of patronizing a business on a Sunday and being the cause of someone else having to work on that traditional day of rest, but I had already trapped myself into the necessity of breaking one of my own ground rules. I needed to beat it on down to the Linville Falls area just to find a decent place to rest myself for the day. The choice between my usual fare of instant grits versus scrambled eggs, bacon, sausage, biscuits, and gravy confessedly played a major role in the decision I had to make.

Janine welcomed me to a table and refused to accept any payment for the meal, forcing me to leave a tip, I hope large enough to cover its cost, to a flabbergasted waitress who only brought me a cup of hot chocolate. Travis, in upgraded attire on his way to church, soon joined me at my table. As I walked back down to the Parkway entrance ramp, Sam and Christa, on their way to the cafe or church or both, tooted their horn in passing and waved like it was the last time they would ever see me. Like Bunnie and Russell, Jean and Edgar, and all the others, these were people to whom I would be forever welded.

Feeling somewhat fatigued and a little guilty about clicking off mileage on my designated day of rest, I fairly ambled rather than strode down the Parkway, relishing the musky smell of botanical maturity in the autumn air. Yes, I *had* swallowed the gift of a handful of raisins. And I *had* called Patty on cell phones owned and offered by others. And I *had* been conclusively certified as a bum by Horton himself. But I *had* resisted the strong temptation to rent a motel room, and I could not imagine any circumstance that would require me to violate my ground rules related to firearms and fires.

Thusly absorbed in the process of self-evaluation and pathetic rationaliza-

The author's home for a night, the barn behind Sam and Christa Poore's store in Pineola, North Carolina. Photo taken June 5, 2004.

tion, I nearly stepped on a little cottontail rabbit. Frozen in that glazed, paralyzed state of fear common to his kind, he was apparently munching on breakfast in tall grass only two feet from the edge of the road when I surprised him. A touch on his head with the tip of my walking stick prompted him back into a thicket and out of the range of my burgeoning road kill log. "Run, Fiver, run," I borrowed from the book *Watership Down*.

Soon thereafter, a southbound vehicle whizzed past, suddenly braked hard, and pulled onto the grass shoulder ahead of me. There was something about this driver's manner of stopping that made me slightly uncomfortable, and a gut feeling told me it had nothing to do with a rabbit running across the road from my blind side. As I approached the car, occupied by an older man and woman, I noticed from the license plate that these folks were from Georgia, specifically Union County. Good old north Georgia mountain people, I hoped.

"Hey, mister. You the feller that's hiking this here Parkway?" he asked rather abruptly.

"Yes sir," I answered cautiously, while furiously attempting to evaluate his body language and state of mind. Wide smiles formed instantly on both of their faces, and my initial anxiety began to dissipate.

"We just read an article about you in the Boone newspaper. Said you said nobody from Georgia waved at you, that they must all be from Atlanta. We just wanted to make sure that somebody from Georgia said hello to you."

John O'Dowd had apparently quoted me verbatim in the *Watauga Demo-*

crat, I realized. But these good people from Georgia, who I immediately thanked and flattered, had left their copy of the newspaper back at the motel. From the sound of things though, it appeared that I had committed the cardinal sin of speaking too loosely to a reporter equipped with excellent shorthand skills. Talk like that could get a man shot on the I-285 beltway around Atlanta. For the remainder of the trip now, I would have to assume a defensive posture in the presence of Georgia vehicles from any of the Atlanta metropolitan counties such as Fulton, Cobb, and Dekalb. Book sales in Georgia, too, I assumed, were doomed.

My plan to spend the afternoon lounging in the Linville River picnic area backfired in my face as well. A breezy, partly cloudy cold front, exacerbated by the natural cooling effect of the Linville River flowing nearby, chilled me to the bone. I moved from table to table in a futile game of tag with the shadows, seeking sunny patches of warmth. Attempting to find the leak in my air mattress by pouring ice cold water over it with bare hands did not help matters. Normally packed with picnickers in better weather, the picnic area was a lonely place on this chilly day in comparison to the sociality I had enjoyed only a day earlier. As the day began to ebb to a close, I began walking down the spur road toward the campground, hoping to find a pay telephone from which I could call Patty before pitching my tent for the night.

Just before I reached the campground, however, a vehicle abruptly intercepted me from behind. "Jump in, and I'll show you my place," yelled Travis Proctor. "And you're welcome to spend the night if you like."

I could have ended my hike right there and lived happily ever after in Avery County. Sam and Christa had mentioned a farm they had for sale. But the story had not yet been completely written. I could have also done the same thing back in 1975, but there the fairy tale would have ended not far past its beginning.

25

Motorcycles

"The way is full of flowers and surprise views, tight turns one
after another so that the whole world rolls and pirouettes and
rises and falls away."
—*Zen and the Art of Motorcycle Maintenance,*
by Robert M. Pirsig

Travis Proctor, on eleven secluded acres of choice mountain land, had created, with his own hands, a paradise retreat of which many dream but few ever
realize. A bold, headwater spring of Lost Cove Creek not only provided a year-
round supply of pure water for his log cabin, but it also fed three small ponds
that spilled successively into each other before racing down the mountain, destined for the distant Atlantic Ocean. Fat trout and catfish filled the ponds, around
which he had transplanted, from the wild, beautiful flowering species such as
bee balm, Turk's-cap lily, and many others. A tiny plantation of Fraser fir, located
in one corner of the property, had been permitted to mature past the point of
marketable Christmas tree size to look as natural as the ones growing high on
Grandfather Mountain. At least one stately specimen was well on its way to
becoming a candidate worthy of a future holiday term at the White House in
Washington, D.C.

Clusters of rhododendron and rock walls, made from native stone, could
have deceived disoriented visitors into believing they were still on Parkway land
and had driven up on that imaginary log cabin which so many still believe is
provided to park rangers free of charge. Oh, that more Parkway neighbors were
like him; one look at how perfectly this homestead fit into the surrounding natural landscape and Stanley Abbott, in another time, would have hired Travis
Proctor as his chief assistant.

Approaching darkness soon ushered our walking tour of the grounds to the

211

interior rooms of his cabin, filled with the trappings of an obviously avid out-doorsman. Graciously shown the refrigerator and shower along the tour route, I was soon cleansed, fed, and seated by the warmth of a newfangled heater, swapping stories with someone with whom I was beginning to understand I had much in common.

A bumping noise behind the cabin interrupted our conversation momentarily. Travis listened intently as another sound mimicked one made by a rocking chair being dragged across the wooden floor of a front porch. Grabbing a flashlight and rushing for the door, he muttered something about a bear that had been making nocturnal foraging visits. I followed him out the door, hoping to get a glimpse of that magnificent wild animal I had not yet seen on my hike that everyone I met was certain I had.

"Must have been the wind," he concluded, much to my disappointment, after an intensive search in the darkness surrounding the cabin. "If you're interested, though, I've got something better than an old she-bear to show you," he added. Not waiting for an answer, he fired up several pieces of computer equipment cluttering one corner of his living room.

Digital photography had become an avocation for which no skill or interest could be discerned by anyone meeting him for the first time. But he was good, very good, to the point that I found myself mildly chastising him for cleverly manipulating unlikely clusters of wildflowers into the foreground scenes of waterfalls. "It's amazing what you can do with this stuff," he confessed with a wry smile, proud to have met someone who, like himself, could detect the faintest disruption in the natural order of things. From the cover of a blind, though, he had genuinely filmed wild turkey strutting about his property while colorful wood ducks fed in the ponds, all of which had been artfully choreographed to beautiful music. We spent half the night enjoying scenes of mountain ranges draped in sunrise and impressing each other with our knowledge of at least the common names of dozens of wildflowers.

For a retired man, he certainly had a nervous energy, and before daylight the next morning, I heard him banging around the cabin. "Let's go, Tim. I'm buying breakfast this morning," came a waking voice in the darkness. My plans for the day required an early start anyway, but "I'd be dadblamed," as Mom used to say, if I was going to let a man who had rescued me from a cold night and had gone to the trouble of copying his art onto three compact discs for me buy my breakfast as well.

Following a hearty meal at a locally historic restaurant in the small community of Linville Falls, during which I was forced to obtain the check from our waitress by stealth and subterfuge, I asked Travis to drop me off at the Linville Falls Visitor Center. Though it represented a lengthy detour from my point last walked on the Parkway, I was determined to hike a dead-end trail all the way out to Erwins View for one more look at the thunderous waterfall and head of the Linville Gorge Wilderness Area. Stanley Abbott was surely thinking about places like this and people like me when he announced, in 1939, that "large areas ... will

Travis Proctor created a paradise retreat adjacent to the Parkway near Milepost 310 in Avery County, North Carolina. Photo taken September 28, 2003.

remain undeveloped so that the adventurous may withdraw from the Parkway traffic to tramp or fish in the unbroken forests."

In the visitor center parking lot, I began the awkward process of finding the proper words to express my gratitude to Travis for his companionship and generosities. Before our farewell reached the point of conclusion, a car drove up and a woman, wearing an Eastern National uniform, stepped from it and began walking toward the visitor center. She looked familiar enough to risk an embarrassing mistake of identity, and with reserved volume and halfhearted effort, I tossed out the bait: "Vivian McKinney, is that you?"

Halted by the question, the woman slowly turned around and looked queerly at both of us. Before she could say anything, I took a cautious step or two away from Travis, volunteering, like a boot camp recruit, to accept my medicine if my assessment had been inaccurate. "It's Tim. Tim Pegram. I lived in the little ranger trailer behind your store one summer. Next to the Medfords."

Her puzzled look quickly vanished, and my offer of a cordial handshake was categorically dismissed in lieu of a bear hug she executed with a style and zest no other person can imitate. "Well, I'm glad to see you finally filled out to be a real man," were her first words, after releasing me only the distance of her extended arms, still clasping my shoulders with the strong, resolute hands of a native mountain woman. As a matter of explanation to my companion, she

Vivian McKinney, at the Linville Falls Visitor Center at Milepost 316.4 in North Carolina, kindly agreed to stow my weighty burden. Photo taken September 29, 2003.

continued. "Travis, this boy and his wife were just skinny little children when they lived up here. Now look at him."

Travis, apparently well acquainted with Vivian, cracked a smile and spared me any further embarrassment with a hasty exit. I walked this singular personality, who had not aged a single day in the nearly thirty years since I had last seen her, to her work station. There, she kindly agreed to stow my weighty burden while I walked, unencumbered as well of the past worries of an uncertain future, the familiar path to a waterfall of many pleasant memories.

By the time I walked the nearly 2½ miles from Erwins View back out to the Parkway proper, noontime had arrived, and I had not yet netted the first real Parkway mile of a new walking week. Still struggling to free myself from the grasp of Avery County, I lingered on the bridge spanning the Linville River, the largest stone-faced and the only triple-arch bridge on the Parkway, watching trout that would have to be caught another day. I still had about two weeks of walking ahead of me.

Only an afternoon of surprising observations permitted me to gradually get my train back on sound tracks headed in the direction of the future.

The occupants of two separate vehicles bearing Georgia license plates waved fervently. Whether they were begging forgiveness for past neglect, chiding me for my recent misstatement to the press, or just plain being friendly in a balancing confirmation of the law of averages I would never know.

This sign, near Milepost 321 in North Carolina, was enough warning to make a man thankful to be on foot. Photo taken September 29, 2003.

My first good view of the massive Black Mountain range, from which sprang Mount Mitchell, the highest point of land east of the Mississippi River, abruptly emerged in the distance. In a couple of days I would be subjected to its unmerciful reputation for producing weather anomalies; snowfall had been recorded at its peak at least once on every month of the calendar.

But it was three successive caution signs that I had never before seen on the Parkway that most captured my attention. One warned, "High Collision Area — Next 3 Miles." Another warned of a "Spiral Curve" ahead. And a third, simultaneously humorous and foreboding with its warning, depicted a stick figure, with arms flailing, being catapulted from the seat of a motorcycle which had lost contact with the road surface in a sharp curve. It was enough warning to make a man thankful to be on foot.

The Blue Ridge Parkway is indisputably one of the most popular motorcycle rides in the United States. Its design, however, plays siren and nemesis for too many unfortunate riders whose extra mile per hour or single second of inattention brings them tragedy. Their pain and suffering always anguished me as a ranger, and I never enjoyed that part of the job which required me to hose down the road surface or notify next of kin. The innocent victims I remember the most, and their collective stories justify my refusal to ever ride a motorcycle again.

One of my favorite instructors in basic law enforcement training took his wife out for a ride on the Parkway one Saturday morning. Witnesses behind him said he was not exceeding the speed limit on a straight, dry road when the rear tire blew out. They also noted that he courageously fought the wobbling bike until the front wheel finally folded into the frame, pitching them both headfirst over the handlebar onto the road surface. His wife died instantly, and he was critically injured, despite the protection of helmets. When I got the call to assist with this accident, I was a short distance away, supervising some young men working on an Eagle Scout project. No one affected would enjoy the remainder of that beautiful spring day.

Another day, I drove up on the scene of an accident involving a car and a motorcycle. A teenage girl, uninjured, was screaming hysterically, despite the attempts of her shaken, but also uninjured, boyfriend to calm her. The front of the car in which they had been riding had sustained a grotesque, V-shaped indentation to its front end, and the windshield was smashed. Parts of a motorcycle laid scattered over the roadway; the front wheel and fork had been completely severed from the frame. Its driver, writhing in pain, laid nearby, and my initial reaction was that I would soon be investigating a fatality. But his injuries miraculously proved to be minor, and when I interviewed him later in the emergency room of a local hospital, I discovered why. In the split second just before colliding head-on with the car, he jumped vertically from his motorcycle as high as he could leap, allowing his body to glance off the windshield over the top of the car. I doubt the young couple in the car ever skipped school, exceeded the speed limit, or crossed the center line on the Parkway again.

I would love to claim authorship of the following statement, which I first heard facetiously uttered by an instructor teaching the tort claims section of our Ranger Skills course at Grand Canyon National Park: "Many citizens of this great land apparently believe that the Constitution of the United States guarantees them the right to die in the national park of their choice."

Despite brochures, signs, and regulations designed to protect visitors from hazards obvious to most of us, a foolhardy few deliberately defy these warnings in reckless flirtations with death. Some choose to camp illegally in the grizzly bear mating grounds of Yellowstone National Park. Others choose to hike the Appalachian Trail through the Great Smoky Mountains National Park in January without proper winter gear. A handful of speedsters on so-called "crotch rockets" attempt to set land speed records every year on the Blue Ridge Parkway.

I always considered myself an equal opportunity ranger and declared private war on these fellows with the same vengeance I exacted on poachers who had nerve enough to set a fire in the park to divert my attention while they treed and shot a bear a short distance from the ranger station. Except for the tedious scaled drawings I would be required to construct of their accident scenes, it mattered little to me if they killed themselves or not. I once even thought it a good idea to close the Parkway periodically to all other traffic just to let them get it out of their systems. But it was the innocent, shaken family they ran off the road while passing a vehicle in a blind curve that brought my blood to a boil. And, as I also did with poachers, I employed every legal trap and trick to stop them.

With their superior acceleration and cornering abilities, those who chose to run could not be stopped and often vanished onto an exit ramp. For them, I once delayed the complete marking of a new patrol car and equipped it externally with only grill lights and insignia on the doors. From the rear, it looked like the sedan of a bona fide visitor, and the lawless bunch would often buzz obliviously past me on a double yellow line. For those who decided to run, I could at least note their license plates for future prosecution. For those who chose to stop, I often thanked them first for so doing.

To every motorcyclist I met on the hike, I waved. Like some of the bicyclists I met, a few were locked into their own little fantasy world of escape and sang past me like I did not exist. Those on glitzy, expensive machines often startled me with two shrill toots of a horn, while I stumbled in their wake of stereophonic country music. A few rugged contemporaries, whose battered lives had somehow rolled past much youthful mischief to a more peaceful state of existence, rumbled past on choppers and answered my wave with a hand of friendship extended in the respected four o'clock position.

All past sinners were forgiven, and a new generation of rangers would now have to enforce the words of Edward Abbuehl, Stanley Abbott's actual chief assistant, to a new generation of daredevils: "It would be a mistake for a visitor to get on the parkway and see how fast he can cover the section."

26

Skulking About

We were within four feet of each other when I first saw him. I came to an abrupt stop, and he simultaneously woke from his nap on a sun-drenched rock. Hoping to make another friendly acquaintance, I offered my best translation into gray squirrel chatter. His tense, flattened body gradually relaxed into a less frightened posture, and soon he was sitting upright trying to decipher my broken "Squenglish." A curious nose sniffed the cold, autumn air to which his sun bath had brought respite, and with fresh courage, he began to inch my way. Cashews and camera became my operative thoughts, as I slowly released the breast and waist straps of my pack and began to let its weight slide down my back. Before it reached the ground, though, some instinctive alarm sent my furry friend scurrying back into the cover of thick woods.

Not only did he forfeit a rich snack, but he missed our parallel stories as well. I wanted to tell him about the nap I once took in the sun underneath Courthouse Valley Overlook on a similarly cold, breezy day. Through fetterbush and dog-hobble I had struggled all morning, chopping boundary with a bush axe over the crest of the world, underneath a weather-stunted canopy of American beech and northern red oak. When lunch time arrived at a perfect, windless spot, I collapsed, with welts on my ears and shins all scratched, onto the sunny carpet of an open patch of wild grass. There, where few had ever walked, between an apple and a sandwich, I tried to imagine, as did Stanley Abbott,

> ...the number of survey men and rodmen and project engineers who fought the sleet and the snow and the wind and cold and heat and snakes and many discom-

forts at comparatively low Civil Service pay, to really grind out the flagging of the road through those mountains, and the survey of that line, and the construction of it.

Then I succumbed to the bathing warmth of an autumn sun and, for a few dreamy minutes, napped like a fattened squirrel, pleasantly dazzled and weary from cutting all morning to provide food for my family, too. A little too weird, he might have thought and perhaps the reason he had run.

Patty had warned me a few days earlier that Dad had threatened to set up a mobile kitchen at an overlook somewhere ahead of me to surprise me with a hamburger and hot dog feast. The prospect had excited me, and I had eagerly looked for him around every curve. "Trail angels" we call them on the Appalachian Trail. Rarely do they make personal appearances, but they are known to leave treats like fresh fruit, cookies, candy bars, and weather forecasts hanging in trees. But too many days and two weekends had passed, and the hoped-for smell of freshly cooked chili and chopped onions eventually dissipated into the thin mountain air. Anticipation, based on bad information, could be a backpacker's worst enemy, especially with regard to good food.

By the time I reached Bear Den Overlook on Monday afternoon, the vision had all but vanished, and I silently forgave Dad for his occasional bad habit of speaking things he really did not mean. That overlook was quite the appropriate place to bury burgers and franks and bad feelings, because it was there that Mom, Dad, Patty, and I — somewhat lost — had stopped to study a map and eat our picnic lunch in the spring of 1975. A college degree. Another summer job on the Parkway. A borrowed pickup truck. An exit missed back at Linville Falls. And a dad always there when I really needed him and sometimes when I thought I did not.

By nightfall I was camped in a vacant spot in the middle of a Fraser fir plantation. Five ranger cars had fanned me that afternoon. Had they attended a meeting? Some training? Whatever the reason, they had certainly set a density record for my trek, and I was beginning to feel grateful for their disinterest in where I was camping. The tree rancher, too, would never know I had enjoyed the smell of Christmas for an entire night in late September. I should have left some homemade decorations on one of his trees to express my appreciation.

Tuesday promised luck with the early discovery of a four-leaf clover, which I carefully pressed in my spare notebook. By the end of my hike, my collection of lucky charms, begun with a penny found on the second day, would grow by eight more pounded pennies, one squashed quarter, one nicked nickel, and a buckeye shinier than a new piece of furniture. This adventure was certainly no way to make a living but was worth every moment of its living, especially, I noticed, upon passing a wild turkey hen and her young one feeding happily together with a doe and twin fawns not far past the clover.

A wayside exhibit at The Loops Overlook explained why I heard the laborious strain of powerful diesel engines pulling trains the entire previous night. Not long after the rumbling vibrations of one had faded into the stillness of an otherwise quiet night, another could be heard grinding in the distance in a never-ending procession. It was the Clinchfield Railroad winding and climbing over the Blue Ridge through eighteen tunnels, the last of which I had just unknowingly walked over back near McKinney Gap. From the same overlook, too, was a splendid view of a privately owned apple orchard, and there I concluded I could have just as easily enjoyed the industrious, outdoor life of an orchardman or a nurseryman.

Snuggled in the dip of Gillespie Gap, the Museum of North Carolina Minerals marked passage over the ninth fold of my map; two folds remained. Unchanged in appearance, its stone exterior looked the same as it had in 1975. But its quaint familiarity ended abruptly when I stepped through the entrance door into a bustling construction zone and the sounds of electric saws and banging hammers. Stunned momentarily by all the activity, I needed a few seconds to remember the rumor I had heard that it was being remodeled and outfitted with new exhibits.

I was lost. The old counter from which I had greeted thousands of visitors and pointed many of them in the direction of the restroom facilities had disappeared, along with the lapidary demonstration area where Patty had once polished her own fiery opal from a stone in the rough. Disoriented by the changes and my sudden immersion into such noisy, human activity, I dropped my backpack and quickly retreated to a safe corner still open to the public to shop for a post card.

Without warning, I found myself surrounded by Patty Lockamy and some of her staff, whose interest in monitoring the work in progress shifted temporarily to greeting me and quizzing me on the details of my hike. Odd, I thought, how I kept bumping into this busy chief of interpretation at Parkway visitor centers. Our last accidental meeting had been sixteen months earlier at the Peaks of Otter Visitor Center, where its exhibits, too, had been superbly refurbished.

As we chatted, I could not believe my eyes when Mom and Dad walked through the door. My first reaction was that I had become the unwitting victim of a carefully coordinated ambush on the order of a surprise birthday party. But it soon became apparent that the "random" element of my adventure had blossomed into quite an unexpected surprise. Instead of hamburgers and hot dogs, we enjoyed a finer picnic of homemade chicken stew, deviled eggs, fresh tomatoes, chocolate chip cookies, and sodas. Like an arrow shot at a moving target, our chance meeting had missed Bear Den Overlook by only eight miles and twenty hours. On the grand scale of the Parkway, I considered their intersection with my course a direct hit on the bull's-eye with nostalgically symbolic overtones.

"Your Mamaw Corn said if we found you to bring you home," said Mom with a smile. Mamaw was confused and worried at the age of ninety-five but probably would have felt the same way fifty years earlier.

I stared eastward into the distance, where somewhere she still courageously and defiantly walked with the aid of a walker, and guiltily replied, "She just doesn't understand me. Tell her I'll be fine." As I began to climb the steep embankment between the museum parking lot and the Parkway, I turned to wave goodbye to Dad's video camera and saw that look again on Mom's face. It was the same look I had seen one Sunday afternoon when I talked her into driving me up to the interstate highway so I could hitchhike back to the university. Men cannot shake that look from the faces of their grandmothers and mothers and wives as they often plunge forward and do that which they are driven to do.

Under the strain of a grotesquely full stomach and a pack heavier than it had been on the first day of September, I began the steep, southbound climb out of the gap. The aluminum pins attaching the pack to the frame squeaked an annoyingly incessant two-note refrain under the weight of full water bottles, a replenished fuel bottle, fresh trail food, and Mom's care package of cookies, trail mix, and whole apples. Concerned that my next reliable point of resupply was over fifty miles away in Asheville, I had drafted Dad into giving me a ride into the nearby town of Spruce Pine. I was now outfitted with enough supplies to finish the trip, if the weight did not kill me in the process.

My passage through the Little Switzerland Tunnel marked the first one I had entered since the only one in Virginia. The gaping jaws of twenty-four more of them stood in my path, and with some trepidation over what they might offer, I looked forward to an intimate inspection of their design and construction and the unusual sounds that echoed within them. Needless to say, as a boy, I had no tunnels in which to play.

Not far past the tunnel, the village of Little Switzerland presented itself close enough to the Parkway to warrant a brief detour, and I found its tiny post office only minutes away from closing. To Granddaughter Emily went a post card showing a picture of a bear in a tree and a sad explanation that it was the only one I had seen. To Patty went a package of weightier matters: an extra notebook that I had unnecessarily toted over 333 miles; exposed film; all the compact discs Travis Proctor had given me; and loads of business cards and brochures. Separately, to her also, went a post card to remember the Linn Cove Viaduct of an earlier year.

Tempted to eat dinner at the finest inn and restaurant in this displaced little hamlet, I chose instead to sit on a bench in front of it and trim more weight from my pack by eating all the cookies and apples my stomach could hold. Then I waddled about two more miles into the sunset of Backpacker's Paradise and camped with no prior reservation but some apprehension near a suspiciously named place called Gooch Gap.

When I ate and what I ate on the trek did not always coincide with the established norm of our civilized times. That should explain why I was standing at the doorway of the Crabtree Meadows Restaurant when it opened the next morning and ordered a hamburger deluxe for breakfast. Like a song stuck in my head, it was a craving that had been nagging me for several days that finally got satisfied. To my culinary credit, however, I did not order the hot dog I had long imagined, loaded with chili, slaw, onions, and mustard.

I introduced and explained myself to a curious Dick Mullins, who had never experienced an October on the Parkway as a concession manager. "Make sure your freezer is heavily stocked," I warned. "And if you survive until the end of the month, you will not want to see another visitor until May," I added with emphasis to his puzzled look.

With September finally behind me, my Wednesday and October began with an ominously red sunrise, which defied its legendary forecast and, instead, ushered forth another beautifully clear day. Cold weather had finally silenced the last of the noisy katydids and cicadas; large numbers of fluttering juncos now whispered in their places.

Mount Mitchell no longer loomed in the distance. From some vantage points, its dwarfing immensity created the illusion that I could throw a stone across one final, deep valley and strike it. Black Mountains Overlook was one such place, and in its vicinity I met reporter Jimmy Tomlin and photographer Sonny Hedgecock from the *High Point* (N.C.) *Enterprise.* Stung by the lesson learned from my earlier transgression, I answered Jimmy's questions a little more thoughtfully, especially to his portable tape recorder. A few days later I was relieved to learn that our "Long and Winding Road" story had been picked up by the Associated Press and was devoid this time of any errant misstatements on my behalf.

By the time I reached Hewat Overlook, Mount Mitchell looked close enough to reach out and grasp, and I chose the stone curb at the overlook on which to cook an early supper and enjoy the view. A recently purchased foil packet of pink salmon added a new dimension to boring pasta, and its timely consumption further reduced the weight of my pack. But I worried about how many bears had picked up on its strong scent. Stuck with having to carry the empty packet, I rinsed it thoroughly with water and sealed it securely inside a plastic bag and reminded myself to dump it at the next available trash receptacle. Like a real salmon spawning, I had been climbing against the current most of the afternoon and had no interest in being intercepted prematurely before reaching my own primordial destination.

With a sixteen-mile day behind me, I found the graded flats of an abandoned logging road about the only suitable place on which to camp for the night. Luckily, too, it offered shelter from a cold wind that had blown in patches of clouds which had produced a multitude of false sunsets over the Black Mountains. Over my last three miles, I had stared at them in dumbfounded awe and better understood how some earthy cultures had drifted to the idolatrous worship of such imposing natural features. Signs bearing the names of places I had encountered that day autographed the type of country into which I had entered — Wildcares Tunnel, Singecat Ridge Overlook, and Rough Ridge Tunnel. Had I not been so exhausted and fallen asleep so quickly, I might have been spooked by its wildness and the lonely, enveloping darkness only a friendly campfire could have suppressed.

Sometime during what I thought was the middle of the night, the cracking sound of a breaking branch snapped me from my sleep. I quickly rose to a sitting position and tried to focus sleep-encrusted eyes through the additional blurriness created by the mosquito net portals sewn into the roof of my tent. A cloud cover had caused the stars to disappear, yet there was just enough light to barely distinguish the skeletal forms of trees standing over me. Only then did I realize I was looking into the early minutes of dawn.

The sound of something large moving toward me in the dark, invisible distance created an instant, inner panic as I remembered the smelly foil packet still in my possession. Drats! Wishing I had left the thing back at the overlook in one forgivable lapse of environmental etiquette, I mentally prepared myself for an inescapable confrontation with a hungry black bear.

As the sound grew closer, its cadence and vibration became better perceived as the steady march of more than one creature. In the faint light of morning, four men carrying hunting rifles eerily appeared on the graded path. Understanding exactly what they were doing and where they were heading, I waited until the lead man was right in front of my tent before repeating the same words I had spoken many times as a ranger.

"Mornin' boys," I simply said, to which one in the party grunted a reluctant, similar reply. Without breaking stride, they continued their stealthy march in the direction of the park, and this time I just let them keep walking.

Slicing through areas of prime wildlife habitat, the Blue Ridge Parkway tempts the lazy hunter to steal some of its prizes as strongly as does candy to a young boy with no coins in his pocket. Shooting a deer from its center line or trapping a bear within its boundary was never legal; thus came the rub with the rangers.

I was a newcomer to the district when I first met one particularly infamous local poacher. Complaining about another veteran ranger who had allegedly hounded and harassed him for several years but had never caught him, he glibly offered to respect me if I could ever catch him "fair and square."

"But if you ever hook and crook me, I'll get you," he threateningly warned, to which I acknowledged no agreement and casually replied, "I'll do my best."

Catching a poacher actually taking wildlife illegally in the park was a finicky business, and I cannot remember a single case in which I personally witnessed such an act. Encountering hunters with game already shot or with firearms in their possession were the more likely scenarios. Never averse to the practice of matching trickery with trickery, I employed every legal means available to catch or deter them.

Undercover operations for the most boastful and egregious characters I will not mention, along with the finer secrets of the trade. But black thread trip lines made wonderful indicators of ingress and egress to and from suspected places. Decoying radio chatter, transmitted from the comfort of home, had to occasionally substitute for unfunded manpower in order to confuse the clever ones who monitored our frequency. Rangers, most rightfully thought, rarely worked past midnight and then only in emergencies. On the way to the bathroom at two in the morning I had been known to whisper, over channel two, "Bring some hot chocolate. It's getting cold up here."

A few night owls, however, were surprised by our intermittent presence. A shiny patrol car used on a stakeout could be easily rendered invisible with a camouflage parachute. A simple toggle switch could disable the brake lights. Two round pieces of reflective tape could be arranged to appear as the glowing eyes of the largest buck in the woods. Entrapment? Hah! They never found them, and I never mentioned them. Besides, what did they have to do with the probable cause established by the witnessed sound of gunfire and the sight of a muzzle flash blazing from the window of a pickup truck in the middle of the night? Fair game, too, was any moving or equipment violation associated with a motor vehicle. Concealing a rifle or deer within one was awfully difficult once it was stopped.

The park had to be patrolled with the vigilance of a watchdog during the legal hunting season, when bordering lands were deluged with mostly legal game seekers. But throughout that population of genuine sportsmen wandered also the reckless and ignorant minority like a stain on a new sofa. In most cases, they were not difficult to catch.

Deer season was in full swing one mid-December morning when I began my work day earlier than normal at six o'clock. Clear weather and Saturday promised a busy day monitoring the expected flurry of that special breed of once-a-year-weekend hunters. The morning was still dark when I pulled into an overlook and noticed a woman standing near the open passenger door of a pickup truck. Upon noticing me, she quickly jumped into the truck, and the male driver attempted to drive it back onto the Parkway. But the light, required by State law, designed to illuminate the license plate was not working, and I stopped them. Propped on the seat between them was a rifle loaded with twelve rounds of ammunition, one of which was in the firing chamber. Another rifle, similarly loaded, was retrieved from behind the seat. Busted. When they cited a misunderstanding that a state hunting license permitted them to hunt deer from a vehicle on the Parkway, I urged them to bring that defense with them to the courtroom.

I had received information from a supposedly reliable source that a man was running a trap line along a creek which ran several hundred yards through the park. With an understanding that he was checking his traps daily at dawn, I decided to case the area on an afternoon to better develop a trap of my own. Not a single trap could be found, though — not even a boot print in the sand. This was going to be fun. This guy, like any successful trapper, was clever and good. But, unlike his traps, he could not make himself invisible, or so I thought.

Before daylight the next morning, I was waiting for him, but he made no appearance. Nor did he the next morning. Something was wrong. Certain that my presence had not been detected, I concluded that his schedule must have changed and planned a dawn-to-dusk surveillance for the next day.

The leaves had already dropped from the trees, and a bluff overlooking the creek provided an unobstructed, commanding view of a long stretch of it. The waiting game began at dawn. Before noon I had already eaten my lunch and every snack I had brought with me. Wood shavings and whittled castaways were scattered on the ground all around me. I was tempted to doze under the warming massage of an autumn sun but dared not. I had too much time invested in this fellow to let him slip past me, literally, right underneath my nose.

I suppose the sun had dipped to about three o'clock in the afternoon when the natural sounds of the woods were interrupted by the foreign sound of a person walking through it. But the sound was not coming from the now shadowy flats along the creek below me. It was coming from behind me and getting closer every second. I eased from my seated, cross-legged position at the base of a white oak tree to an upright one and carefully peeked around the trunk. A man carrying a shotgun was walking in my general direction.

Apparently he had not seen me; most poachers would have run. His unbroken gait, however, presented two other disturbing options. He had either seen me and intended harm or had not seen me but was capable of doing something accidentally stupid if startled. The state of mind could never be assumed of a man walking through the woods with a gun. Whatever the case, I shrunk myself against the trunk of that tree, unsnapped my holster, and waited.

As he approached, I could find neither the words nor the courage to match the nightmare or fantasy (I cannot remember which) that still plays crazily inside my head. Five surprised hunters. One ranger staring down the barrels of five rifles. No trees between them. As he draws his little six-shooter, he is heard to say, "Drop those rifles or one of you gets two." And they all comply. Too many cowboy movies as a kid, I was eventually diagnosed.

The hunter in this true story, however, walked right past me and took a seat at the base of another tree just a few feet from mine. It soon became clear that the shotgun he had been toting was for squirrels, and the pockets of the military surplus coat he was wearing were for beers. Before permitting him to fire the first shot and finish his first beer, I sneaked up behind him and tapped him on the shoulder, grateful that he had propped the shotgun out of reach against the tree. Moving on to more productive pursuits, I made a reasonably safe assumption that the elusive trapper, if he ever existed, had been sufficiently spooked by rampant rumors that Parkway rangers, despite common misconceptions, sometimes stepped into the woods.

A particular section of the Parkway was technically closed due to a recent snow one winter, but only a flimsy "Road Closed" sign stood in the way of anyone foolish enough to drive past it. Locked gates that would have better enforced the closure were impractical in that area due to numerous private road accesses. Anyone driving through it, other than local residents, was sometimes stopped and warned. So an unattended pickup truck, parked on the road shoulder in prime wild turkey habitat, drew special attention that day.

A quick check on the license plate determined that its registered owner did not live anywhere along the closed section. A few items in plain view about the interior of the truck tripped my adventure switch: an open box of shotgun shells; a blaze-orange vest; an almost-empty foil pouch of chewing tobacco; and an assorted mix of tools, spare motor oil, and leather gloves scattered on the floorboard. Most surprising, however, was the single set of boot prints leading from the truck up the side of the mountain. At last, I had finally stumbled onto an easy case.

As I carefully tracked this person up the mountain, I chastised myself a little for not being more familiar with the boundary line in that area. There was so much of it to learn on both sides of the Parkway. His tracks aimed for the crest of the ridge, and about halfway up it, I halted at the sound of someone scratching out a turkey call. I would now have to be extremely careful for two reasons. Firstly, I was not interested in being mistaken for a wild turkey in the brush by a trigger-happy hunter. Secondly, turkey hunters must remain motionless and camouflaged to effectively lure a turkey within range. If facing me, he would probably see me before I could see him, and he would attempt to flee.

As I carefully inched my way in his direction, it became obviously clear that he had secreted himself within a rhododendron thicket at the crest of the ridge. Every step I took forward had to be carefully planned, not only to be silent but to remain behind the cover of a tree large enough to stop lead. For almost an hour, I stalked him while he continued, unaware, his game of pretender.

At the upper limit of my nerve, I flattened myself behind the last tree large enough to afford protection and shouted into the cold air. "Park ranger. Step forward without your gun." The woods became deathly silent. I could only imagine the thoughts running through his mind. It mattered not to me if he wanted to run. I had his truck covered with a back-up ranger and was game for a good foot chase and wrestle in the snow.

"Sir, I don't have a gun," came a whimpered reply from a man I could not yet see.

"Sure you don't. Come on out anyway," I ordered him. I had found firearms hidden in leaves and thickets before.

This time, however, I found only a tripod and a camera and could not decide if the story was a blooper, a skulker, or one that should have been censored.

27

Bear!

"I followed the bear tracks off the road.... It would be good
for me to wander with him for a while."
— *The Search*, by Tom Brown Jr.

Sufficiently awakened by the four bear-mistaken hunters who had traipsed through the middle of my campsite and the coldest temperatures I had yet experienced on the trip, I forfeited an instant oatmeal breakfast in lieu of a better plan. I was only three miles from the access road to Mount Mitchell State Park, and my travel directory confirmed a vague memory that it featured a restaurant which was open from May through October. More importantly, this crown jewel of the North Carolina state park system demanded that I pay homage to it for more honorable reasons.

Established as North Carolina's first state park in 1915, the unique, natural character of Mount Mitchell and its environs immediately caught the eyes of planners in the Parkway's early stages of planning and development. As late as the 1970s, well-intentioned politicians and government bureaucrats unsuccessfully sought to bring it under control of the National Park Service as either a separate national park itself or as an expanded "widening" of the Blue Ridge Parkway. Little did they understand how deeply it was loved by its rightful guardians and the citizens of North Carolina who had adopted equal, if not better, standards for its preservation and public enjoyment. As a former state park ranger myself, I could almost guarantee that not even a cigarette butt could be found on its trails or developed facilities at the close of business on any Monday of the year. Four other jewels of this adept state park system — Hanging Rock, Pilot Mountain, Stone Mountain, and Mount Jefferson — had teased me from a distance, just out of reach of a reasonable detour on foot. Walking past this one would have been a sacrilege without at least making a courtesy visit to its lofty ranger station in search of familiar faces.

By the time I reached the park's entrance gate near the intersection of the Parkway and N.C. Route 128, I was numb from the cold. The wind was blowing fiercely, and the tops of the mountains above me certified at least subfreezing temperatures; moisture-laden clouds from the previous night had frosted them with a generous coating of rime ice. And I was only marginally prepared for such weather conditions in terms of clothing.

Exactly how long and steep the road was to the top of the mountain I could not remember, but it was tough enough to dramatically alter my plan to hike at least as far as the restaurant. With cold fingers fumbling over plastic zippers that stung, I retrieved every article of outerwear from the depths of my pack. Strategically positioned near the open gate, I hunkered down in the wind under the added protection of rain gear and gloves and stretched my airborne-prone fedora over a toboggan-covered head and hung on to it for dear life. Had it launched from that location, a little over five thousand feet in elevation, I would have never seen it again. As the minutes ticked into quarter-hours, my revised plan to politely flag down a ride quickly degenerated into a sinister plan to leap into the roadway and hijack, if necessary, the first creature I met rolling on four wheels. Like a homeless person, I was cold and hungry. Like a criminal, I was desperate and determined.

I must have waited an hour (or so it seemed) before I finally heard the rescuing sound of a small pickup truck make the turn at the Parkway intersection and start up the grade. It was fortunately being driven by a pleasant-mannered maintenance employee on his way to work at the state park who was not the least bit intimidated by an unshaven icicle blocking his path. The small cab of his truck was filled with gear, and his forced offer of a ride did not extend beyond the open bed of his truck. By the time we climbed up to the restaurant, we were well within the zone where frozen fog, feathered daintily by the prevailing wind, had collected on every exposed object; a few crystals had even begun to form on my eyebrows and facial stubble.

"They're predicting twenty-four degrees down in the valley tonight. No telling what it'll do up here," warned my driver as I clambered feebly out of the back of his truck.

"Thanks. I'll make like a rabbit off this thing as soon as I get breakfast," I forced through gritted teeth, inhibited more than aided by jawbones that no longer swung properly on their frozen hinges.

My driver apparently did not understand that I had strayed into the early stages of hypothermia as he left me at the locked door of the restaurant forty-five minutes prior to its scheduled opening. Too proud to tell him, I thanked him for the ride and found refuge from the wind on the sunny side of the building. In due time, I was spoiled again by the comforts of indoor living and had to force myself from its pleasure to scurry to a much lower elevation before nightfall.

On the walk back down to the Parkway, I stopped at the park office to look up an old acquaintance and instead found a young but friendly Ranger Jonathan

Griffith, who just happened to be heading in my direction. "By the way," I added before we departed company. "Are you familiar with an old logging road about three miles...?" The information about the hunters seemed to make his day.

Much obliged that Ranger Griffith had kindly delivered me back to my point first frozen, I only had to take a few steps before realizing I had turned a sharp corner into another room of the grand cathedral. Not far behind me, the Parkway had jumped ship, never to return again to the geologic formation known as the Blue Ridge Mountains. Instead of following its namesake into north Georgia, it had sidetracked onto the shoulder of the Black Mountains by way of a connecting ridge in its mandated destiny with the Great Smoky Mountains National Park. Drawn into the new scene ahead of me, I forgot it was noon and cold and stepped slowly and reverently across another threshold. This was a time to relish, not rush. Only the sound of a saxophone played a certain way could match the depths of my surrender once again to a park that had long ago captivated my heart.

Second only to the breathtaking jewelry of the graceful bridges and viaduct which adorned Grandfather Mountain, the afternoon ahead of me would bring the most spectacular scenery of the trip. With the 20,000-acre Asheville watershed preserve conveniently to my left, I soon eased off the shoulder of the Black Mountains and meandered into the Great Craggies. Through this fragile, pristine landscape, where motor vehicles are permitted to park only at paved overlooks, I reveled in the freedom to stop as long and often as I liked. Birds of a species I have yet to identify could be seen feeding vigorously on mature seed cones still attached to the limbs of the red spruce. From one point, I was fairly certain that I could see the Great Smokies in one direction and a bald summit on the Appalachian Trail known as the Beauty Spot in another. A perceptive woman at Glassmine Falls Overlook suggested that I soon purchase a copy of Sharyn McCrumb's book, *Ghost Riders*, for an interesting dose of local Civil War historical fiction. The only glitch in the afternoon occurred when, after readjusting the alignment of my spinal cord for several minutes on a new section of guide rail, I noticed a tiny piece of paper stapled to it. Even with my reading glasses I could barely decipher its fine print:

CAUTION: ARSENIC IS IN THE PESTICIDE APPLIED TO THIS WOOD.... Some chemical ... may be dislodged from the wood surface upon contact with skin.... Because preservative may ... accumulate on clothes, launder before reuse.

Gulp. I had gone horizontal on such material at least once each day of the hike and was now legitimately warned and bound to wash my clothes more often. Had I noticed this warning label early into the hike, I would have surely been forced to cancel it.

The ranger was disappointingly locking the door of the Craggy Gardens Visitor Center when I arrived at exactly five o'clock, and he looked old enough and hurried enough to be en route to a scheduled parent-teacher conference that evening at a local elementary school. How well I understood the dutiful struggle between profession and family, having once spent an entire day closing the district due to snow before driving my daughter two hundred miles in just barely enough time to participate in a piano competition. But the restrooms remained open, and I took advantage of the facility for an agonizing shave using the coldest water on earth. The abundant supply of tap water also rendered the area a convenient place to cook supper, and I soon had a small kitchen set up in an unoccupied corner of the parking lot.

In a few minutes, I found myself surrounded by a small crowd of visitors who became quite fascinated with the gizmos and packets that could produce a hearty meal in such a remote place. Politely accommodating their every question to the best of my patient abilities, I felt like the host of a television cooking show with a million viewers watching me. This was not the time to make an embarrassing mistake with flammable liquid. The noodles in my little aluminum pot had just come to a boil when a compact station wagon, driven by a panic-stricken woman, veered sharply into the parking lot.

"I just saw a bear cub cross the Parkway about a half-mile back," she screamed through a narrow opening in her side window. "Lock up your food and get in your cars now. Its mother can't be far away." She then sped out of the parking lot as rapidly as she had entered it and continued her northbound flight.

I continued to stir my noodles and prepared to add a serving of freeze-dried beef to the dish as the fidgety crowd began to nervously disperse. "What will you do?" asked one concerned gentleman as his wife tugged the sleeve of his jacket in the direction of their car.

Past the point of no return with regard to an empty stomach, I tested the noodles for softness and pondered his question for a few seconds. I had truly walked myself into a jam this time. Although I had lollygagged a surprising thirteen miles for the day, I was now at a higher elevation than I had been at the entrance gate to the state park, and a cold night was quickly approaching. If I could get past that bear cub and its alleged mother, I could descend at least a thousand feet before dark. Finding a place both flat enough to pitch a tent and out of the wind in that part of the country posed an even greater challenge. In the most nonchalant disguise I could muster, I finally answered his question.

"Well, I plan to eat my supper sitting right here on this curb and hope not to burn my tongue in the process. Ya'll take care." Four bearless miles later, I found the only flat ground within a ten-mile radius and slept safely and soundly in the mild comfort of an unusual thermal inversion about four thousand feet above the dangers of high tide and loggerhead turtles.

"Have you ever read Bill Bryson's book, *A Walk in the Woods*?" would have to be ranked as one of the most frequently asked questions directed to me on the trek. Fortunately, I had read this book but only at the prodding insistence of a neighbor who had thrust it upon me. Originally prejudiced by the startling, face-to-face stare of a black bear on the book's cover, I had avoided the book simply because, like the hysterical lady in the station wagon, it seemed to over-state the likelihood of even seeing a black bear, much less being attacked by one. A book whose cover (specifically designed to promote sales) depicted such a misleading representation had seemed as blasphemous to me as society's frequent use of the term "hillbilly" to characterize mountain people. Once I looked past the cover, however, I was captured by the accuracy and humor associated with the author's attempt to hike the entire Appalachian Trail, and I laughed at my every mistake he had duplicated. Perhaps he *had* walked every day in fear of a bear lurking behind every rock and tree. For that possibility alone he had earned my sympathy and forgiveness.

Black bears, generally speaking, are quite frightened of humans and prefer a solitary life in the wilderness. A visitor to the Parkway is far more likely to see bear signs (Bearwallow Gap, Bear Den Overlook, Bear Pen Gap Overlook, Bear Trap Gap Overlook, Bear Trail Ridge Overlook, et cetera) rather than signs of a bear. Rarely do the skittish majority of them ever threaten to harm a human being. For them, the rules of encounter are fairly simple: avoid surprising one; avoid cornering one; never attempt to lure one closer with food; and never posi-tion oneself between a mother and her cub. Their natural shyness, however, can be occasionally compromised by a hungry stomach and the luring smell of humankind vittles.

Blaze had developed an unhealthy fondness for the facilities located near the Mount Pisgah section of the Parkway. He was the only black bear I had ever met with a patch of white fur on his breast. Hence, the nickname. One of those animals who had grown lazy from the intentional and unintentional availabil-ity of the wrong kinds of food, he had even been known to feed on the fatty foam floating on a nearby sewage lagoon. His predecessor cousins with similar habits had been responsible for the placement of warning signs in the campground and the use of bearproof trash cans throughout the entire developed area of Mount Pisgah.

I had just gotten comfortable in front of the television set when the tele-phone rang one June evening. The manager of the Pisgah Inn reported that a bear was causing problems near the employee quarters located near the restau-rant. By the time I arrived with the culvert trap, the news had worsened. Blaze had attempted to force his way into the kitchen of the restaurant, and the chef and his crew were not happy. Neither was I. This was not the first time Blaze had been trapped in that area for relocation. His last known address had been the Great Smoky Mountains National Park over fifty miles away, but a bear research team from North Carolina State University had lost contact with him due to a malfunctioning radio collar. How had he found his way back to his favorite snack bar? Bears, members of the research team later told me, could memorize the sequence of smells as easily as a child could remember the way to grandma's house by the sequence of visual landmarks. This 230-pound nuisance needed to be driven to a more distant home by way of a very circuitous route, and I was more than willing to work half the night to help him find one.

The sturdy trap, constructed from a large piece of metal culvert pipe mounted onto a mobile trailer, was baited with an onion sack filled with delicious table scraps scavenged from the kitchen. Left privately to his own devices, Blaze was securely padlocked within its hollow cell in just a few minutes.

About one o'clock in the morning, the trap containing its reluctant cargo was returned to its reserved parking place at the Balsam Gap ranger station. Arrangements would have to be made the next morning for his new home. When I arrived for work early the next day, Blaze was wide awake and irritable. The maintenance employee who had missed the memo and parked in his usual place next to the trap was also in dire need of a sedative and ready to kill me as well. Sadly enough, Blaze was eventually harvested during the legal bear hunting season in the faraway corner of a remote national forest, a regrettable victim of man and himself.

One morning, I was patrolling a section of the Parkway where it coursed through the Cherokee Indian Reservation and noticed the canopy of a small tree shaking vigorously at eye-level. The bottom two-thirds of the tree was not visible due to its position below the road grade over a steep embankment. I found a place to park on the shoulder and peeked down the mountain to investigate.

For several minutes, I enjoyed the astounding scene of a bear that had discovered a payload of wild grapes hanging from vines that had ensnarled a tree. With the agility of a twelve year-old boy, he reached out from the trunk of the tree to pluck clusters of ripe fruit with his paws. Anyone who has ever seen a bear stripped of its hide and fat would have to agree that they very much resemble the form of a physically fit human being. For that reason alone I would be reluctant to ever kill one.

As a ranger, though, I had to respect the fact that bear hunting was a time-honored tradition in the Southern Appalachians neither an act of Congress nor the use of military force would ever be able to stop. If a properly licensed hunter chose to hunt bear during the legal season on lands bordering the park, I respected his right to do so and let that remain his own business. Once that hunt or hunter, legal or otherwise, found its way into the park, I made it my business with a vengeance.

A bear hunt was the last thing I expected to encounter one snowy November morning as I patrolled through a gated, closed section of the Parkway. A good six inches of new snow had covered the roadway, powdery enough to permit a vehicle to drive through it softly and silently. These were the days for which rangers lived — snow, no visitors, and the rare opportunity to surprise a bobcat or other unwary critter. A man standing in the middle of the road holding a rifle was not expecting to encounter me either.

Miles away from the nearest road access, he jumped over a steep embankment with the speed and panic of any bobcat I had ever spooked — right into the trap of a blackberry thicket that would have stopped a train. Seeing no need for me to make the same mistake with a man twice my size, I took advantage of his predicament and flipped the switch on my public address system.

"If I have to come in there and get you it's going to be a whole lot worse" (for me, I estimated more truthfully). "So just come on out," I blared to half of Jackson County while this brute of a man furiously attempted to unload his gun, hoping, perhaps, that an unloaded weapon would somehow legalize his presence in the park. The sound of bear dogs baying in the distance compounded his predicament like the telltale "clank" of a lid set too clumsily on the rim of a cookie jar. And this was one grateful ranger that a rifle had jammed and its owner was docile. To express my appreciation for his cooperation, I even gave him a ride in a warm patrol car. At the end of that day, at least, the score remained: Ranger Bears—1, Poached Hunters—Nothing.

28

Sunday Solace

"Turn away thy foot from the sabbath ... and I will cause
thee to ride upon the high places of the earth."
— Isaiah 58:13–14, King James Version
of *The Holy Bible*

On Friday morning, I awoke to the pleasant realizations that I had survived
the overexaggerated dangers of the night and was about to experience the easi-
est walking day of the trek; my projected path was downhill nearly all the way
to Asheville. As I began the gentle, 2,500-foot descent into civilization, I tried
not to think about the fact that, in a couple of days, I would have to regain all
of that elevation and more. This day, however, was *the* present in terms of time
and *a* present in terms of a gift, and I resolved to focus on its immediacy and
savor whatever experiences it was about to deliver. The time had come to knock
my transmission out of gear and coast all the way to the next restaurant.

I had only taken a few steps from my campsite when Milepost 369 made its
modest appearance around a slight curve in the road. An obscure landmark for
a hurried traveler, for me it was the starting line for my last hundred miles. As
the Parkway and I wormed our way down the Craggies on a predominately south-
eastern exposure, the chilly mountain air, warming quickly by the rising sun,
was filled with the energetic sounds of life in the wild.

A huge pileated woodpecker launched into flight from a tree right in front
of me. I had heard their distinctive call almost every day of the trek but had seen
only faint glimpses of their red-headed forms high in the canopies of mature
forests. Close enough this time to briefly study the distinct, contrasting lines of
its coloration, this bird — just like the wood duck — reminded me of a robotic,
paint-by-number creation whose artist had deliberately failed to color some
carefully selected patches on a snow-white canvas. In no way could I suggest,

following this daring pose for me, that the costume of this bird or that of its regal cousin was in need of any further completion.

A pair of ruffed grouse, invisibly camouflaged on the ground and instinctively endowed with the patience of a soldier under orders not to shoot until the whites of the eyes of the opposing enemy could be seen, ambushed me with such an explosive burst of flight that a man with an unhealthier heart would have deemed it a tasteless invitation to a cardiac event. I feared that our species would soon become extinct if grouse ever developed the ability to hunt man. I had only killed one of the tasty birds in my life, a fat hen who tragically underestimated the clearance underneath my approaching patrol vehicle. The experience had caused me to wonder how many poachers had aimed the same gun whose trigger I had unwittingly pulled.

Hunting dogs, chasing the fresh scent of a bear, bayed high on the ridge above me, and I halfheartedly hoped to see the hounded prey come crashing down the mountain for an encounter as close and vivid as I had enjoyed with the woodpecker and grouse. Perhaps it was the very individual I had so hoped to avoid just a few hours earlier. But the prospect of my first bear sighting faded when the sounds of the chase turned and evaporated on the opposite side of the ridge. Like an unexpected meeting of two ambassadors of rival countries in the men's room at the United Nations, awkward and tense would have best described our impromptu conference that never convened.

The panoramic view at Lane Pinnacle Overlook soon presented itself as a fitting location for a restful journal entry — one of hundreds I had already taken. Having experimented with every conceivable object and posture, I had found the sleeping bag strapped to the bottom of my backpack to be the most comfortable seat for such business.

At this overlook, I chose also to flush my radiator by drinking as much of my overstock of water as I could hold, careful not to waste a single drop from the three bottles I had topped off back at the visitor center. Carrying it temporarily in my stomach rather than on my back, just as I had done with those weighty apples and chocolate chip cookies, seemed far more efficient when its availability and abundance was certain; I was only ten downhill miles from the sure-bet watering hole of the Folk Art Center. Filling all of my bottles at every available source had become a standard operating procedure for me as the result of some harsh lessons of previous experience. Flanked by the requirements of the precious fluid for both a supper and breakfast, one night between water sources too far apart guaranteed misery even when all other conditions were favorable. The open facilities and abundance of natural springs scattered along the length of the Parkway, however, had made water management on this particular backpacking trip a far less treacherous enterprise than one of a more wilderness nature. For this and many other reasons, obvious perhaps only to me, I had already crowned this trek the ultimate backpacking experience.

While I was forcing down the last few slugs of water that my saturated body could hold, a four-wheel-drive vehicle rolled smartly past the overlook. Its male driver, straining his neck to look back at me, braked hard as if he had just missed an intended stop. Apparently realizing he had overshot the overlook, he continued driving and disappeared from view. In a few seconds, though, the same vehicle, having reversed its direction somewhere down the mountain, reappeared and pulled into the overlook. Its driver, noticing me seated at my makeshift desk with no vehicles in the overlook, had assumed that I needed assistance and had driven back to offer his help. A brief explanation of my motorless presence caused him to shut off the engine and leap from his vehicle, excitedly eager to share our companion stories.

Chris Quill, you see, was a flatlander who had driven across the state from his home near zero elevation at Wrightsville Beach, N.C. A kitchen manager at a locally famous seafood restaurant, he only received two weeks of vacation per year and had taken a solitary journey to see, for the first time in his life, the mountains of western North Carolina. Many young men in their early to mid-twenties take similar, soul-searching odysseys at that stage of their lives.

Like a kid excited over seeing snow for the first time, he breathlessly shared that he had camped the previous night at the Linville Falls Campground and had just enjoyed a spectacularly clear view from the summit of Mount Mitchell. Mutually enjoying the experiences told to each other, we must have talked for an hour. On his next trip to the Linville Falls area, I urged him to visit a place known as Wiseman's View for an exhilarating peek into the Grand Canyon of the East — the Linville Gorge. Hump Mountain, Crabtree Falls, Graveyard Fields, and Sliding Rock, too, were hastily added to his must-see list; there was not enough time to name and describe them all. Kindred spirits, we had both discovered this region at about the same age, and I could see my own youthful exuberance for these mountains reflected through his very eyes. This was one young man that Dr. Jolley, who once worried over the millions that would never receive or take the opportunity to visit the Parkway, could cross off his list. A repeat visit, in this case, was a certainty in the offing.

By the time I reached Haw Creek Valley Overlook later in the afternoon, I had crossed the tenth fold of my map; only one fold remained. From its vantage point I could see the forested swath through a large valley where the Parkway hooked eastward around the city of Asheville. Beyond the valley, a ridge formation gradually gained elevation all the way to Mount Pisgah, along which the Parkway snaked and climbed, crisscrossing in many places the old wagon road that George Vanderbilt had constructed to get from his mansion at Biltmore to his hunting lodge high on Buck Spring Gap. On the distant horizon stood the beckoning beacon of Cold Mountain at the dead-end edge of the Shining Rock Ledge. I was excited. The most accurate map available was unfurled before me, and I could see half the distance to my destination. With the remainder of the route already memorized on software tissue, a hard-copy map was no longer essential; a homecoming was in the making.

As my long descent gradually tapered onto flatter ground, the unbroken forest to my right produced a strangely foreign sound that caused me to initially wonder if I had been walking too alone, too long. Like the creeping edge of a slowly rising flood on a dry plain, the gentle sound of soft music gradually saturated every space between the ground and the treetops. Church bells? Chimes? Had I descended from the highest level of heaven to the lower estate of another? Then it abruptly stopped. Had I now descended right into the pit? Not until I detoured at U.S. Route 70 in search of pizza was I relieved to discover that the music had flowed from the nearby Veterans Hospital.

Darkness overtook me in the company of paycheck-day laughter, good food, and a jukebox that never ceased playing mostly unfamiliar country tunes. Long after my meal had been completed, I played the silly game of "linger," repeatedly delaying my departure until I heard a song that I knew. Toby Keith's "Courtesy of the Red, White and Blue" finally released me from my little mock prison; defiantly and triumphantly I burst through its walls into the blinding glare of neon and headlights. Fatigued and under the influence of too much pepperoni, I settled for the first tent site my flashlight could find despite the disturbing presence of the three-leaved poison ivy vine. Trapped between the constant highway noise of U.S. Route 70 and Interstate 40, I spent a restless Friday night amid the additional annoyances of barking dogs and back porch lights from nearby private residences.

Quite honestly, I did not wake up on Saturday morning looking forward to my low-elevation walk through a tunnel of trees, heavy traffic, and a fourteen-mile gap between scenic overlooks. Few rangers, too, had ever enjoyed working this glorified commuter route located directly under the all-searching eye of the local headquarters staff. Unlike my twice-maneuvered passage through similar perils of the Roanoke Valley, I had at least timed this stretch to avoid a weekday — better, too, as a visitor rather than as a ranger. With grim determination, I pulled on my boots, adjusted the drawstring on my trousers to a waist size I had not experienced in years, and began the day like it was an inescapable chore.

I had not yet reached my third mile when the appearance of a new sign demanded that I detour onto a slightly ascending entrance road to see a Parkway headquarters building that had only been a dreamy concept on my last day of employment as a ranger. From the 1934 dining room of Stanley Abbott's apartment in Salem, Va., to leased commercial space, first in downtown Roanoke, Va., and later in downtown Asheville, N.C., park headquarters had finally found a home within the borders it managed.

Perched peacefully on a bench of Hemphill Knob, its empty parking lot and locked doors quietly reminded me that my visit had disappointingly coincided with a weekend. I would have to settle for a photograph of its exterior and a peek through the windows of what had been aptly named the Gary E. Everhardt Headquarters Building. Mr. Everhardt had been the park superintendent during my entire tenure as a permanent ranger and had presided over the Parkway's fiftieth anniversary and its long-delayed dedication and completion around Grandfather Mountain. A former director of the National Park Service, he was best known for his political acumen that could bring dreams such as this building to fruition. I best remembered him as a man that I respectfully feared but with whom I was still permitted to speak frankly.

As I began to walk away from the entrance door of a facility designed and dovetailed into the landscape by none other than the son of Stanley Abbott himself, I heard the muffled sound of keys rattling against glass. The metallic thud of a locking mechanism being released was quickly followed by the sound of a familiar voice.

"Hey, Tim. Do you have time for a tour?" Once again, it was the ever-busy Patty Lockamy who, in the process of attending to catch-up work on her day off, had seen me wandering about the place. Was I ever thrilled.

My day thusly encouraged, I rather enjoyed and cheered onward an unidentified ranger who darted back and forth most of the day stopping speeders fallen victim to his radar gun. Blue lights and an occasional bump on the siren were still in my blood. How refreshing it was to rediscover the ranger spirit of visibility and hustle.

Near Milepost 387, I unexpectedly found a little cascading stream on Parkway Left, hidden just enough by the autumn foliage to discreetly serve as a makeshift bathing spa. By all appearances, it had been created for just such a purpose.

A ledge was situated perfectly on which to place my pack in an upright position for access to all the necessities. A small bush was located perfectly on which to hang my clothes. A natural basin pooled enough water to make a thorough sponge bath possible while a five-inch long salamander and I worked around each other. Teeth were brushed. Hair, best not described, which had not enjoyed such cleanliness since Travis Proctor's cabin, was finally shampooed. Every aforementioned attention was accomplished conveniently, too, under the warm, drying effects of dappled sunlight and a mild afternoon, just in time for a more civilized appearance at a restaurant near the Parkway on U.S. Route 25. Having satisfied a craving for fried chicken, I successfully resisted the temptation of a nearby twelve-movie theater and prodded myself like a stubborn mule back onto the Parkway.

Not until several months after I had completed the trek did I have an occasion to travel westbound on Interstate 26 to lend specific attention to the details of its intersection with the Parkway. For travelers driving up a long grade, the tall Parkway bridge casts a striking pose against a clear, blue sky. Add a setting sun to the background and the catalyst of the darkened silhouette of a man outfitted with a hat, a walking stick, and a backpack to stimulate a most effervescent social reaction.

Grade separation structures the civil engineers call them. They permit the Parkway to cross over or under intersecting highways, making it possible for a visitor to drive its entire length without the interruption of either a stop sign or red light. At overpasses I had taken advantage of shelter from the rain; had rested from the heat of the day in cool shade; had uttered words out of context to nobody just to hear them echo; and had studied the beauty of many adorned with native stone facings. At underpasses I had rested safely on the convenience of abutments while snacking; had waved on occasion to someone passing underneath me; and had silently cursed every wobbly driver and wind gust I met that nudged me too close to their edges. Over the short and shallow ones I had ambled nonchalantly. Over the lengthy and lofty ones I had crossed steadfastly and quickly — until this one.

About halfway across this dizzying underpass, I glanced eastward down the length of Interstate 26 for the cause of so much horn-blowing. Only then did I realize that some animal had not strayed onto the freeway. With heads strained upward and arms waving wildly, they were all honking at me! The truckers were most impressive with short blasts from their air horns, and I suspected that I symbolized the roaming freedom of their occupation. I stopped and turned to face them. To each one that tooted I waved my hat high in the air. The feeling surfaced first as a giggle and soon swelled into uncontrollable laughter. That almost-forgotten excitement of a little boy on Christmas morning was resurrected, and I began to play another game of linger. Delaying my passage for one more honk that progressed to ten, I finally advanced to the south end of the bridge, hoping that nobody had reported me to the rangers as a potential jumper. By nightfall I was safely positioned to begin checking off a long list of "lasts" — my last Sunday, my last Monday... my last trail meal, my last mile.

A night in the woods can bring frightening experiences due to things both unseen and unknown — sounds, mostly, but sometimes disturbing sights. On my first dark night as a Boy Scout and my first experience with snipe hunting, I discovered tiny bits of fox fire scattered all over the ground in the woods. A luminous fungus sometimes found in decaying wood, it glowed greenly and eerily like the cooling remnants of a meteor shower and scared me more than the imaginary snipe I was determined to catch with my open sack. Education and experience eventually reduced my fears of the night to a manageable list. I could now chuckle, rather than cringe, when a family of voles decided one night on the trek to play tag on and around my tent. Harmless, too, was the sound of what I call "tree grit" that falls from the sky. Minute pieces of tree bark or star dust or something, it makes faint little popping noises when it lands on dry leaves and taut tents. Throughout the last Saturday night of my trek, I could have sworn I was sleeping underneath a giant salt shaker which dispensed, in slow motion, bits of a substance I think I will forever leave to the imagination just for the mysterious fun of it. Hurrah for the single millimeter of protection afforded by modern-day tents! And more reasons to sleep in one rather than under the stars.

The practically frictionless interaction of smooth, synthetic surfaces rubbing against each other is the primary reason I select a level site on which to camp. Otherwise, the slightest slope will create a slippery, nocturnal struggle between the fabric of my sleeping bag, mattress pad, and tent floor, with the inevitable result of all of us migrating downhill, bunched into a wadded heap by morning. When forced to camp on a slope, however, I have learned that positioning the foot of my tent against the trunk of a tree permits me to brace myself with my feet against these slip-and-slide tendencies. In just such a position did

I find myself waking on Sunday morning, flat on my back, staring up the entire vertical length of a crooked sourwood tree.

My internal alarm clock understood, without having to set it, that my rest day had arrived, and it was the grinding sound of squirrels busily cutting acorns high in the trees above me that eventually awakened me rather than the usual light of dawn. I just laid there and listened to their work and their chatter, knowing I could delay breakfast and, due to warmer weather, would not even have to wear gloves to prepare it. The top of the tree under which I rested shook gently from the impact of a fat squirrel landing in it, and he slowly began to work his way headfirst down the trunk in my direction. My broken "Squenglish" brought us to a face-to-face standoff that lasted several seconds before he scampered, his jaws packed tightly with acorns, back up the tree. This was going to be a beautiful day on which to rest and ponder.

The luck of my stride had landed me very close to a facility I had never before visited that sounded perfect for a Sunday layover — the North Carolina Arboretum. Following a leisurely breakfast in bed, I began the short walk to it and was soon humored by the words someone had spray-painted on the Parkway bridge spanning the French Broad River. "STOP DRIVING, START LIVING," it boldly declared in large letters on the pavement. While my experiences of the past thirty-five days had left me somewhat sympathetic to the message, I hoped that the rangers and posterity understood that I neither endorsed nor constructed such tacky graffiti. I had every intention of saving my words and philosophies for the tidier medium of a book.

The gatekeeper refused to accept any payment, even a prorated portion of the standard admission fee of $6.00 per car, insisting that anyone who had walked that far to visit the arboretum should see it free of charge. Not far past the gate, a security guard cautioned me that I had a long, uphill mile ahead of me and demanded that I accept her offer of a ride. A lady at the Visitor Education Center offered to stow my pack safely behind the reception counter so I could explore the grounds unencumbered. I was overwhelmed, again, by everyone's kindness.

For the entire day I roamed and relaxed in the peaceful quiet of streams, pools, and gardens. I studied every sign and label that described the plants. I sketched drawings of a trellis and a border fence that I thought might work in my garden at home. I noted that my yard, in the process of becoming a manicured forest, still lacked the global balance of the gingko and American hornbeam trees. I found a snack bar loaded with pizza, soda, and ice cream bars. I watched a special slide program about orchids and learned that its expert presenter cultivated such masterpieces for a living just a few miles from my home. Following his presentation, I met a member of the Carolina Mountain Club while munching on the complimentary refreshment of chocolate chip cookies. I called Patty from a pay telephone and together we chatted. And in the comfort of a rocking chair near the end of the day, a seeker of high places proved that, regardless of one's religious persuasion, resting every seventh day could be a nourishing boon to both body and spirit.

29

Balsam Gap
District Revisited

"It's so peaceful here. I'd put this day on my list."
—*Ghost Riders*, by Sharyn McCrumb

Though not very hungry from all the junk food my calorie-deprived body had absorbed like a sponge over the last three days, I forced down a healthy serving of rice before retiring to bed on Sunday night just to load up some carbohydrates for the next day. The way I remembered it, there was no break in the steady climb from the French Broad River all the way up to the Mount Pisgah recreation area. My map and reference materials confirmed that I had about a three thousand-foot climb over a fifteen-mile incline to reach the place where I dearly wanted to spend Monday night. My day of rest could not have come at a better time, and having acquired a little experience and proficiency with daily exertive calculations, I figured the goal to be doable. The prospect of fine food, a hot, soapy shower, and a much needed laundry had, once again, crept in to assume dictatorial command of the plan.

Sometime during the night, an unexpected shower forced me to dash out of my tent to cover it with the rainfly accessory. I had come to enjoy telling time by the heavens and watching shooting stars, squirrels, and satellites through the netted windows of my synthetic little house at any expense. And trust me. Running around in the cold darkness in my underwear, getting rapidly wet, and finding every thorny protuberance on the ground with my bare feet was always considered a high price to pay for such grand entertainment. The portentous sound of solid raindrops gradually reduced in volume to the quieter patter of drizzle by daybreak and stopped altogether by the time I finished breakfast and started walking.

A backpacker facing a long, uphill day, could not have ordered more ideal conditions than the cool, overcast weather that prevailed.

In only a couple of miles the road grade actually leveled out somewhat, and for the remainder of the day, I was pleasantly surprised by every level platform — even a couple of downhill stretches—just a few years of absence had eroded from my memory. Just at the point when I thought that life could not get any better, I almost stepped on a humongous copperhead as the Parkway climbed back into the wilds of the Pisgah National Forest. A closer inspection with my walking stick, though, determined it to be another road kill, and in a terror-stricken rage, I hung the bloody carcass on a conspicuous tree limb near the road-way to warn all the unwary motorists of what dangerous "bear" country they had entered. "Should have done that with the other two copperheads and rat-tlesnake," my journal recorded.

About halfway through the Grassy Knob Tunnel, I realized the necessity of my flashlight at the blackout point and found it quickly in its readily accessible, designated place in my backpack. This proved to be the only tunnel out of twenty-six in which I could not see, from within its bowels, at least faint light at either end. Perhaps it was the same tunnel in which Harold Peters had crashed his bicycle. As a ranger, I had learned the hard way to burn my headlights con-stantly when driving through this stretch of one tunnel after another.

As the natural light began to reappear in front of me, I decided to stow my flashlight, which had been courteously employed on low beam, of course, in the closer reach of my trouser pocket; Pine Mountain Tunnel, almost twice the length of this one and the longest on the Parkway, was not far ahead of me. As the light ahead grew brighter, a vehicle that sounded a bit louder than normal rumbled slowly into the tunnel behind me. I assumed it to be a motorcycle whose driver was fumbling for the headlight switch, and I continued walking. But I quickened my pace through the last hundred yards of the tunnel when it became clear that the deafening machine was not going to overtake me and seemed to be playing a sick game with my blind side. Not until I stepped into the safety of daylight, a little worried and greatly irritated, did I look back to face the behemoth — a monstrous Cyclops with one blinding headlight for an eye.

The maintenance man driving the huge front-end loader, who was push-ing the machine to its apparent limit of ten miles per hour, just barely nodded with a who-are-you, back-to-work-Monday scowl. Had its driver been Charles Ballard, he would have at least dimmed his "eye" and offered me a ride in the bucket. My first choice of hands on any fire crews I mustered, his morale-boosting humor was worth more than his muscle; even the exhausted and down-spirited words that proceeded from his mouth were funny in that singularly distinct drawl of his.

From Bad Fork Valley Overlook, big old Mount Pisgah made its first appear-ance since Friday back at Haw Creek Valley Overlook. I could understand, from many walks to its summit, how the rich valleys below this biblically named mountain could likewise be confused with an ancient Promised Land. With every step I advanced in its direction, more familiar became the landmarks as the memories of six years of rangering in the area began to flash exponentially into view. Ferrin Knob Tunnel No. 1. Ferrin Knob Tunnel No. 2. Ferrin Knob Tunnel No. 3. All had been shot through the same mountain whose name had nothing to do with slang references to international visitors but everything to do with a local abundance of ferns. By eleven o'clock I was halfway to my goal and was thoroughly enjoying the scenery.

Suddenly, terrible, repressed memories surfaced along a stretch that had not even been my assigned district; administrative boundaries did not exist for any emergency on or near the Parkway. Bam. Bam. Bam. Cast before me again came the horrific Saturday morning discovery of a drug-related murder and another person critically wounded at Big Ridge Overlook. Both had been shot in the head. My pace quickened beyond normal. Lightning popped all around me again on top of some unnamed ridge as I began a frantic, solo attack on a wildfire while still wearing my Class-A uniform. CPR could not revive a heart attack victim at Mills River Valley Overlook. As a helicopter transported her to a local hospital, I could still hear her husband, in denial, thanking me for saving her as I drove him to the shattering words of an emergency room doctor in my patrol car. Faster and faster I walked, fleeing tragedies, tunnel monsters, and dangers looming only in my head, until I breathlessly reached the obsolete district boundary line known as the Buck Spring Tunnel.

I stepped across this imaginary threshold into the calmer sense of what had once been known as my professional home — the Balsam Gap District. Nine tidy districts on the Parkway had now been compacted into four in the comically perpetual cycle of reorganization. Oblivious to these grafts and amputations so arbitrarily drawn onto paper, the Parkway topped out and meandered peacefully into my goal for the day with plenty of daylight remaining.

I stepped into the Mount Pisgah gas station/camp store only to learn that the showers I was certain had been proposed several years earlier were still not available. But the building had been slightly remodeled to offer 24-hour access to a laundry facility, and I became happier. I noticed, too, a printed announcement that the little building was soon to become only a camp store. Gasoline would not be available after the current season due to environmental concerns associated with its storage and delivery. Hurrah for the extra protection afforded to one of the oldest heath bogs in the Southern Appalachians and the lessened likelihood of a backpacker getting scorched in a tunnel by an errant tanker truck driver.

Still miffed by the absence of a long-anticipated hot shower, I moped into the restroom to salvage some vestige of respectable appearance to match my plan for an elegant evening. The sponge bath proved to be no more and no less than could be expected in the reduced privacy of a public restroom. I had walked too far to be mistaken for a perverted vagrant, and I doubted that the closest Federally-approved lockup offered a menu. But the temptation to shampoo my hair in the sink overwhelmed me. I performed the task quickly so nobody would see me and carefully cleaned up the evidence. Only then did I discover how swiftly a homeless person can walk into any restroom equipped with an electric hand dryer and walk out with clean, dry hair. Wearing a complete set of clean clothes saved just for the occasion, I stepped to the curb like a millionaire on the streets of New York City. Had the service been available, I would have hailed a taxi for the hundred-yard jaunt across the parking lot to the Pisgah Restaurant.

In the process of being seated at a table, I requested a location slightly beyond the mainstream of diners in a quiet corner by a window. Presentable enough not to dramatically shock the ambience, I, nevertheless, did not want to disturb the peace of more polished customers or crowd them with the bulky appendage hanging angularly from one of my shoulders. Too, I had surrendered to a tenderly contemplative mood requiring only a smidgen of privacy for some reflective journal entries. If the solitude of wilderness had taught me anything, it was that I could never survive long without the company of people even though half of me was genetically identical to the main character in the movie *Jeremiah Johnson*.

Thus far, I had patronized every single restaurant operated by a concessionaire on the Parkway but had bridled my wallet to the enjoyment of only the economy sections of their menus. Since this was the last such available facility on the Parkway, I decided that the time had come to celebrate my progress and splurge on a meal finer than the hamburger I had eaten out of kilter for breakfast back at the Crabtree Meadows Restaurant. Patient restraint and perfect timing now justified the appropriate choice of salad, ribeye steak, rolls, and baked potato for this reward dinner.

Perched at almost five thousand feet on the crest of the Pisgah Ledge, I had a view from my table just as inspiring as one from the rim of the Grand Canyon, only on a smaller scale. The sleepy sun had been yawning all day behind a curtain of clouds, and just before it pulled the cover completely over its head for the night, it splashed a momentary beam of light into the valley below me. As the light faded, the ridges and valleys of a lower elevation gradually changed from the colors of red, yellow, green, and brown to that inspiring shade of purple majesty before finally disappearing into blackness. Only then did I focus on the feast before me, while the recorded voice of Alison Krauss softly haunted me with "Ghost in This House" in the background. How, I wondered, could the purest voice of the bluegrass blues genre so effortlessly draw three syllables from the word "smoke"?

In the dim light of the restaurant her music continued, causing my mood to struggle between the narrow difference in melancholy and pensive. Words and their combinations I had never before experienced translated into a language that only I could interpret. Through "Dreaming My Dreams with You," I offered the Parkway my sincerest apology for having left it so abruptly so many years ago. And in the most mellow moment I have ever experienced in my life,

Alison Krauss became the vicarious voice of the Parkway singing words of welcome and forgiveness back to me through the opening lines of "Stay."

Royally enriched in body and spirit, I discreetly removed the faint remnants of meal and emotion from my fingers and face with an unsullied cloth napkin and reached for my journal. What a rich history of overlapping memories this place called Mount Pisgah had afforded me. I had been privileged to critique the campfire programs of seasonal rangers I had hired and trained in the same amphitheater I had presented programs myself as a seasonal ranger. Would Blaze's grandchildren still have an ax to grind and find me and my full pack of food later that night in the nearby campground? My writing hand could not keep pace with the flood of thoughts that came streaming. A couple, perhaps in their thirties, finished their meal and walked toward my table.

"We noticed your backpack and journal and thought you might be someone we'd like to meet," the man cautiously explored. Tony and Melissa Wilder, from Kingsport, Tennessee, had temporarily escaped the rat race of living for a retreat at the Pisgah Inn, and I had apparently been carefully studied during the course of their own meal.

"Please have a seat," I graciously replied, as we introduced ourselves to each other and proceeded to lose track of time in the details.

My waiter must have walked past our table two or three times, clearing his throat at each pass, before I realized the staff was trying to close the restaurant. We were the last three customers remaining. The Wilders would never know just how much their company had meant to me on that uniquely mellifluous evening.

30

Swinging Snow Gates

"We have spent nearly all winter opening or closing snow gates."
— Author's personal journal entry of
January 22, 1982

Having closed the restaurant at a late but respectable hour, I stepped from warm fuzziness into the cold uncertainty of a dark night, legitimately worried about spending it in the campground just across the street. I did not have the luxury of securing my food in the trunk of a car, as did most tent campers in this area frequented by opportunistic bears prowling for an easy meal. Stringing it up in a tree was not an option either; bears were more agile than humans in that respect.

Postponing the inevitable risk of my vulnerable circumstances a little longer, I proceeded back to the camp store to attend to some pressing laundry chores. With only sixty miles remaining, the clean set of clothes I had just changed into would easily carry me to my destination. I would then have another clean set in which to more respectfully meet Patty — hoping, too, that she would honor my request to bring with her another fresh set from home. I had truly become bored with a limited wardrobe that was beginning to show its mileage — faded, threadbare, and torn. Exposed to the same elements longer than they had ever before endured, my suntanned arms and face were noticeably beginning to assume a similar weather-beaten character. But, unlike the lifeless strands of fabric that comprised my clothing, this amazingly resilient body possessed the uncanny ability to duplicate and heal itself at the cellular level in utter defiance to the thrashing it was receiving and the uncertain length of its mortal existence. My little experiment with endurance now confirmed that the human body, cast in whatever proportion of beauty or deformity allotted to it, was a far better deal than being born a wad of cotton.

Held loosely hostage by the timed cycle of a coin-operated washer, I fought boredom by reading every label, sign, and notice in sight. Sufficiently enlightened on hours of operation, product ingredients, and other mundane matters of minutiae, I nearly fell asleep listening to the rhythmic drone of the dryer tossing my delicates like they were the assorted contents of a fresh garden salad.

The time must have been close to midnight when I finally extracted myself from the safe arms of solid walls and wandered into the deathly quiet, seemingly vacant campground. Had I not been so intimately familiar with the area, I probably would have merely snickered at the bear warning sign posted near its entrance.

Thinking that I might be the only person camping in the tent loop, I chose a prominent campsite so the rangers, if the worst case scenario unfolded, could easily locate my scattered remains the next morning. Perhaps the cover of Bill Bryson's book *had* been justified. But I was pleasantly surprised to find that a sturdy, bearproof, metal container had been installed next to the tent pad for my safety and convenience. With the additional peace of mind of a life insurance policy in full force, I placed all of my food in it and gave no further thought to Blaze's descendants before quickly surrendering to sleep.

Refreshed and gratefully intact the next morning, I saw absolutely no advantage to the economic sense of preparing a meager meal of grits or oatmeal within a stone's throw of a restaurant. I had survived my justified fears of the night, and with an embedded penchant for warped logic in matters of nourishment, considered that important accomplishment just cause for another celebratory reward meal. Unlike the previous evening, I accepted the table randomly chosen for me and found myself at a window seat, surrounded on three sides by a healthy host of equally hungry, bleary-eyed visitors, most of whom had enjoyed the luxury of a hot shower in their motel rooms within the past twenty-four hours.

A little girl about three years old, too young and innocent to understand the dangers of strangers, soon began to flirt with me, which forced her mother and father to engage in some polite but guarded conversation with me that otherwise probably would never have occurred. An old geezer seated behind me coarsely complained to his waitress that the soft, instrumental Beatles music playing in the background was too loud and won his preference of volume. A person, deprived of all other time and directional bearings, could have absolutely concluded, from the mood of almost everyone in the dining room, that the sun on the distant horizon was undoubtedly rising instead of setting. Although I did not rush my meal of scrambled eggs, sausage, hash browns, toast, and cold skim milk, wispy remnants of clouds down in the valley and clear, blue skies overhead offered a splendid invitation to more congenial company of a different sort. Improved human temperament and the rising sun could catch up with us farther down the road.

I was now back in territory familiar enough that I could almost remember the name and sequence of every overlook and gap remaining on the trip. Repetitive patrols had imprinted them to memory as effectively as the homemade flash

Lone Bald Overlook, Milepost 432.7 in North Carolina, is country notorious for its bitterly cold temperatures and deep snows during the winter. Photo taken about 1985.

cards I used in college had chiseled the scientific names of trees onto the same gray matter. Should the dreaded Alzheimer's disease ever creep into me, my final babblings in the advanced stages of dementia will quite certainly and accurately equate *Aesculus octandra* with Buckeye Gap.

Entry into the old home district had also brought me back again into the company of the harbingers of higher elevations—mixed natural stands of red spruce and Fraser fir. In fact, the next thirty miles of Parkway would roughly bobble in the forty-five hundred to six thousand-foot range through country notorious for its bitterly cold temperatures and deep snows during the winter months. General weather forecasts of scattered snow flurries for the surrounding lower elevations often translated into six inches of snow up in these parts. Such conditions required its closure more frequently and for longer periods of time than any other section of the Parkway. A lover of winter weather and its unique challenges, my appointment to work in it had been accepted with great excitement and anticipation. Hoping that foul weather, though, would steer clear of my path for the next few days, I plunged headlong into a beautiful day, propelled by a real breakfast and confidence in a body that had already endured every physical challenge that I knew nothing ahead of me could exceed.

Only three miles into my last Tuesday, I unexpectedly crossed paths again with my new friends from Tennessee at Cold Mountain Overlook. Tony and

I crossed paths again with Tony and Melissa Wilder from Tennessee at Cold Mountain Overlook, October 7, 2003, at Milepost 411.9 in North Carolina.

Melissa appeared to represent a generation from which the passage of time had finally cleansed the rancor generated by the decision to route not an inch of the Parkway through their own fine state. They also had begun another day of exploration and discovery, and the awe-struck look in their eyes bore silent agreement that the Parkway had indeed been routed properly. What a perfect opportunity our chance encounter at this particular location offered me to further enrich their visit with a few details the little overlook sign could not offer.

Almost the entire eastern flank of the geologic formation known as the Shining Rock Ledge was framed clearly before us. Beginning at a point to our left, where this long, high ridge first came into view, I walked them across its crest with the tip of my index finger. From the pure white quartz outcrop from which the area derives its name, we panned slowly to the right across the ruggedly rocky stretch known as The Narrows. We then descended into one of those places dreaded by backpackers—Deep Gap. Up, up we then ascended, past the unlikely oasis of spring water not far from the crest of Cold Mountain. At its rounded summit our tour halted, and I attempted to describe, as if standing upon it, the view I remembered from one lovely day and one meteor-riddled night high in the remote heart of the Shining Rock Wilderness Area. I urged them to read the recently published, highly acclaimed novel *Cold Mountain* by Charles Frazier. The author, I explained, was ancestrally linked to the region, from which the

Howard Inman, of the Bethel community of Haywood County, North Carolina, October 7, 2003, at Pounding Mill Overlook at Milepost 413.2 in North Carolina.

inspiration for his book had sprung. I had already read it three times myself and had committed a treasured copy of it to my sparse hardback library. Dared I also tell them how I had discreetly memorialized the main character of this book? Would they understand why I had carved the words "INMAN WAS HERE" on a scrap of wood and had wedged it in the fork of a tree high on the top of this mountain? Not even two miles farther down the Parkway, I experienced one of the most coincidental moments of my life.

Construction engineers and landscape architects might have feuded between the choice of drilling another tunnel or blasting a huge chunk of rock around the shoulder of a steep ridge near Milepost 413. Any tunnel proponents obviously lost the imagined tussle, which resulted in the creation of a fairly tight loop in the Parkway and the stunning view from Pounding Mill Overlook.

Here was the place where I had spotted a herring gull in a winter storm. Here was the place where many students from a nearby college so frivolously blemished otherwise clean criminal records. Here was the place where I had experienced vertigo in dense fog one night and nearly launched my patrol vehicle over the mountain. Thinking that I was two miles farther down the Parkway, I had missed the curve in the road, inched my way straight into the overlook, and bumped the curb with the front tires. Not until I found the overlook sign with my flashlight on that perplexing night did I realize just where I had, fortunately, gently landed.

Even in the absence of fog, there was something about the presentation of this overlook that drew almost every passing visitor into it like a magnet. Jutting into the sky like the balcony of a grand theater, it offered free and equal seating to both noble and common, wealthy and poor. What a grand model in so many respects this Parkway had become. Adopting the flimsy excuse that I needed a rest and a snack, I steered into it this time deliberately. Seated near the same spot on the stone curb that had saved me earlier from certain disaster, I contentedly munched on trail food and chatted with a small group of curious visitors that had gathered around me.

While thusly engaged in yet another pleasant social experience, an elderly man, at least in his eighties, drove his antiquated pickup truck into the overlook. His quiet, lean presence around the periphery of our gathering caught my attention. Alone, he walked about the grounds with his hands folded behind his back the way a cattle farmer might proudly inspect his herd on a restful Sunday afternoon. His eyes seemed to focus on something beyond the horizon; whether it was on the past or the future I could not discern. Perhaps it was both. But I could tell, from his patient shuffling and curious glances, that he wanted to speak to me. I had lived around these mountain people long enough to know, too, that he was not shy. He was just politely waiting his turn to talk to me about something that was for my ears only. Not until the overlook had been vacated by all the other visitors did he finally approach me.

Despite the tuggings of some kinship already detected between each other, the natural suspicions that had preserved us thus far in life required an immediate disclosure regarding the business with my backpack — there were no hiking trails in our immediate vicinity. When the man learned that I had almost completed hiking the entire Parkway and that I had once worked that area as a ranger, the walls of cautious restraint came tumbling down. His countenance changed to an accepting smile, and he proceeded to tell me that he had helped build the Parkway through that area, including the Devil's Courthouse Tunnel. He was the first person I had ever met who had done such work, and I pumped him for every detail he was willing to share. He described how, using no more than raw muscle and a sledgehammer, he had broken huge boulders into smaller chunks. "We had to bust them down to about the size of your backpack so they could fit into the rock crusher," he clarified with an analogy that my sore shoulders could well understand. I could not hear enough of his story. He could not hear enough of mine. And we politely disagreed over whose story was worthier of preservation.

Photographs and formal introductions were reserved for the concluding moments of our by-invitation-only symposium of eyewitnesses to history and wistful adventurers. When he introduced himself as Howard Inman, a resident of the Bethel community, I was jolted by the revelation. Bethel, I knew, was located near the base of Cold Mountain. I had driven through it numerous times after swinging the snow gates on the Parkway. And Inman? Inman! I had to ask one more burning question.

"Are you, by any chance, related to Charles Frazier?" My question brought a twinkle to his eye.

"Yes. We are some distant relation," came his proud reply. A movie, based on Frazier's book, was due to premier in a couple of months.

I took a picture of him standing in front of the huge rock face around which the Parkway had been carved. He had probably labored over some of the very chunks which had been explosively peeled from it. No wonder that he visited the place often. And then, as awkwardly as we had met, we departed from each other's company. Benumbed by the experience, I continued my journey.

Midafternoon was rapidly approaching, and I had only seven miles to my credit when I strolled into Cherry Cove Overlook. A solitary man, armed with a pen and notebook, was gazing into the sky in an attitude of serious, scientific contemplation. As had Harvey's Knob Overlook with respect to migrating hawks, this overlook had developed a widespread reputation as *the* place to observe monarch butterflies fluttering to their annual wintering grounds in Mexico. An interpretive display at the overlook and various sources of published literature might have spawned — and had undoubtedly perpetuated — this notion that I had always dismissed as a myth. Perhaps this low notch in the Pisgah Ledge really did funnel these critters into the path of least resistance through this part of the Appalachians. But I had never seen any more of them there than from any other overlook on the Parkway. In fact, I had seen just as many of them fly through the wide-open spaces past the fishing piers on the Outer Banks of North Carolina during the same time of year. "At times the sky is darkened by their numbers" was the sarcastic line that professional rangers were better advised not to use on the average, inquisitive visitor. Only those prejudged to be of exceptionally keen humor ever heard it from me.

When the guy surprisingly announced that the monarchs were crossing through the gap at the rate of 636 individuals per hour, I became a thunderstruck believer and, upon taking closer notice, was finally thrilled to witness the glorious, reputed spectacle. The sky never actually darkened, but I became so excited over the steady stream of orange wings that I remarked to two young men who had just driven into the overlook, "Man. Just look at these jokers pouring through here today," like I had never doubted the allegations of their profusion. Jeff Schmerker and Benjamin Hicks, reporter and photographer respectively, had been searching for me while I had been searching for butterflies.

Representing *The Enterprise Mountaineer*, a local newspaper serving the Haywood County area whose fringes I was now skirting, their youthful exuberance reminded me of two high school students who had escaped a boring classroom in exchange for a cool field trip. Benjamin, displaying every idiosyncrasy one would expect from a member of a yearbook staff, worked quietly in the background with his camera. Jeff, appearing to be distracted from his assignment by the scenery into which he had escaped, fired odd, disjointed questions and worried me somewhat with what appeared to be a noticeable deficiency in stenography skills.

Most young people, however, eventually surprise their older, so-called wiser critics with manifestations of refreshing brilliance and unimaginable achievement. Thus did this pair fool me until I gasped at their creation a few days later. The colorful, detailed article they produced so accurately described the spirit of my adventure that I was compelled to recommend to their editor that they receive a hearty Christmas bonus for their work. With a correctness nearly as keen as Benjamin's camera, Jeff quite surprised me with numerous verbatim quotes, including another verbal slip that could have qualified me for a visit from the men in white coats. Regarding my response to the many people who kept asking me if I had ever read *Cold Mountain*, I told him, "I tell them I'm Inman." And, in one forgiving statement, which stretched the truth closer to their age than my own, I was graciously described as appearing "more dashing than the typical long-distance hiker." Perhaps my body and accouterments had not degraded to the condition with which my own eyes viewed them. I was certainly not "blasted and ravaged, worn ragged and weary and thin," as the fictional Ada had viewed her Inman at the end of his long journey.

Crossing the eleventh and final fold of my map, I managed to log seven more miles that day under skies that did eventually darken — not from the shadows of millions of butterflies, but from a weather system that dropped fog and drizzle onto my party like the lid on a coffin. How terribly I had looked forward to seeing again the savannah-like openness of Graveyard Fields and the unique shades of color that were reliably splendid even on years plagued by autumnal mediocrity. The thrill, too, of watching a golden eagle soar in the sky or a peregrine falcon scream in for a kill would also have to be postponed to a more cooperative day. Wild country, these parts were considered dangerous, also, to the inattentive explorer. I had managed more than one search for hikers who wandered too far from the Parkway to become disoriented and lost in the Dark Prong drainage. The "Bermuda Triangle of the Parkway" some of us affectionately called it.

By the time I reached the Devil's Courthouse Tunnel, the path in front of me had become so utterly dark that only the absence of echoing footsteps confirmed that I had passed completely through it. Once again, I had trapped myself in steep, thick country where finding a suitable campsite, even in daylight, could be difficult. A plantation of red spruce trees, located near Mount Hardy Overlook, offered an option, and I veered into its protective shelter. Within its clean, dark understory, I pitched my little tent with the aid of a flashlight whose batteries had been reserved for just such necessities.

In collaboration with the United Daughters of the Confederacy, the U.S. Forest Service had planted 125,000 red spruce seedlings on fire-ravaged lands in the early 1940s to commemorate the same number of men who served in the Civil War from North Carolina. Quiet, deathly quiet remained the memorial forest that night, while I slept, surrounded by stately specimens I imagined to represent Inman and two great-great-grandfathers of my own: John A. Corn and John Fletcher Pegram. They were all deserving of honor — not for their common cause, but for what many of them had been individually forced to suffer due to circumstances completely beyond their control. I could not pack up fast enough the next morning to escape the symbolic sadness of the whole rotten affair and the brutal scolding of a red squirrel in whose territory I had so rudely intruded. Breakfast could be better enjoyed just around the next curve.

There were some days I would have argued that Beech Gap was the coldest, windiest place on the Parkway, especially the day a strong north wind momentarily tipped my patrol vehicle onto its two right wheels while I drove through it. Funneled into the gap between Mount Hardy and Little Sam Knob, it could race up the drainage known as the West Fork of the Pigeon River with the force of a hurricane. Such conditions, compounded by bitterly cold temperatures, could make a lone ranger's passage through the snow gates at this particular location a challenging experience.

I learned pretty quickly to park beyond the reach of the swinging arms of any snow gate. Once they were loosed from their moorings and out of one's grasp, a gust of wind could wrap them around their hinges. A ranger could hardly be blamed for a collision with a runaway rooster, but headquarters frowned on any ranger who permitted a snow gate to fly into a headlight. Until I figured out a couple of ways to anchor and prop them, joining the two flailing arms of a snow gate proved about as easy as forcing love with a shotgun wedding.

I also learned pretty quickly that neither warm hands nor forced breath were any match for the locks on the gates at Beech Gap; the least bit of fog would creep into them at night and freeze them tighter than a weld. Matches, candles, even cigarette lighters proved fairly useless in thawing the locks if the slightest bit of wind was stirring. Frustrated enormously one morning, I began an experiment with the use of heat that advanced abruptly to the overkill stage of twisted rolls of flaming newspaper. Albeit messy and dangerous, this approach proved to be highly successful if the uncontrollable flames could be rushed from the interior of my patrol vehicle to the stubborn lock quickly enough. Dissatisfied with the probability that I would eventually set myself or the woods on fire, I stumbled upon and adopted the clean efficiency of a portable propane torch, despite its proclivity for producing mysterious burn scars on my gloves, pants, and various interior parts of my patrol vehicle.

Seated at a picnic table located just south of Beech Gap, I sipped on a serving of hot chocolate which was slightly tainted with the flaky remnants of instant grits. Trail economy sometimes was not a pretty sight; neither was the weather on that overcast, misty morning. I had always wanted to enjoy a meal at that location, which was more likely to be used by fair weather visitors better blessed with fried chicken, potato salad, and blue skies. Both the north and south snow gates were visible from my vantage point. I had worried, as a slightly middle-aged ranger, that I might not be able to handle them when I became an old, arthritic man. Now I was grateful that I would never have to wrestle with them again.

One rainy, winter afternoon, a report came in to the Vinton ranger station that the Parkway was icing up on Bent Mountain. Forfeiting the opportunity to chain up the rear tires on my two-wheel-drive patrol car in the warm, dry comfort of a garage, I proceeded posthaste in that direction. Closing Section 1-N in the early stages of an ice storm was critically important in preventing a rash of motor vehicle accidents and in reducing the number of reports I would have to write. With a good fifteen miles of solid road ahead of me, I could at least get the closure signs flipped at the U.S. Route 220 intersection and, if I was lucky, could make it to the top of the mountain without the assistance of chains. Experience had already taught me that it could be done with the proper mix of finesse and momentum.

True to the report, I encountered black ice about halfway up the mountain. To this day, I am certain I could have made it to Adney Gap without chains had I not met that pickup truck. I had just negotiated a sharp curve when I noticed a slight skew in the truck's course and a bright, left headlight easing into my lane. Its driver was desperately trying to maintain control. I let up on the accelerator and steered to the right just enough to avoid a head-on collision. Luckily, we missed each other, but I lost my momentum and came to a spinning stop right in the middle of the road.

Frustrated and shaken, I shoved the transmission into the "park" position and applied the emergency brake. Before I could decide whether there was enough sight distance in both directions to safely mount the chains where I was parked, an odd sensation came over me. The car was now sliding in a strangely disorienting motion on the icy, tilted surface. Not only was it sliding backward, but it was heading for the narrow road shoulder and an unobstructed plunge of several hundred feet down the mountain. I pumped the foot brake to no avail and silently cursed the fact that, of all the miles of guide rail that had been planted along the Parkway, this one treacherous spot had for some reason been neglected. Remembering, from past investigations, the damage and injury such a ride could inflict, I made a split-second decision to spare myself the agony by jumping ship.

Hollywood had made it look so simple. All I had to do was depress the release button on the body restraint system, open the door, and leap from the vehicle. As I was about to execute the final stage of that maneuver, I realized that the lap belt and shoulder harness had hooked my gun holster. Ironically, two of the most important pieces of equipment available for my safety and preservation had conspired to facilitate my destruction. I now faced another crucial decision with only milliseconds left to make it. Should I attempt to untangle myself and proceed with the leap? As the horrific vision unfolded of my body being slung like a rag doll, tethered at the waist, against metal and rocks, I opted for the alternative. For the second time in my life, I was certain I was about to die, and I elected to do so by hanging onto the steering wheel with a death grip as long as I could.

The right-rear tire bit the shoulder first, causing the front of the car to snap to the right. With whitened knuckles, I gritted my teeth and prepared myself for the violent tumble. But both right tires ground into the dirt and gravel like a sharp file against coarse metal. Surprised by the abrupt stop, I opened my eyes and leaped from the car. Heck, I had two feet to spare! Only then did I exhale. As I proceeded to mount the chains and complete the task at hand, I had to remind myself again and again that I really was employed in the profession to which I had so doggedly aspired.

The entire Balsam Gap District was locked down due to a winter storm that had dumped several inches of snow even on the Parkway's lowest elevations. In the highest elevations, some sections of the road were windswept and barren while other sections were clogged with snowdrifts several feet deep and wide. Half a day was about my limit in responding to the never-ending flow of paperwork through my in-box. "Nastygrams" (correspondence from headquarters) and messages from the "note ghosts" (fellow employees I saw on an intermittent basis due to opposing work schedules) demanded more time than I ever thought would be required of a district ranger.

Following lunch and a rowdy game of checkers with one of the maintenance men, I decided to leave the warmth of a hot wood stove and announced to anyone who chose to listen, "I have some important government business to attend to up at Mount Pisgah. Bye." As I warmed up my heavy-duty, four-wheel-drive patrol vehicle, this oft-repeated ritual was countered with some serious head shaking followed eventually by sincere, concerned advice. Like the fatherly desk sergeant on the hit television series, *Hill Street Blues*, someone always, always reminded me to be careful and to watch out for that curve at Milepost 430 — another place in dire need of a guide rail.

Escaping the confines of my office was not the only reason I felt it necessary to patrol the district in such conditions. Snow gates were frequently vandalized, and I constantly worried that an innocent visitor might assume that a dry road near a dangling gate meant there were no dangers ahead. Cross-country skiers were also known to explore several miles back into these closed areas, and their welfare needed to be monitored. The sooner a potential rescue path could be punched through those areas, the better, was my philosophy. There were many reasons for me not to feel guilty over leaving the paperwork pit to create powdery explosions busting through snow drifts on a sunny, winter afternoon.

The locks on only two of the six gates out to Mount Pisgah were frozen, and I made the turnaround by midafternoon. Punching the first set of tire tracks through the area, I had done so cautiously and conservatively, avoiding lumps certain to be fallen rocks hidden by the snow and taking the path of least resistance around or through the drifts. On the return trip I could drive a little more boldly through a path already carefully blazed.

With about two hours of daylight remaining, I eased up to a huge snow drift that was located on a level stretch of road near the final descent into Balsam Gap. My original route around its tapered edge was precipitously close to a steep drop-off, and I did not feel comfortable following my tracks in the reversed direction. Besides that, I was in a gamy mood for some experimental adventure. I bumped the mountain of snow with the front of my vehicle just to make sure it was still soft enough to penetrate. A snowdrift loaded with sleet or one that had melted some and had settled was better left alone. Estimating it to be about twelve feet high and fifteen feet deep at the center of the road, I judged from prior experience that a speed of 30 mph would get me through it. Wrong.

I knew as soon as I hit that beached albino whale that my mental calculation of its density was grossly in error. So there I sat, high-centered about three feet above the pavement, surrounded by the pure white entrails of the beast that had swallowed me. I rolled down the window and dug upward, pulling snow into the interior of the vehicle in the process. There was no one around for miles to be humored, but I know I must have looked like a prairie dog emerging from its mound when my head finally popped through the top of the drift. Too proud to call for help, I climbed back through the window and wormed my way back to the cargo bay to retrieve a shovel. What? No shovel in this shared vehicle? A hard hat proved to be a poor substitute for a shovel and... The sun had already dipped below the horizon and the temperature had begun to plummet when I finally freed my terrified steed from the fluffy blubber.

31

The Main Event

"It seems that Hollywood discovered the Blue Ridge Parkway."
—"Must See Movies," *Ridge Runner*
Newsmagazine, February 1990

I was familiar enough with the weather along the Parkway to know that lousiness would eventually be replaced with splendor. Sometimes this transition occurred abruptly; sometimes it took forever. A climb out of dense, low-elevation fog could suddenly bring one into clear, blue skies with a splendid view of "cotton-filled" valleys below. An unhurried low pressure system, however, could delay any transitional relief for days and drag the most robust of spirits into a mild depression. Few things pained me more as a ranger than the sad faces of a poor mill worker and his family whose precious few days of Fourth of July vacation were ruined by the latter. I, too, had timed myself right into the middle of one of those disappointing systems at the worst possible juncture — the final days of my trek through the climactic high country of my old district. Donned once again in full rain regalia, I tightened the waist strap of my backpack and marched forthrightly into the soup. At least it was not snowing, albeit not many degrees from it.

Neither the weather nor my mood permitted a detour from my breakfast table at Beech Gap out onto the wild, undisturbed flats of Tanasee Bald, the reputed home and farm of Judaculla, the slant-eyed giant of Cherokee folklore. Had the dreams of early planners been completely realized, an extension of the Parkway into Georgia would have been constructed right through the middle of it, along with a gas station, coffee shop, and picnic area. Implementation of those ideas, fortunately, many would say, never made it beyond the drawing board and a capped wellhead.

Driven by reports of extensive poaching, I had ventured into that mysteri-

A climb out of dense, low-elevation fog could suddenly bring one into clear, blue skies with a splendid view of "cotton-filled" valleys. Photo taken about 1985 from Waterrock Knob Overlook, Milepost 451.2 in North Carolina. The crest of the Great Smoky Mountains is in the background.

ous territory one day, determined to locate a neglected section of the park boundary. Certain that I had truly discovered the edge of the earth, I finally extracted myself from some of the most dangerous, forsaken country I had ever explored. One stood a better chance of finding the bleached remains of the original survey crew than that elusive line. Superstition, of course, had nothing to do with my decision to never walk back into that area again.

Four miles into the morning, the curve at Milepost 426 vividly reminded me of every inch and second of a harrowing ride I took one afternoon. Most of my close calls driving on snow and ice on the Parkway had resulted from too much accelerator while trying to maintain momentum driving up steep grades, resulting occasionally in heart-stopping spinouts. Deep snow in closed sections or the urgency to close a section still shallow in accumulation was usually to blame in those instances. Rarely, however, did I ever lose control of a patrol vehicle going downhill. Slow speed and gentle brake action, aided by chains, on all four tires if necessary, usually got me safely to the foot of every grade I attempted to descend.

Haste, a momentary lapse of short-term memory, and the distraction of a deer, however, sent me descending too fast into this curve that afternoon after having just driven over a two-mile section of dry road. Intermittent patches of snow and ice proved far more dangerous to me than a blanketed roadway, and when I hit this one, I basically bid fair adieu again to this wonderful life. Skillful driving, I am certain, is not the power that kept me between the ditches and eventually pointed me forward until the tires, slightly out of kilter, barked briefly at their joyous reunion once again with a dry road. I had been completely and unequivocally out of control for a distance longer than I care to quantify.

From Haywood Gap, I prepared myself for a long, steady climb to a familiar Parkway landmark. With every foot gained in elevation, the weather conditions deteriorated proportionally. Misty rain progressed to a steady drizzle; dark, overcast skies degraded to dense fog. While my uphill exertion and protective rain gear kept me comfortably warm, a group of northbound motorcyclists, dressed in the finest of rain gear, looked as cold and stiff as icicles. One of them, evidence would soon suggest, was probably smarting from a very recent, unplanned meeting with a guide rail. The descriptive adjectives formerly applied to them as an estimation of their body temperature would soon be replaced with those more indicative of an altered mood — humble and stern.

Analyzing old motorcycle accident scenes had become a fairly routine mental diversion for me on the hike. Direction of travel, point of loss of control, points of impact, probable damage, and probable extent of injuries could often be determined. The accident scene I discovered at a guide rail just north of Cowee Mountain Overlook was no different than most of them, except for the fact that it was very, very fresh. Before striking the guide rail, a downed, northbound motorcycle had ripped chunks of turf out of the narrow shoulder, and the exposed soil was still fairly dry when I found it. My prediction to Patty had almost been realized again. A new oddity at this scene, the meaning of which I did not understand at the time, was the discovery of an eight-of-hearts playing card. I picked it up, looked at it and, for reasons I cannot explain, dropped it uncharacteristically back on the ground like it was a nasty piece of litter that I would rather not handle.

Less than a mile farther down the Parkway, I stepped into Richland Balsam Overlook and promptly negotiated a reciprocal, picture-taking agreement with two other weather-rejected visitors of the motorcyclist variety. A large, rustic sign, perhaps the most photographed one on the Parkway, marked an elevation of 6,053 feet — the highest point on the motor road. For me, it also symbolized the high-water mark of my ranger career and a psychological threshold which created the pleasant illusion that the remainder of my trek would be mostly downhill. Equally proud of our airy, intimate association with this most extraordinary Parkway, I proudly posed in front of it with my walking stick while they proudly posed with their bikes. All three of us now had documentary proof, for any unbelievers back home, that we had conquered "Mount Parkway" in our own individual ways under less than ideal conditions. Brothers, of sorts, I thought we had become through a liberal stretch of the imagination.

With visibility now reduced to less than a hundred feet, I begged them to drive carefully and told them about the accident scene I had just discovered a

Intermittent patches of snow and ice proved far more dangerous to me than a blanketed roadway. Photo taken about 1985, near Milepost 426 in North Carolina.

short distance down the road. Their silence and wry grins directed at each other suggested that they lent little credence to any authority I might be on such matters. What would I know about the art of motorcycle riding? I was not one of them. I was a mere walker! Before leaving, however, they were thoughtful enough to enlighten me with some information apparently sacrosanct in the biker world. Some riders, they told me, carry a deck of playing cards and drop one card at every location where their motorcycle hits the ground. If they survive long enough to drop the fifty-second card, they never ride again. As my two new acquaintances roared back into the fog, I pondered the odds associated with that superstition and concluded that being born a cat was a much safer bet.

Richland Balsam Overlook seemed to be the perfect place for seasonal ranger Richard Griffin and I to snag the yet unidentified, unsuspecting target. Unlike a hidden surveillance trap, we positioned ourselves in full view of the passing public that eventful Tuesday morning. We were searching for some people whose travel plans were more relevant than their physical descriptions. Visitors were randomly stopped and questioned in such an unusual and friendly manner that the worst of which we could be accused was nutty nosiness. It was a tricky operation that reminded me of an old television series in which someone was carefully selected each week to receive a gift of a million dollars.

Richland Balsam Overlook symbolized the high-water mark of my ranger career and a psychological threshold which created the pleasant illusion that the remainder of my trek would be mostly downhill. Photo taken October 8, 2003, at Milepost 431.4 in North Carolina.

Headquarters had projected that, sometime during the week of September 28-October 4, 1986, the Parkway's 400-millionth visitor would elusively trip a traffic counter somewhere in the park. Faced with the impractical task of pinpointing exactly when and where that event might occur on such a sprawled boundary with dozens of access points, a truly brilliant plan was formulated. Sometime during that week, an individual or couple would be identified in each of the nine Parkway districts on which to lavish the symbolic honor. The selection criteria were subjectively simple — find people willing to accept the honor whose travel plans permitted them to enjoy its fruits. The participation of dozens of businesses, organizations, and media services along the entire length of the Parkway guaranteed the rolling event to produce a positive public relations bonanza for the park and region. Nine district rangers were entrusted with the delicate selection process.

Ranger Griffin and I were apprehensively excited about the "other duties as assigned" section of our official job descriptions that brought us to Richland Balsam Overlook that morning. "We'll know them when we see them" was about the only advice I could give to my young, eager-to-please partner. Carefully concealing our intentions and the gifts we were bearing, we began an awkward process that would instantly elevate someone from the status of anonymous visitor to that of celebrated guest.

Jack and Edna Gaither appeared a little surprised when two armed park rangers instructed them to stop their car. They later told a reporter from a local newspaper that they were fairly certain that they had not broken any laws. They had not, of course, and in a few short minutes, Ranger Griffin and I nodded at each other in absolute agreement that we had found our couple. Recently retired, neither of them had ever before visited the Blue Ridge Parkway. En route to Washington, D.C. from their home in Lancaster, Texas, they had just entered the Parkway that morning in Cherokee and planned to drive its entire length. Would their schedule permit them to linger in the area for two or three days? Yes!

We then escorted the surprised couple to the Pisgah Inn, where they were honored in a small ceremony and presented a surprise package that included a certificate, special badges, books, postcards, and complimentary meals and lodging at the Pisgah Inn and other local establishments. The looks of gratitude on their faces were all the thanks we needed. Sandwiched between the Parkway's fiftieth anniversary celebration in 1985 and its dedicatory celebration in 1987, this event became one of the sweetest experiences I ever enjoyed as a park ranger.

Monitoring commercial filming operations, though, never ranked high on my list of favorite ranger activities. Most of them came in the form of car and truck commercials along with a host of concerns and problems: disrupted work schedules; oversized equipment requiring escort through tunnels; low-flying helicopters; fog machines; temporary road closures; alterations and damage to park resources; and visitor complaints. Despite the fact that they brought an air of excitement to an otherwise mundane work day, I never grieved over a film crew's departure — until one chilly April morning, when a little snow flurry precipitated the rapid demobilization of a small army of support vehicles and staff from their staging area at Richland Balsam Overlook. Apparently satisfied with the footage accumulated the previous day under better weather conditions, they scurried off the mountain like sunbathers caught in a shower.

The excitement surrounding the filming of a 2½-minute scene from the movie *Made in Heaven* was contagious and even brought members of the headquarters staff down to the district. Co-producer David Blocker, son of Dan Blocker (Hoss Cartwright on the television series *Bonanza*), and actors Timothy Hutton and Debra Winger were in town to be met. Only a surprise visit from Kelly McGillis, who co-starred in the movie but was not in this scene, would have made the experience any finer for me; her eyes had slain me in *Top Gun*. No better backdrop could have been found for Elmo's down-and-out encounter with Emmett just south of Richland Balsam Overlook. Only a visit to this section of the Parkway — on a clear day — and a viewing of the movie can explain why. Just try to avoid asking a bothered ranger, late in the summer season, what killed all the trees.

I never really understood how this movie bombed at the box office. It was one of the most beautifully written, artfully directed movies I had ever seen. Or perhaps I had become unalterably biased by the charm of Kelly McGillis and the fact that a fraction of it had been filmed in a place dear to my heart. Despite all the headaches of which they remind me, I still enjoy spotting familiar Parkway scenes when they flash briefly across the television screen during commercial breaks. The orchestrated absence of center line reflectors, side striping on the edge of the roadway, and clutter in the distance are the dead giveaways.

32

Local Comparable Rate

"I have given careful consideration to your memorandum ... requesting a possible move from your government quarters ... and you may proceed with your plans."
— Memorandum from Gary Everhardt, Superintendent, to author

From the looks of the weather, my trek seemed destined not to conclude with the sunny, happy ending of a good movie. Even more disturbing than the now steady, healthy raindrops was the inordinate distribution of bear scat deposits along the roadway. There were too many of them too close together. The frequent presence of yellowish-orange piles of digested mountain ash berries indicated that I was either very close to one diarrhea-stricken bear or had stumbled into a one-course family reunion of the lovable creatures. In either case, the thoughts of surprising one from a downwind position in the now dense fog were not pleasant. Neither was the prospect of pitching my tent in the midst of either scenario without the protection of a bearproof container for my food. Even though it meant a twenty-mile day, pushing myself all the way to the Balsam Gap ranger station seemed to be the more rational choice for my thirty-eighth night on the trail. I had planned to stop there anyway to say hello to any remaining familiar faces. At the least, I could, relatively free of bearish worries, unfurl my foam mattress and sleeping bag under the dry protection of an open carport if one of the ranger quarters happened to be unoccupied.

I had walked hardly a mile past Richland Balsam Overlook when a ranger vehicle slowed to a stop and its female driver asked, "Hey, mister. You okay?"

It sounded like such a silly question coming from someone who, despite the fact that we had not seen each other in several years, should have instantly recognized me. Had I really aged that much? Armed with little more than a college degree and an enthusiastic introduction, Marcia Bowers had confidently marched herself into my office one day looking for a job opportunity. Even though she had no prior experience in park operations, the fact that she owned her own Christmas tree farm, could operate just about any piece of logging equipment, and had qualified herself for a seasonal law enforcement commission had caused me to take notice that this was no ordinary applicant. I had taken her under my wing, and she eventually worked herself into a permanent ranger position. With no intention of playing any mind games like I had done with Ranger Schula, I hesitated momentarily to permit Ranger Bowers to get her bearings. The direction she took startled me.

"Sir. I asked you if you were okay," came a stern, impatient utterance at a decibel level that demanded an immediate response to the question still suspended between us. The title "mister," used formerly in a conciliatory sense, had also been strategically replaced with a more aggressive connotation of the title "sir." Her sudden change in demeanor was effective enough to make a baby cry and get the attention of a grown man. I had trained her too well for my own good.

When I bent slightly forward to make better eye contact with her through the open window, water streamed from the brim of my fedora like a mini-waterfall onto the ground. "You don't recognize me, do you Marcia?" I hinted, remembering how well my get-up might be concealing my true identity.

When she finally recovered from the shock of seeing an unexpected ghost from her ranger past, she quickly formulated a simple rescue plan. "Listen. I've got to make a run up to Mount Pisgah. When I come back through here, I'll give you a ride down to the ranger station. No way are you going to spend the night out in this mess."

Though late in the game, another ground rule came to mind, and I decided to never protest the instructions of a woman carrying a gun. In a matter of minutes, I had twice upgraded my room for the night from a wet tent in bear-infested country, to an airy carport, to at least the top of a table in the enclosed, dry comfort of the employee break room. Suddenly, my pack did not feel as heavy, and the weather did not seem as gloomy. I could slow my pace and, in the glaring absence of panoramic vistas, could at least enjoy a few pleasant memories of movies of my own making that *had* concluded with happy endings.

Months of planning and hard work had preceded the dedication ceremony of the Roy Taylor Forest Overlook on June 9, 1984. Retired U.S. Congressman and honoree Roy Taylor, North Carolina Governor Jim Hunt, and a host of other dignitaries were expected to attend. The district maintenance staff had heroically braved cold, stormy weather in the months preceding the occasion to build a scenic observation platform, erect a monument, and pave a short trail. As the date of the event approached and the frenzy surrounding its execution intensified, so too came an increase in the number of calls from headquarters emphatically reminding me of an additional, critically important assignment—

provide a veil for the monument and materials for the ribbon-cutting ceremony. The nagging diminished somewhat when I began to tease the callers that I was giving serious consideration to replacing the "Tarheel Blue" ribbon with one of "Wolfpack Red" color. At the conclusion of the ceremony, which came off without a hitch, Superintendent Everhardt, another N.C. State University alumnus, shook my hand vigorously and exclaimed, "You made the Parkway look good today." I would never forget that remark and the proud look of approval in his eyes. And all agreed that baby blue better matched the occasion and the sky on that beautifully, sunny day.

Two young men at Licklog Gap Overlook seemed unusually startled by my sudden appearance in a patrol car one morning. The district had been plagued recently by thieves breaking into cars parked at overlooks, and the fact that these men were rummaging through the contents of a bulky, leather handbag, for some reason, did not give me the impression that they were looking through their own gear for a clean pair of socks. I stopped to investigate, whereupon they immediately surrendered the suspected loot with a hasty explanation that they had just found it lying in the roadway. Sure.

Carefully concealing my suspicions, I played along with their story and pretended to treat their report as a routine lost and found incident. When I explained that they could eventually be awarded the property if its owner could not be located, they cooperatively provided enough information for me to locate them later. Future arrest warrants, quite honestly, were more on my mind than any reward for convenient honesty. With no matching reports of stolen property on file, I thanked the men for their help and permitted them to leave. Their home state of West Virginia was not that far away if I had to go looking for them later.

In addition to several expensive items of camera equipment, the bag also contained a checkbook on which was printed enough information to identify and later contact its owner. But George Warwick Jr., an attorney from Anchorage, Kentucky, quickly dashed my plans for a road trip to the coal country and exonerated the young men by reporting his loss the same day to another park employee. His property had not been stolen, as suspected. He had driven out from under it after leaving it on the trunk of his car! My per diem dreams of West Virginia vanished quicker than they had formed.

In a complimentary letter, Mr. Warwick later speculated that, even though the men might have eventually turned in his property, my timely presence apparently had a "salutary effect on their consciences." And more important to him than anything in the bag, he said, was the return of his fifty-year-old Boy Scout pocketknife.

I had already passed Grassy Ridge Mine Overlook and had begun the steep descent into Balsam Gap when Marcia stopped about two hours later on her return trip from Mount Pisgah. The steady rain had progressed to a downpour, and I was more than grateful to be rescued from its uncomfortable dreariness following a modest, fourteen-mile day. Before I could inquire about carport availability for the night, the little dickens surprised me with another unexpected declaration. She had already made arrangements with the maintenance foreman for me to spend the night inside one of the vacant ranger quarters. Perhaps still mindful of my former fussiness as a supervisor, she quickly added that the heater was still working to mitigate any inconvenience I might find with the fact that the residence was not furnished and that the water supply had been shut off for the season. But time, life experience, and the trail had tumbled and polished me into a much more mellow fellow. How could I complain about sleeping on the dry floor of a warm, carpeted room on such a dreadful night? Indoor plumbing, too, had now become, for me, more of a curious novelty rather than an expected amenity.

Our close proximity to each other in the front seat of a heated patrol vehicle probably made her more aware than I of a troubling circumstance in dire need of rectification. I had distanced myself ten days and 127 miles from the last hot shower for which no number of cold sponge baths could properly substitute. As we drove up to the locked entrance gate at the ranger station, Marcia startled me with another surprise announcement made in a subtle, diplomatically directive manner. "Your old office is now a women's restroom. They also put a shower in it. You're welcome to use it while I run into town and pick us up a pizza." What?!

I knew the first day I reported for duty at Balsam Gap that our ranger office — not much larger than a walk-in closet — was way too small to accommodate a cadre of four permanent rangers supplemented by an even larger staff of seasonal employees. It was one condition that I absolutely refused to tolerate, and I immediately began a campaign for relief. Following much spilled blood, more spacious digs in another part of the building were eventually acquired, and the last time I saw the original ranger office it had been converted to a storage room.

Like the long line of insensitive male planners, architects, and managers that had preceded me on the Parkway, I never gave much thought to the fact that the entire maintenance-ranger complex was equipped with only one bathroom. Our "knock before entering" policy seemed to work pretty well until some of the female employees began to mildly complain that the addition of a women's restroom was just as important as getting more square footage for a ranger office. Attempting to defuse the issue in a humorous manner, I posted a sign on the bathroom door one day after carefully calculating the affected male-female ratio. Mondays, Wednesdays, and Fridays were reserved for males, it stated. Tuesdays and Thursdays were reserved for females. Users would operate on a first-come, first-serve basis on weekends. I had ruffled enough feathers fighting the bureaucracy for a larger office and had no intentions of engaging in another battle that involved knocking holes in walls and installing new plumbing.

Evolution had certainly manifested itself in some interesting, even peculiar ways up and down the Parkway. The grass around several miles of guide rail, once trimmed by a small army of humpbacked employees equipped with hand clippers, was now whacked quickly and efficiently by a piece of plastic cord spun by a two-cycle engine suspended from one person wearing enough safety equipment to be mistaken for an astronaut. Rangers, once required to hide their sidearms in the glove boxes of their patrol cars, were now equipped with automatic weapons. And, in the most ironic, mutational twist of them all, I now reveled in soapy delight in almost the exact place where I had once fretted over work schedules, evaluations, and paper cuts. Hurrah to all the once-oppressed, pioneer women of Balsam Gap whose perseverance had made my hot shower possible! My rude intrusion into their newly acquired space had technically been legal; the day was, incidentally, a Wednesday.

The weather did not improve any on Thursday, and I chose to linger the full day and another evening at Balsam Gap to visit with old friends and catch up on more than a dozen years of news. Despite a sixty percent chance of rain predicted for Friday, however, I rose early with an impatient determination to resume my journey. Taut trail legs were not only screaming for a workout, but I could smell Milepost 469 and a huge personal victory only two days in the distance.

Hoping to scrounge a free northbound shuttle back to my point last walked, I stood ready with my backpack at the ranger station as the maintenance staff began to arrive for the last day of their work week. Still poking and teasing each other with good-hearted humor in the established tradition of the district, they were as excited as school kids looking forward to the approaching weekend. Their own supervisor, Marshall Lovedahl, abruptly forestalled the efforts of anyone planning to dive too quickly into their assigned responsibilities when he drove onto the scene with a wide grin and a sack full of sausage biscuits. I always knew that his untiring work ethic and even temperament would fairly qualify him someday for the position which he now held. He had obviously learned also the fine art of morale management and insisted that I take a second biscuit for the road. I knew better than to refuse his offer and graciously thanked him for also arranging a ride for me back to Grassy Ridge Mine Overlook. So much had changed at Balsam Gap yet so much had remained the same.

I could hardly wait to begin my own day under skies that, although threatening in appearance, were at least devoid of fog and precipitation for the moment. I had only one specific goal for the day — to reach the Waterrock Knob Visitor Center before closing time. There were two items whose purchase I had postponed for this, the southernmost visitor center on the Parkway. Attaining that goal would first require a steep, six-mile descent of about two thousand feet followed by a steep, eight-mile climb of almost twenty-five hundred feet. My unscheduled day of rest could not have come at a better time in preparation for what would be my last passage through another "deep" gap not so named. Otherwise, every ounce of bone, muscle, and connective tissue from my waist to my toes would likely have coalesced into mush by the end of the day.

As I began my day coasting merrily downhill with a renewed spirit and fresh legs, the appearance of every curve and overlook once again triggered memories in multiples like forgotten scenes from an old, once-familiar movie. Steestachee Bald Overlook had been the scene of a hair-raising rope rescue of a man who, in the process of trying to impress his lady friend, had climbed himself into a frozen panic on an unstable rock cut. Of all people, Mike Sneed, Bud Carter's mechanic counterpart at Balsam Gap, was caught red-handed one Saturday afternoon gathering morel mushrooms in what I thought was my own secret patch — an overgrown apple orchard near the foot of the mountain. As I approached the bridge carrying the Parkway over U.S. Route 23–74 at Balsam Gap, the disgusting smell of hot brakes reminded me of another October afternoon at that same location. One distraught lady. Each front wheel on fire. One small fire extinguisher. Two-shot odds. Poof. Poof. One vehicle, minus front brakes, saved from a fiery death. Downshift that automatic transmission, milady. Downshift it next time.

By noon, I was well on my way up the last challenging grade of my trek, headed toward Waterrock Knob at a blistering pace I knew not was in me. To that second sausage biscuit I gave all the credit. A couple from Miami, Florida, approached from the south and slowed to a stop. When I realized that they were videotaping me, I tossed in a few candid, informative lines at no extra charge. I was bewilderedly thrilled that they were so pleasantly thrilled to record such a spectacle, given all the available scenery. Happy, too, that the day had not yet brought rain, I spurred myself upward with the strength and determination of an orchestra being directed to crescendo. Only two miles from the top, near the same place where Patty, Laura, and I had often enjoyed picking wild blueberries together after supper on Monday evenings, the faint sound of a siren far below me broke my pace and, in a couple of minutes, almost broke my spirit.

I could see the ranger vehicle almost two miles away as it snaked its way rapidly up the mountain. Its engine and transmission strained and groaned to their maximum limits as its driver negotiated the steep grade past slower vehicles and through sharp curves toward some unknown emergency. With hand signals, I attempted to slow and forewarn the drivers of northbound vehicles of that which they could neither see nor hear but would momentarily meet. When Marcia screamed past me, she was in the delicate process of passing a slower vehicle in a slight curve where visibility was very limited. I could tell from the expression on her face and the way she was clenching the steering wheel with both hands that she was tapping her driving skills to their limit. Someone, somewhere, was in dire pain or danger that afternoon; she had never been prone to hot dog just for show. As she raced out of sight around the next curve, I just stood there as helpless as the day I had been born.

A few steps later I hit an emotional wall as hard as any runner ever hit that intangible, physical wall near the eighteen-mile mark of a marathon race. For reasons I cannot explain, I was suddenly overcome with emotion. Perhaps my heart just ached for the unknown pain and suffering suggested by flashing blue lights and the desperate sound of a wailing siren. Perhaps the memory of our private blueberry patch made me long to have Laura back again just one more day as my little girl. Perhaps I had physically pushed myself too hard up the mountain that day and had discovered my mental and physical limit for long distance hiking at 449 miles. Perhaps I had seen myself behind that steering wheel and wanted, just one more time, to be a park ranger again. Or perhaps I remembered the evening of June 21, 1998, when a cable news channel flashed a brief message across the bottom of my television screen that a park ranger had been killed that Father's Day afternoon in a shootout on the Blue Ridge Parkway near Cherokee, N.C. Until I learned differently, I feared that Marcia, almost another daughter to me, had been the victim.

Instead of lying down in defeat in the middle of the road, as Elmo had done in the Parkway scene in *Made in Heaven*, I decided, with dogged stubbornness, to walk out the tears and pains that were inexplicably consuming me. Two miles later, they were all finally wrung out when I stepped into the safe harbor of the Waterrock Knob Visitor Center — just in time to avoid a fast-moving, ferocious squall that pounded the aged, stalwart mountain with wind and rain. There, I finally purchased a hardback copy of Sharyn McCrumb's *Ghost Riders* and the Blue Ridge Parkway's official walking stick medallion. The extra weight of the book was no longer a consideration; I was in desperate need of some good reading material. The medallion, as far as I was concerned, had been genuinely earned.

Despite the fact that I was now emotionally and physically exhausted, a prompt closure of the visitor center forced an involuntary resumption of my walk. The rest of the day, at least, would be gentle; the rain had stopped and the next few miles were downhill. As clouds and fog threatened to bring the light of day to a premature close, Marcia stopped to explain her prior hurry. A man had been seriously injured when his motorcycle struck a truck head-on near Milepost 467. "Tim. It's the only thing about this job that rattles me," she lamented. I know. How well I know. Just hang in there and be careful.

By the time I reached Soco Gap, utter darkness and thick fog had overtaken me. Had I not been intimately familiar with the area, I would have never found nor ventured down the narrow, paved path that appeared to disappear into the forest. Before settling for the night, I had to walk down it one more time to take a peek at the last ranger quarters in which we ever lived.

Under ideal circumstances amid pristine weather, the usual visitor monologue at scenic overlooks went something like this: "I always wanted to be a forest ranger (a common misstatement of professional title). I can't believe you actually get paid to do this job. On top of that, you get to live in a little log cabin somewhere in the park free of charge. Right?" I always had to carefully restrain myself from dashing to bits the idyllic image of the life of a *park* ranger and the widespread myth that government quarters were furnished at no cost, especially in the presence of little children who might be gazing upon me with dreams of their own.

Rental charges, in fact, were partially based on a complicated formula that used the local comparable rental rates as an integral part of the computation. The fact that the Parkway coursed through many areas where such rates were artificially inflated due to the seasonal tourist industry usually guaranteed a hefty bite from modest wages. Despite the fact, however, that rent was neither free nor cheap and that "required occupancy" was a general condition of employment for rangers, most of us eagerly moved into them as a matter of convenience and initially enjoyed the romanticized life of living within the park and being near the action. Our little family had the privilege of experiencing the joys and challenges of Parkway housing at their widest extremes— modern and suburban, rustic and remote.

Known for the special funding program which made them possible, the cluster of five "Mission 66" homes, located near the Vinton ranger station, looked more like the finer quarters reserved for officers on a military base than the imagined ranger cabin in a unit of the national park system. Fairly modern and comfortable, they were strung in a single line along a narrow strip of land adjacent to the Parkway with enough room for spacious lawns, gardens, and fruit trees. Uniquely embedded within the surrounding suburban community, we were close enough to a local high school to hear the marching band practice on weekday afternoons and the crowd cheer touchdowns on Friday nights. We were also close enough to the city of Roanoke that large commercial jets, making last-minute corrections on their final approach to the airport, often appeared to be gunning their engines in an effort to clear the summit of Stewarts Knob, near whose foot we lived a goodly life.

At one point, we shared this housing cluster with an assistant superintendent, my first-level supervisor, my second-level supervisor, and another ranger of equal rank. For the most part, we lived together peacefully. We had to; we worked with and for each other. The fact that my preschool daughter fell in puppy love with my second-level supervisor's son of the same age did not hurt matters. Neither, too, did the fact that both daughters of the assistant superintendent were excellent baby sitters when Patty and I needed a night out together. I could have passed, however, on Laura's revelation to their father one day that her daddy was "out on the Parkway shooting people." Mr. Stokes was of the old school of park managers who did not believe that park rangers should be visibly armed. I thought Laura had been asleep all those nights when I, upon the advice of my firearms instructor at the police academy, had "dry fired" my handgun at the television screen during commercials to practice proper sighting while developing a steady hand.

We lived in this blissful arrangement for almost six years while the realization that we were chucking a considerable sum of money into a bottomless pit

Parkway Assistant Superintendent and next-door neighbor Dick Stokes holds the author's daughter, Laura, who once told him her daddy was "out on the Parkway shooting people." Photo taken about 1981 in driveway of ranger quarters at Milepost 112.0 near Vinton, Virginia.

began to fester like an ulcer that could not be relieved. Before we were able to execute a plan to begin building equity for the future, a promotion moved us, literally and figuratively, to the opposite end of the Parkway housing spectrum.

When Jim Davey, a founding stockholder and employee of The Davey Tree Expert Company, purchased 640 acres of land in the Soco Gap area in 1935, his vision of building a self-sufficient farm and lumbering operation was already on a collision course with the route of the Parkway. Before the State of North Carolina could acquire the property for transfer to the Federal government, Davey had already built a spacious, rustic home and several other smaller buildings. Mountain Dew Farm — so called due to a number of abandoned whiskey stills discovered on the property — employed members of the local community and was often visited by friends and relatives of the Davey family in its heyday. What had once been used as a guest house eventually became a ranger residence and the setting for a most memorable experience for our family.

We moved into the little ranger cabin, located high on Soco Gap, in the month of February. At the foot of the mountain to the east rested the town of Maggie Valley; to the west sat the town of Cherokee. Both slept through the winter months but bustled with tourist activity during the summer months.

Our sixteen months in the ranger cabin at Soco Gap is more fondly reckoned in terms of two winters. Photo taken about 1985 at Soco Gap, elevation 4340 feet, at Milepost 455.7 between Maggie Valley and Cherokee, North Carolina.

Considering our seemingly isolated location, I considered it a priority for the entire family's sanity to get our television set up and running as a first order of business. Snow was falling when I mounted the rotary antenna and the tall, metal mast against the side of the rustic, wooden structure. Half of a local channel, and when atmospheric conditions were just right, usually at night, a Spanish-speaking channel out of El Paso, Texas, made the job hardly worth the numbing effort. My next priority was to figure out which of the many moving boxes, stacked to the ceiling in quarters deemed immediately too cramped, contained our vast collection of jigsaw puzzles and board games.

We soon learned, however, that our new home was not quite as isolated as it appeared. We were already adjusted to the 24-hour chatter on the park radio, but having a park telephone in our residence was a whole new experience. With the number listed in the business section of the telephone directory, it rang constantly, and we were patiently polite with the lady from South Carolina who called almost daily during the winter months to check on cross-country ski conditions. Dozens of sledders played in the snow just out of sight of our home on the open embankments where the Parkway intersected U.S. Route 19. Good-hearted park employees, like Charlie Norman, stopped by to make sure we were comfortable and never failed to favor Laura with a shiny new quarter in exchange for a cup of hot chocolate. Lost visitors frequently found our discreetly concealed driveway and wandered to our door seeking directions. Game wardens stopped to chat. Poachers sneaked around to see if I was on duty. Trucks backfired like cannons after cresting the gap on their way down the Cherokee side of the mountain. Large military transport planes nearly shook the house off its foundation making surprise, lights-out training runs through the gap at night. A bear cub once paid us a visit. Flying squirrels rudely played tag with each other on the roof, in the attic, and within the chestnut-paneled walls of our home from dusk to dawn. Chipmunks scurried across our driveway like ants on a hot sidewalk; their numbers have probably not yet recovered from Hershey's decimating hunts. Soco Gap, indeed, would have never been considered a lonely and depressing place if only the long periods of rain and fog could have been removed from its reality.

The simple fact of living at an elevation of almost 4,500 feet also provided some novel, unforgettable experiences. Bags of potato chips swelled like balloons on the ride from the grocery store down in Waynesville back up to the house. High altitude instructions, typed in small print on the backs of cake mix boxes, suddenly became applicable. Trilliums, growing by a small creek next to our house, were fashioned by Patty into a beautiful corsage for Laura to wear to a piano recital. The finest cool-weather crop of cabbage and broccoli I ever cultivated was devoured by groundhogs with the precision and thoroughness of a sharp razor. In exchange for getting the bus route extended all the way up to our house, we volunteered to become the weather eyes for Mr. Bembry, the principal at Smokey Mountain Elementary School and accepted his calls at five o'clock in the morning with grace. The rubber seal on my truck's oil filter cracked one night under the strain of minus fifteen degrees Fahrenheit while Hershey maintained an unyielding position by the door of the wood stove and reminded us, with his scowl, that Siamese cats did not easily tolerate cold weather. A snowstorm, which eventually accumulated to a depth of twenty-nine inches, prompted Laura and me into its fierceness one day to escape a bad case of cabin fever. Pretending to be survivors of a plane crash, we traipsed through deep snow for almost a mile. Under the safe, sprawling arms and shelter of a huge hemlock tree, we built a small fire over which we cooked a half-pound of bacon with forked sticks. What we could not eat we hung on the lowest branches and watched the hungry chickadees eat happily within our reach.

We only lived in the ranger cabin at Soco Gap for sixteen months before we were finally relieved of the requirement to live in it. That length of time is now more fondly reckoned in terms of two winters.

33

Cased and Unloaded

"Except as otherwise provided ... the following are prohibited:
Possessing a weapon."
> —*Code of Federal Regulations*, Title 36,
> Volume 1, Chapter 1, Part 2, Section
> 2.4(a)(1)(i)

The weapons of which I am about to speak are of the firearm variety, specifically handguns, shotguns, and rifles. Until I became a ranger on the Parkway, I never realized just how many Americans vigorously exercised the constitutional right, afforded to them by the Second Amendment, to keep and bear arms.

In the early hours of a February morning, only five vehicles passed through one of our random checkpoints during a three-hour period; a total of six firearms were nonetheless encountered. A few minutes after this activity was discontinued, two freshly spent shotgun shells were found lying in the roadway about eight miles from the checkpoint. Though we could never prove as much, they were strongly suspected to have been fired from a double-barreled shotgun confiscated from one of those vehicles.

The possession and use of firearms within units administered by the National Park Service is a somewhat convoluted issue. Authorized local, State, and Federal law enforcement officers, of course, are permitted to carry them in the performance of their official duties. (A man I once charged with possession of a loaded handgun unsuccessfully argued that his status as a paid informant for a law enforcement agency he refused to identify fell within this provision!) Superintendents of parks may issue permits with certain restrictive conditions that allow the possession and use of firearms under special circumstances. Hunter access to contiguous lands and support of research activities are specific examples of such allowances. Generally speaking, however, a visitor to the Blue Ridge

Parkway cannot possess a firearm unless it is unloaded and rendered temporarily inoperable, packed, cased, or stored within a motor vehicle in such a manner that will prevent its ready use. Expecting to find peace, refuge, and tranquility in such places, wildlife and visitors alike appreciate compliance with this most basic park regulation. One would think that its obvious necessity and nearly universal acceptance would make the life of a park ranger much simpler and safer. Wrong.

A report that someone was discharging a firearm in the tent camping section of the Roanoke Mountain Campground prompted my hasty advance in that direction one warm, summer evening. En route, I hoped I was not about to experience the dreaded domestic disturbance I had heard so much about in training. Statistically, such incidents had not been portrayed as particularly conducive to the better health and welfare of law enforcement officers.

The absence of any curious onlookers and the fact that only one vehicle was parked in the general area described in the report calmed my worst fears somewhat. As I cautiously stepped out of my patrol car, two distinct sounds rang clearly through the night air — the innocent call of a whippoorwill and the crisp, crackling noise of a small-caliber gun. From the last campsite located at the end of a short spur ridge came also the drug and alcohol-induced laughter of a man and woman. As I inched my way down the trail in their direction, at least three more shots rang out. Each shot seemed to coincide with the intermittent call of the whippoorwill. My advance became low and slow from one large tree to the next one. The glow from their roaring campfire eventually shed all the light I needed on a situation in dire need of immediate correction.

Close enough to finally see the small, semi-automatic handgun, I watched in disbelief as the man extended his arm upward and fired into the dark treetops. When he attempted the next shot, the gun jammed. With a large tree between me and him, I saw an opportunity to terminate his folly and announced my presence and ordered him to drop the gun. His quick compliance was apparently his only wise choice of the night. "That confounded bird was bothering us," he loudly complained in the face of multiple charges.

The time was exactly high noon (the report can verify it) when I drove into Roy Taylor Forest Overlook one Saturday. Had the man standing beside a litter can been a little bit taller, I could have easily mistaken him for Clint Eastwood in one of his more modern movies— John Wayne had he been wearing a cowboy hat. His walk, however, was neither determined nor swaggered as he comically attempted to sidestep his way toward his car, parked about fifty feet away, with a most unnatural gait. No amount of twisting and turning, though, could hide the 9-mm handgun, loaded with fifteen rounds of ammunition, which was noticeably strapped against his right hip.

He said he was just wearing it for protection as he cooperatively halted, assumed the frisk position against the hood of my patrol vehicle, and was disarmed. I believed him. I truly did. He even volunteered to tell me that he also had a shotgun stored in the trunk of his car.

After making a determination that he was not a convicted felon, that there were no outstanding arrest warrants on file for him, and that neither gun was stolen, I decided to release him with an option to forfeit a modest fine. He probably did not notice my slight flinch when, while preparing the violation notice, he told me he was employed by the U.S. Postal Service.

On another Saturday, during the busy month of October, another man proved to be far more subtle and slightly less cooperative. He was sitting on the tailgate of his truck with two other men when I first approached him at Graveyard Fields Overlook. I saw the can of beer he attempted to hide between his legs before I saw the gun. Tucked discreetly in a shoulder holster underneath his open jacket, it was not immediately noticed until he twisted his body slightly during our conversation. Somehow I had to gauge his state of mind and let him know that I knew he was armed. Positioning my right hand close to my own holstered revolver, I casually asked him what type of weapon he was toting.

"A thirty-eight pistol," he drawled in an uncomfortably measured tone.

Caught in a face-to-face standoff of my own making that I now had to win, I proceeded to what I thought was the next most logical step and asked him to place his hands in the air. He did not, and the sullenly, solemn expression theretofore displayed on his face began to slowly transform into a wicked, challenging smile. Liquid courage and a fraternal audience seemed to be clouding his better judgment. Game time had come to an end.

Time seemed to stop as the adrenalin rush and the will to survive another day overpowered my logical thought process and caused me to do something I had never before practiced. To this day, I am still surprised at the uncontrollable reflex which shot my hand inside his jacket and snatched the gun from his possession. This incident was the only time in my career that I ever drew down on a man with his own gun, albeit ever so briefly. He and his buddies, I think, were equally surprised. Thank goodness for that other guiding hand of protection that kept all of us from getting hurt that day.

Same overlook. Different date. Ten o'clock in the evening. Another ranger and I had responded to a report of a "disturbance of some sort" in the Graveyard Fields area and were walking down a trail which led to a waterfall. Not too far down the trail, we met two young men walking back toward the overlook. One of them made a herculean, yet futile attempt to conceal a bulky piece of drug paraphernalia inside his coat. An unwieldy water pipe and a small amount of marijuana were immediately seized.

After being advised of his rights, he volunteered this startling statement: "Before you go any further, I have a loaded gun on me." And he did — a semi-automatic handgun loaded with six rounds of ammunition. He said it belonged to his grandfather and that he only carried it for protection. Where had I heard that line before?

During the remaining period of our association with him that evening, he repeatedly stated, in his youthful ignorance, that he and his friend had just come up to the Parkway to "get high." Only the tender age of sixteen years prevented him from incurring more serious charges and being taken to jail that night.

Trees and rock slides never made convenient appointments with the park staff when they decided to come crashing down on the Parkway. The large oak tree that blocked both lanes of travel had at least landed during the evening hours when visitor traffic was light. But the behemoth — about three feet in diameter — had to be removed immediately to prevent an accident and a likely tort claim. Summoned from the comfort of their own homes and television sets, two members of the maintenance division agreed to assist me with the job.

Within two hours we had the roadway cleared, and I began the hour-long drive back to the ranger station slightly overdabbed with the distinct essence of burnt gasoline and two-cycle engine oil. Despite the uncomfortable irritation caused by flecks of wood that had invaded my clothing like fleas on a dog, I was determined to make a thorough, inquisitive patrol en route back to the ranger station. Mischief would not be expecting to meet a ranger at that hour of the night.

When I first saw the man standing in front of his parked truck, the head-lights of which were fully illuminating him, I made an instant, definitive decision to drive right past the overlook; he was holding what appeared to be a military assault rifle. Radio reception was iffy at best at that location, and as badly as I wanted to keep him under observation, I knew the safer course was to pretend I did not see him. Bearing only a six-shooter and a shotgun, I was severely outgunned no matter how quickly I could reload. A backup posse would have to be mustered from a safer distance.

Upon recognizing my patrol vehicle, however, he quickly walked to the left side of his truck, opened the door, tossed the weapon on the seat, closed the door, and walked back to the front of his truck. I hit the brakes and contemplated a possible change of plan. He remained in his headlights. My roving spotlight could find no other people in the immediate area. I took a cautious, calculated chance and pulled into the overlook.

What I found on the front seat of his truck caused my heart to skip a beat. An AR-15 rifle, loaded with twenty rounds of ammunition, was ready to fire with one round already seated in the firing chamber. Found also on the seat was an ammunition clip containing twenty more rounds.

The following morning, I contacted a special agent with the Bureau of

Alcohol, Tobacco and Firearms for instructions on how to determine if the rifle had been converted from semi-automatic to fully automatic. To the credit of its owner, it had not been. After describing the events of the previous evening to the agent, he then paralyzed me with a chilling theory and this suggestion: "You might want to contact the Drug Enforcement Administration. They probably know your district better than you do."

I was sitting low in the seat of a privately owned vehicle one summer evening at Roanoke Basin Overlook, pretending to be just another visitor enjoying the night air. Two other rangers, each driving separate patrol cars, hovered nearby, waiting for my signal to pounce on whatever mischief might unknowingly present itself to my view. The disguise was just another vigorous enforcement technique we occasionally used along a section of the Parkway prone to problems much more serious than a marijuana cigarette; during a recent summer, the superintendent had ordered that section to be gated and closed at night due to a rash of homicides.

The sound of loud music pierced an otherwise calm night as a vehicle blasted into the overlook and parked about ten yards to my left. From the sounds of excited conversation and laughter spilling also from the car, several young people appeared to be having a most enjoyable evening. I sank a little lower in my seat and tuned my antennae to their voices and the movements of their barely visible forms, which were distorted by the faint light. Underage possession of alcohol was my worst-case assessment for the whole bunch. This would be a simple, bothersome exercise of written warnings for teenagers while leaving the more stringent discipline of grounding to their parents' discretion. Then came the shocking debauchery of my most well-intended assumption.

A young man, seated in the right-front passenger seat, extended his right arm into the sky at a 45-degree angle and yelled, "Just let a park ranger pull in here now!" I could not shrink small enough. He was clearly holding a handgun. Had they just robbed a convenience store? Did they have an ax to grind with a ranger who had just given them a speeding citation? Or had this young man just developed an untimely case of diarrhea of the mouth?

I slowly rolled up my side window and adjusted the volume of my portable radio to its lowest discernible setting. The time had come to call in the cavalry, and I gave both rangers specific details about the suspects and specific instructions on how to enter the overlook. They could not have executed the takedown more perfectly.

As my two cohorts burst simultaneously into the overlook from opposite directions and flooded the suspect vehicle with enough blue, red, and white light to stun its occupants with the effectiveness of a percussion grenade, I slipped, unnoticed, out my right-front door. As we emptied the car and began a search for the handgun, profuse complaints were muttered regarding the necessity and legality of our actions. I ignored these comments until we found — a pellet gun!

Confused, angered, and embarrassed, I stepped up on the stone curb to an imaginary podium and solemnly addressed the entire group. "See that car over there? I was sitting in it when this toy was aimed over its roof a few minutes ago."

Not another word of complaint followed and not a single parent took issue with anything the rangers said or did that tragedy-spared evening.

I had forgotten how deceptively long and steep the southbound climb out of Soco Gap really was; the steep grades in every direction out of that gap had nearly extinguished my love for jogging a few years earlier. Fatigued more than anticipated from the previous nineteen-mile day which had been punctuated with an emotional sprint over Waterrock Knob, I labored through the compounding malaise of dense fog and drizzle. In search of autumn color, traffic was already heavy that mid-October Saturday morning, and I dodged it blindly and continuously while struggling to maintain my balance along a narrow, lumpy road shoulder. With only thirteen miles remaining to complete the trek, I was disheartened by the weather and was somewhat reluctant to bring my adventure to a close under such gloomy conditions. Involuntarily as much as deliberately, my pace slowed to that of a sloth as I lumbered through the lethargy and contemplated my options.

Had the weather been more cooperative, I would have certainly detoured a little more than a mile off my course out the Heintooga Spur Road — a less traveled, backdoor entrance to the Great Smoky Mountains National Park — to enjoy a special treat. From Mile High Overlook, one can behold much of the breadth and immensity of this natural treasure to which the Parkway links and owes half the inspiration of its conception. Instead, I continued climbing through the fog past Wolf Laurel Gap to a crest in the road and welcomed the physical relief offered by the Parkway's abrupt change to a downhill course. My day instantly improved by a fraction more than half of a whole. It brightened even further at Bunches Bald Overlook upon meeting amateur photographer Jim Fletcher, who invited me to visit his Web site in a few days to view some photographs he took of me and to read a commentary he planned to write about our fortuitous meeting in the clouds.

Miraculously, just past Milepost 460, I descended out of the soupy mist into the sunny warmth of a beautiful day. To my left and right, I could finally see the colorful hills and coves below me and the very heart of the Cherokee Indian Reservation. So many members of this quietly noble tribe of Native Americans had befriended me during the years I had worked and lived in the area: Jim Cooper, Henry Otter, Ronnie Blythe, Peggy Jenks, Driver Pheasant, and others. Just recalling their names and faces warmed my spirit as quickly and effectively as the sun drove me out of my rain gear. Reminding myself of the civilized comforts of life awaiting me in the nearby town of Cherokee, I concluded that the day had now qualified itself worthy to become the final day of my trek. I coasted onward.

I left my own private memorial to a park ranger that I had never known personally but whose spirit I had just felt strongly, October 11, 2003, at Big Witch Gap, elevation 4160 feet, at Milepost 461.6 in North Carolina.

Not far past Big Witch Gap, I paused near the crest of a hill at the gated entrance to the Barnett Knob fire tower road. A harsh memory shattered the peace I had finally found in the day.

There, on an early June morning, I had approached the right side of a parked vehicle which was blocking the gate. A young man was curled up in a sleeping bag on the back seat. Apparently startled from his sleep, he looked directly at my face through the side window and began groping wildly for something that he could not seem to find.

I saw the semi-automatic handgun about the same time he reached between the two front seats in an attempt, I presumed, to grab it. Had I not already noticed that the right door was unlocked, training and reflexes would likely have caused me to pump six rounds through the window glass as soon as I saw the end of the barrel. Instead, I opened the door and grabbed the gun before it could be pointed in my direction. I nearly boiled over with fear and fury as the man frantically screamed that he was only looking for his glasses. I eventually found them for him, peered through them, and nearly collapsed from the realization that I had almost shot someone that was very close to being legally blind. He was only twenty-four years of age.

From the crest of the hill, I looked back down the path I had just walked. Big Witch Gap was still within sight, and there I had just left my own private memorial to a park ranger that I had never known personally but whose spirit I had just felt strongly.

Much farther north, in a quiet courtyard, the Parkway headquarters building in Asheville safely embraced a more formal, fitting memorial — a replica of a dress Stetson resting peacefully on a large stone and these words:

> ON JUNE 21, 1998, WHILE
> PROTECTING VISITORS FROM HARM
> UNITED STATES PARK RANGER
> JOSEPH D. KOLODSKI
> WAS SLAIN IN THE LINE OF DUTY
> HIS SERVICE AND SACRIFICE
> TO THE NATIONAL PARK SERVICE
> AND THE PEOPLE OF THIS COUNTRY
> WILL NEVER BE FORGOTTEN

I turned my back to the past and looked in the opposite direction to the south. Less than seven miles and not a single uphill step remained between me and Milepost 469. The road ahead of me looked so much more inviting than the one I had traveled.

34

Milepost 469...

"And that which is for him to say lies as a load on his heart
until it is delivered."
                        —"Representative Men: Goethe; or, the
                        Writer," by Ralph Waldo Emerson

In a memorandum dated June 8, 1934, Chief Landscape Architect Thomas
C. Vint expressed some concerns about the proposed route of the Parkway to
Arno B. Cammerer, director of the National Park Service:

> There is a good deal of feeling of isolation to one driving over a mountain
> road.... It is a question in our minds whether the average person would enjoy
> driving over its entire distance.

Little did Mr. Vint know that the Blue Ridge Parkway would soon become the
most visited unit of the National Park Service. Little did he know that hundreds
would be followed by thousands who would drive its entire length and proudly
boast of their unofficial membership in the "469-Miler Club." Little did he know
that a sentimental adventurer would someday walk every foot of its scenic
splendor.

Along the steep descent over the final miles, I continued to be satisfied,
soothed, and startled by the perpetual flow of random observations. Large clusters of seed from the angelica plant wobbled heavily on the ends of their tall stalks
like overladen bowls of wild oatmeal begging to be eaten. Another gurgling pipe
spring divulged its secret location; I now knew the whereabouts of every single
one of them and had partaken of refreshment from their every spout. Still strewn
with fresh, indisputable evidence, the scene that had so rattled Ranger Bowers
the previous day remained clearly distinguishable. Ugly, irregular stains of gasoline and antifreeze on the pavement marked the location of a violent collision.

Ripped from its moorings on a motorcycle, the jagged remains of an instrument panel were found lying face down in a ditch. The needle on the speedometer rested legally at 43 mph; the tachometer was frozen suspiciously on 10,000 rpm.

A young neighbor's bicycle wreck in front of my house one day had been my most serious encounter with trauma since my days of rangering on the Parkway. A panicked neighbor, whose faith in my first aid skills stemmed wholly from my Parkway experiences, summoned my immediate assistance. Only by cutting off the pedal of his bicycle with a hacksaw was I able to free Matt Johnson's foot that had somehow become tightly wedged between the pedal and the frame. Even so, he suffered neither a broken bone nor a cut requiring stitches. His tears and screams, nevertheless, had rudely reminded me of one aspect of a noble profession that I would never miss.

As my remaining distance diminished like the closing seconds of a countdown which could no longer be aborted, I succumbed to the enigmatic human tendency to summarize and quantify a few details of trivia. An overweight body had been trimmed considerably; scales would later confirm the loss of thirty useless pounds. In another odd, unplanned coincidence with a common Biblical reference to measurement, I had spent exactly forty nights on the trail. Eight of them had been spent directly under the stars in reckless disregard to abrupt weather changes and crawling critters. An escalating fear of sudden showers and snakes had forced me within the walls of my tent for twenty-four of them. Eight evenings had been enjoyed under the more comfortable and less vulnerable roof of one type or another through the hospitality of others. Ten real showers averaged to a thoroughly clean body every four days. Five real laundries averaged to a thoroughly clean set of clothes every eight days. The memorial road kill log had burgeoned in stunning diversity and proportions to include: one turtle; one mole; one tunnel monster (too dark to tell but identifiable by the smell); two mice; two opossums; two deer; three chipmunks; three raccoons; five birds; six squirrels; six voles; nine frogs; fourteen unidentified pancakes; fifty-eight salamanders (mostly red efts); and seventy-one snakes (including three copperheads and one timber rattler). I felt fortunate to have completed the trek unscathed and in the best physical and mental condition of my life.

Along the last mile, a family from Cordele, Georgia stopped and asked if I needed any assistance. They had never heard of a newspaper reporter by the name of John O'Dowd, and I challenged them to later read a book to see how perfectly they had fit into its ending. And, as Milepost 469 came into view, a couple riding in the last southbound car to pass me responded to my wave by honking wildly and waving through the open roof of their T-top. Their license plate indicated they were from Cobb County, Georgia. Georgians north and south — even from the frenetic, sprawling metropolis of Atlanta — had fully redeemed themselves from my wearied ramblings.

I had learned some new and important lessons on this trek. A sturdy pair of boot socks would last about five hundred miles, and rain gear only creates an illusion of dryness. What I already knew, that I now understood more clearly,

was that the gift of human kindness could swell the soul with even more joy than could the most beautiful scenery on the earth.

The colorful tops of the mountains still sparkled brightly with sunlight as the shadows in the valley foretold the close of another October day. The crickets and cicadas sang the final verses of their songs in the face of an inevitable winter. Finally, I knelt by the peaceful, flowing waters of the Oconaluftee River to kiss Milepost 469 and the Parkway a proper goodbye. I could hardly wait to get home; my head was about to burst with a book it had already written.

Appendix:
Noted Parkway Locations
and Author's Schedule

Date of Passage	Milepost	Parkway Landmark
Sept. 1	0.0	Rockfish Gap (elev. 1909')
	0.0	U.S. Route 250 Underpass
	0.0	Interstate 64 Underpass
	5.8	Humpback Rocks Visitor Center
	6.0	Humpback Gap Overlook (elev. 2360')
Sept. 2	15.4	Love Gap (elev. 2597')
	19.0	Twenty Minute Cliff Overlook (elev. 2715')
Sept. 3	29.0	Montebello Ranger Station
	31.4	Stillhouse Hollow Overlook (elev. 3000')
	34.4	Yankee Horse Ridge Overlook (elev. 3140')
	35.7	Rocky Mountain Viaduct
Sept. 4	38.8	Boston Knob Overlook (elev. 2508')
Sept. 5	53.1	Bluff Mountain Tunnel
	55.9	Dancing Creek Overlook (elev. 1300')
	60.8	Otter Creek Restaurant
	60.8	Otter Creek Campground
Sept. 6	62.5	Lower Otter Creek Overlook (elev. 685')
	63.1	Otter Lake Overlook (elev. 655')
	63.6	James River Visitor Center
	63.7	James River Bridge

Date of Passage	Milepost	Parkway Landmark
	74.7	Thunder Ridge Overlook (elev. 3485')
	75.2	Arnold Valley Overlook (elev. 3510')
	75.3	Arnold Valley Overlook (elev. 3700')
	76.5	Apple Orchard Overlook (elev. 3950')
Sept. 7	(Sunday layover)	
Sept. 8	78.4	Sunset Field Overlook (elev. 3474')
	85.6	Peaks of Otter Lodge & Restaurant
	85.9	Peaks of Otter Visitor Center
Sept. 9	89.4	Upper Goose Creek Valley Overlook (elev. 1925')
	91.0	Bearwallow Gap (elev. 2258')
	92.1	Purgatory Mountain Overlook (elev. 2400')
	95.2	Pine Tree Overlook (elev. 2490')
	95.3	Harvey's Knob Overlook (elev. 2524')
	99.6	Great Valley Overlook (elev. 2493')
Sept. 10	105.8	U.S. Route 460 Overpass
	106.9	Norfolk & Western Railroad Overlook (elev. 1161')
	109.8	Read Mountain Overlook (elev. 1163')
Sept. 11	112.0	Vinton Ranger Station
	112.9	Roanoke Basin Overlook (elev. 1250')
	114.7	Roanoke River Bridge
	114.8	Roanoke River Overlook (elev. 985')
	118.6	Bandy Road Overpass
	120.3	Roanoke Mountain Loop Road
	120.4	Mill Mountain Spur Road
		0.1 Gum Spring Overlook (elev. 1445')
		1.3 Roanoke Mountain Campground
	121.4	U.S. Route 220 Underpass
	122.4	Buck Mountain Road Underpass
Sept. 12	136.0	Adney Gap (elev. 2690')
Sept. 13	143.9	Devil's Backbone Overlook (elev. 2687')
	144.8	Pine Spur Overlook (elev. 2703')
	154.1	Smart View Overlook (elev. 2564')
Sept. 14	(Sunday layover)	
Sept. 15	154.5	Smart View Picnic Area
	165.3	Tuggle Gap (elev. 2752')
Sept. 16	167.1	Rocky Knob Ranger Station
	168.0	Saddle Overlook (elev. 3380')

Date of Passage	Milepost	Parkway Landmark
	174.1	Rocky Knob Cabins
Sept. 17	176.2	Mabry Mill
	176.2	Mabry Mill Restaurant
	188.8	Groundhog Mountain Picnic Area
Sept. 18	189.1	Pilot Mountain Overlook (elev. 2950')
	189.9	Puckett Cabin
	193.7	Orchard Gap (elev. 2675')
	199.4	Fancy Gap (elev. 2925')
	200.7	Interstate 77 Underpass
Sept. 19	206.1	Piper's Gap (elev. 2759')
	212.7	Blue Ridge Music Center
	215.8	Va. Route 89 Overpass
	216.0	Chestnut Creek Bridge
	216.9	Virginia–North Carolina State Line
Sept. 20	217.5	Cumberland Knob Recreation Area
	218.6	Fox Hunter's Paradise Overlook (elev. 2805')
Sept. 21	(Sunday layover)	
Sept. 22	232.5	Stone Mountain Overlook (elev. 3115')
	234.0	Deep Gap (elev. 3193')
	235.7	Devil's Garden Overlook (elev. 3428')
	237.1	Air Bellows Gap (elev. 3729')
	238.5	Brinegar Cabin
	238.5	Doughton Park Recreation Area (north entrance)
	241.1	Bluffs Lodge
	241.1	Bluffs Restaurant
	242.0	Ice Rock Cliffs
Sept. 23	248.9	Laurel Fork Viaduct
	251.5	Alder Gap (elev. 3047')
	258.7	Northwest Trading Post
Sept. 24	264.4	The Lump Overlook (elev. 3465')
	267.8	Betsey's Rock Falls Overlook (elev. 3400')
	268.0	Benge Gap (elev. 3296')
	276.4	Deep Gap (elev. 3142')
	276.4	U.S. Route 421 Underpass
Sept. 25	288.0	Aho Gap (elev. 3722')
Sept. 26	294.0	Flat Top Manor
	295.8	Julian Price Memorial Park (north entrance)
	296.4	Price Picnic Area

Date of Passage	Milepost	Parkway Landmark
	296.7	Price Lake Overlook (elev. 3380')
	298.6	Holloway Mountain Road Underpass
	304.0	Linn Cove Viaduct
Sept. 27	308.3	Flat Rock Overlook (elev. 3987')
	310.0	Lost Cove Cliffs Overlook (elev. 3812')
	315.6	Camp Creek Overlook (elev. 3443')
Sept. 28	(Sunday layover)	
Sept. 29	316.4	Linville Falls Spur Road
		0.5 Linville Falls Campground
		1.4 Linville Falls Visitor Center
	316.5	Linville River Picnic Area
	316.6	Linville River Bridge
	323.0	Bear Den Overlook (elev. 3359')
Sept. 30	327.5	McKinney Gap (elev. 2790')
	328.6	The Loops Overlook (elev. 2980')
	330.9	Gillespie Gap (elev. 2819')
	330.9	Museum of North Carolina Minerals
	333.4	Little Switzerland Tunnel
	335.4	Bearwallow Gap (elev. 3490')
	336.3	Gooch Gap (elev. 3360')
Oct. 1	336.8	Wildacres Tunnel
	339.5	Crabtree Meadows Restaurant
	339.6	Crabtree Meadows Campground
	342.2	Black Mountains Overlook (elev. 3892')
	345.3	Singecat Ridge Overlook (elev. 3406')
	347.9	Hewat Overlook (elev. 4175')
	349.0	Rough Ridge Tunnel
	351.9	Deep Gap (elev. 4284')
Oct. 2	355.3	Mount Mitchell State Park Spur Road
	361.2	Glassmine Falls Overlook (elev. 5200')
	364.5	Craggy Gardens Visitor Center
Oct. 3	372.1	Lane Pinnacle Overlook (elev. 3890')
	380.0	Haw Creek Valley Overlook (elev. 2720')
	381.0	Folk Art Center
	382.5	U.S. Route 70 Underpass
Oct. 4	383.6	Interstate 40 Underpass
	384.1	Parkway Headquarters
	388.8	U.S. Route 25 Underpass
	391.8	Interstate 26 Underpass

Date of Passage	Milepost	Parkway Landmark
	393.5	French Broad River Bridge
Oct. 5	(Sunday layover)	
Oct. 6	397.1	Grassy Knob Tunnel
	399.1	Pine Mountain Tunnel
	399.7	Bad Fork Valley Overlook (elev. 3350')
	400.9	Ferrin Knob Tunnel No. 1
	401.3	Ferrin Knob Tunnel No. 2
	401.4	Ferrin Knob Tunnel No. 3
	403.6	Big Ridge Overlook (elev. 3820')
	404.5	Mills River Valley Overlook (elev. 4085')
	407.3	Buck Spring Tunnel
	407.7	Buck Spring Gap Overlook (elev. 4980')
	408.5	Mount Pisgah Gas Station/Camp Store
Oct. 7	408.6	Pisgah Inn & Restaurant
	408.8	Mount Pisgah Campground
	411.9	Cold Mountain Overlook (elev. 4542')
	413.2	Pounding Mill Overlook (elev. 4700')
	415.7	Cherry Cove Overlook (elev. 4327')
	418.8	Graveyard Fields Overlook (elev. 5120')
	422.1	Devil's Courthouse Tunnel
	422.4	Devil's Courthouse Overlook (elev. 5462')
Oct. 8	422.8	Mount Hardy Overlook (elev. 5415')
	423.2	Beech Gap (elev. 5340')
	423.5	Courthouse Valley Overlook (elev. 5362')
	425.5	Buckeye Gap (elev. 5377')
	426.5	Haywood Gap (elev. 5225')
	427.6	Bear Pen Gap Overlook (elev. 5560')
	428.5	Bear Trap Gap Overlook (elev. 5580')
	430.4	Bear Trail Ridge Overlook (elev. 5872')
	430.7	Cowee Mountain Overlook (elev. 5850')
	431.0	Haywood-Jackson Overlook (elev. 6020')
	431.4	Richland Balsam Overlook (elev. 6053')
	432.7	Lone Bald Overlook (elev. 5625')
	433.3	Roy Taylor Forest Overlook (elev. 5580')
	435.7	Licklog Gap Overlook (elev. 5135')
	436.8	Grassy Ridge Mine Overlook (elev. 5250')
Oct. 9	(Rain layover at Balsam Gap Ranger Station)	
Oct. 10	437.0	Deep Gap (elev. 5260')
	438.9	Steestachee Bald Overlook (elev. 4780')

Date of Passage	*Milepost*	*Parkway Landmark*
	442.8	Balsam Gap Ranger Station
	443.1	Balsam Gap (elev. 3370')
	443.1	U.S. Route 23–74 Underpass
	444.6	The Orchards Overlook (elev. 3810')
	451.2	Waterrock Knob Visitor Center (elev. 5718')
Oct. 11	455.7	Soco Gap (elev. 4340')
	455.7	U.S. Route 19 Underpass
	458.2	Heintooga Spur Road
		1.3 Mile High Overlook (elev. 5250')
	458.2	Wolf Laurel Gap (elev. 5100')
	459.5	Bunches Bald Overlook (elev. 4925')
	461.6	Big Witch Gap (elev. 4150')
	462.3	Barnett Knob Fire Tower Road
	465.6	Rattlesnake Mountain Tunnel
	469.0	Oconaluftee River Bridge (elev. 2000')

Chapter Notes

Abbreviations used in the following notes:

BRPG: *Blue Ridge Parkway Guide* (by Lord)
BRP: Blue Ridge Parkway
HAER: Historic American Engineering Record
MP: Milepost
TBRP: *The Blue Ridge Parkway* (by Jolley)

Chapter 1. Once Upon the Parkway

Page 3   "Without a diary": McCullough, *John Adams*, p. 617.
Page 4   The representation from Greek mythology is known as Pegasus.

Chapter 2. Door Number Three

Page 5   "I've never intended": Kelly, *How Close We Come*, p. 153.
Page 5   "wear adequate foot coverings": Werner, "Doctor's Bag," p. 11.
Page 6   "In a way I own it all": Allen and Jones, *The Good Old Boys*, <http://www.imdb.com/title/tt0113196>.

Chapter 3. Twelve Years, Eight Months, Forty-One Days

Page 8   "I learned this, at least": Thoreau, *Walden*, p. 440.
Page 11   First resident landscape architect: Quin, "BRP/HAER," p. 33.
Pages 11–12   "Now we are coming in here ... I can't imagine": Abbott, interview, pp. 2, 14.
Page 12   "beads on a string": ibid., p. 2.
Page 12   Chief assistant: Quin, "BRP/HAER," p. 39.
Page 12   "frosting on the cake": Abbuehl, interview, p. 33.
Page 13   Land purchased: Quin, "BRP/HAER," pp. 76–77.
Page 13   Land donated: Lord, BRPG, MP 316.5.

Chapter 4. Deliberately, Reflectively, Randomly

Page 19   "Although many people": Fletcher, *The Man Who Walked Though Time*, p. 7.
Page 19   "That's all I have to say": Roth, *Forrest Gump*, <http://www.imdb.com.title/tt01098301>.
Page 20   "People think that if a man": Melville, letter, p. 141.

Page 21   Original plans: "General Development Plan," Drawing PKY-BR-PO-2003-B, 8
               June 1939.
Page 23   Spent a year making preparations: Fletcher, *The Man Who Walked Through Time*,
               p. 9.
Page 23   Congressman Jesse P. Wolcott: Jolley, TBRP, pp. 122–24.
Page 24   The calculation of a vertical distance of over nine miles is derived from data
               found in: "Bicycling," BRP information brochure. Tom DeVaughn of Trout-
               ville, Va., is credited in this brochure for providing the relevant statistical
               data.
Page 24   Local paper headline: Lee, "A 469-mile nature hike — Oak Ridge man preparing
               to hike the Blue Ridge Parkway."
Page 24   Another headline: Pegram, "Man plans to hike entire Parkway."

Chapter 5. Means of Engagement
Page 25   "There are some enterprises": Melville, *Moby Dick*, p. 235.
Page 25   Boys need "wood to chop": Attributed to Dirk Christiansen, a friend from
               whom I first heard this wise phrase at an adult Boy Scout leadership training
               seminar.

Chapter 6. Milepost Zero
Page 36   All quotes and factual references to the Mill Mountain "star": Weems, "Monthly
               Narrative Report — November 1949," p. 2.
Page 37   General Stonewall Jackson once sneaked: Lord, BRPG, MP 0.0.
Pages 37–38   Early proposed name for the BRP: Jolley, TBRP, p. 127.
Page 38   Mountain Top Tavern: Lord, BRPG, MP 0.0.
Page 39   Original BRP route concept: Jolley, TBRP, pp. 23–25.
Page 39   Transfer of construction unit 1-A: Quin, "BRP/HAER," p. 91.

Chapter 7. One Manpower
Page 43   "Make an honest evaluation": "Bicycling," BRP information brochure.
Page 44   Valentines postmarked from Love, Virginia: Lord, BRPG, MP 15.4.
Page 45   Sun will set on the mountain: ibid, MP 19.0.
Page 48   Twelve days earlier ... 21-speed machine: Brennan, "Same goal, different method,"
               pp. A-1, 8.

Chapter 8. Boston Knob Overlook
Page 50   "Here is a tranquil scene": Lord, BRPG, MP 38.8.
Page 50   About a third of the Parkway: Quin, "BRP/HAER," p. 63.
Page 51   "A little thing like that": Girzone, *Joshua*, p. 236.
Page 52   "ordinary course of life": ibid.
Page 53   Accidental creation of an overlook: Jolley, TBRP, pp. 117–118.
Page 53   Overlooks referred to as "balconies": Abbott, interview, p. 16.
Page 53   Nettle Creek drainage: Lord, BRPG, MP 38.8.

Chapter 9. Spooked
Page 56   "But what troubled me most": Brown Jr., *The Tracker*, p. 118.
Page 60   Battery Creek Lock: Quin, "BRP/HAER," pp. 188–89.
Page 62   Mac Dale hired as second BRP ranger in 1938: Liles, "Early Rangers of the Blue
               Ridge Parkway," p. 17.
Page 62   "And everybody in Roanoke": Dale, interview (reel 263), p. 11.

Chapter 10. Ranger Bloopers
Page 66   "You put your tongue on a pump handle": Keillor, *Lake Wobegon Days*, p. 480.
Page 67   Once thought to be the tallest mountain: Parker, "Sharp Top," p. 9.
Page 67   A piece of stone from its summit: ibid.

Chapter 11. *Taking Flight*

Page 78   "It takes a lot more": Cash, Epps Jr., and Yonay, *Top Gun*, <http://www.imdb.com/title/tt0092099>.

Page 80   BRP courses its namesake: Quin, "BRP/HAER," p. 7.

Page 80   Bill Austin quote: Abbott, interview, p. 12.

Page 80   "one panorama following right on another": ibid.

Page 80   "The Parkway does not exclusively follow the skyline": Abbott, "The Blue Ridge Parkway — A New Element in Recreational Planning."

Page 82   Eagle, osprey, etc.: Lord, BRPG, MP 95.3.

Page 82   Historic flight of Wilbur and Orville Wright: Kelly, "Wright Brothers National Memorial."

Chapter 12. *Stills and Fields*

Page 84   BRP extension to Cartersville, Ga.: BRP, "The North Carolina–Georgia Extension of the Blue Ridge Parkway: A Report to the Congress of the United States."

Page 85   Stanley Abbott formally complained: Quin, "BRP/HAER," pp. 73–74, 111.

Page 87   Loss of fencing: ibid, p. 148.

Page 88   When Mac Dale reported for duty in 1938: Liles, "Early Rangers of the Blue Ridge Parkway," pp. 17, 19.

Page 88   "It got to be sort of a game": Dale, interview (reel 263), pp. 15–16.

Page 89   Granville Liles begins work on the BRP: Liles, "Early Rangers of the Blue Ridge Parkway," pp. 17–18.

Page 89   "Upon his arrival at the blockade": ibid, p. 18.

Page 89   By the spring of 1940: ibid.

Page 89   Liles attends FBI Academy: Liles, interview (1971), p. 5.

Page 89   "whole countryside burned over": Liles, interview (1964), p. 14.

Page 89   "And I on this particular occasion": ibid, pp. 14–16.

Page 90   Rangers Barrow, Dale, and Campbell: Liles, "Early Rangers of the Blue Ridge Parkway," p. 17.

Page 90 $9,959 per year: This author's actual salary effective 23 April 1978.

Page 91   "laurel hells": Lord, BRPG, glossary.

Page 93   "Now, I got caught in this thing": Weems, interview, p. 77.

Chapter 13. *Ranger Mischief*

Page 96   "And I about made up my mind": Twain, *The Adventures of Huckleberry Finn*, p. 271.

Page 98   Dedication of the Roanoke River bridge: Eden, "Acting Superintendent's Annual Report," p. 1.

Page 98   160 feet below: calculation derived from "Blue Ridge Parkway Log."

Page 101   "right smart view": Lord, BRPG, MP 154.5.

Chapter 14. *Beware of Dog*

Page 109   "I've also always wanted to": Sparks, *The Guardian*, p. 721.

Page 109   Six-span, structural steel bridge: Quin, "BRP/HAER," p. 119.

Page 111   "too little money for proper upkeep": Abbott, interview, p. 38.

Page 113   "Evicted": Atkin, "Evicted — Abandoned dog loses his home on Blue Ridge Parkway."

Page 113   A few days later another article appeared: ibid, "And now Dawg has disappeared."

Page 113   "For the record": ibid.

Page 114   Complimentary article: ibid, "Parkway patrol," pp. B-1, B-8.

Chapter 15. *Gone Awry*

Page 117   "Inman looked at the lights": Frazier, *Cold Mountain*, p. 205.

Page 119   Completed in 1960: Dikigoropoulou and Dubin, "Historic American Engineering Record," sheet 2.

Page 119	References to Michelangelo's statue of David: Bucci, Lachi, and Paolucci, *David — Five Hundred Years*, pp. 78–79; and Riding, "Questions for 'David' at 500 — Is He Ready for Makeover?" <http://www.floria-publications.com/italy/news>.
Page 120	"To provide ample room": Jolley, TBRP, pp. 110–11.
Page 120	Problems with road access easements: Evison, "Finding a Route for the Blue Ridge Parkway," p. 12.
Page 120	"hot dog and gasoline shanties," Abbott, "The Blue Ridge Parkway — A New Element in Recreational Planning."
Page 120	"There will be adverse forces later": Abbott, interview, p. 38.
Page 121	Hurrah to the U.S. Forest Service: Quin, "BRP/HAER," p. 97.
Page 121	Hurrah to North Carolina: ibid.
Page 121	Hurrah to the Asheville City Council: ibid, p. 98.
Page 121	Plaza to the Galleria dell'Accademia: Bucci, Lachi, and Paolucci, *David — Five Hundred Years*, pp. 78–79; and Riding, "Questions for 'David' at 500 — Is He Ready for Makeover?" <http://www.floria-publications.com/italy/news>.

Chapter 16. Disorderly Conduct

Page 122	"It is hoped that word": Weems, "Monthly Narrative Report — September 1945," p. 3.
Page 125	"The heavy body glides": Lord, BRPG, MP 408.0.
Page 127	Sections 1-A through 1-W: Jolley, TBRP, p. 107.
Pages 127–28	Problems with disorderly behavior: Weems, "Monthly Narrative Report — September 1945," pp. 3–4.

Chapter 17. Clocking Butterflies and Bumblebees

Page 131	"Some wonderful things to observe": Parkway safety flier.
Page 132	"a managed museum of the American countryside": Quin, "BRP/HAER," p. 9.
Page 132	No paved roads: Jolley, TBRP, p. 11.
Page 134	Dimensions of timber guide rails: Quin, "BRP/HAER," p. 115.
Page 135	"At the order of the Secretary": "40 M.P.H.," p. 2.

Chapter 18. Not of This Earth

Page 141	"In a narrow country we suffer no more": Reece, *Better a Dinner of Herbs*, p. 214.
Page 142	Proposal to establish rest areas: Abbott, memorandum, p. 1.
Page 144	Conscientious objectors: Quin, "BRP/HAER," pp. 81, 211.
Page 144	"et for breakfast": Dale, interview (reel 263), p. 11.
Page 148	"The big thing while I was chief ranger": Dale, interview (reel 264), p. 11.
Page 151	"Gossip almost always does more harm": Brotherton, "Memorandum: Words of wisdom from the Director."
Page 151	"If you are prevented": Brotherton, "Informational Memorandum No. 78-25: Nationwide Post-Attack Registration of Federal Employees."
Page 154	"Eloise and I": Dale, interview (reel 263), pp. 56–57.

Chapter 19. Weathering Isabel

Page 155	"And everybody knows": Bragg, *Ava's Man*, p. 18.
Page 155	Newspaper headline: Lee, "A walk through memory lane," pp. 1–2.
Page 156	"The Scenic": Abbott, interview, p. 16.
Page 159	"centrally located bath house": "Blue Ridge Parkway Directory & Travel Planner," p. 26.
Page 159	Rocky Knob Cabins originally built as a pilot project: Abbott, "Monthly Narrative Report — March 1941," p. 2; and Quin, "BRP/HAER," p. 174.
Page 159	Rocky Knob Cabins upgraded: Quin, "BRP/HAER," pp. 215–16.

Page 160   General George Pickett: Will, "America's Shifting Reality," p. A-25.
Page 161   "I give Mac Dale ... credit for saving that mill.": Weems, interview, pp. 66–67.
Page 162   Imaginary suspension bridge: Quin, "BRP/HAER," pp. 223–24.
Page 162   Weeks and Cox quotes: "The Shenandoah-Smoky Mountain Parkway," pp. 9–10, 12.
Page 163   Life of Orelena Hawks Puckett: Parkway interpretive sign located at the Puckett Cabin, MP 189.9.

Chapter 20. Crossing Paths

Page 166   "Sometimes he thought he heard voices": Frazier, *Cold Mountain*, p. 58.
Page 167   Only double-arch bridge: Quin, "Highways in Harmony."
Page 167   Italian and Spanish masons: Quin, "BRP/HAER," p. 122.
Page 167   "the most distinctive architectural features": ibid, "BRP/HAER," p. 117.
Page 168   State line surveyed by Peter Jefferson: "Blue Ridge Parkway" map/brochure.
Page 169   Cross paths with the legendary Daniel Boone: Lord, BRPG, MP 285.1; and Quin, "BRP/HAER," p. 151.
Page 169   Cross paths with a mustered force: Lord, BRPG, MP 330.9; and Quin, "BRP/HAER," pp. 149–50.
Page 169   Army of General Griffith Rutherford: Lord, BRPG, MP 441.9; and Quin, "BRP/HAER," p. 282.

Chapter 21. Death of a Chorus

Page 170   "There have been no serious accidents": "Good Record for the Parkway Visitor," p. 3.
Page 170   "never had a monster like this": Abbuehl, interview, p. 21.
Page 171   "crusty old gentleman": Howland, "Mr. Browning Moves Mountains."
Page 171   Senator McKellar threatens to withhold funding: Jolley, TBRP, pp. 61, 64.
Page 171   Presentation of photo album: ibid, p. 72.
Page 171   Influence of Josephus Daniels: ibid, pp. 66, 72.
Page 171   Bear hunts and fishing trips: ibid, p. 66.
Page 171   And an hour before the final hearing: ibid, pp. 78–79.
Page 171   Robert Marshall's tour and recommendation: ibid, pp. 76–77.
Page 172   In his precise, fair style: ibid, pp. 79–82.
Page 172   Senator McKellar ... fired a strategic shot: ibid, p. 82.
Page 172   "I shall take my head between my hands": McKee, "N.C. Presses Claims For Parkway At Hearing," p. 1.
Page 172   Parker dam controversy: "Arizona Sends Troops To Halt Federal Works," p. 1.
Page 172   Trouble brewing in other parts of the world: "France Alarmed at Rapid Growth of German Fleet," p. 1.
Page 172   But the dominating story of the day: Brown, "Ickes' Decision Placing Route for Parkway," p. 1.
Page 172   Pack Murphy farm: Quin, "BRP/HAER," p. 70.
Page 173   Stone walls built by force of slavery: Parkway interpretive sign located at Greenstone Overlook, MP 8.8.
Page 174   Parkway key chain token: "ENJOY THE VIEW — WATCH THE ROAD."
Page 174   Parkway safety poster: "Do you know what a descending radius curve is?"

Chapter 22. Finding at Last, the Wild Asparagus

Page 177   "Why go fishing for mountain trout": Gibbons, *Stalking the Wild Asparagus*, p. 1.
Page 179   Children's children: *The Holy Bible*, Proverbs 17:6, p. 829.
Page 180   Travel directory advertised a private campground: "Blue Ridge Parkway Directory & Travel Planner," p. 33.
Page 187   Lemonade from the sumac tree: Gibbons, *Stalking the Wild Asparagus*, p. 91.
Page 187   Acorns from the white oak tree: ibid, pp. 10–13.
Page 187   Ingesting the leaves of poison ivy: ibid, pp. 284–85.

Chapter 23. Pure Harmony

Page 189   "There had to be a good deal of wandering away": Evison, "Finding a Route for the Blue Ridge Parkway," p. 13.

Pages 190–91   Parkway engineers had limited themselves: Quin, "BRP/HAER," p. 111.

Page 191   160 extra miles: Roughly calculated with the aid of a yardstick and the BRP "strip map" and including a gross vertical addition of eighteen miles (nine miles uphill and nine miles downhill).

Page 192   *Starry Night*: Reference to the famous painting by Vincent van Gogh.

Page 193   President Truman's press conference: McCullough, *Truman*, p. 822.

Page 194   All references to the Cone family and Flat Top Manor: Quin, "BRP/HAER," pp. 246–52.

Page 194   "park and pleasuring ground in perpetuity": Lord, BRPG, MP 293–295.5.

Page 195   "find something for this house" (pressure to move park headquarters to Flat Top Manor): Weems, interview, p. 53.

Page 197   "S-and-one-half" curve measuring 1,240 feet in length: Quin, "BRP/HAER," p. 124.

Page 197   Largest water feature on the Parkway: ibid, p. 252.

Page 197   Tallest mountain along the Blue Ridge proper: ibid, p. 255.

Page 197   Higher route vs. lower route: ibid, pp. 92–93.

Page 199   The distraction of the Korean conflict: ibid, p. 86.

Chapter 24. Derailed in Avery County

Page 200   "For I was an hungred": *The Holy Bible*, Matthew 25:35, p. 1233.

Page 202   "He thought, that, if waked from a trance": Emerson, eulogy, p. 27.

Page 203   Beatitude related to the meek people of the earth: *The Holy Bible*, Matthew 5:5, p. 1192.

Page 203   Story of the poor widow: *The Holy Bible*, Mark 12:41–44, p. 1264.

Page 203   "The poor never have enough for themselves": Girzone, *Joshua*, p. 54.

Page 209   "Fiver" is the fictional name of a character, who also happens to be a rabbit: Adams, *Watership Down*.

Chapter 25. Motorcycles

Page 211   "The way is full of flowers": Pirsig, *Zen and the Art of Motorcycle Maintenance*, p. 370.

Pages 212–13   "to tramp or fish in the unbroken forests.": Abbott, "The Blue Ridge Parkway — A New Element in Recreational Planning."

Page 214   Description of Linville River bridge: Quin, "BRP/HAER," p. 118.

Page 217   Actual chief assistant (as opposed to Travis Proctor): Quin, "BRP/HAER," p. 39.

Page 217   "It would be a mistake": Abbuehl, interview, p. 35.

Chapter 26. Skulking About

Page 218   "Prohibited: the taking of wildlife": *Code of Federal Regulations*, 36 CFR 2.2(a)(1), <http://ecfr.gpoaccess.gov>.

Pages 218–19   "the number of survey men": Abbott, interview, p. 26.

Page 220   It was the Clinchfield railroad: Lord, BRPG, MP 328.6.

Page 222   Newspaper story: Tomlin, "Long and winding road," pp. E1, 8.

Chapter 27. Bear!

Page 227   "I followed the bear tracks off the road": Brown Jr., *The Search*, p. 150.

Page 227   Travel directory advertised a restaurant: "Blue Ridge Parkway Directory & Travel Planner," p. 43.

Page 227   Federal efforts to acquire Mount Mitchell State Park: Quin, "BRP/HAER," pp. 267–69.

Page 229   Parkway jumps ship: Lord, BRPG, MP 354.

Page 229   Asheville watershed: ibid, MP 355.4–366.
Page 229   "CAUTION: ARSENIC": untitled, undated warning label.

Chapter 28. *Sunday Solace*

Page 234   "Turn away thy foot from the sabbath": *The Holy Bible*, Isaiah 58:13–14, p. 931.
Page 237   From the 1934 dining room: Quin, "BRP/HAER," pp. 39–40, 105–6.
Page 238   Grade separation structures: ibid, p. 117.

Chapter 29. *Balsam Gap District Revisited*

Page 241   "It's so peaceful here": McCrumb, *Ghost Riders*, p. 204.
Pages 242–43 Name origin of Mount Pisgah: Lord, BRPG, MP 407.4.
Page 243   Name origin of Ferrin Knob tunnels: ibid, MP 400.9–401.5.
Page 243   Printed announcement: Brown, letter.

Chapter 30. *Swinging Snow Gates*

Pages 249–50 Ancestrally linked: Frazier, *Cold Mountain*, jacket cover.
Page 253   "more dashing than the typical long-distance hiker": Schmerker, "Hiking the
            Blue Ridge Parkway," p. B2.
Page 253   "blasted and ravaged": Frazier, *Cold Mountain*, p. 321.
Page 254   125,000 red spruce seedlings: Morriss, letter; and "Unveiling of Memorial
            Marker," program leaflet.

Chapter 31. *The Main Event*

Page 258   "It seems that Hollywood": Pegram, "Must See Movies."
Page 258   Reputed home and farm of Judaculla: Lord, BRPG, MP 423.7.
Page 258   Proposed development of Tanasee Bald: "Roads and Trails Map," Drawing
            PKY-BR-TB-2050, 1 January 1942.
Page 258   Capped wellhead: Quin, "BRP/HAER," p. 282.
Page 263   They later told a reporter: Barrett, "Texas couple parkway's 400 millionth vis-
            itors," p. A3.

Chapter 32. *Local Comparable Rate*

Page 265   "I have given careful consideration to your memorandum": Everhardt, mem-
            orandum.
Page 267   In a complimentary letter: Warwick Jr., letter.
Page 272   Special funding program: Quin, "BRP/HAER," p. 89.
Page 273   All references to the Davey family and Mountain Dew Farm: Buxton, "His-
            toric Resource Study—Davey Farm."

Chapter 33. *Cased and Unloaded*

Page 276   "Except as otherwise provided": *Code of Federal Regulations*, 36 CFR 2.4(a)
            (1)(i), <http://ecfr.gpoaccess.gov>.

Chapter 34. *Milepost 469...*

Page 284   "And that which is for him to say": Emerson, "Representative Men," p. 746.
Page 284   Vint memorandum: Quin, "BRP/HAER," p. 41.

Bibliography

BLUE RIDGE PARKWAY PLANS AND DRAWINGS

"General Development Plan, Peaks of Otter Park, Blue Ridge Parkway." Drawing PKY-BR-PO-2003-B, 8 June 1939. Located in Asheville, N.C.: Blue Ridge Parkway Engineering and Technical Services files, Cabinet 3, Rack 3-A-9.
"Roads and Trails Map, Tennessee Bald, Part of the Master Plan for Blue Ridge Parkway." Drawing PKY-BR-TB-2050, 1 January 1942. Located in Asheville, N.C.: Blue Ridge Parkway Engineering and Technical Services files, Cabinet 3, Rack 3-B-4D.

BLUE RIDGE PARKWAY REPORTS AND PUBLICATIONS

"40 M.P.H." *Blue Ridge Parkway News*, Vol. V, No. 2, December-January 1941–42.
Abbott, Stanley W. "Monthly Narrative Reports—January 1941–March 1947." Located in Asheville, N.C.: Blue Ridge Parkway Archives.
"Bicycling." Blue Ridge Parkway information brochure, April 1988.
"Blue Ridge Parkway." Official map/brochure for the Blue Ridge Parkway, also known as the "strip map." U.S. Government Printing Office, 2003.
"Blue Ridge Parkway Directory & Travel Planner." 54th ed. Blue Ridge Parkway Association, Inc., 2003.
Blue Ridge Parkway investigative report files (including unsolicited letters which became attachments to same). Various mentioned. 1978–1990.
"Blue Ridge Parkway Log." Blue Ridge Parkway, Division of Resource Planning and Professional Services, April 1995.
Buxton, Barry M. "Historic Resource Study—Davey Farm," February 1990.
Eden, James M. "Acting Superintendent's Annual Report," 1966. Located in Asheville, N.C.: Blue Ridge Parkway Archives.
"Good Record for the Parkway Visitor." *Blue Ridge Parkway News*, Vol. IV, No. 6, July-August 1941.
"The North Carolina-Georgia Extension of the Blue Ridge Parkway: A Report to the Congress of the United States." Asheville, N.C.: Blue Ridge Parkway, June 1963. Located in Asheville, N.C.: Blue Ridge Parkway Library.
Parker, Jamie, Interpretive Ranger, Blue Ridge Parkway. "Sharp Top." *Parkway Milepost*, Fall-Winter 2004–05.
Pegram, Tim. "Must See Movies." *Ridge Runner Newsmagazine*, Vol. 4, No. 1, February 1990.

Weems, Sam P., Superintendent, Blue Ridge Parkway. "Monthly Narrative Reports— April 1944–October 1963." Located in Asheville, N.C.: Blue Ridge Parkway Archives.

BOOKS

Adams, Richard. *Watership Down.* New York: Avon, 1975.

Bragg, Rick. *Ava's Man.* New York: Vintage, 2002.

Brown Jr., Tom. *The Tracker* (as told to William Jon Watkins). New York: Berkley, 1979.

_____. *The Search* (with William Owen). New York: Berkley, 1982.

Bucci, Cristina, Chiara Lachi, and Antonio Paolucci. *David — Five Hundred Years.* New York: Sterling, 2005.

Emerson, Ralph Waldo. Eulogy of Henry David Thoreau as edited by Philip Van Doren Stern in *The Annotated Walden.* New York: Barnes & Noble, 1992.

_____. "Representative Men: Goethe; or, the Writer" as edited by Joel Porte in *Ralph Waldo Emerson — Essays & Lectures.* New York: Literary Classics of the United States, 1983.

Fletcher, Colin. *The Man Who Walked Through Time.* New York: Vintage, 1972.

Frazier, Charles. *Cold Mountain.* New York: Atlantic Monthly Press, 1997.

Gibbons, Euell. *Stalking the Wild Asparagus.* New York: David McKay, 1974.

Girzone, Joseph F. *Joshua.* New York: Touchstone, 2003.

The Holy Bible. Authorized King James Version. Salt Lake City, Ut.: The Church of Jesus Christ of Latter-day Saints, 1979.

Jolley, Harley E. *The Blue Ridge Parkway.* Knoxville: University of Tennessee, 1995.

Keillor, Garrison. *Lake Wobegon Days.* Large print ed. Thorndike, Me.: Thorndike, 1986.

Kelly, Susan S. *How Close We Come.* New York: Warner, 1999.

Lord, William G. *Blue Ridge Parkway Guide.* 2 vols. Birmingham, Al.: Menasha Ridge, 2004.

McCrumb, Sharyn. *Ghost Riders.* New York: Dutton, 2003.

McCullough, David. *John Adams.* New York: Simon & Schuster, 2001.

_____. *Truman.* New York: Simon & Schuster, 1992.

Melville, Herman. *Moby Dick.* Edited in *The Best of Herman Melville.* Secaucus, N.J.: Castle, 1983.

Pirsig, Robert M. *Zen and the Art of Motorcycle Maintenance.* New York: Bantam, 1984.

Reece, Byron Herbert. *Better a Dinner of Herbs.* Athens, Ga.: University of Georgia Press (as a Brown Thrasher Book), 1992.

Sparks, Nicholas. *The Guardian.* Large print ed. New York: Warner, 2003.

Thoreau, Henry D. *Walden* as edited by Philip Van Doren Stern in *The Annotated Walden.* New York: Barnes & Noble, 1992.

Twain, Mark. *The Adventures of Huckleberry Finn.* New York: Washington Square, 1962.

CORRESPONDENCE

Abbott, Stanley W., Resident Landscape Architect, Blue Ridge Parkway. Memorandum for Mr. Hall, 27 June 1939. Located in Asheville, N.C.: Blue Ridge Parkway Archives, RG7, Series 41, Box 57, Folder 17.

Blue Ridge Parkway memoranda files. 1978–1990.

Brotherton, James R., Acting Superintendent, Blue Ridge Parkway. Memorandum to all employees: "Words of wisdom from the Director," 26 August 1986.

_____, Administrative Officer, Blue Ridge Parkway. Informational Memorandum No. 78-25 to all employees: "Nationwide Post-Attack Registration of Federal Employees," 14 November 1978.

Brown, Daniel W., Superintendent, Blue Ridge Parkway. Letter to Parkway guests, 1 October 2003.

Everhardt, Gary, Superintendent, Blue Ridge Parkway. Memorandum to Park Technician Tim Pegram: "Request to move out of Park quarters," 27 January 1981.

Melville, Herman. Letter to Nathaniel Hawthorne, 17 November 1851. Edited by Merrell R. Davis and William H. Gilman in *The Letters of Herman Melville*. New Haven: Yale University, 1960.

Morriss, D.J., Forest Supervisor, Pisgah National Forest. Letter to Mrs. R.N. Barber Sr., 13 August 1956. Located in Asheville, N.C.: Blue Ridge Parkway Archives, RG 5, Series 27, Box 34, Folder 5.

Warwick Jr., George W. Letter to Gary Everhardt, 28 March 1985.

Ephemera

"Do you know what a descending radius curve is?": Blue Ridge Parkway safety poster, undated.

"ENJOY THE VIEW — WATCH THE ROAD." Blue Ridge Parkway key chain token, undated.

"Some wonderful things to observe...." Blue Ridge Parkway safety poster, undated.

"Unveiling of Memorial Marker." Program leaflet, 11 August 1956.

Movies

Allen, J.T., and Tommy Lee Jones (teleplay writing credit). *The Good Old Boys*, 1995. <http://imdb.com/title/tt0113196>. 19 May 2006.

Cash, Jim, Jack Epps Jr., and Ehud Yonay (screenplay writing credit). *Top Gun*, 1986. <http://imdb.com/title/tt0092099>. 24 May 2006.

Roth, Eric (screenplay writing credit). *Forrest Gump*, 1994. <http:www.imdb.com/title/tt01098301>. 22 May 2006.

Newspaper Articles

"Arizona Sends Troops to Halt Federal Works." *The Asheville* (N.C.) *Citizen*, 13 November 1934.

Atkin, Jerrie. "Evicted — Abandoned dog loses his home on Blue Ridge Parkway." *Roanoke* (Va.) *Times & World News*, undated clipping.

_____. "And now Dawg has disappeared." *Roanoke* (Va.) *Times & World News*, undated clipping.

_____. "Parkway patrol." *Roanoke* (Va.) *Times & World News*, 9 September 1979.

Barrett, Ginny. "Texas couple parkway's 400 millionth visitors." *The* (Waynesville, N.C.) *Mountaineer*, 1 October 1986.

Brennan, Shannon. "Same goal, different method." *The* (Lynchburg, Va.) *News & Advance*, 4 September 2003.

Brown, Walter. "Ickes' Decision Placing Route for Parkway in N.C. Hailed as Great Victory by Entire State." *The Asheville* (N.C.) *Citizen*, 13 November 1934.

"France Alarmed at Rapid Growth of German Fleet." *The Asheville* (N.C.) *Citizen*, 13 November 1934.

Howland, Ralph. "Mr. Browning Moves Mountains; Once Even Changed Ickes' Mind." *The Charlotte* (N.C.) *Observer*, undated clipping. Located in Asheville, N.C.: Blue Ridge Parkway Library, vertical files, R. Getty Browning file.

Lee, Becky. "A 469-mile nature hike — Oak Ridge man preparing to hike the Blue Ridge Parkway." *Kernersville* (N.C.) *News*, 30 August 2003.

_____. "A walk through memory lane." *Kernersville* (N.C.) *News*, 23 October 2003.

McKee, Robert. "N.C. Presses Claim for Parkway at Hearing." *The Asheville* (N.C.) *Citizen*, 19 September 1934.

Pegram, Tim. "Man Plans to Hike Entire Parkway." *The Floyd* (Va.) *Press*, 28 August 2003.

Riding, Alan. "Questions for 'David' at 500: Is He Ready for Makeover?" *New York Times*, 17 July 2003. <http://www.floria-publications.com/italy/news>. 29 May 2006.

Schmerker, Jeff. "Hiking the Blue Ridge Parkway, one memory at a time." *The Enterprise Mountaineer*, 13 October 2003.

Tomlin, Jimmy. "Long and winding road." *High Point* (N.C.) *Enterprise*, 5 October 2003.
Werner, Dr. Arnold. "Doctor's Bag." *Technician* (N.C. State University), 27 March 1974.
Will, George F. "America's Shifting Reality." *Washington Post*, 4 November 2004. <http://www.washingtonpost.com/wp-dyn/articles/A239>. 30 May 2006.

ORAL HISTORIES

Abbott, Stanley W. Interview by S. Herbert Evison, 1958. Transcript of tape 55. Located in Asheville, N.C.: Blue Ridge Parkway Library.
Abbuehl, Edward H. Interview by S. Herbert Evison, 9 April 1971. Transcript. Located in Asheville, N.C.: Blue Ridge Parkway Library.
Dale, Mac. Interview by S. Herbert Evison, August 1980. Transcript of reels 263 and 264. Located in Asheville, N.C.: Blue Ridge Parkway Library.
Liles, Granville B. Interview by S. Herbert Evison, 1971. Transcript of tape 80. Located in Asheville, N.C.: Blue Ridge Parkway Library.
_____. Interview by S. Herbert Evison, 1964. Transcript of reels LXX, LXXI, side 1. Located in Asheville, N.C.: Blue Ridge Parkway Library.
Weems, Samuel P. Interview by S. Herbert Evison, 16 July 1971. Transcript of tape 79. Located in Asheville, N.C.: Blue Ridge Parkway Library.

OTHER GOVERNMENT REPORTS AND PUBLICATIONS

Abbott, Stanley W. "The Blue Ridge Parkway — A New Element in Recreational Planning." *The Regional Review*, Vol. III, No. 1, July 1939.
Code of Federal Regulations — Title 36. U.S. Government Printing Office. <http://ecfr.gpo access.gov>. 1 June 2006.
Dikigoropoulou, Lia M. and Elisabeth Dubin. "Historic American Engineering Record NC-42." National Park Service, 1997.
Kelly, Fred C. "Wright Brothers National Memorial." National Park Service information brochure. U.S. Government Printing Office, 1961.
"The Shenandoah-Smoky Mountain Parkway and Stabilization Project Parkway Hearings." Public Works Administration, 1934. Transcript. Located in Asheville, N.C.: Blue Ridge Parkway Library.
Quin, Richard, Historian, National Park Service. "Blue Ridge Parkway — HAER (Historic American Engineering Record) Report No. NC-42." Washington, D.C.: U.S. Department of the Interior, National Park Service, HABS (Historic American Buildings Survey)/HAER Division, 1997.
_____. "Highways in Harmony: Blue Ridge Parkway." U.S. Department of the Interior, National Park Service, HAER (Historic American Engineering Record), 2000–02. Brochure.

PERIODICALS

Evison, S. Herbert. "Finding A Route for the Blue Ridge Parkway." *National Parks Magazine*, September 1969.
Liles, Granville. "Early Rangers of the Blue Ridge Parkway." *The State*, July 1988.

Index